COMMUNISM IN RUMANIA

1944-1962

GHITA IONESCU

Issued under the auspices of the
Royal Institute of International Affairs

OXFORD UNIVERSITY PRESS

LONDON NEW YORK TORONTO

1964

Oxford University Press, Amen House, London E.C.4
GLASGOW NEW YORK TORONTO MELBOURNE WELLINGTON
BOMBAY CALCUTTA MADRAS KARACHI LAHORE DACCA
CAPE TOWN SALISBURY NAIROBI IBADAN ACCRA
KUALA LUMPUR HONG KONG

Printed in Great Britain by
Willmer Brothers and Haram Ltd.
Birkenhead

To

V B T

Contents

Abbreviations

Analele:	*Analele Institutului de istorie a Partidului de pe langa CC al PMR.*
An. Stat.	Rumania, Institutul central de statistica. *Anuarul statistic al RPR.*
CC:	Central Committee.
Comintern Journal:	*For a Lasting Peace. For a People's Democracy.*
Inprecorr:	*International Press Correspondence.*
D. Ger. FP:	*Documents on German Foreign Policy, 1918–1945, from the Archives of the German Foreign Ministry,* published jointly by the British Foreign Office and the U.S. Department of State, Series D (1937–45).
JCE Aff.	*Journal of Central European Affairs.*
PCR, *Documente:*	Partidul Comunist din Romania. *Documente din istoria Partidului Comunist din Romania.* 2nd. ed. 1953.
PMR, *Documente:*	Partidul Muncitoresc Romin, CC, Institutul de Istorie a PMR. *Documente din istoria Partidului Comunist din Romania.* 4 vols. 1953–7.
Rezolutii:	PMR, *Rezolutii si hotariri ale Comitetului Central al PMR.* 2nd ed. 1952.
RIIA, *Documents* and *Survey*	Royal Institute of International Affairs, *Documents on International Affairs* and *Survey of International Affairs.*
RWP:	Rumanian Workers' Party.
Sc. :	*Scinteia* (formerly *Scanteia*).
RPR:	Rumanian People's Republic.

Acknowledgements

I should like, first, to express my thanks to the Royal Institute of International Affairs which in 1955, through the then Director-General, the Hon. C. M. Woodhouse, extended to me an invitation to undertake the research work and write the study which was the first draft of this book.

I was most fortunate to be able to benefit from the advice of eminent scholars who were kind enough to read the manuscript or part of it and made most valuable observations and suggestions. Professor Hugh Seton-Watson, of London University, Dr G. H. Bolsover, Director of the School of Slavonic and East European Studies, London University, and Mr John Campbell, Director of Political Studies at the Council on Foreign Relations, have read various versions of the manuscript and have constantly helped me by pointing out errors of fact or interpretation. Those which remain in the book are entirely my own responsibility. To Mr F. W. Deakin, Warden of St Antony's College, Oxford, Professors Philip Mosely and Henry Roberts, of Columbia University, Professor Leonard Schapiro, of the London School of Economics, to whom the manuscript was submitted in earlier and rougher versions, I am profoundly indebted for guidance and advice badly needed at the beginning of my work. Mr C. Visoianu, Mr A. Cretzianu, and Dr Sabin Manuila helped me greatly by their comments on the first drafts of the Introduction and Part 1.

My thanks go simultaneously to Miss Hermia Oliver, of Chatham House, whose careful editing, revision, and criticism contributed much to the final version of the text, and to Mr J. F. Brown, who at an earlier stage checked the style and who allowed me to consult his Rumanian research work and studies at Radio Free Europe, when I was working on Chapters 12 and 13 of the present book.

I have pleasure in thanking the staffs of the library and press library of Chatham House, and of the libraries of the Council on Foreign Relations, New York, of the Centre de Documentation, Paris, of Transport House, London, of the Institute of Social History, The Hague, and of the New York Public Library and the Staats Bibliothek, Munich, for the assistance they gave me in finding first-hand documentation for a work for which, from many points of view, research had to be started from scratch.

Miss Geraldine Sheehan, Mrs Rozeta Metes, and Mrs Malila Szabados helped at various stages in the work of typing and correcting different parts of the book.

To my wife, without whom this book would not have been typed or even written or undertaken, it is dedicated.

G.I.

Note on Orthography

The author regrets that it was not possible to use the specific Rumanian accents in this work.

In addition to the ordinary vowels and consonants, the Rumanian language has three vowels (a, a, i) and two consonants (s and t).

a represents an indeterminate vowel and is pronounced like *a* in 'marine' or *e* in French 'je' when not stressed, but almost like ŭ in 'murmur' when stressed.

â and *î* represent the same sound, which is somewhat like the hollow sound of *e* in 'children' or *i* in 'pencil' (or like the Russian *i*). Since the advent of the communists to power, *â* has been replaced by *î* (e.g. the name of the communist newspaper *Scânteia* was changed to *Scînteia*). In this study both forms of the vowel are used because the subject-matter is not confined to the post-communist history of Rumania, but to avoid confusion, either *a* or *i* is consistently used in one and the same name. In the case of publications, however, the spellings current at the time must be used.

ş represents 'sh' as in 'shut'
ţ represents 'ts' as in 'hats' } represented by s and t in this work

Preface

THIS book seeks to connect three different but interacting groups of events. First, there are the international events which have basically determined the changes affecting the countries of Eastern Europe; second, the events in Rumania itself which were produced more directly by the people and rulers of that country; and third, the events which led to the formation and development of the Rumanian Communist Party and the rôle it has played in the relations between Rumania and the Soviet Union.

The international events have already been extensively described and analysed, some of the more important works being included in the Select Bibliography appended to this study. Consequently only those international events which had an obvious or ultimate effect on Rumania—in this case the adjectives are by no means synonymous—are dealt with here. Internal events in Rumania, especially those during the inter-war years, have also been described many times from many angles, and a satisfactory mosaic can be pieced together from these works. Here, therefore, they will be given necessary but brief attention. Their importance to this study is in the light they throw on, and the setting they provide for the formation and development of the Rumanian Communist Party.

There is no reliable history of that party in any language, least of all in Rumanian. For any potential historian before the war it was both negligible and elusive. Negligible because it was so minute, and elusive because from 1924 to 1944 it was outlawed, and even before that it had concentrated its ineffectual activities in the 'underground'. Since 1944 the party has become its own historian. The result has been the all too familiar profusion of narratives, documents, heroism and villainy.[1] Some of it is, of

[1] During the CC plenum of 28 Nov.–5 Dec. 1961 it was announced that the party was once more going to rewrite its history, in the words of N. Ceausescu, to give 'a scientific history of the party, putting an end to the idealization and superficial analysis on which it is based today'.

course, of value, but the party historians who have undertaken the task have worked under the party's strict control. The result is a confused perversion not only of Rumanian communist history but also of Rumanian history. This book is an attempt to describe and analyse Rumania's history under communism and to put it in its national and international perspective.

In the main, this survey has been kept, deliberately, on a strictly chronological basis. The principal reason for this was the author's conviction that in the case of small countries international affairs play a decisive rôle in internal politics. In Rumania's case, this is true also since she became part of the Soviet bloc in Eastern Europe, relations between the people and the rulers being considerably affected by agreement or disagreement between Russia and the Western Powers on the fate of the countries of Eastern Europe. Moreover communist politics are like all politics in being a result of hesitations, consultations, attempts, and withdrawals, in which in Eastern Europe the strategy of the Soviet Union plays the decisive part. The phases of internal development are thus short, uncertain, often contradictory, and undoubtedly less relentlessly economically determined than communist historians would believe them to be. They are the fruit of sudden decisions for the whole bloc, sometimes of refusals or counter-orders. To enable the reader to follow this chequered pattern, the implementation of main policies such as collectivization, industrialization, and cultural evolution are described in their various changing and sometimes contradictory phases. This, of course, may inconvenience some readers who prefer the customary method of synoptical treatment under subjects such as agriculture, industry, labour, &c. It is, however, hoped that the index will help readers who wish to follow main developments in any particular field.

August 1963

G.I.

I

Introduction: A History of the Rumanian Communist Party

THE RUMANIAN COMMUNIST PARTY BEFORE THE FIFTH CONGRESS 1917–32

ACCORDING to official communist history,[1] the Rumanian Communist Party was founded on 13 May 1921 and after some years of intermittent activity was finally established at the Fifth Congress in 1932. From this date its continuity can be traced. Specifically communist activity, however, began in Rumania immediately after the Bolshevik Revolution and became more recognizable as such after the formation of the Third International on 4 March 1919. Until 1921 the communists operated within the small but growing Social Democratic Party, a party which they tried unsuccessfully to capture.

The Social Democratic movement was founded in 1893 in the Old Kingdom of Rumania where it followed closely on the emergence of a small working class, a class which had appeared earlier in the more speedily industrialized Transylvania and Bukovina, then provinces of the Austro-Hungarian monarchy. In Transylvania as early as 1866 the 'General Workers' Association of Self-Education' was publishing syndicalist literature in six languages, including Rumanian.[2] The first socialist journal to appear in Rumanian was *Contemporanul* in 1881. In 1880 'workers' circles' were founded. These 'circles' held their first general congress on 31 March 1893, when the formation of a Social Democratic Party of the workers of Rumania was decided upon.

Two groups of young intellectuals were mainly instrumental in founding the new party. One group was chiefly inspired by socialist ideas from France, the other from Russia. From 1893

[1] See Bibliography, p. 358 below.

[2] The first workers' organization in Rumania was the 'House for Insurance and mutual help of the printers', founded on 24 August 1858.

until the end of the century it was the first group which held the ascendancy. The most notable French-inspired intellectuals were V. G. Mortun, the Radovici brothers, Iosif Nadejde, and G. Diamandi. They were nicknamed 'the generous' and were all sons of rich middle-class or aristocratic families. Together with others, they held that Rumania was in the incipient stages of the industrial revolution and were convinced of the inevitable superior strength which this would bestow upon the workers. The instruments for the social and political advance of the workers were to be the working-class organizations which were envisaged as ranging from the utopian-idealistic 'brotherhoods' and the rather romantic Fourier-type phalansters to fully fledged trade unions and syndicates which were then being founded, though as yet on a very small scale. This group had a certain backing from the Rumanian workers who favoured its 'economistic' methods as the best means of organizing and protecting themselves against pressure from the employers and the bourgeoisie.

But the 'generous' became disillusioned by their inability to put Marxist theory into Rumanian practice, especially into the essentially agrarian structure of the country. Many of them at the beginning of the twentieth century joined the Liberal Party.[3]

The leadership was then assumed and retained till the end of the First World War by a second group, led by Christian Rakovsky and Constantin Dobrogeanu-Gherea. Rakovsky[4] was perhaps the most brilliant and cosmopolitan of all the Balkan communist personalities. Born in 1873, a Bulgarian from the Dobruja, he and his family had moved to Rumania when he was seven. Educated at Geneva, Berlin, and Montpellier, he had been attracted to Marxism at an early age and became active in socialist circles in

[3] See further below, pp. 35 f. The first split occurred in 1899 when V. G. Mortun left the Socialist Party, justifying his decision with such considerations. See also 'Documents from the Archive V. G. Mortun, 1907–18', *Studii*, no. 3, 1957. M. Roller, the official historian of the Rumanian Communist Party, tried to show in 'The Working Class and 1907', *Analele*, no. 2, Mar.-Apr. 1957, that even the Socialist Party under Rakovsky's influence was indifferent towards the peasant revolt of 1907 and that only a fraction, led by M. G. Bujor, took sides openly with the peasants. On the other hand Trotsky, in a portrait of Gherea in *Nase slova*, 7 June 1915, said that Gherea and Rakovsky started to reorganize a new Rumanian Social Democrat party after the Russian Revolution of 1905.

[4] For more on Rakovsky see J. A. Rothschild, *Rakovsky* (St. Antony's College, Oxford, Feb. 1955); C. N. Clark, *Bessarabia, Russia and Roumania* (N.Y., 1927); C. T. Petrescu, *Socialismul in Romania* (Buch., 1946); and L. Fischer, *Men and Politics* (N.Y., 1941). Zubcu Codreanu, Zamfir Arbore, and Dr Russell (who held an American passport) were other young Russian revolutionaries who took residence in Rumania.

both Rumania and Bulgaria. In 1893 he represented the Bulgarian Social Democratic Party at the Zurich Congress of the Socialist International and five years later was a regimental doctor in the Rumanian army. In 1900 he had gone to Russia but had soon been expelled. In 1905 he had become editor of the Social Democratic newspaper *Romania muncitoare* and in 1907 represented the Rumanian party at the Stuttgart conference of the Socialist International. For his attitude toward the peasant revolt of the same year he was refused permission to re-enter Rumania, being branded as an 'undesirable alien'. Nevertheless in 1913 his friend Trotsky was still describing him as the 'leader and organizer of the Rumanian workers' and he remained so until 1917.

Dobrogeanu-Gherea was a Russian of Jewish origin; his real name was either Cass or Katz.[5] Born in 1855 in the market town of Slavianka in the Ekaterinoslav district, he first studied in Kharkov but because of his activities in revolutionary student circles he was forced to leave Russia. He arrived in Iasi, the capital of Moldavia, in March 1875. As the leading theoretician of the party, Dobrogeanu-Gherea tried to find a short-cut between the agrarian structure of Rumania and the need for socialism, by adjusting the Menshevik theory and proposing the *ad hoc* theory of 'neo-serfdom' (*neo-iobagia*).[6] He stressed the disparities between the 'legal' and the 'real' country, between the set of codes and institutions bestowed upon Rumania by her ruling class and the low standard of living and the scant political freedom. He argued, even before the agrarian reform of 1919, that the redistribution of the land alone would not be enough, unless the farmers were also given the capital and credit to work their land efficiently. Rumania, he argued, first needed a bourgeois-democratic revolution which, by bringing more capital and ensuring a more rapid industrialization, would create conditions in which the country could prepare itself for socialism.

It was under the leadership mainly of these two men that the Social Democratic Party continued during and after the war

[5] In the Great Russian Encyclopaedia (vols 21–22, 1906–7) his name was given as Michael Nikitivich Katz. He himself, however, in a letter to the historian Iorga of 9 Jan. 1892, giving his *curriculum vitae,* gave his name as Constantin Cass. Two more complete studies of Dobrogeanu-Gherea's youth have recently been published in Rumania: I. Vitner, 'C. D. Gherea', *Viata romaneasca,* nos. 11 & 12, Nov. & Dec. 1956, and 'C. Dobrogeanu-Gherea', *Studii,* no. 3, 1957.

[6] See *Neo-Iobagia* (Buch., 1908). The other important work by Dobrogeanu-Gherea is *Studii critice* (Buch., 1921, 2 v).

years. The First World War presented it, as it did all socialist parties, with great problems of ideology and internal discipline. It had been represented at the Zimmerwald conference in September 1915, but had not endorsed Lenin's thesis.[7] Moreover even the socialist newspapers *Lupta* and *Socialismul*[8] were far more in sympathy with the Allies than with the central powers. However, Rakovsky and Dobrogeanu-Gherea wrote articles directed against the Tsarist empire, which they described as a predatory neighbour, the traditional source of danger. The plight of Bessarabia was repeatedly cited in their articles as the image of what would happen to Rumania herself, should she ever have the misfortune to come under Russian occupation.[9]

Rumania's entry into the war on 27 August 1916 was greeted with general acclaim throughout the country. The somewhat equivocal attitude of the party leadership met with a strong challenge from the rank and file. There was also considerable pressure from the Rumanian sections of the Transylvanian branch of the Hungarian Social Democratic Party and of the Bukovinian branch of the Austrian Social Democratic Party. These sections had yielded to the strong popular feeling of Rumanians in these areas for a reunion with the Old Kingdom. Furthermore, with the February Revolution led by Kerensky, the ideological grounds for opposing alliance with Russia seemed to have been removed. Finally, support for the war was made more palatable by King Ferdinand's proclamation of April 1917. The king promised the troops, as 'sons of peasants', that an agrarian reform would be carried out and the land redistributed. This gave the Bratianu government some basis of popular support and a progressive appearance.

What attitude to adopt towards the war itself was not the only problem which beset the party from 1916 to 1918. It was plagued

[7] Rakovsky and Alexandru Constantinescu were the delegates. Rakovsky was also the leader of the 'Zimmerwaldian' section of the Rumanian Socialist Party. His booklet *Les Socialistes et la guerre* (Buch., 1915) and his article in *Lupta* are strongly pacifist.

[8] An incomplete collection of these two Socialist newspapers during the First World War may be consulted at the Institut voor Social Geschicht, Amsterdam.

[9] 'Our French comrades assure us that the Allies, including Russia, are fighting for the principle of nationality. We who live in Eastern Europe in immediate propinquity to the Muscovite Empire ask liberty to doubt that'—Rakovsky in *Lupta*, 2 Jan. 1915. Also in *Lupta zilnica*, 16 May 1915: 'Russia wants, apart from the Banat and Northern Bukovina, to keep also a territory through which she could tie Bukovina to the Banat. This means the submersion of our country in the Slav element, equivalent to its disappearance as an independent state.'

also by considerable internal difficulties. The holding of a new congress and the election of a new Central Committee were long overdue and indeed frequently demanded by the rank-and-file. But the remaining members of the Central Committee and its Secretary-General, Ilie Moscovici, declared that this was impossible in the circumstances, when communications were interrupted and when police restrictions had been so intensified that a great many of the leaders, among them Rakovsky, were under arrest. The war years did bring considerable and influential additions to the party, mainly through common cause being made with the Transylvanian and Bukovinian branches of the Hungarian and Austrian parties. But increases in numbers meant also increases in factionalism. This became marked especially at the end of the war. Some of the new branches were tainted with what the 'maximalist' element considered as 'reformism' and there was a growing division between these branches and those who considered that the only source of inspiration was the Russian Bolsheviks.[10]

Rakovsky and the 'Rumanian' Group in Odessa

The February Revolution caused the complete collapse of the Russian armies on the Rumanian front. During the nine months between the two Russian revolutions collaboration between the Russian and Rumanian governments was cordial enough. Part of the Rumanian funds and gold reserves was transferred to Moscow and some administrative, military, and even industrial units were evacuated to Odessa.[11]

The Rumanian Social Democrats were committed to the idea that the end of the Tsars meant the end of Russian imperialist ambition. They also claimed that the democratic revolution in Russia would have internal effects in Rumania as well. The most categoric statement of this new policy was first made on 16 April 1917, when a great demonstration took place in Iasi on the occa-

[10] In Rumanian communist history this phase is described as a setback to the advance of the revolutionary ideas which were coming from Russia. Thus: 'The official reorganization of the Socialist Party at the end of 1918 brought a large number of new people into the movement. But at the same time the opportunist trends which existed before the war were intensified. The opportunist section was strengthened by hard-boiled reformists like Grigorovici (Bukovina), Flueras, Jumanca (Transylvania) &c. Thus did the reformist group crystallize in our country's working-class movement' (M. Roller, 'The Revolutionary Impetus among the Masses in Rumania in 1917–21', *Analele*, no. 6, Nov.-Dec. 1957).

[11] V. Liveanu, 'The Influence of the February 1917 Russian Revolution on Rumania', *Studii*, no. 1, Jan.-Feb. 1956.

sion of the funeral of one of the socialist leaders, Ottoi Calin. Mihai Bujor, a former lawyer who was later to become one of the officers commanding the revolutionary Rumanian battalion in Russia, demanded that the 'bourgeois-democratic revolution in Russia be extended also to Rumania'.[12] On 1 May 1917 further demonstrations took place and the demonstrators stormed the prisons and released Rakovsky, who fled to Odessa. Similar incidents took place also in Galati, Tecuci, and other towns in unoccupied Rumania.

In June a 'Rumanian Social Democratic Committee for Action' was formed in Odessa by Rakovsky, Bujor, Zadik, Gheorghe Stroici,[13] Alexandru Nicolau, and others who had fled there, fearing imprisonment in Iasi. From its inception, this Committee was in close touch with the Russians and was distrusted by the majority of Rumanian Social Democrats, who accused it of being Russian-dominated. On 8 July the Rumanian Social Democratic Party publicly disavowed the Committee, stating that 'its activity is not in accord with the past and present policies of the Rumanian social democracy'; it also denounced in the same terms the 'illegal' groups of the Committee. These groups were small cells, hastily recruited and serving primarily to distribute pamphlets and manifestoes and the newspaper *Lupta,* which was later published in Odessa.[14]

Yet these pamphlets and manifestoes were not uniformly revolutionary in the Bolshevik sense. A manifesto published in July 1917 was still rejecting the idea of armed insurrection and claimed that the bourgeois-democratic revolution was the final goal of the movement. It also stressed the importance for the Rumanian people of attaining national and territorial unity.[15] On 10 October 1917 *Lupta* still maintained that the Russian February Revolution 'had altered the aim of the war and transformed an imperialist war into a just one'. These and similar sentiments reflected the differing views and interpretations which were still prevalent in the Russian revolutionary movement at the time.

But with the coming of the October Revolution, any wavering

[12] Ibid. [13] See below, p. 357. [14] Liveanu, in *Studii*, Jan.-Feb. 1956.

[15] 'A manifesto of the Committee of the summer of 1917 underlined rightly the need for a democratic revolution but proclaimed that "the overthrow of the Russian Tsarism is the first step which we must take towards the remodelling of Rumania, for her territorial defence, for her national aggrandizement and for her democratic progress".' The manifesto stressed that the democratic transformation was necessary for the 'territorial defence and the country's territorial fulfilment' (ibid).

among the Odessa group came to an end, at least as far as its attitude toward the war and Bessarabia was concerned. For one thing, immediately after the revolution Rakovsky was appointed Governor of Odessa on Trotsky's recommendation and entered the service of the Soviet Union.[16] As one of the leaders of the pre-war Revolutionary Balkan Federation, Rakovsky had frequently denounced the dangers of Russian imperialism in the Socialist International. But now he reversed his position and henceforward advocated the incorporation of Bessarabia, by force if need be, into the new Soviet Union.

In January 1918, on the initiative of the newly formed Rumanian Revolutionary Committee, a revolutionary Rumanian battalion, with its headquarters in Odessa, was formed under the command of Bujor and Vasile Popovici; a naval unit was formed, led by Stroici. In the spring of the same year the first collection of booklets and publications issued by a body calling itself 'the Rumanian group of the Communist Party' also appeared.[17] The collection was put out under the imprint of the 'Revolutionary Library in Moscow'. Later a further collection appeared called the 'Communist Library', this time published by the 'Rumanian Revolutionary Communist Committee'. In this collection the Soviet constitution, speeches of Lenin and Trotsky in 1918, and an analysis of the political situation by Rakovsky were published. One booklet, *The Book of the Slaves,* by A. Costin, was written in language borrowed exclusively from popular religious vocabulary, with the obvious aim of appealing to the peasants. It was an incitement to revolt. Half the subsequent books in this collection were published in Cyrillic characters, although the language was Rumanian.[18] Later, and especially after the Hungarian communist revolution in 1919, the texts were for the most part translations of Bela Kun's articles and manifestoes.[19] The adaptations and Rumanian references were largely Transylvanian in character. Rakovsky took an active part in exalting Bela Kun's revolu-

[16] Fischer, *Men and Politics*, contains many details about Rakovsky's final phase in Soviet Russia during the Trotskyite purge.

[17] Some copies of this collection may still be consulted in the library of the Centre de Recherche et de Documentation Française, Paris.

[18] The same procedure is now applied for the books and publications of the Soviet Moldavian Republic, including Bessarabia.

[19] *Cine va plati rasboiul?* (Who will pay for the cost of the war?) by Bela Kun was the first booklet in the series of the Revolutionary Library, published in 1918 in Rumanian in Moscow.

tion,[20] urging the Rumanian revolutionaries to form a bridge between Hungary and Russia. A delegate of the Rumanian revolutionary battalion in Odessa was present at the foundation on 26 December 1918 of a 'Rumanian Communist group' in Budapest which in turn also contained an initial 'Magyaro-Rumanian group' made up of Transylvanian prisoners of war who had merged in Siberia on 24 March 1918.[21]

The Rumanian battalion in Odessa was most active in the period before Brest-Litovsk, when Trotsky's revolutionary army was being made ready to resist the Germans. Later it was sent to the Crimea, where it was disbanded in what seem to have been unpleasant conditions for all its leaders who elected—or were forced—to return to Rumania. (In this connexion it is significant that none of the members of the Odessa group was imposed or even proposed by the Russians in 1920 for the new leadership of the new Rumanian Communist Party.) Two of the old leaders, Stroici and Bujor, were among the many to be arrested and tried for treason when they returned. Bujor was sentenced to hard labour for life after his return in January 1920 and later lionized in socialist and communist manifestoes. He was released under an amnesty in 1934 and subsequently tried to reconcile the Socialist and Communist Parties without adhering to either. Since the communists came to power he has been treated with veneration and has held various honorary posts.

Politically the activity in Odessa became more confused; it is still impossible to unravel some of the events which took place. The publishers of the Rumanian texts, which since August 1919 had included the new official newspaper *Scanteia* (Spark),[22] were now described as 'the Rumanian section of the Russian Communist Party'. According to Deutsch,[23] who bases his research primarily on documents in Moscow, the origin of this section is to be found in the early foreign sections or groups formed in Moscow in March–April 1918 by Czech, Rumanian, and Magyar prisoners

[20] V. A. Varga, 'From the History of the Revolutionary Solidarity of the Rumanian and Magyar Popular Masses', *Analele*, no. 3, May-June 1957. In the manifesto of the Rumanian communist groups soldiers were asked to refuse to take part in military expeditions for the crushing of the revolution in Hungary. See PMR, *Documente*, i. 117–18.

[21] See 'Recollections by Former Volunteers', *Lupta de clasa*, May 1951.

[22] Three weekly numbers appeared altogether in Odessa, the last on 17 Aug. 1919.

[23] 'On the Activity of some Revolutionary Rumanian Groups in Soviet Russia, 1918–21', *Analele*, no. 5, Sept.–Oct. 1957.

of war. Deutsch states that the Rumanian section had been formed in Moscow by Rumanian soldiers and civil servants who had been forcibly detained there. To these was added a group of Transylvanian soldiers of Rumanian origin, prisoners of war from the Austro-Hungarian army. This latter group was 'much more to the left' than the original Rumanian one, which preferred to consider itself as a Rumanian syndicalist unit. Under the influence of the Transylvanians 'the Rumanian Revolutionary Peasant Party' was formed and edited in Moscow a newspaper in Rumanian called *Foaia taranului* (The Peasant's Journal). A part of the committee of this Peasant Party, however, asked the Central Committee of the Russian (Bolshevik) Party on 13 April 1918 to recognize it as a Rumanian group of that party. In July 1918 a delegation of the Military Committee (Battalion) arrived in Moscow from Odessa. *Pravda* of 6 August 1918 noted their arrival and described the Revolutionary Committee as 'the supreme organ of the revolutionary Rumanian movement'. There were thus three groups which now comprised (or contested) the leadership of Rumanian communism—the Moscow group, the Odessa Committee, and the so-called 'maximalist group' from Rumania itself. This last-named group represented the extreme left-wing faction of the Rumanian Social Democratic Party. On 14 October 1918 a conference in Moscow was arranged between representatives of these three groups, the maximalists being represented by Alexandru Constantinescu,[24] one of the pioneers of Rumanian socialism. The conference decided to intensify the publication of revolutionary literature in Rumanian and to unify the Rumanian communist propaganda in Russia.

> From an organizational point of view [says Deutsch] this meant the symbolic union of the revolutionary movement from Rumania with that from Transylvania. The continuous preoccupation of the Rumanians in Russia with the reunion of Transylvania with Rumania meant at the same time the pledge to create a communist party able to put an end also to the capitalist regime in Rumania.[25]

Behind this involved explanation one can detect the fact that, after Rakovsky's arrival in Moscow from Odessa, a Rumanian conference was summoned and that Rakovsky, informed also by Constantinescu and other emissaries from Rumania, convinced the Russian Bolshevik Party that the communists of Transylvania

[24] See below, p. 351. [25] In *Analele*, Sept.–Oct. 1957.

should be active within the future Communist Party of Rumania, the union of Transylvania with Rumania being taken as a *fait accompli*. A communiqué issued at the end of the conference stated that 'through the fusion of the Rumanian Communist group, the Transylvanian group and the Bessarabian group into a single organization, the Rumanian section of the Russian Communist Party has come into existence'.[26] While it is clear that the Russian Bolsheviks wanted to unite the new Rumanian group with the branches of the former Hungarian and Bulgarian parties, active now on Rumanian soil, there is evidence that the fusion between these extremist elements and the 'Rumanians' was effected only much later. But for that one must return to the activity of the illegal maximalist groups in Bucharest, Iasi, and Moscow. But before leaving the Rumanian communist activities on Russian territory, it should be noted that on 22 March 1920, i.e. one year before the formation of the Rumanian Communist Party in Rumania, it was decided to re-form the foreign groups of the Russian Communist (Bolshevik) Party. These 'bureaux' continued to work in Moscow throughout the history of the pre-war Rumanian Communist Party. This explains why, as will be seen, some of the most active persons and indeed *éminences grises* in communist affairs in Rumania were sometimes not even members of the Rumanian Communist Party Central Committee. It also explains why, even as late as 1944, Ana Pauker could defy certain decisions of the Rumanian Party Central Committee from Moscow where she was head of a 'Rumanian bureau'.[27] This duality of power in Rumanian communist activities remained from the beginning their most characteristic feature.

The Rumanian Communists and the Third International

During the period covered by the events just related in Odessa and Moscow, the most important development within the Social Democratic Party at home was the deepening rift between the maximalists and the rest of the party. The maximalists were so called because ideologically they stood for the immediate dictatorship of the proletariat by a revolution that was to ensure to the

[26] Quoted on the cover of the 11th pamphlet in the Revolutionary Library series, *The Soviet Republic* (with preface by Lunacharsky). On this pamphlet the publishers called themselves for the first time 'The publishing house of the Rumanian group of the Russian Communist Party'.

[27] See below, p. 79.

workers' state all the means of production. Their position was thus indistinguishable from that of the Russian Bolsheviks.

The ideological extremism of this group was matched by the extremism of the tactics which it urged in the struggle against the bourgeois governments and the war. Here again it was at bitter variance with the main body of the socialists. The maximalists were in favour of immediate and continuous actions regardless of the sacrifices entailed; the bulk of the socialists wished to protect themselves and the workers they represented against reprisals by the police and the army which would have been much too costly measured against any advantages gained. Through the leadership of the party, which they controlled, they therefore advocated a policy of caution. But the maximalists defiantly continued to organize small demonstrations and coups on the Leninist principle that, in order to gain control of the party, they must be in a state of perpetual activity. In the hope of achieving this they were prepared to risk giving the authorities the pretext for destroying the whole movement.

The October Revolution in Russia spurred the maximalists on to even greater action. From then on, they called themselves communists and maintained that they as 'communist groups' were in command of the party. Their agitation became dangerous after the withdrawal of German troops from Bucharest in November 1918 when for a time the government had only one regiment of troops in the city. After being responsible for a printing strike and other disturbances, the maximalists organized a serious demonstration led by one Constantin Ivanus on 13 December in which troops fired on the crowd. Some people were killed and others were injured. Among the injured was I. C. Frimu, a local worker and one of the maximalist leaders. This incident, insignificant in comparison with what was going on at the same time in Bulgaria and Croatia, to say nothing of Germany and Austria-Hungary, was the closest Rumania came at the time to a 'revolutionary situation'. With so few troops available, Bucharest would almost certainly have fallen to a determined movement based on solid support. But the majority of the workers, though by no means contented with their lot, were averse to revolution and the Social Democrats had no revolutionary intentions. Indeed, they disclaimed all responsibility for the incident and for the strike which led to it.

One person, however, gloried in the episode. This was Ana Rabinovici, to become famous by her married name of Pauker.[28] This formidable daughter of a Moldavian Rabbi took an active part in organizing the demonstration. In 1951, over thirty years later, in a study of Pauker published for the thirtieth anniversary of the party, it was stated that 'the Communists alone deserve all the credit' for the action.

The formation of the Comintern in March 1919 brought the pressure of the communist groups to a climax. They demanded of the Social Democratic Party an immediate affiliation with the Comintern and the launching of an insurrection throughout the country. They also demanded that a congress of the Social Democratic Party be convened. In May 1919 a conference was held at which a new programme was drafted. It was a compromise document, reflecting the profound differences within the party, but at the same time it contained statements once again revealing a western orientation which showed a victory of the moderates over the extremists.[29] The spirit of the 'generous' was still active in the party. It was, however, decided to send the programme to the Comintern, although affiliation was not asked for, nor was it promised to change the name of the party to 'Communist'.[30]

But the compromise reflected in the programme was not sufficient to overcome the serious divisions within the party. There were four main groups. The extreme right wing, led by Dunareanu, was in favour of immediate reunion with the Second International. When his motion to this effect failed to win the necessary majority, Dunareanu and many of the trade union leaders withdrew from the party and later formed a new Social Democratic Party. In this they were joined by the Bukovinians, led by Grigoro-

[28] See below, p. 355.

[29] The programme, published in *Socialismul,* 27 Mar. 1919, was the 'Statement of Principles' of 9 Dec. 1918 of the Rumanian Socialist Party (text in *Documente,* i) but even more westernized. The 'Statement of Principles' asked for the take-over of the means of production by the working class and for peace; it paid due homage to the Russian Revolution. But as a communist historian (Pompiliu Matei, 'The Workers' Movement in Rumania, 1918–21', *Studii,* no. 5, 1957) asserts: 'the Statement resembled in great measure the programme of the old Socialist parties of Western Europe'. He points out that the main political analysis is focused upon developments in the west, while only a little is said about the impact of the Russian Revolution.

[30] In a letter dated 10 Dec. 1920 sent by the Executive Committee of the Rumanian Socialist Party to Zinoviev, the President of the Third International, published in *Kommunist international,* no. 16, 1921, together with the minutes of the fateful meetings of Nov. 1920 at which the 'Rumanian case' was discussed by the International.

vici, and the Transylvanians, led by Jumanca. These two sections had for some time been at odds with the party of the Old Kingdom because of what they considered to be their too lenient attitude toward the communist group. The second main group of the party can be described as belonging to the centre. It was led by two intellectuals theoreticians, Dr Ghellerter and Serban Voinea,[31] who combined Dobrogeanu-Gherea's social theory of neo-serfdom with Kautsky's views on the means of action open to socialist parties. Moving to the left, the third group was headed by two workers, Alexandru Constantinescu and the Bucharest trade union leader, Gheorghe Teodorescu. Both these men had remained in Bucharest throughout the war and the occupation. Their attitude towards the means of gaining power was rather equivocal. Having experienced clandestine action for a considerable period, they did not see in parliamentary institutions a necessary prerequisite for socialist victory. But, on the other hand, neither of them advocated immediate communist revolution. The differences between this group and the extreme left-wing maximalists were rather of emphasis than of principle and at the October conference in Moscow in 1918 Constantinescu had actually led the maximalist delegation. The maximalists themselves, who comprised the fourth group, were now led by Alexandru Dobrogeanu-Gherea,[32] the son of Constantin, and by Boris Stefanov[33] who, like Rakovsky, was a Bulgarian from the Dobruja. This group was joined by a considerable number of intellectuals, among them the young Lucretiu Patrascanu;[34] many of them were of Jewish origin, like Marcel Pauker[35] and his future wife, Ana Rabinovici. The Secretariat of the party, in the hands of a triumvirate formed by Ilie Moscovici,[36] Gheorghe Critescu-Plapumaru,[37] and Constantin Popovici,[38] tried to preserve some kind of

[31] Serban Voinea (Beuve) was already at this time considered to be one of the outstanding theorists of the socialist movement in Rumania, largely because of his work on *The Marxist Oligarchy* (Buch., 1926).

[32] See below, p. 352. [33] See below, p. 356. [34] See below, p. 354.

[35] See below, p. 355.

[36] Secretary-General of the Socialist Party from the war years until the late 1930s, Moscovici, the learned son of a Rabbi, all his life had a reputation for staunchness and doctrinal orthodoxy, although he lacked either intellectual originality or political courage. His ideology is expressed in 'Lupta de Clasa si Transformarea Sociala', in Inst. de stiinte social, *Doctrinele partidelor politice* (1928).

[37] Fellow worker of A. Constantinescu, but much younger than he, this picturesque character was the first active Secretary-General of the party. See further below, p. 21.

[38] Secretary of the General Trade Union Committee. The other leaders of the

unity by remaining as aloof as possible from the controversies.

But the speed of events only brought out the internal divisions more clearly. The non-interventionist attitude adopted by the Transylvanian Social Democrats towards the part played by the Rumanian army in the crushing of Bela Kun's revolution enraged the International, which had ordered the party to help Kun and to sabotage the action of the Rumanian government. This failure on the part of the Rumanian Social Democrats brought them into considerable disrepute and the Hungarian and Bulgarian Communist Parties in particular began a campaign against Rumania and her working class within the International, which persisted for many years. The grievances were later compounded when, in the electoral campaign of May 1919, powerful Bukovinian and Transylvanian Social Democratic organizations concluded a pact with the People's Party of General Averescu. The complaint here was that Averescu had been in command of the Rumanian army at the end of the war. These 'social-patriotic deviations' served as a useful pretext for the communist groups to demand that the ideological line be strengthened. The Social Democratic Party was invited to send a delegation to the International to discuss further collaboration. In their new organ, *Lupta de clasa,* which first appeared on 4 July 1920, these communist groups continually urged that the party should seek 'affiliation with Moscow.'[39]

In the meanwhile they continued their violent agitating tactics. These culminated in the attempt at a general strike in October 1920. The attempt, directed by Stefanov, failed after a week but caused some loss of life and a considerable amount of governmental repression.[40] An act of open terrorism was to follow on 8 December 1920 when the Senate building was blown up and this time many people were killed. This desperate act led to harsh

groups, according to present communist historiography, were Constantin Ivanus, Pavel Tcacenco, P. Becheanu (in Bucharest), Leonte Filipescu, &c. But in his speech on the 30th anniversary of the party (as published in *Lupta de clasa,* May-June 1951), Gheorghiu-Dej said that the groups 'were led by Comrades Ana Pauker and Vasile Luca, as well as by the unforgettable fighters', and then gave the names only of those who had died. Since then the names of Pauker and Luca have been eradicated.

[39] PMR, *Documente*, i. *Lupta de clasa* was published by the Bucharest section of the Socialist Party which had already asked for affiliation to the Third International on 25 Jan. 1920.

[40] Contemporary communist authors such as Roller and Pompiliu Matei do not conceal the fact that the strike, although a failure, helped to crystallize the difference of views between the socialists and communists and to push the latter towards key positions in the party apparatus.

reprisals by the authorities and seriously offended public opinion. It also had the most serious repercussions within the party.[41] Even before the terrorist activity, the calling of the general strike had been enough to cause the Transylvanian, Bukovinian, and many of the Old Kingdom organizations to break away and form a new Social Democratic Party.

At about the same time as this serious defection, a delegation of the remaining members of the old Social Democratic Party had been in official negotiations with the Third International. It was composed of six members, four from the Old Kingdom party: Alexandru Dobrogeanu-Gherea, Constantin Popovici, Gh. Cristescu, and D. Fabian (editor of *Socialismul*) and two from Transylvania: E. Rozvany and I. Flueras, a right-wing trade union leader. They were received for the first time at a public session of the Comintern on 11 November 1920.[42] Bukharin asked them five questions: Was it true that they had concluded certain agreements with Averescu? What had the party done to oppose the bourgeois régime? What could they show that they had done in support of the Hungarian Soviet Republic? Why did they not call themselves a Communist Party and why had they not yet held a congress? The answers of the delegation were apologetic, acknowledging the mistake of having believed that Averescu could be a democrat, but defending with some dignity their difficulties in working among a non-socialist and western-orientated people. They were then told to submit these answers in writing so that they could be discussed at the next meeting.

When this took place on 24 November[43] Bukharin objected that Flueras, who had been sitting with the Rumanian delegation, had not only been a collaborator of Averescu, but also a member of the Rumanian peace delegation in Paris and Versailles. Zinoviev, who was presiding, expelled him and made some insulting personal remarks; Fabian, on behalf of the Rumanian delegation, apologized for the inclusion of Flueras. The real reason for expelling Flueras was that he was the most outspoken member of a very stubborn delegation which the Russians decided to break at the very outset. That they did not succeed entirely in doing so is proved by the contents of a letter of reply written by the Executive

[41] See account in Petrescu, *Socialismul in Romania.*
[42] *Kommunistische international* (German ed.), no. 16, 1921.
[43] Ibid.

Committee of the Social Democratic Party, dated 10 December 1920.[44]

This letter, written in Moscow, probably by Cristescu, Popovici, and Rozvany, acknowledged the wish to collaborate with the International and reiterated some of the excuses already put forward at the public meeting. But it struck back at the International on several points. The authors criticized it for not having read the programme of the party carefully enough. Zinoviev had derided the Rumanian socialists' alleged preoccupation with having enough trained midwives in the villages to counter the high infant-mortality rate. The letter reminded Zinoviev that this was not a preoccupation but an incidental point which had been mentioned along with more basic problems, ranging from the ownership of the means of production to that of establishing the workers' and peasants' state. The writers considered a calumny the jibe that their party 'loved Russia more now because it had given Transylvania back to the Rumanians rather than because it had given to the world the revolution which would free the whole of mankind'.[45] As for immediate revolution in Rumania, they considered that the recent experience in Hungary had shown how premature the notion was. Finally, they declared that it was untrue to say that the masses wanted them to affiliate to the International. The Rumanian 'masses' were completely indifferent to the problem. It was they who had tried with great difficulty to interest these non-revolutionary masses in communist ideology.

The revised minutes of the meeting of the International[46] started with an equivocal preamble in which it was stated that 'in so far as the members of the Rumanian socialist delegation only today returned from a study-journey in the district of the Don, near Moscow', they could only now give the answers to Bukharin's questions, which had increased to six. These alleged answers of the Rumanian delegation were self-accusations of a kind which were to become familiar later to all communist parties. Thus to the question as to why the party still called itself socialist, and not communist, the Rumanian delegation is alleged to have admitted that this was because the leadership of the Rumanian Social Democratic Party, unlike its rank and file and the working class as a whole, was not communist. To the question why the Transylvanian comrades had collaborated with the Rumanian govern-

[44] Published ibid. [45] Ibid [46] Ibid.

ment of occupation in that province, the answer said to have been given was that the Transylvanian party leaders considered the annexation of Transylvania by the bourgeois Rumanian government had been a 'liberation from a foreign yoke'. Finally, to the last and additional question as to why the delegation had not told the International sooner about the internal conflicts within the party, the answer was that the communist groups, led by Boris Stefanov, Fabian, and Dobrogeanu-Gherea, were the genuine party and were now on the way to being recognized as such.[47]

It is very unlikely that these answers were agreed by the whole delegation. Probably Dobrogeanu-Gherea and Fabian agreed to sign the answers. On behalf of the communist groups they probably pledged themselves to bring the entire Social Democratic Party into affiliation with the Third International and to a genuine communist discipline and had gone back on any pledge made to the party. They were received personally by Lenin on 5 December.

Organizing the 'Groups'

In January 1921 the delegation returned home. In February, at a General Council, the split became official.[48] It was agreed that a new congress should be convened in May. In the interval, however, the communist groups tried very earnestly to come to an agreement among themselves and to form a united body which could carry the majority with it to the Third International at the coming congress. A secret conference of these groups was called in Iasi between 3 and 6 March in a house in Sararia Street.[49] According to the official minutes, since published, 'representatives of the Communist Party and delegates from Moldavia, Muntenia, Oltenia, Dobruja, and Banat took part', and of the Bessarabian C.P.[50] The absence of the 'Transylvanians', although they had been reported as having united with the other wings in Odessa and although the group from Budapest had allegedly returned to Transylvania in 1919,[51] was due to the fact that, while Hungarian irredentists of any social class refused to join a Rumanian party, the majority of the Transylvanian industrial workers remained loyal to the Social Democratic Party, to which they had belonged since before the war.

[47] Ibid.

[48] S. Darvicu, 'Conferinta dela Iasi a grupurilor comuniste din Romania, Martie 1921', *Analele*, no. 3, May-June 1956.

[49] Ibid. [50] Ibid.

[51] Varga, in *Analele*, May-June 1957.

Two other separate groups were to join later. One was the 'Bukovinian' which again, as in the case of the Transylvanian, comprised a high percentage of non-Rumanian elements, especially Ukrainians. But here again, however, the great bulk of the workers preferred to remain with Grigorovici and his Social Democrats. The other was the 'Organization of Communist Jews'. This Yiddish-speaking group had no links with the young intelligentsia of the party, which was also largely Jewish but which ignored religious or racial differences.

It was apparent from the first that the responsible and commanding section of the future Rumanian Communist Party was to be the Bessarabian one. At the Iasi conference of the groups, it was stressed that 'through their revolutionary fervour, their intransigence, their discipline and their sacrifice, the Bessarabian communists have been held up as an example to the whole working class of Rumania'.[52] Also the Bessarabian Communist Party, which had always led an illegal existence, had nevertheless maintained steadfastly 'the general line of conduct' which was to serve as a fruitful example to all communist organizations in Rumania. According to early histories of the party, neither the communist nor the socialist organization of Bessarabia had ever been affiliated with the Rumanian Social Democratic Party. Thus the Bessarabian group, because of its many links, especially organizational and financial, with the Russian party and government, wielded a preponderant influence from the beginning. The policy of 'self-determination up to secession', which was later to become one of the main causes of the party's unpopularity, was insistently forced upon it by the powerful Bessarabians. When these communist groups had merged, a Central Committee was elected which directed the still precariously joined segments in their attempts to take over the Social Democratic Party at the coming congress.

The Foundation Congresses, 1921 and 1922

The Congress opened on 8 May 1921, on a hill in Bucharest called Dealul Spirei, near the parliament buildings.[53] The proceedings were typical of the conditions in which the Rumanian Social Democratic Party had to work. The combined pressure of

[52] Darvicu, ibid. May-June 1956.
[53] PMR, *Documente*, i.

the communist 'groups', together with that of the police, working from within as well as from outside, helped to create a confusion beneficial to the communist elements. During the first days of the Congress, 9–11 May, most of the delegates showed a growing reluctance to adopt the idea of becoming a 'Communist Party', but the police provocateurs joined forces with the leaders of the groups to force the issue. According to C. Titel Petrescu, three of the most fervent advocates of affiliation were the police agents Rusu, Gheorghian, and L. Neagu, who hoped to bring about a schism and to justify the intended arrests. Then, on 12 May, the police decided to act from outside. They closed down the Congress and arrested those who had voted for affiliation. They also arrested some who, like Stoiculescu, declared later at the trial (known as the 'Dealul Spirei trial') that they had neither known of nor recognized the theses of the New International, or, like Ilie Moscovici himself, the secretary of the party, who opposed the resolution adamantly.[54] Thus the confusion brought about by the mass arrests on 12 May benefited those communists who had escaped the police. On 13 May these met in hiding and, assuming that affiliation had already taken place, sent on behalf of the whole party a message of solidarity with the Third International. But the party was described as 'socialist-communist', and no Central Committee had been elected. Again, since the better-known political and trade union leaders were under arrest, the lead was now taken by two heterogeneous groups. In the provinces fanatical irredentists from the ranks of the national minorities saw in the revolutionary violence of communism a pretext for terrorism. In Bucharest and the Old Kingdom it was the young intelligentsia under Marcel Pauker which, through their control of the organization and of the party publications that were now published in Bucharest, took over the leadership. This was to have an enduring effect upon the evolution of the party.

A second Congress, or rather a continuation of the first, was held in secret the following October in Ploesti. It began as a conference but in the course of its debates was transformed into a Congress. Those participating took the name of the 'Communist Party of Rumania, section of the Communist International'.[55]

[54] Petrescu, *Socialismul in Romania*.

[55] PMR, *Documente*, i. See also A. I. Loglin, 'On the Importance of the Second Congress of the RCP', *Analele*, no. 3, May-June 1957, and Matei, in *Studii*, no. 5, 1957. Both authors recognize that although the 2nd Congress was important in

The statutes—still called provisional—were similar to those of the Third International. Although never published with the other documents and resolutions, it is known that they were similar to those readopted in 1924 and unchanged until 1948. They stressed the need for a clandestine organization and for bases of work in 'factories and work-cells' rather than in the streets and districts. These two points, together with the unpopular policy of 'self-determination', though perforcedly adopted by the new party, never received its wholehearted approval, and were the cause of a continuous and deepening rift with the International. The party was soon forced into complete illegality by the authorities, but in 1921 it was felt, especially by the 'Rumanian' element, that it was better to have more surface and open propaganda work. On this, both the 'workers' wing', led by Constantinescu and later by Cristescu, and the intellectuals under Marcel Pauker and Dobrogeanu-Gherea were agreed. But the regional wings of the party, led by the Bessarabians, imposed the doctrine of underground work. They recommended that all party members should join the trade unions and try to win them from within. The prospect of capturing the unions, however, seemed very remote. At a congress of trade unions in Sibiu just previously the communists had suffered a serious defeat and it was this defeat which led those party members connected with trade union work to conclude that concentration on the 'factories and work-cells' offered little chance of success in view of the Social Democratic hold on the bulk of organized labour.

It was at this October Congress that a unified Central Committee was first elected. The following can be recorded as being among its members: A. Constantinescu, Gh. Cristescu, Marinescu, A. Dobrogeanu-Gherea, Marcel Pauker, G. M. Vasilescu Vasia, Boris Stefanov, Moise Kahana, D. Fabian, Ana Pauker, Bela Brainer, and others from the Old Kingdom. From the regional organizations Tcacenco and Petre Borila[56] from Bessarabia, Elek Koblos and Berger from Transylvania, and B. Donchev and Colev from Dobruja were the outstanding members.[57]. A unified com-

that it adopted some 'provisional' statutes, especially that of the title of 'Communist Party, section of the Communist International' (which was what Moscow wanted above all), the communist programme was not adopted in its most fundamental aspects, particularly in regard to agrarian policy.

[56] See below, p. 350.

[57] There is no evidence of how the work was divided and who formed the Politburo. The 'unions' of Bessarabian, Ukrainian, and Bulgarian 'peasants' were

mission for press and publications was also set up with the task of seeing that the Rumanian publications of the party carried the same material and followed the same line as the publications in Russian, Ukrainian, German, and Yiddish. This was designed to take care of the run-away Bucharest 'sectarian' intellectuals.

But in order to ensure the unity of the party as an organization a new Secretary-General was elected in the person of A. Constantinescu. A few months later he was arrested and Cristescu became the Secretary-General. This picturesque demagogue, who always wore a red bow-tie and was nicknamed 'the mattress-maker' after his trade, was certainly not the man to give the party the toughness the Bessarabians demanded. The soapbox was his favourite political means of action. His approach to clandestine work was 'moderate'; to 'self-determination' reluctant. As to his relations with his fellow workers, he was highly sceptical.[58] Lozovsky stated in the Communist International in 1926 that Cristescu had openly declared that 'owing to its cowardice and indifference the majority of the Rumanian proletariat stands aside'.[59] But the fact that both Constantinescu and especially Cristescu were among those who did not enjoy the confidence of the Russians and yet were elected shows that even in a party as artificial as was the Rumanian, the influence of the International was as yet weak and that, in order to maintain any such party in existence in Rumania, it had to compromise.

As for the 'sectarian' intellectuals of Bucharest, they continued not only to run the party's open publications but also to challenge the validity of the International's new points on Rumanian problems. Marcel Pauker took part in the debates of the Fourth World Congress of the Comintern in Moscow where he opposed Varga's policy on the agrarian problems of South-East Europe, especially with regard to Rumania.[60]

already at work in villages with a strongly irredentist programme. Members of the CC of the party were directing them, e.g. Tcacenco and Borila in Bessarabia and Donchev in Dobruja. Yet these 'unions' were not responsible to the leadership of the RCP.

[58] Loghin (*Analele*, May-June 1957) makes it clear that the greatest mistake of the 2nd Congress had been to maintain the 'moderate' Cristescu in the central position. See also N. Goldberger, *Lupta partidului comunist din Romania* (1952).

[59] *Inprecorr*, Mar. 1926. It is true that party membership had fallen considerably. In April 1924, for instance, the Komsomols had only 17 circles with 1,500 members and 7 groups with 79 members in the whole of Rumania (PMR, *Documente*, i).

[60] *Inprecorr*, 24 Nov. 1922 (Report on 4th World Congress).

The Third Congress

The Third Congress of the Rumanian Communist Party, which took place in mid-September 1924, was influenced by three factors. Stalin was already assuming control of the International, which had held its Fifth Congress in the previous June. The Bulgarian communist uprising of September 1923 had ended in failure. The Rumanian Communist Party itself had been forced by the government into an illegality which was far from welcome to its rank and file. These three events were to have a bearing upon the new structure of the party created at the Congress.

The ban on the party had been partly the outcome of a diplomatic incident. The negotiations for resuming diplomatic relations, which the representatives of the Rumanian government had opened in Vienna in March 1924 with the Soviet representatives, had ended in failure over the Bessarabian question. The problem of Bessarabia was the only post-war legacy of the enlargement of Rumania which had not been solved by the subsequent peace treaties. On 25 October 1917 a Moldavian 'Military Committee' had proclaimed the historical and political autonomy of Bessarabia, annexed by Tsarist Russia in 1812. On 9 April 1918 the newly formed National Council voted by an overwhelming majority for the union of Bessarabia with Rumania. This decision was recognized internationally by the Paris treaty of 28 October 1920, signed by France, Great Britain, Italy, and Japan, although Japan did not ratify it. The new state of the Union of Soviet Socialist Republics had made a special point of not recognizing the accession of Bessarabia to Rumania.[61] This refusal, however, did not mean that the Soviet Union on occasion could not be fairly reassuring on the subject of her immediate aims towards the area. Even before the negotiations in Vienna in 1924 between the Soviet and Rumanian delegations, Rakovsky had confided to Louis Fischer that 'Litvinov would have agreed to recognize a *de*

[61] On 1 May 1919 the Soviet govt had given the Rumanian govt an ultimatum signed by Chicherin, People's Commissar for Foreign Affairs, and Rakovsky, President of the Council of People's Commissars and People's Commissar for the Ukrainian SR, demanding that Rumanian troops in Bessarabia should withdraw. The ultimatum was to expire in 48 hours. It expired without any further move from the Soviet govt. On the contrary, on 13 Aug. 1921 the Soviet govt through the same two signatories sent another note to the Rumanian Govt in which it assured the latter of the peaceful intentions of Russia and of the Soviet Ukraine and stated that orders had been given to the Russian troops near the Dniester to avoid any action likely to give the appearance of aggression (*Soviet Russia,* 1921; published by the Soviet Legation in Washington).

jure Rumanian sovereignty over Bessarabia but that he, Rakovsky, backed by Stalin and Chicherin, preferred to maintain Bessarabia as a Soviet *irredenta*.[62]

It was this hard line which prevailed, and the Russian delegation in Vienna refused to endorse any formula which might be interpreted as an acknowledgment of Rumania's rights over Bessarabia. The press and mass organizations of the Rumanian Communist Party were accordingly instructed to open a particularly strident campaign in favour of the Soviet viewpoint. The anger which such a campaign aroused among Rumanian public opinion played into the hands of the Liberal government which had a long-sought pretext for banning the party. This it did on 11 April 1924.

But the sharpening of the conflict over Bessarabia gave rise to stronger Russian action. In the summer of 1924 a 'Moldavian Republic' was proclaimed across the Dniester. In September irredentist agitations were provoked by the communists in Russian-inhabited villages in Bessarabia. The Rumanian Ministry of the Interior, with G. Tatarescu as Under-Secretary, decided to call out the troops, which led to tragic results in the village of Tatar-Bunar. The revolt of Tatar-Bunar, which afterwards spread to other Bessarabian villages involving some 4,000 people, was later presented by the Communist Party as a new peasant revolution and as the first establishment of a Moldavian Republic in Bessarabia.[63] It was rather a local irredentist episode. It had been provoked by the Union of Revolutionary Peasants of Bessarabia which was the new kernel of the Communist Party's Bessarabian wing.[64] The revolt afforded on the one hand the opportunity for Tatarescu to provoke some ugly anti-Semitic incidents in Rumania. On the other it offered the first opportunity for concerted action abroad by the Rumanian communists, this action being led by Dobrogeanu-Gherea. The 'trial of the peasants' was widely reported in the communist world press. The French writer Barbusse attended the trial.

[62] *Men & Politics*, pp. 134–5.

[63] It was the Moldavian Autonomous SSR that became a constituent Moldavian SSR only on 2 Aug. 1940 after the conquest of Bessarabia and Northern Bukovina as a result of the ultimatum of 27 July 1940. The aim of the proclamation of the Moldavian Republic in 1924 was therefore also irredentist.

[64] The only communist known to have taken part in it is Borila, at the time of writing Deputy Chairman of the Council of Ministers and member of the Politburo. Pavel Tcacenco, who died in 1927, seems to have been prominent in the action.

The Congress had been publicly announced for February 1924, but instead took place clandestinely in mid-September. The Comintern sent a representative. Two representatives of the Balkan Federation, Dimitrov and Kolarov, also attended. The Congress reaffirmed that the party should adopt a basically illegal character. The fact that the Rumanian government had by this time banned the party was cited by the International as proof that it had been right all along to stress the vital importance of an underground organization.

A further ruling called for an intensive recruiting campaign among the working class. But here the leaders admitted that the Rumanian workers showed less and less desire to join or even to collaborate with the Rumanian Communist Party. In the trade unions, they pointed out, the Cluj congress of September 1923 had ended in yet another victory for the Social Democrats. This victory marked the end of any communist hope of winning the bulk of the organized workers, who either remained loyal to the Social Democratic or to the National Peasant Parties, or else chose to remain politically independent or apathetic. But the International had instructed the party in November 1923, shortly after the Cluj defeat, to begin the establishment of revolutionary trade unions, the so-called 'unitary' unions. By 1924 no progress had been made. It was evidently this failure which provoked the crushing comment at the Congress from the Comintern representative that the 'Rumanian Communist Party is not yet a truly communist party, with a clear communist ideology, with strict proletarian discipline and with deep links with the broad working class'.[65]

On social lines, the Congress recommended work among the peasants. Politically it pressed for close collaboration with the left wing of the National Peasant Party and the creation of a 'Workers'-Peasants' Bloc', as a front and electoral organization.

Finally, on the national question, it again insisted that the party must convince the masses that 'it is vital for the bringing about of the revolution and for the true independence of Rumania that the efforts of the subjugated minorities should be backed on the principle of self-determination up to complete secession from the existing state'.[66] This was a further victory for the irredentists and was but an echo of a resolution passed at the Fifth Comintern

[65] PMR, *Documente*, ii. [66] Ibid.

Congress the same year. This Congress had considered it 'essential to intensify communist work among the Magyar population of those territories annexed to Czechoslovakia, Rumania, and Yugoslavia and that the Communist Parties of those countries should launch the slogan of self-determination up to secession from the states which had annexed them'.[67] The Congress also approved the slogans advanced by the Rumanian Communist Party for the separation of Bukovina and Dobruja from Rumania.

It must have been at this moment that the Transylvanian wing, which had hitherto refused to collaborate, entered the party. It at once received full honours. This moment also saw the beginning of the activity of the Bessarabian, Bukovinian, and Dobrujan Revolutionary Organizations which were to act as the revolutionary irredentist bodies. The Dobrujan Revolutionary Organization was established in 1925 by a group of Bulgarians, among whom were Colev and Dmitri Kroshneff. It was Kroshneff who in 1935 became the editor of the illegal newspaper *Scanteia,* thus continuing the tradition of Rakovsky and other Bulgarians within the Rumanian Party.[68]

The Congress dismissed the existing Central Committee and denounced the existence within the party of both 'right-wing opportunist deviations' and 'liquidationist-intellectual left-wing tendencies'. In terms of personalities, the right wing meant Cristescu and Boris Stefanov.[69] The left wing, led by Dobrogeanu-Gherea and Marcel Pauker, was for the moment only rebuked. But the International was already beginning to prepare the case against them as 'Trotskyists', through their association with Rakovsky and the inspiration they derived from him. A new Secretary-General was found in Elek Koblos, who was considered suitable on two counts. He was a Hungarian and a worker, a carpenter by trade. For four years he was to represent the Rumanian Communist Party at the congresses of the International under the name of Badulescu. Ana Pauker was the mistress of Koblos and is

[67] Resolution of 5th World Congress, *Communist International,* Dec. 1924–Jan. 1925.

[68] For biography of Kroshneff see *Sc.,* 16 Oct. 1956.

[69] At the plenary meeting of 28 Nov.–5 Dec. 1961 Gheorghe Stoica singled out Boris Stefanov as the person most responsible for the 'defeatist line' of the 3rd and 4th Congresses. He said that animated by Dobrogeanu-Gherea's theory of 'neo-serfdom' Stefanov advocated a line whereby the CP should have a 'parallel and simultaneous' line with the other Rumanian parties and not try to solve social, economic and political problems which were not yet ripe by insurrectional methods.

believed to have given him a good deal of help and support. Kereszi-Krisan was one of the Political Secretaries, under the name of Alexandru Georgescu.

The Fourth Congress

Such was the unpopularity and impotence of the party that its situation continuously deteriorated and the International soon realized that it must again intervene, this time more openly and rigorously.

'Bolshevization' of the party had been decreed by the Central Committee and Control Commission in July 1925, but without any perceptible result. According to a report published by these two bodies in December 1925,[70] the setting up of factory cells and trade union fractions had made no progress, leaders and rank and file alike suffered from 'legalist delusions' and 'practised only a kind of Sunday underground'. Moreover they showed a regrettable tendency to confuse the Workers' Peasants' Bloc, the legal electoral platform established in 1925, with the party itself. The report repudiated the leaders' defence that the party did not have enough strength to carry on the underground activities assigned to it and denied that attempts at the 'most elementary illegal action, such as the distribution of clandestine manifestoes' were invariably followed by disastrous reprisals.[71] In 1926 the number of regional organizations had been reduced to half the number which existed in 1924 by order of the Central Committee and Control Commission themselves.

In 1926 the International once again drew very severe conclusions in its resolutions. 'The Party', it stated, 'will not make a single step forward if it does not succeed in acquiring communist ideology and Bolshevik tactics.' It again complained of the existence of left deviations, which threatened to isolate the party from the masses, and of the much more dangerous right deviation. What the Rumanian party lacked was personal discipline. More of this and the deviations would soon disappear.[72] Yet the Inter-

[70] 'For the Bolshevization of the Rumanian CP', PMR, *Documente*, ii.

[71] Yet such an action on 10 Dec. 1924 had been followed by 800 arrests, including many members of the CP. Thus 'one of the reasons put forward by the liquidatory group is that the party being underground cannot be a mass party and so becomes a romantic section cut off from the masses'. Also: 'Some members believe that we have endangered the legality of the party by launching much too radical slogans of self-determination.' (Rep. of plen. mtg. of CC, Dec. 1925, PMR, *Documente*, ii).

[72] Ibid.

national hesitated to deal drastically with the leaders. There may have been two reasons for this. One was the instability within the Russian party itself, due to the Trotskyist opposition. This instability may have produced a desire on the part of Stalin not to offend parties elsewhere. Rakovsky's elimination from the Russian party in November 1927 was to give rise to especial anxiety about the reaction of the Rumanian party, and Koblos's declaration of solidarity with the Stalinist leadership on 23 November 1927 was therefore very welcome.[73] The second, more immediately compelling, reason was that the leaders of the International themselves realized that the Rumanian party was in no position to stand a drastic purge of leadership.

But by the time the Fourth Congress was held in September 1928 it was obvious that the leadership would have to be changed yet again. Koblos and the Central Committee had committed what was at that period a cardinal sin in the eyes of the Comintern. The Congress[74] admitted that the party had made a great ideological mistake with respect to the slogan of self-determination up to secession. The Central Committee and its 'renegade' Secretary-General had allowed the slogan to be replaced by the 'Rothermere-catchword of a federative republic of workers and peasants of Rumania' in Transylvania, Bukovina, and Dobruja. In other words, Koblos and his fellow Hungarians had been trying to serve the interests of the Magyar government in Budapest and not those of the International. Other resolutions once again frankly admitted the serious situation of the party.[75] 'The party is passing through an acute crisis in leadership' and 'its mistakes have led the party to the decomposition of its leadership, to the refusal of members to continue active work and to intrigues, calumnies, and fractionalism'.

At the end of the Congress the leaders of the right wing, Koblos, Berger, and Koloman Muller, were dismissed and the left wing, Dobrogeanu-Gherea and Boris Stefanov, were again only ad-

[73] He insisted on the necessity of a special campaign against the activities of Rakovsky. 'The Rumanian Communists', he said, 'would have to expose all the more energetically the activity of Rakovsky because he was so popular in Rumania.' Then followed on 1 Dec. the statement of the Balkan Federation that the Rumanian, Bulgarian and Yugoslav CPs had no Trotskyite adherence (*Inprecorr*, Jan. 1928).

[74] Resolution of 4th Congress (PMR, *Documente*, ii.).

[75] Ibid. The implication being that the bourgeois govts of Hungary and Bulgaria were using the Rumanian CP to further their anti-Rumanian policies, for which there might be some evidence.

monished. In fact, although the International, partly through Marcel Pauker, had managed as usual to manipulate the Congress, it was unable to provide any new leaders for the party. The heterogeneous and artificial group broke into more and more fractions, animated by personal dislikes and antipathies. Marcel Pauker formed from the outside a powerful group which under his clandestine name of 'Luximin' claimed to represent the party. His main associates were Dobrogeanu-Gherea, Vasile Luca,[76] and Boris Stefanov. Thus, as a result of the decisions of the Fourth Congress, two main factions, the Luximin and the Barbu,[77] both claiming to represent the Central Committee, struggled with one another. This situation endured in utter confusion, paralyzing any activity, for another two years. In 1930 the International once more was called upon to intervene, this time most drastically and a new Congress, the Fifth, was convened in 1932.

THE BACKGROUND OF THE WORLD CRISIS, 1929–33

While Rumania's tiny Communist Party was being torn by internal dissensions, the world as a whole was being shaken by a crisis which was to give the extremist right and left movements their greatest opportunity since the end of the war. The agrarian countries of Eastern Europe were more severely affected by the world economic crisis than, in some ways, any other part of the world. They were affected as agricultural producers, for their exports dwindled away partly because of increased western purchases from Canada and other non-European countries, and partly because of Soviet 'dumping'. The crisis also produced a catastrophic fall in agricultural prices everywhere. Unsold crops rotted in the fields and the attempts of various governments to assist producers by state purchases, loans, or mortgages came rapidly to an end because of the precarious financial situation. At the same time, and for the same reasons, a greater discrepancy between agricultural and industrial prices developed, the 'scissors' again taking on a threatening reality.

The Eastern European countries also suffered a blow by the abrupt stoppage of the flow of financial and industrial capital

[76] See below, p. 353.

[77] In the accusations against Vasile Luca published in 1952 it was said that 'in 1929-30 Luca received orders and financial help from the *Siguranţza* to foster the treasonable clique of Marcel Pauker, the former enemy of the communist movement and Trotskyist agent' (*Rezolutii*).

from Western Europe. The collapse in May 1931 of the Kredit-Anstalt in Vienna, through which much of the European capital and credit had been channelled to the Austro-Hungarian territories, brought down with it a series of important banks in all these countries. As a result credit, especially agricultural credit, had to be even more severely restricted. Agricultural investment dried up almost completely.

Moreover when Great Britain went off the gold standard in September 1931 a tendency towards autarky and protectionism in Central and Eastern Europe arose. Thus began the phase of economic nationalism which was to contribute so much to the spread of political nationalism.

In Rumania the crisis struck at an already weak economic structure. The discrepancy between the standard of living in the towns and that in the villages was largely due to the way in which capitalism had come to Rumania.

Even in 1929 Rumania was not a fully capitalist country. Virgil Madgearu's definition, given in 1940,[78] that Rumania was 'a semi-capitalist state with a peasant economic structure' was the most adequate. What this definition implied was that in spite of the speedy industrialization which had taken place between 1919 and 1939, agricultural production was still by far the most important factor in the economy. This was strikingly noticeable even in investments, which were more than double in agriculture what they were in industry and trade combined.[79] But the structure of agriculture had markedly changed since the agrarian reform. Instead of the neo-serfdom described by Dobrogeanu-Gherea, Rumanian agriculture was dominated by millions of individual peasant holdings which employed no hired labour but were worked by the owner and his family and which formed—again to quote Madgearu—'a quite specific economic texture in which the classical categories of capitalism, wage, profit, and rent were totally absent'. But agrarian reform had also produced its own problems. The great majority of the plots of land of under 3 hectares could not feed the owners and their families, who were forced to work on the larger estates; and even the more prosperous peasants were

[78] In his *Evolutia economie i romanesti*. See below, p. 55 n. 39 on the political personality of Madgearu.

[79] The value of agricultural technical investment in Rumania was 1,000 lei per hectare, in Bulgaria 2,000, in Germany 15,000, and in Switzerland 42,000 (ibid. p. 69).

short of machines, tractors, ploughs, tools, and fertilizer. This was undoubtedly one of the major causes why Rumanian per capita agricultural production was among the lowest in Europe.

Modern agricultural implements could not be bought because the price paid to the peasant for his produce was so low and there was a great dearth of agricultural capital and even of credit upon which to draw. To combat this unsatisfactory rural situation the growth of Rumanian industry should have done two things. It should have provided cheaper and more abundant goods for agricultural producers and should have absorbed much of the surplus labour from the countryside. The density of the agricultural population in Rumania was in 1930 among the highest in Europe: 94.3 to the square kilometre of arable land as compared to 37.5 per square kilometre in Denmark, for example.[80]

But the industrialization carried out before the First World War had been both inadequate and badly directed. At first capital was foreign in origin and accordingly went first to those industries which could most usefully produce goods for export, such as oil and timber or flour mills and sugar factories.[81] Up to 1916 Rumanian capital still represented less than one-sixth of the total industrial investment—and out of this small fraction, state capital played the greatest part owing to the nationalization of the rapidly developing railways. In the oil industry the share of Rumanian capital remained, even up to the outbreak of the Second World War, only 27 per cent of the total.[82] Thus national income did not increase proportionately with the volume of export. Instead, industrialization helped to destroy the local crafts and industries, which could not stand up to the crippling competition offered by manufactured or imported goods, and did not help agricultural producers as much as it should have done. It did not produce more plentiful supplies of cheaper goods, which was what they needed, and it did not attract enough of the unemployed agricultural workers.[83]

After the First World War industrialization was placed on a better footing. The new western provinces were rich in mineral resources and were themselves more highly industrialized than

[80] W. E. Moore, *Economic Demography of Eastern and Southern Europe* (1945).

[81] N. P. Arcadian, *Industrializarea romaniei* (1936), which is also the best account of the industrialization of Rumania.

[82] N. C. Jordan, *The Rumanian Oil Industry* (1955), p. 11.

[83] See Arcadian.

the Old Kingdom. Yet even after the incorporation of these provinces the workers represented only 10 per cent of the total population of Rumania. The second favourable post-war development was the consolidation of Rumanian financial capital.[84] Western capital was now less eager to expand in the new Eastern European countries than it had been before the war. Finally, the emergence of the peasantry, now landowners themselves, and thus potentially consumers, directed the attention of the industrial producers and financial investors towards this new, natural, and permanent market. In 1929, with the price of agricultural products still high, the 'scissors' between agricultural and industrial prices were gradually closing. The National Peasant Party's economic policy was also concerned with the direction of industry towards consumer goods and agricultural implements.[85] The stabilization of the currency, with the help of French loans, was effected in February 1929.[86] It was hoped to modify the foreign trade, fiscal, and credit policy of the Liberals and to encourage as far as possible agricultural producers and consumers. This trend was apparent not only in Rumania but in nearly all the agrarian countries of Eastern Europe.

That these countries realized that they had much in common was shown during the 1920's by two separate though parallel movements. First there was the Green International,[87] grouping together all the agrarian parties of the region in a common quest for collaboration and regional integration, and second, the unity shown by the Eastern European governments at the League of Nations, pressing for a European plan in which Western and Eastern Europe could mould the continent into a more self-contained economic unit. By the end of the 1920's it seemed that some success might be reached in the second effort. The Briand Plan, the most articulate of these various schemes, was given priority in the discussions at the League, greatly to the displeasure of the Soviet Union and of her satellite communist parties, who denounced it as another attempt on the part of the imperialist powers to encircle her.

[84] RIIA, *South-Eastern Europe* (1939).

[85] Madgearu, *Rumania's New Economic Policy* (1930).

[86] The monetary reform took place on 8 Feb. 1929; it stabilized the leu at 10 mg gold.

[87] See Bureau international agraire, *La Politique étrangère et l'organisation internationale des agriculteurs* (Prague, 1925); W. B. Bizzel, *The Green Rising* (N.Y., 1962). For the doctrinal background of the Green International see D. Mitrany, *Marx against the Peasant* (1951).

Thus, at a time when the world economic crisis was already beginning, it seemed that Rumania had grasped the significance and the causes of many of her economic weaknesses and social injustices and was groping toward their solution. It was the National Peasant movement which seemed most capable of solving them.

The National Peasant Government

The coming to power of the opposition party, the National Peasants, in 1928 could have meant the beginning of the solution of the structural, social, and economic maladjustment of Rumania.

The National Peasant Party was formed through the union of the Peasant Party of Muntenia, Moldavia, and Bessarabia, with the National Party of Transylvania. Actually they first collaborated in the government of September 1919 as two separate and not yet entirely merged parties. The former had appeared in the Old Kingdom at the end of the war, after the agrarian reform. Its programme was based largely on the doctrine put forward by the Bessarabian C. Stere, a Rumanian who, like the Russian Dobrogeanu-Gherea, had come to Rumania after having suffered in Tsarist prisons. His doctrine as expounded between 1905 and 1912 in the pages of *Viata romaneasca* was populism (Narodnikism) adapted to conditions in Rumania.[88] It stressed the paramount importance of the rural population and production, denounced the 'parasitic' industrialization promoted under the influence of foreign capital which was directed primarily towards exports, and produced more expensive goods than could be imported thus being of no benefit to the bulk of the population, the peasantry. Stere also advocated a gradual integration through concentration upon the economic and cultural needs of the countryside and through the creation of a genuinely democratic system.

When Bessarabia joined Rumania Stere, although handicapped in the eyes of Rumanians by the fact that he had supported the war on the side of the Germans, became the natural leader of the Peasant Party in that province.[89] The Bessarabians

[88] The series of studies 'Social Democratism sau poporanism' in *Viata romaneasca* in 1907 and 1908 is the main source for his doctrine. The early Peasant Party programme, *Proectul de program al partidului taranesc din Romania* (1921) contains many of Stere's attitudes.

[89] He had not taken part in Marghiloman's administration. But in a newspaper

understood and believed his contention that his patriotic duty as the representative of a people oppressed by Russia was to oppose her, until she granted them freedom. The electoral strength of the party increased. In the Old Kingdom it was organized by Ion Mihalache. A peasant teacher whose contribution to doctrine was insignificant, Mihalache insisted upon the importance of peasant co-operation as a means of improving agricultural production in an underdeveloped country.[90] The theoretician of the movement was Virgil Madgearu, an economist who was to become the spokesman and planner of the National Peasant Party in economic, financial, and social policy and theory.

The Peasant Party was at a disadvantage in the political field by the electoral laws and methods then in force and by the fact that it existed in only three of the provinces. But its union in October 1926 with the National Party, the direct descendant of the Rumanian parliamentary majority in the Austro-Hungarian empire, made it a real political power.

The National Party was not, as was the Peasant Party, a class party and it actually had little concern with ideology for its own sake. Its main political inspiration was of a national and political character. Its most outstanding personality, Iuliu Maniu, found his main inspiration in his belief in the need for a consolidation of the union of Transylvania with Rumania and in his religious faith—he was a Greek Catholic. Born in 1873 in the strongly clerical town of Blaj, Maniu had studied law at the university of Vienna. Though he was still a young man in 1918 it was he, more than any other Transylvanian leader, who must be credited with the reunion of this province with the Old Kingdom. Maniu, like many Transylvanians, combined strength of character with political pragmatism; he tended to distrust intellectual brilliance and considered genuine day-to-day democratic practices more valuable than sweeping modern reforms on paper. The National Party too was aware of the discrepancy between the promises of the centralistic administration in Bucharest and its achievements. It advocated the immediate adoption of a law for decentralization. But although not class-minded and composed of various

Lumina, published in Bucharest during 1916, he had denounced the dangers of fighting on the same side as Russia, which he regarded as the main expansionist Power in Eastern Europe.

[90] Mihalache's practical peasant doctrine is best expressed in *Noul regim agrar* (1925).

social elements, the party did acknowledge the primacy of the peasant class in Rumania. It was on this basis that it united with the Peasant Party, but whereas the Peasant Party wanted to establish a genuine democracy in order that the peasants as a class could assume power, the National Party accepted the coming to power of the peasant class through a wholly democratic system which, in its view, was the ultimate essential.[91] Only two years after the fusion, the National Peasant Party swept to victory on 12 December 1928, gaining about 80 per cent of the votes. The opposition remained powerless for two years.

The Other Parties

The Conservative Party had almost disappeared in the great changes brought about by the land reform and by the outcome of the war. The power of the landowning class which had been its bulwark disappeared with the expropriation of the large estates. Also, the traditional orientation of the party towards Germany, as opposed to the Liberal attachment to France, was a further handicap to them after the Allied victory.[92] Thus only a remnant of the party was kept in existence under the leadership of A. Marghiloman.[93] Marghiloman had been the head of the Rumanian administration which remained in Bucharest when the Germans occupied it in 1916. Other former Conservatives rallied round General Averescu after the war. Averescu had helped to suppress the peasant revolt of 1907, but at the end of the war he became a popular figure through his victorious campaign against the German army. His 'People's Party' came to power in 1920 and

[91] Partidul National Taranesc, *Principiile, programul si statutele* (1926). A new administrative law applying decentralization was passed in 1926.

[92] The most outstanding personalities of this party, the literary critic Titu Maiorescu and the landowner Petre Carp, had both been educated in Germany and had both acquired a great respect for the thoroughness of German culture. In politics as well as in economic and social problems the two schools of thought, 'German' and 'French', were almost psychologically opposed to each other. The francophils, who were the great majority, considered that the racial and historic links of the Rumanian people with France justified her paramount influence over Rumania's contemporary destiny. The germanophils advocated 'realism' as opposed to the 'superficial idealism' of the others. They showed that there was a mutual economic interest between industrial Germany and agrarian Rumania; that the political interest of Rumania *vis-à-vis* Russia could be better safeguarded through an alliance with Germany; and that Rumania, in need of technicians, should send students to the German engineering schools and universities rather than to the French schools of law and literature.

[93] A. Marghiloman, *Note politice* (1931).

remained in power until the end of 1921, during the period when Take Ionescu, a francophil lawyer and diplomat, worked with Benes to bring into being the Little Entente. The party was also in power in 1926-7. The two former wings of the Conservative Party were bitterly opposed on foreign, social, and economic policy. Marghiloman was in principle opposed to the agrarian reform bills introduced by Bratianu and his administration in 1919. Averescu, on the other hand, in 1920 passed the final bill, which was a compromise between the claims of the Peasant Party and the initial reforms as proposed by Bratianu.[94] The strength of Averescu's government lay in the cluster of talents he gathered around him. The most notable of his supporters, apart from Take Ionescu, was the young Nicolae Titulescu who, between 1920 and 1921, was his Minister of Finance and in 1926 and 1927 his Foreign Minister. Later, from his new post as Rumanian Minister in London, he stepped on to the international stage by defending the Rumanian land reform against the Hungarian landowners at the League of Nations. Averescu's party disintegrated after its fall in 1927.

The Liberal Party governed the Rumanian kingdom during the war and, apart from brief periods in 1919 and 1920–1, right up to 1926. They were responsible, therefore, for most of the very important foreign and domestic decisions taken during the period and Bratianu's influence over King Ferdinand was such that even when in parliamentary opposition he remained the monarch's chief personal adviser. The steady progress achieved and the growing successes harvested during these years must be laid to the credit of this party and, implicitly, of the Bratianu family. Ion C. Bratianu, the last of the dynasty, was the Prime Minister under whom the decision to pass universal suffrage and the agrarian reform (which he had advocated since 1913) were taken. These had been pressed upon him by a group of progressive young men around him, some of whom were the former 'generous' socialists, V. G. Mortun, Diamandi, and the Radovici brothers. Yet the peasants did not show their gratitude by supporting the Liberal Party. It was still in the main supported by the middle classes, who formed the weakest link in the political structure of Rumania and thus were unable to win the majority of votes for

[94] For the history of the agrarian reform in Rumania and its various phases see Mitrany, *The Land and the Peasant in Rumania* (1930).

the party of their choice. Affected by the rapid economic development of the country and by the appearance of the 'new' and more impatient generation, the middle classes themselves rapidly separated into upper and lower strata with ever more antagonistic attitudes, ways of life, and political tendencies.[95]

The intellectuals among them, who from the foundation of the Rumanian Kingdom had always been attracted by the progressive planks in the party's platform, now looked to other parties. The party became increasingly the party of the Rumanian-owned—as opposed to foreign-owned—banks, industries, and trade enterprises. Nevertheless it still had the experience which inspired confidence and Ionel Bratianu personally possessed the prestige accruing to a successful Prime Minister. When in his last years he had to face the electoral pressure of the new voters, made up of the peasants and citizens from the new provinces (whom he and his party had helped to free), this seemed to him a proof of the ingratitude of history to which he was determined not to bow. He and his party grew steadily more authoritarian. He died in 1927, leaving as his successor his brother Vintila Bratianu,[96] a man of great integrity but no flexibility. He was followed by I. G. Duca, a talented writer and politician, with a melancholy and hesitant cast of mind.[97]

Although nationalism was the common denominator of all the political parties in Rumania, except for the Social Democrats, those political parties with an exclusively nationalist programme were, in the 1920's, of little electoral significance. One of these was the National Democratic Party which resented the influence of foreign powers and denounced the mercantilism of the Liberals' foreign and economic policy. This party was centred mainly in a group of teachers and intellectuals, dominated by the historian N. Iorga. As an historian and ideological leader, Iorga had been famous even before the First World War both in Rumania and abroad. During the war he was one of the most ardent and inspiring believers in final victory over the Germans. As a politician, however, he was inept and vague. His ideas had much in common

[95] On the process of separation of the layers of the 'bourgeoisie' see also Stefan Zeletin, *Burghezia romana, origina si rolul ei istoric* (1928).

[96] The main advocate of integral economic nationalism. He served as Minister of Finance in the Liberal govt after the war.

[97] His study on liberalism in Rumanian Soc. Inst., *Doctrinele partidelor politice* (1928) is still one of the best works on the Rumanian Liberal Party's general policy.

with fascism, but he himself by breeding and temperament was alienated by the dictatorial brutality of fascist regimes.[98]

The other nationalist party was the League of National Christian Defence, founded by A. C. Cuza, a Moldavian economist and professor.[99] Cuza preached unadulterated anti-Semitism, attributing to the Jews all the evils which beset the world. Though opposing insurrection as a policy, he was not averse to encouraging his young followers to indulge in hooliganism and violence. In 1927 his League split into two irreconcilable groups and this was the signal for the most magnetic personality of his followers, Cornelius Zelea Codreanu,[1] then aged twenty-eight, to form yet a third extreme right party. Codreanu called it the League of the Archangel Michael and on 24 June 1927 invited all those who 'believed unconditionally' to join him. Codreanu was the son of Bukovinian parents. His mother was of German and his father of Polish descent. From early youth he had been fired with the sense of mission to 'save' Rumania and Christendom from the horrors of communist revolution, led by world Jewry. He attributed the success of the communists to their terrorist methods and their new conception of 'direct action'. He urged that these same methods should be used against them, if not by the authorities, then by the 'patriotic' elements. Codreanu's first exploit was in 1924, when he murdered the Prefect of Iasi. He was triumphantly acquitted of his crime the same year, a year in which the communist irredentist armed movements in Bessarabia and Dobruja had particularly inflamed nationalist passions in Rumania. His reputation, especially among Rumanian youth, rose to new heights. Within himself this action created a complex of 'punishment and remorse' which he tried to present later to his disciples as a philosophy of life. Youths who 'believed unconditionally' and flocked to his banner were for the most part white-collar workers, unsuccessful students, and various dilettanti transformed into political zealots.

The 'League' and the Communist Party, the two opposite extremes, had two main points in common. One was their determina-

[98] J. C. Campbell, 'N. Iorga', *Slavonic & E. Eur. R.*, Nov. 1947.

[99] His influence on the Rumanian students was very strong but he had little following in the country. His speeches in parliament and his lectures at the university contrasted strangely with his primitive political doctrines and methods. He was a scholar of German formation.

[1] Author of *Pentru legionari* (1937) (in German trs, *Eiserne Garde*, Berlin, 1939).

tion to seize power by any method and to institute a dictatorial régime. The other was their dissent from the general foreign policy of Rumania, which was predicated on a fear of communist Russia, and later of Nazi Germany, and a desire to insure herself against any potential revisionism on the part of Hungary or Bulgaria. The 'Little Entente' in 1921 between Rumania, Czechoslovakia, and Yugoslavia, the alliance of 1920 with France, the traditional ally, the alliance with Poland and Rumanian diplomacy at Geneva were mainly designed to protect the country from a variety of possible encroachments.

Outwitting the National Peasants

Buffeted by the world crisis, the government of the National Peasant Party showed an increasing weakness. The social and economic problems which it had promised to solve had now become so aggravated by the international situation as to be almost unsoluble. Peasant economics entered into the vicious circle of unsold crops and lack of credit; the state was forced to raise taxes in order to buy some, at least, of the crops and to reduce wages and salaries in order to declare moratoria on debts, thus creating yet another vicious circle. The underpaid industrial workers had also cause for complaints. By the end of 1929 there had already been widespread strikes among the mineworkers at Lupeni, which had led to clashes with the police and some bloodshed.[2] But since one of the answers to the financial crisis was a lowering of all wages, the unrest could not be stopped. It spread throughout the trade union movement and was particularly rife among the railwaymen.

Unrest, however, was by no means confined to the workers. Many intellectuals and students found themselves unemployed. They had expected much from the National Peasant Government's promises of investments in social and cultural plans in which their talents would have been fruitfully used. In their bitterness they turned to extremist solutions, most of them leaning towards some vaguely nationalist, authoritarian administration.

[2] The strike began in Aug. 1929 among the miners of the Jiu valley. The national Peasant govt had to use troops to prevent the workers from capturing the electric plant at Lupeni. Some workers were killed. This was not an entirely communist-directed movement. The lack of communist initiative in this episode is shown in the resolution of the International of Aug. 1930: 'The Party Committee prevented the workers of the whole mining district from joining the fighting workers of Lupeni, arguing that the Lupeni action had been instigated by provocateurs' (*Inprecorr*, 18 Sept. 1930).

These were difficult problems enough for the National Peasant government to face. But the most serious blow to it, and to parliamentary democracy in Rumania, was the return of Prince Carol.[3] In 1926 Carol had renounced his right to the throne and one year later, on the death of King Ferdinand, Carol's son, Michael, was proclaimed king, a council of regency being appointed to exercise his prerogative. Carol left the country with his mistress, Magda Lupescu, and promised never to return. With his personal unreliability, his extravagance, and his love of power, he was unsuited to the rôle of constitutional monarch. Yet after his father's death, and more particularly after the death of the Liberal Prime Minister Ionel Bratianu, Carol asked for permission to return. Among the rank and file of the Peasant Party, especially among the younger members who resented Bratianu and his authoritarian methods, there was great sympathy for Carol. Many National Peasants thought that he would be 'their' king, in the same way as Ferdinand, in their eyes, had been the Liberals' king, and that this would be an enduring political asset. This was despite the fact that already at the time the Yugoslav and Bulgarian monarchs had set up their dictatorships, directed largely against the agrarian parties.

Carol returned, with Maniu's permission, on 6 June 1930 and after an easy coup d'état on the 8th was proclaimed king. On discovering that the king was continuing his association with Mme Lupescu Maniu, who had in principle supported the return of Carol, resigned on 1 October 1930.

Immediately on attaining power, Carol showed a marked tendency to see the national problems of the country simply in terms of what suited his own personality and what benefited his own person. He began to move against the political parties both by undermining them from within and by more direct onslaught. Using his considerable force of personality and a rare genius for intrigue, he attached to his personal circle many of the younger Liberals and National Peasants. From without, his method of attack against the democratic parties was to encourage the extreme nationalist and anti-Semitic groups, among them the burgeoning group around Codreanu. His own speeches came more and more to express quasi-fascist and corporatist tendencies. Fin-

[3] H. Bolitho, *Rumania under King Carol* (1938) and A. L. Easterman, *King Carol, Hitler and Lupescu* (1940) are both 'authorized 'biographies.

ally, he encouraged non-party men to come to power, so that after Maniu's resignation and the securing of the foreign loan by the National Peasant government under Mironescu,[4] he succeeded in forming a government of 'coalition' in April 1931, under the historian Iorga.

Iorga was actually in power when elections were held in April 1931. These were blatantly unfair and enabled Iorga to gain a majority which, in spite of his alliance with the Liberals, he would never have won otherwise. The 1931 elections were an irreparable blow to the real constitutionalism which had been growing in Rumania largely through National Peasant influence, insistence, and example. They saw the rise to national status of extremist parties. The National Democratic Party did surprisingly well in Bessarabia and other agricultural regions. The 'Workers'–Peasant' bloc', behind which the communists had shielded themselves since being outlawed in 1924, gained in the industrial districts of Transylvania and Bukovina. Five communist deputies were actually elected, but their elections were immediately invalidated. One of them was a young lawyer, Lucretiu Patrascanu, a former associate of the young Dobrogeanu-Gherea and Marcel Pauker and one of the few intellectuals in the party.

The Communist Party itself had, against this background of turbulent events in Rumania, been undergoing substantial changes which were to have a profound effect on its future. It is to these changes that we must now return.

The Varga Report on Rumania

On 26 February 1929 the International Press Correspondence (Inprecorr), the new organ of the Third International, published a report on the 'economic problems of the new Rumania', by the Hungarian economist, Eugen Varga.[5] This had been followed in August 1930 by the publication of the International's own resolution on Rumania. These two documents, published at a time when Stalin was reformulating the policy of the International, were highly significant. They led to the complete reorganization of the Rumanian party at its Fifth Congress in January 1932.

Varga stated that 'Rumanian industry has developed, but the

[4] A university professor who belonged to the category of Rumanian scholars who, although not active in politics, belonged to certain parties as specialists or cultural personalities.

[5] *Inprecorr*, 26 Feb. 1929.

progress made by it is not great and alters nothing in the fundamental character of the country as an agrarian state'. There were indications of a 'vigorous industrialization' which had led to the broadening of the social and economic bases of the country. As a result,

instead of reserving to a small group of native bourgeoisie the exploitation of all the working classes, poor peasants, workers, medium farmers and petty bourgeois and, by means of the usurious banking system, also that of the bourgeoisie of the new provinces, the party now in power will enable a far broader class of the bourgeoisie in town and country to enjoy the fruits of such exploitation.

The admission of foreign capital on equal terms with that of domestic capital meant for the medium and petty bourgoisie a 'mitigation of the usury hitherto carried on by the Rumanian banking clique', while for the wealthier peasant class it meant cheaper industrial goods and a better sale for their products at home and abroad. From an international point of view, nevertheless, it would be wrong to consider Rumania as a semi-colonial country. Like every other debtor country, 'it is to some extent dependent on its creditors, but the position of a debtor country could hardly be compared with that of a semi-colonialist country'. Finally, there came the summing up which stated that 'the fact that Rumania is an important link in the imperialist system is bound to be strikingly demonstrated in the inevitable collision between the capitalist world and the Soviet Union'.

This political conclusion was emphasized accordingly in a political report to the International on Rumania by T. Marin.[6] Marin argued that it was the supreme, if not the sole, duty of the party henceforth to see that the imperialists could not use Rumania as a strategic base against the Soviet Union but to aim at making her a permanent friend of the Soviet Union. This would ultimately depend on 'the degree of the revolutionary struggle of the masses themselves under the leadership of the Communist Party'.

The Fifth Congress

On 18 September 1930 the Political Secretariat of the Communist International published its resolution on the 'unprincipled

[6] 'The Role of Rumania in Intervention against the USSR', *Communist International,* 15 May 1931.

fractional struggle and on the revival of the Communist Party in Rumania'. It stated that in the Rumanian party a 'fractional struggle devoid of all principle' had broken out. This had led to the splitting of the party leadership and later to that of a number of party organizations. At a crucially important moment, it continued, the whole activity of the party had been paralysed. Only with the aid of the International had it been possible to set up a provisional party committee for the restoration of the unity of the party and of work among the masses.

The outbreak of the fractional struggle, continued the resolution, had not been preceded by any differences on political principles in the party committee. Even members of the Central Committee had only learnt later of this struggle. The party had achieved some organizational successes after its Fourth Congress. These successes, however, did not in the least correspond to the objective possibilities for the growth of the party and the extension of its mass work. Such possibilities had been offered by the intensification of the political and economic crises and primitive peasant and workers' movements, which frequently assumed revolutionary forms, as well as by the growing discontent of the 'toiling masses of the oppressed nationalities'.[7]

In the most important industrial districts and big factories of the Old Kingdom and Transylvania (Bucharest, Valea Prahovei, Timisoara, Resita) the party organizations, and in particular the factory cells in the trade unions, were at best extremely weak. Further, in the most important agrarian districts, with the exception of Bessarabia, hardly any party organizations were in existence, even where the party possessed some influence with the agricultural workers and semi-proletarian peasantry, as for example in Bihor, Valea Mures, Bukovina, and Dobruja.

As a result of its 'bureaucratic sectarian' methods, the Central Committee, the resolution stated, had become not only isolated from the broad proletarian and peasant masses but even from the party membership. The prevailing form of instructions consisted in sending out directives and circulars, without any connexion with the vital questions of the working and peasant masses. The consequence of this had not only been that the party had not prepared for the mass struggle, but it was also unable to place itself at the head of spontaneously arising political struggles, as in

[7] *Inprecorr*, 18 Sept. 1930; *Lupta de clasa*, May-June 1951.

Lupeni, Buhusi, the peasant unrest in Bessarabia, the movement of the war-wounded, and so on.

This was perhaps the strongest indictment of the Rumanian party ever issued by the Comintern which, as has been seen, had not been noted for its benevolence to the Rumanian communists. It was also a sign that the International, through Stalin, really meant business. The need for a radical reorganization of the party along Stalinist lines was underlined by the fact that the Rumanian communists were fighting 'at one of the most important outposts of the Comintern and of the international proletarian revolution'. They were 'fighting in a country which is intended by international imperialism to serve as an advance guard in the coming war against the Soviet Union'.

Working through the faithful 'Bessarabians', the International struck at both right and left of the incoherent party. Among the leftists immediately dismissed were Dobrogeanu-Gherea and Marcel Pauker. The two were to meet again in Moscow in 1934, when both were going to be victims of the Trotskyist purge. This put an end to the domination of the old intellectual group. On the right the International broke the influence of the 'Transylvanians'. The Hungarian 'nationalists', Koblos and Berger, were purged. Vasile Luca was also demoted.

Finally, the International summoned another Rumanian Congress for January 1932. This was the Congress which, according to present Rumanian communist historiography, laid down the main ideological, political and organizational foundations of the party and was the starting-point of the real Communist Party in Rumania. It rebuked both the 'opportunist right-wing elements' for the maintenance of the Dobrogeanu-Gherea theory of 'neo-serfdom', according to which Rumania was facing a bourgeois-democratic revolution, and the 'sectarian left theory' which maintained that a proletarian revolution was imminent. It put forward its own Leninist theory of the historical position of Rumania which, in its more advanced phase, is the theory which still applies today. This theory was that Rumania was ripe for a bourgeois-democratic revolution, *but one which would be carried out by the proletariat in alliance with the peasantry.*[8]

[8] PMR, *Documente,* ii, and PCR, *Documente.* On the internal discussions within the Comintern about the agrarian problem and on relations between peasants and the party see Mitrany, *Marx against the Peasant,* ch. 12. On the theory of the possibility of a revolution in Rumania led by the workers in alliance with the peasants

In the political field, the Congress pointed out the existence of a revolutionary wave caused by the deterioration in economic conditions. It ordered the party to take the lead in exploiting such a favourable situation and not again to fail as it had done between 1929 and 1932. The Congress candidly admitted that the unrest among the workers had developed spontaneously, unsponsored and undirected by the communists. (The most remarkable in the chain of workers' demonstrations—that of the mineworkers of Lupeni on 5 August 1929—had been described by Vasile Luca, who was supposed to be in charge of it, as 'police provocation', a view afterwards condemned by the party and the International.)[9] The party, too, had failed either to guide or to extend the actions of the workers in Arad, Bucharest, Resita, and Buhusi. The Congress urged that communists should take over the direction of such events and win over the working class, which was still led by the 'social-fascists'. Above all, the party was to make political capital and use of the social and economic unrest in the sense that 'every action of the party, every economic fight, action of the unemployed or of the peasants against this must be linked organically with the struggle against war'.

A new leadership emerged at the Fifth Congress. Among those who now took over the party were Boris Stefanov, just released from prison, Foris, arrested soon afterwards, Koffler, Iosif

see N. Petrovici, 'The Problem of the Character of the Revolution as disclosed by Party Literature (up to the 5th RCP Congress)', *Analele*, no. 1, Jan.-Feb. 1958, which gives a comprehensive account of the struggle between the followers of Dobrogeanu-Gherea, who maintained that the peasantry should first be emancipated from the backward social and economic conditions in which it was kept; and the Leninists, who believed that the situation was ripe after the First World War for a bourgeois-democratic revolution led by the workers and peasants, which would later be transformed into a proletarian, socialist revolution.

[9] In April 1929 the Unitary (communist) Trade Unions held their General Congress to discuss the problem of turning to good account the growing discontent of the workers and of fostering the 'unification', under communist leadership, of the workers' syndicates. Vasile Luca, who had just been elected to the CC, was in charge of the Congress on behalf of the party (Luca, *Uber den Kongress der Einheits Gewerkschaften in Temesvar* (1952) and RWP, *Vasile Luca* (1951), also *Istoria RPR*). When the police tried to close the Congress, the members, after the death of a worker, barricaded themselves in the trade union building and were only arrested after a siege. The Unitary Trade Unions were then dissolved. The main trade unions took no part in the action. In his speech at the 30th anniversary of the party Dej said that 'the Congress of the Unitary Trade Unions held in 1929 in Timisoara called the proletarian masses to the struggle. Through Comrade Vasile Luca's voice the party called on the workers to organize a large mass action'. This acknowledgement contrasts sharply with the later pronouncement that in 1929 Luca led a factionist struggle and was a treasonable defeatist (*Sc.*, 3 June 1952).

Chisinevschi,[10] Patrascanu, Luca, Bela Brainer, and Iosif Ranghet.[11] A new Agitprop group formed by Mihai Roller, Leonte Rautu,[12] and A. Buican was put in charge of the 'Stalinist indoctrination' of the party and the intelligentsia, while a new group of youth leaders appeared in the persons of Nicolae Ceausescu,[13] Miron Constantinescu,[14] Alexandru Barladeanu, Constanta Craciun, and Sorin Toma. Later Constantin Parvulescu,[15] who was in prison at the time of the Congress, and Ana Pauker, who returned in 1934 after a six years' stay in Russia, joined the leadership. In 1935 Kroshneff was added.

Not long after the Fifth Congress the party had an opportunity to act on the fierce exhortation for industrial action to which it had been subjected. It rose to the occasion with a desperation and a success unique in its pre-war history. The effects of the depression had caused considerable industrial unrest in Rumania and the workers had very genuine grievances. In particular there was considerable bitterness among the railway workers who, being classified as civil servants, were not allowed to strike in order to better their condition. It was against this background that a young railway electrician called Gheorghe Gheorghiu began to attract attention as a militant communist. He came to the notice not only of the railway workers but also of the railway management. Gheorghiu had attended, as communist representative from Galati, a national conference of railwaymen in that city in March 1931. Soon afterwards the railway authorities transferred him to the Transylvanian town of Dej. He tacked on the name of this town to his prosaic surname of Gheorghiu and became Gheorghe Gheorghiu-Dej.[16] It was not long before he was to be projected on to the national and even the international scene.

At a second national conference of railwaymen in March 1932, only two months after the Fifth Communist Party Congress, Dej was elected Secretary-General of the National Committee for Action of All Railwaymen. Agitation among the railwaymen continued, as did growing unrest among the working class in general. This dissatisfaction led to the calling of a general strike on 2 February 1933. King Carol's method of dealing with this was to use a show of force. His government, a National Peasant one which

[10] See below, p. 351. [11] See below, p. 356. [12] See below, p. 356.
[13] See below, p. 350. [14] See below, p. 351. [15] See below, p. 354
[16] See below, p. 352.

had been formed in spite of Maniu's refusal to participate, proclaimed a state of emergency. On 4 February Dej was arrested and the next day communist-led workers stormed the railway workshops at Grivita, a working-class suburb of Bucharest. On 16 February the army was called in and a number of workers, including some communists, were killed. It was a deplorable incident which was immediately exploited by the communist press abroad. Thus the Grivita legend was created, a very useful one for the Communist Party.[17] Dej became a communist hero, although it was not he who had played the stirring part in the final incident, since he was gaoled two weeks earlier. It was another railway worker, Constantin Doncea, who led the storming of the workshops. Other communist workers such as Ilie Pintilie,[18] Chivu Stoica,[19] Gheorghe Vasilichi, and Dumitru Petrescu also played important parts in the whole series of events. But it was Dej, and to a lesser extent Pintilie, who reaped the glory.[20] Dej himself was not as popular among his fellow workers as men such as Doncea and Vasilichi, but he was more favoured by the party leaders because of his more compliant attitude toward them. Grivita made him, and his reputation survived twelve years in prison. He was released in 1944.

FASCISM AND ANTI-FASCISM IN RUMANIA, 1933–9

Hitler's rise to power in Germany in January 1933 was to have a decisive effect on Rumanian internal and external politics. Internally his rise led inexorably to a polarization of political forces. In foreign policy it led to the clashes of those forces who resolutely opposed him and those who for various reasons counselled an alliance or association with him. Fascism or anti-fascism, at home and abroad, was the theme of the 1930's. In this dilemma Rumania was, of course, far from being alone.

The Rumanian who, from the day the Nazis came to power, concentrated all his energies and attention upon the need for Rumania and for Europe to offer resistance to Hitler was Nicolae

[17] PCR, *Documente*; Chivu Stoica, *Eroicele lupte ale muncitorilor ceferisti si petrolisti din 1933* (1953) and in *Analele*, no. 1, Jan.-Feb. 1958.

[18] See below, p. 356. [19] See below, p. 357.

[20] Yet the tactics employed by the RCP must have been criticized in some quarters of the International because in an article in *Inprecorr* (no. 68-69, 1933) it was stated: 'We must criticize the theory according to which strikes, followed by the seizure of the factory, are "inferior" forms of struggle. It is obvious that such strikes . . . as for instance the railwaymen's strike in Rumania, are not an inferior form but a sharper form of the fight by strikers.'

Titulescu.[21] For more than four years, from April 1932 to August 1936, Titulescu was at the helm of Rumania's foreign policy. He had already been Foreign Minister in 1927 and 1928 and then Rumanian Minister in London and President of the League of Nations for two consecutive years, the only representative who ever had the distinction of being re-elected to that office. But in 1932 he interrupted his diplomatic career and resigned his London post in protest against his government's clumsy attempts to renew direct diplomatic relations with Soviet Russia,[22] without first ensuring that Russia pledged herself to a recognition of the status of Bessarabia. A preliminary integration of Soviet Russia into Europe's defensive policy, if her offers of co-operation were to be believed, was thought necessary by Titulescu, not only *per se* but also as a consolidation of a future front against the ultimate aggressor. This aggressor he was convinced would be Nazi Germany.

Hitler came to power on 30 January 1933. On 15 February Titulescu, Benes, and Jevtic, the three Foreign Ministers of the Little Entente, strengthened this diplomatic instrument. They transformed it into a more permanent triangular partnership with a standing council of its Foreign Ministers. They agreed also on the necessity of co-ordinating more closely both foreign and trade policies, a co-ordination which could have evolved into a loose form of federative association.[23] Indeed, both Benes and Titulescu were inspired by the conviction that the union of small countries could curb the power politics which had been responsible for the instability of Eastern and Central Europe. Alone, Titulescu embarked upon the creation of the Balkan Entente. Together with Benes, he played a great part in June 1933 in countering the suggested Four-Power Pact put forward by Fascist Italy. Musso-

[21] He expressed his views very clearly in a speech at the opening meeting of the Balkan Entente, 11 June 1936: 'We shall never renounce, for the sake of any of the Great Powers or of all the Great Powers together, the principle of the equality of states, that is the sovereign right to decide our own fate and to refuse decisions concerning us in which we have been involved without our consent' (Titulescu, *Discursuri* (June 1936)).

[22] Vaida-Voevod had actually instructed the Rumanian Minister in Warsaw to enter into consultations with the Soviet representative about a Soviet-Rumanian non-aggression pact, similar to that signed by Poland on 1 Jan. 1932. Titulescu's strong views on this subject had been expressed in an article, 'Rumania and Bessarabia', published in the *Nineteenth Century*, June 1924 (pp. 791–803). Rakovsky, on being appointed Soviet Ambassador to Paris in 1925, answered Titulescu's article in the booklet *Roumanie et Bessarabie* (Paris, 1925).

[23] The 'Pact of Organization' of 15 Feb. 1933 (see RIIA, *Survey, 1933*, pp. 203–5).

lini tried to persuade France and Britain to join Italy and Germany in a pact designed to replace, by a directory of great powers, many of the functions of the League of Nations Covenant. The opposition of the Little Entente and of Poland put an end to this first attempt to replace the Covenant. The final text of the Four-Power Pact signed in June 1933 was divested of all its anti-League provisions or aims.

On 3 July 1933 Soviet Russia signed a Convention defining Aggression with seven border states : Afghanistan, Estonia, Latvia, Persia, Poland, Rumania, and Turkey.[24] On the next day, 4 July, Titulescu persuaded Russia to sign the same convention with the Little Entente, the borders of two of whose states, Czechoslovakia and Yugoslavia, were not contiguous with those of Russia. The network of guarantees which Titulescu inspired was entirely consistent with the League Covenant. The spirit of the Covenant was invoked in Rumania's new relations with Moscow.

After Germany's withdrawal from the Disarmament Conference on 14 October and from the League on 21 October 1933, Titulescu's preparations for establishing the Balkan Entente were quickened. On 12 October he visited Sofia and met with the final refusal of Bulgaria to join such a body, which was designed to replace the ineffectual Balkan conference of which she was a member. Bulgaria's revisionist claims against Rumania, but even more against Yugoslavia and Greece, determined this refusal. The remaining solution was a pact between Turkey, Yugoslavia, Greece, and Rumania, promoting common defence in case of aggression against any one of them. The Balkan Entente, finally signed on 9 February 1934 in Ankara, did not, however, measure up to this requirement.[25] Through secret, annexed protocols, Greece stated that she would not act jointly with the other three states in the eventuality of a conflict with Italy, and Turkey explicitly excepted herself from any commitment in the case of a conflict between Rumania and Soviet Russia. The only real mutual agreement, therefore, was to act in case of aggression by Bulgaria.

Fascism in Rumania

Titulescu's defensive action against Germany was being rapidly

[24] See below, p. 51.

[25] RIIA, *Survey, 1934*, pp. 508 ff.; see also A. J. Kerner and H. N. Howard, *The Balkan Conference and the Balkan Entente, 1930–5* (Berkeley, 1936).

outflanked by the penetration of Rumania from within by the German Fifth Column. The first echelons of this octopus-like apparatus for South-East Europe had already arrived in Rumania and made their presence felt in industry, the press, politics, and elsewhere. The collusion between them and the Iron Guard was clearly only a matter of time.

Banned in 1931 by the Iorga government, the Legion of the Archangel Michael had been re-formed under the name of the Iron Guard and had prospered politically. But had it not been for Hitler's rise to power, the Guard would probably always have remained on the lunatic fringe of Rumanian political life, swinging inconclusively between the monastic and terrorist tendencies of its rank and file.

Hitler's *Sicherheitsdienst,* which at once became active in Eastern Europe, detected the potentialities latent in the confused movement.[26] One of the first pieces of advice that the Guard received from the Nazis was to direct its attention towards the workers. The first months of 1933 were also those of the great workers' unrest. A. Vaida-Voedod's National Peasant government, which had handled the grievances of the workers with an impatience obviously inspired by Carol and his military advisers, had only exacerbated them. Many young workers began to look about them for more extremist solutions than those offered by the democratic parties; and for creeds which offered less affront to their national feelings than did communism.

The Guard began to recruit a surprisingly large number of workers, apart from a growing number of members from other social strata. Simultaneously it acquired, with obvious financial ease, great speed in organizing its cadres and in transforming itself into a more modern-seeming revolutionary party. Duca, the head of the Liberal Party, was asked by the king to form a government, after Vaida's fall from power on 14 November 1933. Titulescu made it a condition of his remaining in the cabinet that drastic measures be taken against the Iron Guard. Before the elections, Duca dissolved it. Three weeks after the elections which brought him to power on 30 December 1933, Duca was assassinated by three young Macedonians, members of the Guard.

[26] See among other works Walter Hagen, *Die geheime Front* (Vienna, 1950), an interesting account of the action of the particular assignments of the *Sicherheitsdienst* in Rumania.

This crime had many consequences, among them the internal disruption of the Liberal Party, in which the pro-Carol wing led by Tatarescu, who was made Prime Minister, took predominance over the constitutionalists, led by C. Bratianu, the third and last surviving brother of Ionel.[27] The democratic parties were caught in a pincer movement between Carol's action from above and that of the Guard from below. In spite of the fact that his mistress was Jewish, Carol encouraged the Guard until the moment when it turned against him. Thus during the arrest and trial of Duca's murderers, Codreanu, who had been indicted as the 'moral author' of the crime, took refuge in the house of Cernovodeanu, Mme Lupescu's cousin.

Anti-Fascism

This situation gave birth to a spontaneous anti-fascist movement in Rumania. Professors, scientists, writers, lawyers, students, and workers formed active groups opposed to the growth of fascism. These groups, however, had great difficulty in acting, because they were suspected of being communist-inspired. Carol's policy was to persecute them on the assumption that they were not only infiltrated but led by communists. It was a convenient pretext because anti-fascism was one of the communists' most popular slogans. Ana Pauker, who returned from Moscow in 1934, was entrusted with this campaign together with Kroshneff who, from 1935, had been secretary in charge of the Agitprop (agitation and propaganda) and editor of the illegal *Scanteia*. As in the case of the workers' movements and strikes, the Communist Party claimed a monopoly of anti-fascism.[28] They abused the good faith of genuine democratic anti-fascists by techniques which have since become all too familiar. True democrats were urged to sign communist sponsored manifestoes, while independent writers and journalists were asked to contribute articles to sporadic publications and lawyers were asked to defend prominent communists in the in-

[27] C.I.C. Bratianu, also known as Dinu, had kept out of politics as long as his two brothers were alive. When he entered them, taking over the leadership of the party at a moment in which it was threatened from within as well as from without he was already an ageing man. He behaved with great dignity and integrity, even if without the necessary vigour and imagination. He died in a communist prison.

[28] P. Constantinescu-Iasi, *Organizatii de masa legale conduse de Partidul Comunist din Romania* (1952), is a typically distorted account of the influence of the RCP on the anti-fascist movement in Rumania. An article in the anniversary issue of *Lupta de clasa,* Apr. 1961, by Ileana Vrancea even tries to show how the CP influenced from within the literary criticism of Rumania between 1930 and 1940.

creasingly frequent trials. The more important of these trials were that of the railwaymen, after Grivita, the joint trial of Constantinescu and Ilie Christea, and that of Ana Pauker herself. Ana Pauker was arrested, together with Alexandru Moghioros,[29] Liuba Chisinevschi, Alexandru Draghici,[30] and others on 4 July 1935. According to her official biography,[31] it was decided in international circles that her trial was to be an important anti-fascist demonstration. It took place in Craiova on 5 June 1936, as the government thought that Bucharest was too explosive a place for such a demonstration. It gave her the opportunity she longed for of attracting world-wide publicity. She was sentenced to ten years' imprisonment.

But the most consistent Rumanian anti-fascist action was still that carried on with increasing determination by Titulescu in the diplomatic sphere. On 9 June 1934 Rumania re-established diplomatic relations with Soviet Russia. This was done without the formal solution which Titulescu had sought of the problem of Bessarabia. But on the one hand consultations on the subject were intermittently renewed between Litvinov and himself, as their mutual confidence grew, and by 1936, when Carol dismissed Titulescu, he had already initialed with Litvinov a pact in which the Soviet Union recognized Rumania's right to Bessarabia.[32] On the other, bilateral initiatives had been preceded by the signature, on 3 July 1933, of the Convention Defining Aggression, concluded between the Soviet Union and most of her Asiatic and European neighbours, among them Rumania.[33] The text of the Convention stated that the invasion of territory was an act of aggression, and in an annexed report it was clearly stated that by 'territory' was meant that territory over which a state exercised *de facto* authority. The renewal of diplomatic relations was followed at once by Russia's entry into the League of Nations, which took place on 18 September 1934. Titulescu and Benes had been very active in bringing this about. They considered that it strengthened the League and at the same time made of it and of the Covenant the

[29] See below, p. 354.

[30] See below, p. 352. [31] RWP, *Ana Pauker* (1951).

[32] See C. Radu, *La Bessarabie* (1944), pp. 42–43. The draft initialed on 21 July 1936 by both Litvinov and Titulescu mentioned in art. 3 that Russian troops would never cross the Dniester without the formal consent of the Rumanian govt and would withdraw (art. 4) whenever requested to do so by that govt.

[33] On 4 July it was also signed by the Little Entente *qua* Little Entente, a symptomatic formality.

most adequate buffers between the Soviet Union and her neighbours. Benes and Titulescu also made great personal efforts to further the final conclusion of the pacts of mutual assistance between the Soviet Union and France on 2 May 1935 and between the Soviet Union and Czechoslovakia on 16 May. The part that Rumania might be called upon to play in the latter treaty was very important. If Poland refused Soviet troops permission to cross Polish territory to come to the aid of Czechoslovakia, would Rumania grant this privilege? It was a question which could not be solved as rapidly as Titulescu[34] desired because of the opposition he met on this point both in the country and from the king.

Carol and the Extremists

Carol's hostility to Titulescu increased and only the fear of showing his hand too soon prevented him from dismissing him at the time of the Italo-Abyssinian conflict and of the strong anti-Italian attitude adopted by Rumania within the League. Rumania was quick to oppose Italian aggression, an opposition which could have caused considerable economic sacrifice since Italy was an important buyer of Rumanian oil. Titulescu's speeches and personal interventions during that crisis of the League earned him the bitter enmity of Mussolini. A year later his attitude towards the remilitarization of the Rhineland by Germany and his appeals that the League should act against what was clearly the disruption of the Versailles order made him a marked enemy of the Reich. The Iron Guard, now called 'The All-for-the-Fatherland' Party, a name taken after it had been banned because of Duca's murder, declared that twenty-four hours after it attained power, it would sign an alliance with Nazi Germany and fascist Italy. It also denounced Titulescu as the prime enemy of Rumanian interests. Carol, who still thought that he could collaborate with the Guard and who found Titulescu's policy far too 'idealistic', dismissed him on 29 August 1936.[35]

But at that time the Spanish Civil War was able to provide the Rumanian extremist parties with a direct, if distant, battlefield.

[34] He had lately been particularly attacked for his part in trying to make the Franco-Soviet and Czech-Soviet pacts workable. Rumania would have allowed Soviet troops to pass through her territory in defence of Czechoslavokia. In this connexion see E. L. Woodward and R. Butler, eds., *Documents on British Foreign Policy*, 3rd ser., vol. vi, and Georges Bonnet, *Défense de la paix* (Geneva, 1946), vol. i.

[35] He died in March 1941 in the south of France. He devoted the years 1937–9 to drawing the attention of the western democracies to the inevitability of a final Nazi-Soviet rapprochement. In this respect, see his lecture to the House of Commons,

The Rumanian Communist Party recruited 600 volunteers and led regiments, companies, and batteries in the International Brigade. Those who took part in these operations included Petre Borila, Burca, L. Rautu, Gheorghe Stoica, Stelian Moraru, G. Vasilichi, A. Buican, and G. Katowsky (Valter Roman).[36]

The Iron Guard, while it sent no contingent to Franco, sent a number of its leaders who fought as individuals. On 13 January 1937 in the battle of Majadajonda two of them were killed. They were Ion Motza, who was Codreanu's first lieutenant and, although fanatical, the most genuinely visionary and least violent of all the leaders of the Guard, and Vasile Marin, an intellectual. The return of the bodies and the funerals gave the Iron Guard a most dramatic occasion for display. From that moment its ranks were swelled by new contingents of Rumanian youth, attracted by the idea of serving a cause and of 'committing' themselves. As in all totalitarian movements, there were among the rank and file many innocents in search of sublimation.

In the autumn of 1937 Tatarescu, the Prime Minister, faced new elections, confident that he would win an easy victory because the popularity of the National Peasant Party was challenged by a formidable electoral rival in the Iron Guard and because he thought the king's personal influence on behalf of the government would tip the balance. He was mistaken on both counts. The Iron Guard and the National Peasants made a pact in November 1937 whereby they agreed not to attack one another during the elections. The pact applied everywhere with one exception. This was in the district in which Titulescu was the candidate for the National Peasants, and here the Iron Guard opposed him bitterly and relentlessly.[37] Controversial as this agreement may have

[36] At the plenary meeting of the CC of 28 Nov.–5 Dec. 1961 many speakers, especially Borila and Valter Roman, spoke at great length of the persecution to which the Rumanian communist volunteers in Spain were afterwards submitted by Anna Pauker and Vasile Luca. They said that following the Stalin-Rakosi line, Pauker and Luca saw 'potential Rajks' in all the former volunteers in Spain and treated them as suspects and spies. They praised Dej for having protected them when they were under attack and for actually saving their lives. They emerged once more as a 'group', linked not only by their past experience but also by their common views.

[37] On 29 Nov. 1937 Codreanu made a statement to the press in which he said: 'I am against the big democracies of the west. I am against the Balkan Entente. I have no respect for the League of Nations. I am for a foreign policy which will link us to Rome and Berlin' (A Hillgruber, *Hitler, König Carol und Marschall Antonescu* (1954). This German historian had access to the German documents and was also helped in his research by the explanations and details given to him by Dr Fabricius.

been, it proved to be too strong in reality even for Tatarescu's electoral methods. The government was defeated in December 1937. This was to be the last parliamentary election in a Rumania still free enough to defeat the government in power.

In these developments the Communist Party once more proved how unprepared it was for even the most elementary of political tasks. Its influence was barely perceptible and, when it was, even in its own electoral front organization, the Workers'-Peasants' Bloc—later called the Democratic Union—its decisions were ultimately catastrophic. Thus, during the elections, carrying out the same policy of a popular front, it tried to unite its Democratic Union with the National Peasant Party. But since the National Peasants had made an electoral pact with the Iron Guard, the communist leaders divided into two camps, the 'revolutionaries' in favour of acting with the National Peasants and the Bessarabians and others opposed to the idea, not so much because of the incongruity of collaborating under any circumstances with fascists, but because of the inspired hint that certain of King Carol's ministers and officials could be useful to the Soviet diplomats. The first course of action prevailed, but was later criticized.[38]

Carol dissolved the newly-elected parliament as soon as the results were made known and on 7 December 1937 instituted a government of his own, based on the non-totalitarian, anti-Semitic party of Octavian Goga and Cuza, with Goga as Prime Minister and with General Ion Antonescu as Defence Minister. But in spite of their hope of winning some popularity with a few mild anti-Semitic laws and of the help lent by the German Ambassador, Wilhelm Fabricius, it soon became clear that the Goga government could not last. It resigned on 10 February 1938. Carol, now obsessed with the idea of becoming the leader of the nationalist movement and of youth, announced on 27 February that the old constitution was suspended. This was the beginning of his own dictatorship, based on a kind of royalist-corporative doc-

[38] There is a veiled reference to this moment in Patrascanu's *Sub trei dictaturi* (Buch., 1946), where he says: 'The decision taken by the leaders of the Communist Party was to give help and assistance in the electoral campaign as well as in the elections themselves to the National Peasant Party. This was a mistake which was bound to have grave consequences.' And Constantinescu-Iasi: 'The leadership of the Democratic Union has not sufficiently branded Maniu's treason and has underestimated the danger of the Iron Guard against whom the main fire should have been opened (*Organizatii . . . legale*).

trine.[39] His hope that his own movement would subtract from the Iron Guard its main support was, however, not fulfilled. Codreanu decided to launch an active campaign of terrorism and propaganda against the king. Hitler's successes in the diplomatic field, especially after the *Anschluss* of 13 March 1938, made the Guard even more determined to come to power. The conflict between Carol and Codreanu grew rapidly; after a new outbreak of terrorism, Carol had him arrested on 15 April, on the accusation of instigating criminal acts. On 27 May 1938 he was sentenced to ten years' hard labour.

During the following November Carol set off on an official journey across Europe, inaugurating his personal diplomacy based on neutrality. Although he stated that he believed that England and France would eventually defeat Germany, he thought that his duty was to keep Rumania out of the conflict. He visited Paris and London and ended his tour with a surprisingly successful visit to Hitler. He promised the latter increased economic collaboration but evoked Rumania's paramount interest in Transylvania and discussed the problem of the strategic importance of the Carpatho-Ukraine as a possible direct territorial and military link with Germany.[40]

On his return, Codreanu with other Iron Guard leaders was shot; the official version stated that this happened during an attempt to escape on 30 November. The general belief was that, after his conversations with Hitler, Carol felt himself strong strong enough to liquidate Codreanu. But he had misjudged badly. Codreanu's death raised an unprecedented storm between the Third Reich and Carol's administration. The *Völkischer Beobachter* violently attacked the king. Nazi dignitaries sent back the decorations which Carol had given them. Diplomatic relations might have been endangered had not the Rumanian government showed a greater pliancy in the negotiations for a Germano-

[39] See, for instance, Mihai Farcasanu, *Monarhia sociala* (1938), a work inspired by the idea of a modern conception of active rule by the king. But the main source of these corporatist conceptions must be found in the works and the influence upon Carol of the Rumanian corporatist philosopher and economist, Mihail Manoilescu.

[40] 'The King of Rumania emphasized that Rumania desired good relations with all powers, but desired especially to maintain and consolidate the good relations with the German Reich that existed today': memo by the Foreign Minister, 'Conversation of the Führer and the King of Rumania in the presence of the Reich Foreign Minister, Berchtesgaden, November 14, 1937', *D. Ger. FP*, ser. D, vol. v, Doc. 254.

Rumanian economic pact in which the Germans were highly interested.[41]

The Effects of Carol's Dictatorship

In internal politics, the dissolutions of the political parties affected the democratic ones much more adversely than they did the totalitarian. The National Peasant, National Liberal, and Social Democratic Parties were now virtually helpless, but the change was advantageous to the totalitarian parties.

Codreanu's assassination did not bring with it the dissolution of the Iron Guard as Carol had expected. It brought naturally a certain confusion and disorganization; but then disorganized and confused the movement essentially was, not only because of the 'illegality' in which it had found itself at least from 1934, but also because of its very nature. Composed of a hard insurrectional and terroristic kernel and an amorphous and naïve rank and file, the former found it easier to act in the violent conditions thus created and augmented by the persecution to which Carol had subjected the Guard. Public opinion had little to choose from in a duel in which justice was in either case absent.

This was indeed a period in which a short-lived neutrality brought to the upper strata of Rumanian society a precarious prosperity. Foreign trade was characterized by an active competition between Germany and Britain and France.[42] Morbidly protected industrialization under the pressure of the need to rearm was forcing the state to buy expensive and unnecessary products. The Malaxa and other concerns which had sprouted under these artificial conditions and which were the favourite customers of the German industries were the main beneficiaries of these orders.[43]

[41] 'On Dec. 5 Wiehl telegraphed Clodius [the Deputy Director of the Economic Department and the Reich's economic negotiator in Rumania and South-East Europe] that he should conclude the economic negotiations in Bucharest as soon as possible since it was not desired that they be upset by a further demonstration of German displeasure which was planned. This was to be the return to Rumania of certain Orders and decoration which had been given to German leaders' (ibid. p. 349).

[42] The total value of the volume of foreign trade of Rumania in 1937 reached a record height of 31,568,357,000 lei and a favourable balance for Rumania of 11,283,609,000 lei. In 1938 it fell to 21,532,580,000 and 2,764,750,000 lei respectively (*Bréviaire statistique de la Roumanie, 1940*, p. 188).

[43] Dr Fabricius telegraphed the German Foreign Ministry on 7 October 1938 stating that he had learned confidentially that the Council of Ministers held a meeting four days earlier to discuss the expansion of economic relations with

A Communist Party would be expected to thrive on such a situation, but once again the Rumanian communists found themselves ill prepared. The leaders were divided on the issue as to whether the party should denounce the king's party as an instrument of terror and dictatorship; or to infiltrate it from within, so as to exert pressure on its foreign policy, encouraging it to oppose the Reich and to lean towards Moscow. This was a most unrealistic attitude: it served only to encourage opportunist members and fellow-travellers to have it both ways, benefiting lavishly from the positions offered to them by Carol, from ministerial portfolios to leading posts on his party newspapers, and yet also being on the list of the Communist Party. Such behaviour was later severely criticized as opportunist by the reorganized Central Committee.[44]

Two Ministers

Carol's position of 'neutrality' was only a source of irritation to the Germans. They wanted to replace him, but Fabricius, the German Ambassador, was still looking round for a suitable candidate, or at least one who could assert sufficient influence over Carol. The Guard and its leaders seemed too crude for this tidy-minded manipulator. Fabricius fixed his eyes on Antonescu, but for the moment was content to extort as many advantages as possible from Carol's 'neutralism'. This neutralist policy was carried on by all Carol's governments, which were far from distinguished, but two men emerged during this period who revealed an ability and strength far beyond that of their colleagues. The first was Armand Calinescu, who served in various governments as Minister for Internal Affairs and Minister for Defence and was Prime Minister between February 1938 and September 1939. The second was Grigore Gafencu, who served as Foreign Minister between

Germany. Following a report by M. Malaxa, Malaxa was authorized to communicate with the Junkers firm about the expansion of the aircraft factory at Kronstadt (*D. Ger. FP*, ser. D, vol. v, no. 231).

[44] 'In 1938–9 Vasile Luca contributed to the evolution and application of the mistaken line of the democratic elements entering the monarcho-fascist FRN organization' (*Docs. concerning Right-Wing Deviations in the RWP* (1952)) and 'Our party at that time committed some grave mistakes, the author of which was the traitor Foris, who was then in the leadership of the party. Thus the party ordered the democratic elements who supported it to take part in the parody of elections organized by the king's dictatorship and launched the slogan of "the concentration of the democratic forces from within and without the Front" ' (Gheorghiu-Dej's report on the 30th anniversary of the party, *Lupta de clasa*, May-June 1951).

December 1938 and May 1940.[45] They were both former National Peasants who had left their party out of an impatient desire for action 'from within' which Maniu's long term in opposition could not provide. Calinescu's twin objectives were the strengthening of the army and the eradication of the Guard, both essential if the German plan to take over the country was to be opposed. A sturdy and resolute man, he was never personally popular because of his ruthlessness in action and a somewhat forbidding appearance created by the black monocle which he used to conceal his blindness of one eye. It was Calinescu who lent to Carol the courage and energy he showed at the beginning of his dictatorship.[46] He was assassinated by a posse of the Guard on 21 September 1939 as a belated reprisal for Codreanu's assassination. It was this murder that catapulted Horia Sima,[47] who had taken over the Guard after Codreanu, to prominence. The death of Calinescu showed that he had proved himself.

Gafencu was the architect of 'neutrality'. His slogan was 'guaranteed by London, armed by Berlin'; for a brief period early in 1938 it seemed to be bearing fruit. With an enviable dexterity, this personable, gifted politician followed up the economic agreement with Germany (the Wohlthat Agreement)[48] with British and French guarantees on 13 April 1939. But the satisfaction was short-lived. Gafencu must have realized that the Wohlthat Agreement was but the beginning of Rumania's incorporation into the *Lebensraum* of the Third Reich. As for the Anglo-French guarantee, this was a melancholy gesture. With the complete dominance of Germany and Italy in Central and South-East Europe, it was a diplomatic bluff easy to call and to scorn.

War in Europe

The Nazi-Soviet Pact of 23 August 1939 shattered the in-

[45] Gafencu's personality is well known through his two excellent books, *Prelude to the Russian Campaign* (1945) and *Last Days of Europe* (1947).

[46] Carl Clodius reported on 13 Dec. 1938 that the murder of Codreanu and his followers had changed the situation considerably, and the bitterness in the Iron Guard was tremendous. 'Unless the King should fall victim to assassination, he will probably be strong enough to maintain his power by means of the loyal part of the Army and the security apparatus of the state under the leadership of the ruthless Minister of the Interior, Armand Calinescu' (*D Ger. FP*, ser. D, vol. v, no. 264).

[47] A former Transylvanian village teacher, known for his fanaticism. In 1951 a book appeared in Paris under his signature entitled *Destinée du nationalisme*.

[48] Named after the German negotiator, Helmuth Wohlthat (text in *D Ger. FP*, ser. D, vol. vi, p. 91).

genious edifice of the 'neutralist' leaders of Poland, Rumania, and Yugoslavia. A clue to the future intentions of Moscow and Berlin towards Rumania could have been found in the attitude of the Rumanian Communist Party at that time. Not only did the party immediately, as did all the other communist parties, heap recriminations on Britain and France as 'imperialist powers waging a war against the wishes and interests of the toiling masses', but in the autumn of 1939 Boris Stefanov wrote an article in the *Communist International* (December 1939) insisting that Rumania's interest lay solely in a direct alliance with Soviet Russia, and attacking Britain and France. He ordered the Rumanian communists to return to the out-and-out policy of 'self-determination' of the early years, especially with regard to Bessarabia. The Soviet government was constrained to deny that Stefanov's article represented its views.[49]

The first few months of the war gave some respite to Rumania and even seemed to justify her policy of neutrality, which was officially proclaimed on 6 September. But with the fall of France it was at an end. So was the period of Rumanian history when she enjoyed full territorial and national integrity.

THE COLLABORATION WITH GERMANY, 1940–3

In the hope that the Reich would defend Rumania against the Soviet Union Carol, on 29 May 1940, concluded the oil pact with Hitler, with all it implied in the way of political and military commitments. In a reshuffled government Ion Gigurtu, an industrialist known also to be an active German sympathizer, took Gafencu's place. On 26 June the Soviet government presented the Rumanians with a twenty-four-hour ultimatum demanding the cession of Bessarabia.[50] It was based upon Article 3 of the secret additional protocol of the Nazi-Soviet Pact of 23 August 1939 which stated that 'With regard to South-eastern Europe, attention is called by the Soviet side to its interest in Bessarabia. The German side declares its complete disinterestedness in these areas.'[51] They loyally kept their words. When Gigurtu sought his

[49] 'Although the Soviet Foreign Office publicly denied that Stefanov represented the views of the Soviet Government, the article provided some evidence that the Russian interest in Rumania at this time was not limited solely to the recovery of Bessarabia' (H. L. Roberts, *Rumania* (1951)).

[50] A. Cretzianu, 'The Soviet Ultimatum to Rumania, 26 June 1940', *JCE Aff.*, Jan. 1950, and his *Lost Opportunity* (1957), pp. 41–58.

[51] U.S. Dept of State, *Nazi-Soviet Relations, 1939–41*, ed. R. J. Sontag and J. S. Beddie (Wash., 1948), p. 78.

counsel, Ribbentrop gave him 'stern advice' to yield. Turkey was unable to act and in any case the clause which she had inserted into the Balkan Pact made it inconceivable that she should do so. On 27 June Rumania yielded to the ultimatum and Bessarabia was evacuated in less than a week.

Carol, with a new and entirely pro-German cabinet headed by Gigurtu, with Manoilescu as Foreign Minister, now asked the Germans for guarantees for the future.[52] But the dismemberment was not over and the Germans cynically retained the king, thus forcing him to accept the opprobrium which the territorial 'corrections' would involve. The friends of Germany, such as General Antonescu and the Iron Guard, were discreetly advised not to accept Carol's offer to join the government. On 15 July Hitler asked Carol to negotiate with the Hungarian government on their territorial claims against Rumania. (A little earlier, the Germans had forced negotiations with Sofia which led to the cession of South Dobruja. This was done, however, within the framework of a diplomatic agreement, which also included population transfers.)[53] Negotiations with Hungary reached complete deadlock and Hitler intervened to 'arbitrate'. On 30 August Ribbentrop and Ciano, acting in Vienna as mediators, imposed upon Rumania the cession of Northern Transylvania.[54] The British government, at war with Germany and Italy, immediately declared that it would not recognize the decision.[55]

On the very morning of the signing of the Vienna *Diktat* the Soviet government too, through a Tass communiqué, expressed its dissatisfaction at not having been consulted in the matter, in which, through her interpretation of the Nazi-Soviet Pact, she was interested. Rumania was also warned; and the Rumanian Communist Party this time adopted an attitude very different from the one it had taken over Bessarabia.

In a brochure called *Our Point of View*, published on 3 Sep-

[52] Mihail Manoilescu, the economist and corporatist (p. 55 n. 39), had finally found an outlet for his political ambitions in becoming one of the main German intermediaries with King Carol.

[53] The treaty was signed at Craiova on 7 Sept. 1946.

[54] See *Romania* (N.Y.), Feb., Mar., & May 1956: a series of three articles on the Vienna *Diktat* based on unpublished Rumanian documents as well as all official documents published to date. See also E. Ciurea, 'L'effondrement des frontières roumaines en 1940', *R. d'hist. de la 2ème guerre mondiale,* no. 20, 1955.

[55] By a statement made by the Prime Minister, Winston Churchill, in the House of Commons and by Lord Halifax in the House of Lords. This statement was repeated by the Foreign Secretary, Anthony Eden, on 5 Mar. 1942.

tember 1940, the Rumanian Communist Party stated that: 'through the sentence of the German-Italian imperialists in Vienna, the Rumanian imperialists have ceded to Hungary not only roughly 45,000 square kilometres, but have submitted more than 1 million Rumanian workers and peasants to a foreign yoke'.[56]

On 2 September, on the excuse that military and diplomatic moves made by Russia after and in connexion with the Vienna *Diktat* might be the portent of some action against Rumania, Hitler at last gave his guarantee by sending a German military mission, with troops, tanks, and anti-aircraft weapons and instructors to protect the oil region and to provide the necessary military training for the Rumanian army. Carol had got his guarantee, but it was now worthless. Public opinion, in so far as it could make itself heard, barely reacted when it was learnt that Antonescu, whom he had asked in September to form a new government, had forced him to abdicate. This was a condition of the Iron Guard's agreeing to serve under Antonescu.

Carol left Rumania in haste, taking with him Mme Lupescu, some members of the camarilla, and part of his immense fortune. He was succeeded at this most difficult moment by his son, King Michael, modest, courageous, and with a strong personal sense of duty.

Antonescu's Assumption of Power

The new government was an association of General Antonescu and the Iron Guard under the leadership of Horia Sima. Sima himself was Vice-President and the Guard held, among other key departments, those for foreign affairs and the interior. The Guard wanted to abolish the monarchy but Antonescu had worked out a compromise by the decree of 5 September, which stated that 'the king has given absolute powers' to the Prime Minister. On 6 September 1940 the new king found himself confronted with a government which made it clear to him that he was supposed to be merely a symbol and to take no active part at all in the direction of the state. King Michael then withdrew into silent isolation, but in his broadcasts on New Year's eve, he gave the country, year after year, the feeling that he was watching the situation. Later, during the war, he never endorsed the action beyond the Dniester, and at

[56] PMR, *Documente.*

the end of it he became the inspiration and the leader of all those who were trying to bring Rumania over to the side of the Allies.

General Ion Antonescu[57] was a man of military skill, personal integrity, and principle in public affairs. Aged fifty-eight when he came to power, this son of an army family had risen to fame very young. During the First World War, as chief of the Operations Bureau of the General Staff, he had been responsible for most of the planning of the Rumanian army's resistance to the German army in 1917. After the war he held for many years the post of military attaché in London where he acquired a deep admiration for Great Britain. From 1934 to March 1938 he was Minister of War, but a quarrel with Carol led to his resignation. Thereafter he played a more active part in political life. He at this time established contacts with the Iron Guard, who courted him and soon found that he shared their quest for an absolutist solution in politics based on authority and nationalism.

On coming to power he deliberately assumed greater responsibilities than he needed to. None of his acts, not even the declaration of war, was endorsed by the constitutional head of the state or by the parliament. These acts were personal. They committed the country less than if he had insisted upon maintaining the semblances of constitutional legality. He resembled Pétain in that he was an ambitious soldier, confident that he had come to power to purge the political arena of corruption and to establish a new political order. Like Pétain, he also may have thought that he was acting as a buffer between a foreign power and his own country. Unlike Pétain, however, he was to find enough strength in himself and in the confidence which he believed the people had in him to act decisively against the fascists and to expel them from the government.

The conflict between Antonescu and the Iron Guard soon developed in intensity. By November 1940 it was clear that the Guardists were thoroughly dissatisfied with the pace and depth of the revolution and were angered by the discovery that the General, instead of being the puppet they had hoped, was intent on thwarting their designs. Emerging from the prisons, they were bent on violence.

[57] See Gh. Barbul, *Memorial Antonescu* (1950), a passionate defence by a former member of his staff; H. Lauen, *Marschall Antonescu* (Essen, 1943), a biography by a German official at the time. Hillgruber is the best guide to all German documents concerning Antonescu and his relations with the Germans, above all with Hitler.

On 21 November 1940 Antonescu went to Berlin to sign the Tripartite Pact, to which Hungary had adhered the previous day. His eagerness to sign was mainly because he believed that, after the fall of France, Germany represented 'the west', to which of necessity Rumania must be linked if she was not to be absorbed by Russia. His first meeting with Hitler was successful. By his frankness on the Transylvanian problem, for instance, on which he warned the Führer that the Rumanians would never yield, as well as by his decisiveness, he impressed Hitler as a man to be trusted.

Only two days after his return, on 27–28 November, special posses of the Iron Guard assassinated in their cells all Carol's former ministers and officials who were about to stand trial for participation in Codreanu's murder.[58] Then, in a frenzy, they continued the manhunt of political anti-German personalities, such as the historian Nicolae Iorga and the economist Virgil Madgearu.[59] Reprimands and reprisals were clearly useless. Moreover it was obvious that the Iron Guard itself, with the help of the Gestapo and of the Nazis, was preparing a direct bid for power. The announcement that the Reich was on the point of sending a new Ambassador, exchanging the foxy old diplomatist Fabricius for an *SA-Obergruppenführer,* Manfred von Killinger, was interpreted as a sign that Rumania was due for *Gleichschaltung*.

But by now Hitler had decided on the invasion of Russia. He needed Rumania as a base and as a source of oil. He therefore needed stability. On 12 January 1941 Antonescu was invited to go to Germany, accompanied by Sima. Sima refused and on 14 January Antonescu went alone. He told Hitler that if there were to be war against Russia, Rumania would participate. At the same time he indicated that the situation in Rumania was getting out of hand. The Iron Guard, infiltrated by communist agents, was creating a state of confusion and was obviously intent on civil war. Without committing himself too far, Hitler said that the arrival of his new Ambassador would not mean any change in his policy towards Rumania.

On 20 January, fighting broke out once more; the insurrectionist groups of the Guard occupied various government buildings. At the same time roving detachments pillaged, killed

[58] See *Pe marginea prapastiei* (Buch., 1941), a collection of documents published by the Rumanian govt on the atrocities committed by the insurgents.

[59] They were both shot by teams of former students whom they trusted when they invited them to attend a meeting.

hundreds of Jews, sacked Bucharest, and committed atrocities hitherto unknown in Rumanian history. For two or three days it seemed that the city would fall to them and that they were well on the way to victory.[60] However, when the army, faithful to Antonescu, moved in, the outcome was assured. On 23 January Antonescu's troops counter-attacked. Moreover on the 24th it was learnt that Hitler had spoken in Antonescu's favour. German tanks rolled into Bucharest. The Guard disbanded by order. Many of those who had taken part in the sack of the city were arrested and tried. The leaders, including Sima, were taken by the Gestapo to Germany where they were put in internment camps. They remained there—a constant weapon in the hands of the Nazis with which to threaten Antonescu when he came to resist any of their demands.[61]

On 27 January Antonescu re-formed the government, appointing only military officers and technicians. On 15 February 1941 he abolished the 'National Legionary State' (the title used by the Iron Guard). He announced, however, that his internal policy would still be one of 'active nationalism' and his external policy full collaboration with the Reich. Nevertheless there soon came a moment in March–April 1941 when for the first time Antonescu refused an unexpected German demand. This was in answer to the Yugoslav coup d'état of 27 March 1941, when the Germans decided to invade, occupy, and dismember Yugoslavia. They had already won, after Teleki's suicide, the support of the Hungarian government and to a lesser extent that of the Bulgarians. The Germans expected the Rumanian government, a member of the Tripartite Pact and a military ally, to co-operate as well. Instead Antonescu's answer on 5 April, when the German Ambassador visited him in person, was that Yugoslavia had always maintained friendly relations with Rumania and that the two countries had no territorial claims on one another. Rumania, therefore, would not join in the attack. Instead, she would move her troops to the frontier in order to dissuade the Hungarian armies, entering the Yugoslav Banat, from coming farther into the Rumanian part of that province. This episode gave the Hungarians and the Iron Guard the opportunity to denounce Antonescu's treachery and

[60] *Pe marginea prapastiei.*

[61] The story of the Iron Guard in Germany is best told in Hagen (*Geheime Front*) and in Stefan Palaghita, *Garda de fier, spre reinvierea Romaniei* (Buenos Aires, 1951).

this for a time clouded his relations with Hitler. But great military and economic obligations were at stake, and indeed the Yugoslav episode proved to be only an unforeseen delay in Hitler's preparations for war against the Soviet Union, in which he knew he could rely upon Rumania.

War

The 'holy war' on the side of the Reich for the reconquest of Bessarabia and Northern Bukovina was proclaimed by the Rumanian government on 22 June 1941. The king heard of it through the radio and newspapers. So did the people who, approving of the action for the reconquest of the lost territories, had grave misgivings about the duration of the war and Antonescu's commitments to it. Antonescu took command of the German and Rumanian troops in Moldavia. Mihai Antonescu,[62] appointed Vice-Premier, was left in charge of the government. The Communist Party issued a manifesto denouncing the crime of the Rumanian and German fascists against the peace-loving Soviet Union.[63] But even Maniu, who foresaw clearly the potential disaster of the 'crusade' getting out of hand and believed firmly in Britain's final victory, thought it unwise to deter the Rumanian people from an action which, if limited to Rumanian territory, was both justified and popular.[64]

On 18 July Bessarabia and Northern Bukovina were reoccupied. But instead of immediately calling a halt as the king, Maniu, and Bratianu requested, Antonescu went on. He was carried away by his own military success and by the victories won by the army which he commanded. He also believed that Hungary, which had also taken part in the military operations against Russia, would turn this participation into a political counter in the Transylvanian question. Basically he also knew that if Germany were defeated, Rumania's action in Bessarabia would have been of little avail. He thought that it was better to join in the main effort and thus to

[62] No relation to the Marshal, a young and ambitious professor of international law, Mihai Antonescu served his leader with great devotion and zeal at least up to 1942. See his *Im Dienst des Vaterlands* (1952) and R. Bova Scoppa, *Colloqui con due dittatori* (1949). This Italian Ambassador enjoyed Mihai Antonescu's confidence. See also F. W. Deakin, *The Brutal Friendship* (London, 1962).

[63] PMR, *Documente*.

[64] For all this phase see M. M. Roy, *Roumania: Nazi Satellite; a Study of the Politics and Propaganda of the Antonescue Regime, Sept. 6, 1940–Aug. 23, 1944* (Harvard, 1948) a very detailed dissertation.

bring the whole operation on the eastern front to a victorious conclusion.

On 27 July, meeting Hitler at his headquarters, Antonescu committed himself to helping the Wehrmacht in the territory between the Dniester and the Dnieper, with fifteen Rumanian divisions. On 14 August Hitler asked the Rumanian troops to cross the Dnieper as well, and reluctantly Antonescu agreed.

Disaster then began to overtake the Rumanian armies. Operations at Odessa were far more difficult than had been expected. The city was captured on 16 October, but not before the Rumanians had lost 70,000 men as against a total of 117,000 Germans lost on the whole front. On 30 November 1941 Great Britain addressed strongly-worded notes to Rumania and Hungary. Rumania was enjoined to cease hostilities against the Soviet Union and to withdraw her troops behind the Dniester before 5 December. Antonescu refused. On 7 December the British government declared war on Rumania. On 12 December Rumania and Hungary declared war on the United States. Maniu and Bratianu at once issued a strong protest, showing that Rumania had no interest in those distant lands and that Rumanian troops should be recalled to the Dniester. They pointed out logically that if Antonescu thought that a few Rumanian divisions were so vitally necessary for an ultimate German victory, then he did not believe that Germany could actually defeat Russia. In that case it was even more imperative that Rumanian troops should no longer fight beyond the Dniester. The Rumanian Communist Party issued at the same time a programme for collaboration with the democratic parties, but insisted that Bessarabia and Northern Bukovina should also be evacuated by Rumanian troops.

The winter of 1941 saw the end of Antonescu's hopes of an easy and total victory. The Rumanian share in the war was limited thereafter to six divisions, mostly engaged in operations in the Crimea.

Transnistria

At the beginning of 1942 Hitler, bent on an offensive in the summer, needed as many satellite divisions as he could muster. He made a strong appeal to both the Hungarian and Rumanian governments. This took place just when the Transylvanian problem had again interposed itself between the two countries. Ribbentrop had assured the Hungarians on 8 January 1942 that as far as the Reich was concerned, the Vienna *Diktat* would stand. This provoked Antonescu to inform Hitler that 'all the Rumanian soldiers on the eastern front asked when it would be possible for them to fight finally for Transylvania'.[65] When, in February, Hitler made his new proposal for the Rumanian forces to be given more responsibilities and autonomy in the coming campaign, Antonescu explained that he was fighting in the east in the hope that this would also win for his country the lost territory in the west. Hitler did not reject this interpretation; he simply refused to commit himself.

But Hitler's ambiguity seemed encouraging to Antonescu and he yielded to the German demands. He agreed that Transnistria be put under Rumanian administration, but resisted the suggestion that it be annexed to Rumania. He also decided to allow the Rumanian army to join in the great offensive which Hitler was mounting against Russia in the coming summer, the second of the war. These were his two gravest mistakes. He made them in spite of the opposition of the king who, in his New Year's Day message of 1942, significantly thanked the army for 'having given back to us Bessarabia and Bukovina and thus restored our frontiers in the east'. He also made them in spite of the protests of Maniu and Bratianu. (To their frequent memoranda and protests he replied on 29 October 1942 with 175 pages of personal invective and self-glorification.)

As for Transnistria, on the basis of an agreement signed on 19 August 1941, the entire territory, corresponding to the old Podolia, situated between the Dniester and the Bug, the area around Odessa, and an undefined northern frontier were put under Rumanian administration. But in the words of Alexander Dallin, who has extensively studied the Rumanian administration in this area, 'no mention was made of annexing or incorporating the province into Rumania . . . Hitler would occasionally urge Antonescu to annex Transnistria, Antonescu would delay, fearing that the Germans were trying to lure him eastwards.'[66] In practice, the government of this territory, measuring roughly 10,000 square miles, was totally independent of that of Rumania. A Transnis-

[65] Hillgruber, p. 146.
[66] *Odessa, 1941–4; a Case Study of Soviet Territory under Foreign Rule* (Santa Monica, Calif., Rand Corp., 1957).

trian government was set up on 17 October 1942 in Tiraspol, which was its capital until December 1942, when it moved to Odessa. It was an administration of occupation and as such compared very favourably with the German administration of the Ukraine. In the 1942 summer campaign the Rumanian Third and Fourth Armies as well as the First Rumanian Tank Division were engaged in the advance on Stalingrad. But on 19 November, when the Soviet army started its great offensive for the relief of Stalingrad, it became clear that the Rumanian armies did not have enough air or armoured protection. Their only tanks were captured French or Russian ones. Hitler's promise to provide the Stalingrad 'group' with adequate planes and tanks was never fulfilled. Together with the German Fourth Army, a Rumanian division was encircled within Stalingrad itself. In the debacle which followed the Rumanian losses in dead, wounded, and prisoners were considerable. The defeat lead to retreat and the retreat became a rout. Transnistria was quickly evacuated and even Northern Moldavia and Bessarabia. The war was drawing to a disastrous end for Rumania.

Part I

THE ESTABLISHMENT OF SOVIET CONTROL OVER RUMANIA, 1944-7

2

From Teheran to the Coup d'état of 23 August 1944

THE Teheran Conference, which was held between 27 November and 3 December 1943, brought together Churchill, Roosevelt, and Stalin for the first time. It was the first of the meetings which were to decide upon both the strategy for ending the war and the ensuing world order. It had also to decide upon the fundamental plan of military action for the final phase of the war.

Historians and politicians have differed, sometimes heatedly, on the question whether at Teheran Churchill's plan, or alternatively that of the British Chiefs of Staff, to open a second front in the Balkans was defeated by the Americans and Russians conjointly. This plan was to open a two-pronged attack, even before the launching of Operation Overlord: through Yugoslavia across the Danube towards Hungary and Rumania and, should Turkey enter the war, through the Straits, towards Bulgaria and Rumania.

In the light of the recently published documents of the conference as well as of Churchill's own recollections,[1] the history of this short-lived project seems to be as follows. In preparation for the conference, the American and British Chiefs of Staff drafted separately plans for the final phase of the war. The American Chiefs of Staff, in a statement of United States strategic policy in the Balkan–Eastern Mediterranean region,[2] considered that operations in the Balkan–Aegean area should be limited to the

[1] For the Teheran Conference see especially U.S. Dept. of State, *The Conferences at Cairo and Teheran, 1943* (1961), which contains all relevant documents; W. S. Churchill, *The Second World War*, v: *Closing the Ring*, in which the military agreement is also reproduced in its entirety. For the wartime conferences see RIIA, *America, Britain and Russia*, by W. M. McNeill (1953). For the deeper meaning of the changes which were taking place in the attitudes of America and Britain towards East Central Europe during and after the war see P. Mosely, 'Hope and Failures: American Policy towards East-Central Europe, 1941-7', *Review of Politics*, Oct. 1955. See also Bibliography, pp. 358 below.

[2] U.S. Dept of State. *Teheran &c.*, doc. cc5402, 18 Nov. 1948.

supply of Balkan guerrillas by sea and air transport, minor action by Commando forces, and the bombing of vital strategic targets. They also agreed that it was desirable to bring Turkey into the war at this time, but that this must be brought about without diversion of resources which would prejudice the success of commitments elsewhere. When on 15 November 1942 the Chiefs of Staff submitted these views to Roosevelt he approved them, adding that the paper should be sent to the British.[3] During the first four days of the conference Roosevelt took his stand upon these views.

The basic thinking of the American strategists, that massive and decisive concentration should be given to one area, made its impact upon the conference, although the records show that Churchill and Sir Alan Brooke argued tenaciously that certain Allied forces, held in reserve until the launching of Overlord, should be used for operations in the Balkans. The crucial point of this discussion was reached at the first plenary meeting on 28 November. The Prime Minister is quoted as saying that Turkey's entry into the war would undoubtedly have an effect upon Rumania, from whom peace feelers had already been received, and also upon Hungary and might well start a landslide among the satellite states. He inquired whether any of the possible operations in the Mediterranean were of sufficient interest to the Soviet Union to warrant a two to three months' delay in the launching of Overlord. At that moment Roosevelt said that 'he had thought of a possible operation at the head of the Adriatic to make a junction with the Partisans under Tito and then to operate northeast into Rumania in conjunction with the Soviet advance from the region of Odessa'.[4] Stalin, after further questions about details, replied that in his opinion he questioned the wisdom of dissipating Allied forces for the various operations mentioned, such as Turkey, the Adriatic, and southern France. He said that he thought it would be better to take Overlord as the basis for all 1944 operations. Discussion around these points continued for the next few days, but finally found its 'military conclusion' in the military agreement of 1 December 1943 whereby the three leaders agreed: (1) that the Partisans in Yugoslavia should be supported by supplies and commando operations; (2) that from the military point of view, it was most desirable that Turkey come into the war; (3)

[3] Ibid. p. 195. [4] Ibid. p. 493.

that if Turkey found herself at war with Germany, and as a result, Bulgaria declared war on Turkey or attacked her, the Soviet Union would immediately be at war with Bulgaria; (4) that Operation Overlord be launched during May 1944 and that the Soviet forces should launch an offensive at about the same time; and (5) that the military staffs of the three powers should keep in close touch with each other in regard to the impending operations in Europe.[5] (The second Cairo Conference, 2–7 December 1943, saw the end of the possibility of Turkey entering the war.)

This military plan of action, as finally worked out, entailed the division of the European battlefield into two zones of operation; one for the Anglo-American armies in the west and one for the Soviet army in Eastern Europe. It also entailed the end of any possibility that the western Allies would open a second front in the Balkans in co-operation with Russia. At Teheran they committed themselves only to the main operations in Western Europe.

To take this memorable episode as the starting-point of a history of Rumania under communism does not imply that there existed between the two developments a direct cause-and-effect relationship such as there was, for instance, between the Teheran Conference and the landings in Normandy, or between Vyshinsky's *coup de théatre* in March 1945 and the passing of Rumania under direct Soviet domination. But, however, when one reads the Teheran military agreement one sees that these military moves were the beginning of a chain of events which soon led to other Soviet designs. Any attempts after Teheran to correct or to adjust the status of quasi-occupation which the advancing Soviet armies created when they overran Eastern Europe proved to be fruitless. But taken together with the much more important political statements of the three powers at Teheran, one sees how the western powers regarded the military measures only as expedients to end the war. Afterwards a 'new world order' was to be created by their collaboration with Soviet Russia within the future United Nations.

Immediately after Teheran the Russians embarked upon their preparations for the conquest of Rumania which, with Poland, was the first Eastern European state to fall to their advancing armies. In November 1943 the Russian troops had crossed the

[5] Ibid. p. 651.

lower Dnieper and had come very near to the Dniester. At the Foreign Ministers' Conference held in Moscow the previous October, it had been decided that all the 'feelers' for 'unconditional surrender' on the part of Germany's allies, no matter to which of the three governments they might be directed, should be considered by all three jointly. This, of course, represented a Russian advantage. Rumanian, Bulgarian, and Hungarian emissaries had tried repeatedly throughout 1943 with increasing urgency to contact the western governments, especially the British, in order to negotiate some agreement whereby their countries could surrender to the Anglo-American forces. Immediately after the Foreign Ministers' Conference, the Rumanian Communist Party proposed to the democratic parties a joint plan of action. Now it was more than ever necessary for the communists to press ahead with such a plan, for they sensed that at Teheran it had been decided that during the final phase of the war Eastern Europe was to be under the ultimate control of the Soviet army.

THREE-PRONGED OPERATIONS, JANUARY–MAY 1944

The Russian government allowed two diplomatic contacts to be opened with the Rumanians. On 4 January 1944 F. Nano, the Rumanian Minister in Stockholm, had the first of his meetings with the Soviet chargé d'affaires there, Vladimir Semonov.[6] These talks were held on Soviet initiative and were to continue till the 23 August coup d'état, first with Semonov and then with Mme Kollontai, the Soviet Ambassador in Stockholm, who was instructed to find out what Antonescu would offer, in contradistinction to what was being put forward by representatives of the opposition in Cairo. Had Antonescu agreed to turn his armies against the Germans, it would have provided the Russians with two short-cuts: first, they would have received the immediately effective order of a cease-fire directly from the military commander, and secondly, they would have avoided any political entanglements with the democratic parties, who inevitably brought political and constitutional reservations and conditions into the negotiations. A military dictatorship could have been more easily succeeded by a communist one without the intervention of these parties and the voters. The fact that there were, at least after Teheran, two schools

[6] See F. C. Nano, 'The First Soviet Double-Cross', *JCE Aff.*, xii/3 (1953). This is a first-hand account of the negotiations held between January and July 1944.

of thought among both the Rumanian communists and the Russian officials about what would be the most profitable way of getting Rumania out of the war was confirmed authoritatively in the report of the Rumanian Workers' Party delegation to the Twenty-Second Soviet Congress, presented by Gheorgiu-Dej to the plenary meeting of the Central Committee of 30 November–5 December 1961.[7] He said that Ana Pauker and Vasile Luca, returning to Rumania in September 1944 from the Soviet Union, 'where they had been in emigration', criticized the plan which led to Rumania's withdrawal from the war on 23 August 1944, especially the fact that the Communist Party had joined forces with the democratic parties for this purpose.

> They alleged that it would have been better if the overthrow of the dictatorship had been left to the Soviet army alone, because that would allegedly have made it possible to immediately seize power by the working class without passing through the stage of co-operation with the bourgeois parties.

The Stockholm talks therefore progressed slowly. Nano, after informing his government, received instructions from Mihai Antonescu to the effect that he should keep the channel open, while at the same time refraining from making any concrete offers or suggestions. The Russians maintained this contact without any great pressure.

The second contact was officially made in Cairo. It had been preceded, however, by negotiations in Ankara. There Alexander Cretzianu, ostensibly Minister to Turkey but actually an emissary of the opposition parties, had suggested that the Allies should receive a delegate from the opposition in London.[8] On 1 February 1944, however, he was told that the Allied High Command would agree to receive the spokesmen for the Rumanian opposition not in London but in Cairo. Prince Barbu Stirbey, his uncle, a former Prime Minister, was the first such emissary to arrive in Cairo. Here talks opened on 17 March between him and Lord Moyne for Britain and MacVeagh and Novikov, the American and Soviet Ambassadors to Egypt. This was to become the main line of contact and indeed the one through which the discussions were to be translated into action. It was on 1 June 1944 that the opposition formed a Democratic Bloc, composed of National Peasants,

[7] *Sc.*, 7 Dec. 1961; *Agerpres Inf. Bull.*, 10 Dec. 1961.
[8] See Cretzianu's *Lost Opportunity*, p. 125.

Liberals, and Social Democrats. But even before that King Michael had become the decisive factor in these negotiations. Through Niculescu-Buzesti, a young and courageous official in the Foreign Office, the king received all the information available on the course of diplomatic events. Through Aldea, C. Niculescu,[9] and many other generals he was in close touch with the army; and to him Maniu and the other opposition leaders reported their views on the contacts and negotiations with the Allies, as well as on those which they were undertaking with the Communist Party. Both the democratic opposition and the king were preoccupied by the defence of the territory of Rumania against any form of Soviet occupation. This concern was more and more justified. The new Soviet offensive started on 4 March. It quickly cut across the Ukraine, forcing the Rumanian armies to withdraw behind the Dniester, to the newly-prepared position at Iasi.

On 22 March Antonescu went to see Hitler, taking with him Mihai Antonescu who, the day before, had asked through Cretzianu what views the western allies held on 'the defense of Rumania's territory against the Soviet advance'.[10] The answer of the British Commander in the Middle East, General Maitland-Wilson, did not reach Antonescu before his interview with Hitler.[11] He discussed with Hitler the reorganization of the front and asked that the Rumanian troops encircled in the Crimea be rescued and that the Rumanian armies be massed in Moldavia and Bessarabia. A division of Rumanian territory, north and south of the line Ploesti–Bucharest, was agreed upon, the north being given to the zone of operations of the newly-formed German *Heeresgruppe Südukraine*.[12] On his return on 29 March Antonescu received a further message from Maitland-Wilson informing him that the Soviet government was ready to establish contact with him and stating that if he wanted to come to terms with them, he should

[9] Gen. C. Niculescu, Commander of Bucharest, was the bravest and most lucid of the group of loyal generals who realized that Antonescu was leading them towards final disaster. Like Gen. Aldea, he was arrested early in 1945 by the communists and never heard of again, in contrast to so many pro-German generals who were afterwards used by the communists as their main mouthpiece for the 'reorganization' of the Rumanian army.

[10] Cretzianu, *Lost Opportunity*, p. 129.

[11] '1. You should on no account visit Hitler . . . 2. You should at once surrender to the three Great Powers and order Rumanian troops to oppose no resistance to the Russians' (ibid. p. 130).

[12] H. Friessner (*Verratene Schlachter*, 1955) is the man who can best describe this phase as he was the newly-named commander of the reformed *Heeresgruppe*.

order his troops to surrender to the Russian command who would afterwards help him to build up his own resistance to the Germans. This message went unanswered by Antonescu. By then, too, the Soviet offensive had been halted along the new lines.

The Allies at this point decided to consider the suggestions made by the opposition. On 2 April Cretzianu transmitted to Maniu a message from the Allied Commander in the Mediterranean stating that 'if you overthrow Marshal Antonescu's régime because it has decided not to break with the Germans, Soviet government has now agreed its willingness to treat with you'.[13] The message went on to state that the Rumanian troops should fight alone against the Germans wherever no Russian troops were at hand and that the Allies would 'bring powerful air attacks to bear on such targets as you suggest'. Also on 2 April Molotov made his formal statement at a press conference in Moscow which, reasserting the rights of the Soviet Union in Bessarabia and Northern Bukovina, stated, nevertheless:

The Soviet government declares that it does not pursue the aim of acquiring any part of Rumanian territory or of changing the existing social order in Rumania. It equally declares that the entry into Rumania of Soviet troops is solely the consequence of military necessities and of the continuation of resistance by the enemy forces.[14]

Novikov, who had categorically stated on 5 April that 'so long as the German armies are fighting in Rumania . . . an armistice is impracticable', handed on, at Stirbey's insistence, on 12 April, a text containing the three Allies' 'minimum conditions of an armistice with Rumania'.[15] These repeated the initial demands for the cessation of fighting and the acceptance of the annexation of Bessarabia, but added demands for reparations and for the release of all Allied prisoners of war. The Soviet government promised the return of all, or the greater part of, Transylvania. On 5 April, too, it is to be noted, the British and Americans started their great series of bombardments of the Rumanian oilfields and refineries. These reached a climax in the massive bombing of 5 May, which cut Rumanian oil production by half.[16] This was also a blow to

[13] Cretzianu, *Lost Opportunity,* p. 130.
[14] Quoted ibid. p. 136.
[15] Ibid. pp. 137-8.
[16] Keitel, the German Field-Marshal, called this particular bombing a catastrophe (Hillgruber, p. 189).

Antonescu, for he had always claimed that the proof that the Allies wanted Rumania to continue to defend herself against the Russians lay in the fact that they had never bombed the Rumanian oilfields. Yet this was not the kind of help that Maniu and his emissaries had in mind. What they did have in mind was the obtaining of more precise guarantees in the certain event of Russia's failing to honour her pledges. Maniu asked that all three powers make public their decision to abstain from interference in Rumania, including Northern Transylvania when liberated. He also asked for the presence in Rumania of some token British and American troops as, for example, some airborne divisions. In his message of 7 April he asked that 'this should not be interpreted as a discrimination between the Allied powers' but explained that it was due to the geographical and military situation which, in the prevailing circumstances, made the Middle East Command supremely important for operation in Rumania.

Maniu then sent to Cairo on 27 May a second emissary, Constantin Visoianu, a former Rumanian Minister and Representative at the League of Nations and one of Titulescu's closest friends. Visoianu brought with him a detailed military plan for the airborne Allied troops. He also explained to the Allied representatives the technical and political difficulties of breaking with the Germans without the help of the Allies. He asked for better armistice conditions. On 1 June the Soviet government refused to continue the discussions unless Maniu accepted the proposals already made. On 10 June Maniu replied, agreeing to the proposals, but in the technical details which he sent ten days later through a courier, he insisted on the need to have three Allied airborne divisions dropped in Rumania. But this message, like all those which followed, remained unanswered by the Allies, that is by the Russians, who had now become the decisive party in the negotiations.

Meanwhile the Communist Party had also started to move. The best-known leaders were divided into two groups. One was the group imprisoned in Rumania: Gheorghiu-Dej, Gheorghe Apostol,[17] Chivu Stoica, I. Chisinevschi, Miron Constantinescu, Moghioros, and Ceausescu. The other group, consisting of Ana Pauker, Vasile Luca, Teohari Georgescu,[18] Constantin Parvulescu, Boris Stefanov, Buican, Gheorghe Stoica, Pintilie Bodna-

[17] See below, p. 350. [18] See below, p. 352.

renko, Borila, Dumitru Coliu,[19] and Emil Bodnaras,[20] were in the Soviet Union.

According to the revelations made at the November–December 1961 meeting of the Central Committee,[21] Ana Pauker, who had arrived in Russia in 1940 as the result of an exchange of political prisoners between the USSR and Rumania, formed there with Vasile Luca an 'external bureau' of 'representation' of the Rumanian Communist Party, and she and her associates considered themselves the 'leaders' of the party. Their most important action was the setting up, after 1943, of the 'Tudor Vladimirescu' division of Rumanian prisoners, which was to return to Rumania, fighting alongside the Soviet divisions. But according to the December 1961 revelations, Pauker and Luca wanted the Rumanian troops in Russia to be trained solely as police forces. This accusation can be taken in conjunction with the one already cited, that they tried to persuade the Soviet Government, through Molotov, not to accept Rumania's voluntary withdrawal from the war, but to allow the Soviet army to occupy the country and then set up a communist government supported by that army and by the Rumanian security forces trained in Russia.

With the prison group and the Moscow wing still unable to act, Foris, Koffler, Ranghet, and Patrascanu were the main figures forming a working Secretariat during this period. They did not organize any sabotage or partisan activity and their underground was feeble and ineffective. But they did achieve some political successes. In Transylvania Foris was able to consolidate the hold of the party on the Hungarian pro-Communist MADOSZ organization and on Petru Groza's Ploughmen's Front.[22] In the Old Kingdom Patrascanu had engaged in negotiations with the democratic opposition groups and had also had some success among the intellectuals. Among the latter he formed a group of university professors and lecturers who were later to write outspoken letters to Antonescu demanding that the war should end.[23] The NKDV had dispatched Emil Bodnaras to Rumania, with the task of revitalizing the party, of establishing contact with

[19] See below, p. 351. [20] See below, p. 350.
[21] See Coliu's speech in *Sc.*, 19 Dec. 1961.
[22] See below, p. 353.
[23] Parhon, Traian Savulescu, Mihail Ralea, C. Balmus, Andrei Otetea, C. Stoilov, N. Bagdazar, and A. Profiri were among well-known professors who frequently signed such documents.

Rumanian generals and officers, and of intensifying the contact with the democratic opposition.

Together with Ion Gheorge Maurer[24] and Ranghet, he got in touch with Dej and the other communist leaders in prison. This was done through various subterfuges, the most popular of which seem to have been the meetings in the wards of the prison hospital in the concentration camps.[25] Dej and his comrades in prison demanded that Foris, who was the Secretary-General and whom they denounced as a police *agent provocateur,* be removed from the leadership. The case against Foris was made publicly and forcefully by Dej as early as 1951. But at the plenary meeting of the Central Committee in November–December 1961 the main speakers referred to Foris's treason during the war. According to these, he had been a police agent since 1939 when he had been freed from prison on the understanding that he would fight the Iron Guard. Since that time, he had tried to dissolve the party, denounce its most active members to the police, and dissuade the others from undertaking any action.[26] This kind of public accusation after the war suited the party which had to find some justification, even if such a shameful one, for its total inactivity during the war. Whether or not there was any truth in these accusations against Foris will probably never be known. He remains an enigmatic character with even his ultimate fate unknown, for according to some witnesses he was kidnapped in Bucharest in 1944 and has never been heard of since.

What is known, however, according to present Rumanian communist history, is that on 4 April 1944 Bodnaras, Dej, Ranghet, Stoica, Constantin Parvulescu, and others held a meeting in a hospital prison during which they decided upon Foris's dis-

[24] See below, p. 353.

[25] In his speech at the CC plenum of Nov. 1961 Maurer described how in 1943, when he was detained in the Targu-Jiu camp 'because of Patrascanu's traitorous activities', he saw the arrival of Dej and Stoica at the camp and later served as Dej's emissary with those outside the prison (*Sc.*, 14 Dec. 1961).

[26] 'In these circumstances, when our party was faced with tasks of historic responsibility, the class enemy succeeded in dealing heavy and painful blows to the party with the help of the counter-revolutionary treacherous elements led by Foris, which found themselves at the head of the party. These imperialist agents provoked the arrest of Comrades Teohari Georgescu and Chisinevschi, members of the Secretariat of the CC of the party. These traitors pursued a criminal and perfidious course of action of dissolution and winding up of the party organizations, handed over to the Siguranta and the Gestapo the basic cadres of the party and denounced the sabotage and partisan activities organized by the communists' (Dej, speech at 30th anniv. of the party, *Lupta de clasa,* May–June 1951).

missal as a traitor, acknowledged Dej as the new leader of the party, and decided upon the measures to be taken to make the party active in the last phase of the war. Bodnaras was empowered to continue, with Patrascanu and Ion Gheorghe Maurer, the negotiations with the democratic parties. Dej wrote a letter of instruction to the party cadres. A new provisional Secretariat was formed with Parvulescu, Bodnaras, and Ranghet. It had the task of organizing some partisan and military activities before the arrival of the Soviet army. Even so, the activity of the Rumanian Communist Party, although thus intensified, remained far behind anything that the other Eastern European communist parties produced during and at the end of the war.[27]

The 'Rumanian C.P. bureau' of Ana Pauker and Vasile Luca in Soviet Russia was apparently not consulted on these moves, for when they returned they allegedly questioned the procedure of the 'dismissal of the elected leadership' and Ana Pauker regretted Foris's departure.[28]

CROSSED LINES, 18 MAY–23 AUGUST 1944

One reason for the breakdown in negotiations between the Rumanian opposition and the Allies is to be found in the negotiations on Rumania which were part of Churchill's strategy for countering Russian spheres of influence in Europe by British ones in Greece and Yugoslavia. As part of this design, on 18 May 1944

[27] In April 1944 a group of partisans was allegedly active in the northern districts of Moldavia (Dorohoi-Botosani-Iasi) and in Bukovina. It is easy to see, however, that these were operating in the front line already held by the Russians. This group was called 'Prut' after the river. Another group called 'Carpati' operated between June and August 1944, on the railway line between Ploesti and Fagaras, an important sector for all transport and deliveries between Germany and Rumania. One-third of the members of this group, which numbered probably 25-30 was formed by CP members who had fought in Spain; two-thirds by Rumanian deserters, probably advanced elements of the Tudor Vladimirescu division which had been formed in Russia and which was advancing with the Soviet troops. But a massive action of the Rumanian gendarmerie put an end to the 'Carpati' group's activities of derailing and exploding German oil and armament trains on 26 July 1944 (see Mihai Roller, 'On the Action of the Partisan Group 'Carpati' during the months June-August 1944,' *Analele*, May-June 1957). Another achievement was the formation on the night of 13-14 June 1944, of a 'military revolutionary command' formed by members of the party and by secret representatives of the units of the Rumanian army, whose leaders, as for instance, Gen. C. Niculescu, the head of the Bucharest troops, extended to the practical plane the co-operation accepted on a theoretical basis by the democratic parties with the communists. Bodnaras was active here. Finally, the 'Patriotic Guards', citizen units, were then set up.

[28] Speeches by Ceausescu and Chivu Stoica at the 28 Nov. CC plenary meeting.

Gromyko replied favourably to Eden's suggestion 'that the USSR should temporarily regard Rumanian affairs as mainly their concern under war conditions while leaving Greece to us', provided that the United States would agree.[29] This proposal was mainly occasioned by concern about the fate of Greece. The mutiny of Greek communist sailors under the British flag in Alexandria in April had caused considerable alarm and confirmed previous reports of the British mission in Greece as to the strength and intentions of the communist partisans. The British could not afford in any circumstances to see Greece, holding a key position in the Mediterranean, turned into a communist base, but Rumania 'fell within the sphere of the Russian armies' since the Russians had crossed the Pruth on 29 March. Thus on 30 May Churchill for the first time instructed Lord Halifax to raise the question (mentioning only Greece and Rumania at that stage) with Cordell Hull, and on 31 May sent a personal telegram to Roosevelt.

The American State Department opposed a proposal that 'might appear to favour the creation or acceptance of the idea of spheres of influence',[30] but after the exchange of further messages, in which Churchill gave assurances that the British 'followed the lead of the United States in South America as far as possible' and promised that any arrangement would be provisional only, on 11 June Roosevelt replied suggesting instead the establishment of 'consultative machinery to dispel misunderstandings and restrain the tendency toward the development of exclusive spheres'.[31] But on 13 June he capitulated to Churchill's plea that the arrangements should be given three months' trial, provided that it was made clear that 'we are not establishing any post-war spheres of influence'. This was communicated to the Russians on 19 June and was endorsed by the State Department on 15 July, but with the rider that American interests in the Balkans would in no way be affected by it, thus depriving the agreement of much of its value. 'We were thus unable to reach any final agreement about dividing responsibilities in the Balkan peninsula. . . . We abandoned our efforts to reach a major understanding until I met Stalin two months later. By then much had happened on the Eastern front', concludes Churchill.[32]

Indeed, the suspension of the negotiations in Cairo was

[29] Churchill, vi. 64. [30] Ibid. p. 65. [31] Ibid. p. 66. [32] Ibid p. 71.

clearly a proof of a Russian change of attitude. Throughout June, July, and August they were possibly trying to bring about the direct capitulation of Rumania to the Soviet Union. Hence the intensification of the talks with the Antonescus, via Stockholm, where Mme Kollontai on 2 June made a tempting offer of an armistice;[33] and the preparation of the big summer offensive which was intended to take the Rumanian oilfields. But the Rumanian action of 23 August, when King Michael, on Maniu's advice, decided to take Rumania out of the war interrupted these trends.

THE COUP D'ÉTAT OF 23 AUGUST 1944

The decision to overthrow Antonescu had to be taken quickly for military as well as diplomatic reasons. On 20 August the Russians started their great summer offensive. The defence, organized by the *Heeresgruppe Südkraine,* including some 21 Rumanian divisions, weary of German command, immediately collapsed.[34] Within three days an army group under Marshal Tolbukhin, which attacked from the bridgehead at Tiraspol, was driving fast to the south-west; another army group under Malinovsky, advancing from the north salient, took Iasi on the 23rd. Antonescu knew that this was the end. He had had his last three-hour-long interview with Hitler on 5 August,[35] immediately after Turkey had broken off diplomatic relations with the Reich, a fact that Antonescu thought highly significant. To Hitler's feverish and angry questions about Rumania's intentions, he had countered with other questions of his own: (*a*) concerning Germany's military plans in the event of a collapse on the Moldavian front; (*b*) concerning the possibilities of the Luftwaffe defending Rumania against Allied air attacks; and (*c*) concerning the new German measures against a landing on the Black Sea coast now potentially opened to the Allies by Turkey. The questions remained unanswered. On 22 August Antonescu came back from his headquarters at Slanic to Bucharest, having decided to ask for an armistice on the lines suggested by Mme Kollontai. He requested an audience with the king in order to inform him of this.

[33] Nano, in *JCE Aff.*, xii (1953).

[34] See Friessner. Hillgruber (p. 259) has also a good map of the operations on that front between 19 and 27 Aug.

[35] He was accompanied by Mihai Antonescu and Gen. Steflea, the Chief of Staff. The meeting took place at Rastenberg, where Hitler's train was then standing. Hillgruber (pp. 209-10) gives a good account of this conversation.

Together with Mihai Antonescu, he was received by the king on 23 August, at four o'clock.[36] He stated that it was his intention to ask for an armistice but at the same time he would inform the Germans of this. The king, who had been advised by Maniu to act as quickly as possible and who had already informed Cairo that he intended to act on 26 August, realized that Antonescu's move would simply mean another delay and complication. It would either have allowed the Russians to advance farther in the guise of enemies or induced the Germans to occupy the country outright. The king made a quick decision. He went into the adjoining room and instructed his friends to arrest Antonescu. He formed a government under General Sanatescu, who had been one of his collaborators during the previous months, with Niculescu-Buzesti as Foreign Secretary, General Aldea as Minister for Internal Affairs, and the representatives of the four parties, Maniu, Bratianu, Titel Petrescu, and Patrascanu, Ministers without portfolio. Patrascanu was also to be Minister of Justice.[37] Then Michael broadcast to the nation, announcing that 'from this moment all fighting and hostile acts cease'. He sent a message to Istanbul through a British officer, Lt-Colonel A. G. G. de Chastelaine—who eight months before had been parachuted into Rumania and at once arrested—asking for three airborne brigades to be landed near Bucharest.[38] Then he prepared for the outcome. Not a single move of protest or resistance was registered against Michael's act, either at the front or in the rear. The country was in a mood of stern but hopeful resolution. When the first Soviet tanks rolled into Bucharest on 31 August they were received calmly by the citizens, although only hastily gathered communist cohorts of the 'Patriotic Guard' acclaimed them.

Soviet official interpretation of the coup d'état varied.[39] On 26 August 1944 *Pravda* said that 'Rumania's break with the Axis is important not only for the Rumanian people' but because the

[36] A. G. Lee, *Crown Against Sickle* (1949) is well informed on the details of the king's moves as it is based on some private papers of Queen Helen of Rumania, the king's mother.

[37] This was the first 'operative' department to be received by a communist. The communists' insistence on having such posts at once was characteristic.

[38] Three British officers had thus been captured: de Chastelain, Ivor Porter, and Nicholas Metzianu.

[39] See, for the first version: USSR, *The Great Patriotic War of the Soviet Union*; *The Great Soviet Encyclopaedia* (1949); V. B. Ushakov, *Foreign Policy of Hitlerite Germany* (Moscow, 1961). For the new version: USSR, *The Great War of the USSR for the Defence of the Fatherland* (Moscow, 1962), iv, ch. 9.

whole German defence system in the Balkans had collapsed. Yet afterwards, and even up to 1961, Soviet histories ignored the coup. New Soviet war histories contain a revised version in which the Rumanian action is acknowledged, but the credit for it is given to the communists and Gheorghiu-Dej. As late as 23 August 1946 *Scanteia* described the events of two years earlier by saying that 'the evolution of the political situation in the country and the secret audience of Comrade Lucretiu Patrascanu with His Majesty the King [*sic*] had created favourable political conditions'. On the other hand the present leadership of the Workers' Party reproaches Patrascanu for the fact that while in Moscow in September 1944, with the Rumanian armistice delegation, he held a press conference during which he stated that 23 August was the action of the king, 'without mentioning the part played by the Communist Party.'[40] This *ex post facto* account was even more dramatized by the 'revelations' made by Dej and subsequent speakers at the Central Committee plenum of November–December 1961. These were intended to show how the Dej group had had to struggle with the Ana Pauker group on this very question. It was significant, Dej said, that 'Ana Pauker enjoyed a warm regard, particularly with the dogmatic, anti-Party elements exposed by the CPSU after the Twentieth Congress, and especially with Molotov'. Being entirely divorced from the realities at home, Pauker and Luca

> were surprised by the force and activities of the Party, under whose leadership the people had obtained the historic victory in the armed insurrection which started on August 23, 1944 . . . [They] looked upon it with dissatisfaction and disapproval. Pauker and Luca maintained that the carrying out of the historic act of August 23 leading to the overthrow of the military-fascist dictatorship and the Rumanian army's joining the armed forces of the Soviet Union in the struggle against Hitlerism had been a big mistake.[41]

Borila said the same thing, and that Pauker and Luca claimed that this mistake was profitably used by the bourgeoisie.[42]

The coup of 23 August 1944 was effected by the action of King Michael and the democratic opposition, and was designed to safeguard the country's territorial and political integrity

[40] Valter Roman's speech at the CC meeting 28 Nov. 1961 (*Sc.*, 12 Dec. 1961).
[41] *Sc.*, 7 Dec. 1961; *Agerpres Inf. Bull.*, 10 Dec. 1961.
[42] *Sc.*, 12 Dec. 1961.

and to present the Russians with the *fait accompli* of an independent Rumania, assuming her own share in the final Allied effort against Hitler.

In the history of the Second World War the Rumanian armistice was significant in that it permitted the Russian armies to reach the Bulgarian, Yugoslav, and Hungarian borders within a week. From then on, the Germans had to wage a difficult rearguard action. In the words of Professor Hugh Seton-Watson:

> Had it not been for the Rumanian armistice, the losses of the Western armies in France would have been higher and so would those among the civilian population in Great Britain and the Netherlands from V-bombs. To the whole of Europe and to Rumania, as well, the final defeat of Germany would have brought greater destruction and would have created more bitter resentment than was thus the case.[43]

[43] *La Nation roumaine,* Aug. 1953.

3

Establishing the Zone of Influence, August–October 1944

On 24 August 1944 the Rumanian army was attacked simultaneously by German and Soviet troops.

In Bucharest the German General Alfred Gerstenberg, Commander of the Luftwaffe in Rumania, received orders to 'smash the putsch'. He attacked the city from the air with his Stukas, selecting as targets the palace and ministerial buildings. The next day, the 24th, the German radio announced that Horia Sima had formed a national government which would continue Rumania's fight on the German side.[1] Hitler's order meant that the few remaining elements of the German army on Rumanian soil (the bulk had been removed in the spring beyond the Carpathians and to Poland) were either decimated or taken prisoner by the Russians. In Bucharest the German Embassy was surrounded by angry mobs. Von Killinger, the Ambassador, and his secretary committed suicide.

The German attack on Bucharest was defeated at the end of three days, but the fact that it had taken place hastened the declaration of war on Germany which took place on 26 August. This made it clear that Rumania was prepared to fulfil the conditions of armistice as agreed on 12 June 1944. On 27 August Molotov informed the British Ambassador in Moscow, Sir Archibald Clark-Kerr, and the American Ambassador, Mr Averell Harriman, of the readiness of the Soviet government to enter upon final discussions for the conclusion of the armistice with Rumania. Stirbey and Visoianu left Cairo and a six-man delegation led by Patrascanu and including G. Popp, I. Christu, former envoy in

[1] See Palaghita for the Iron Guard version of this episode. The author describes how the Iron Guard teams from the various concentration camps were brought to Vienna and kept in complete ignorance of their 'mission'. See also Ion Gheorghe, *Rumaniens weg zur satellitenstaat* (1952).

Sofia, and General Damaceanu set off from Bucharest to Moscow where the armistice was eventually signed on 12 September.

SOVIET RUSSIA'S INITIAL BEHAVIOUR

In the meanwhile, however, the Rumanian army was being attacked and disarmed all along the Moldavian front by the Soviet troops. Obeying the king, officers and soldiers offered no resistance from the time of the cease-fire and with some few exceptions, despite often intolerable provocation, were co-operative. Indeed, the discipline shown at this time by the Rumanian army and people, united under the king's command, was irreproachable.[2] The behaviour of Malinovsky's army towards both the Rumanian army and population during the interval before the armistice was deliberately different from that of Tolbukhin's army in Bulgaria in similar circumstances.[3]

That this behaviour was deliberate was confirmed by subsequent Soviet moves. The first may seem trivial but has at least a symbolic significance. This is that although the armistice convention formally recognized that Rumania had broken with the Third Reich on 23 August 1944, at 4 p.m., the peace treaty of 10 February 1947 stated, that Rumania had taken 'an active part in the war against Germany' after the conclusion of the armistice on 12 September 1944. The reason for this disparity can be found only in the refusal of the Soviet Government to account for 130,000 prisoners taken by them during this confused interval and for the enormous war-booty seized by the unopposed Soviet units in Rumania. This consisted of the country's entire war fleet and the major part of its merchant marine, quantities of oil industry equipment—representing one and a half times the yearly importations made by Rumania before the war—half of the available railway rolling stock, and all motor-cars. According to more recent data the total loot taken between 23 August and 12 September may have reached $2,000 million.[4]

The other move made by the Soviet government involved a

[2] Rumanian contemporary historians agree on this point. See 'About the Contribution of the Rumanian Army to the Anti-Hitlerite War', *Analele*, no. 3, July-Aug. 1957.

[3] The author himself, having crossed Bulgaria by car on his way back to Rumania from Turkey, was struck by the difference in behaviour between the two units. The 'occupation' in Bulgaria was kept closely under control and troops and officers gave little reason for complaint. In Rumania, on the contrary, the Malinovsky army behaved like hordes of invaders.

[4] R. L. Wolff, *The Balkans in Our Time* (1956), p. 345.

slower and more involved operation. This was the way it chose its 'collaborators' in the quasi-occupied country. From the first, the Soviet authorities made it clear that only total subordination of the interests and sentiments of the Rumanians to those of the USSR could be considered 'collaboration', however outrageous the demands of such a collaboration might be. They did not conceal their opinion that for the time being the country must be kept in a state of administrative dependence and economic subservience as a former enemy which had caused great harm to the Soviet Union. The military representatives insisted that politics was not their concern; and that they did not care for the agitation of the Communist Party of Rumania which only disturbed production. They wanted goods and services: and selected their personnel from people approved by the NKDV, whatever their political allegiance before or during the war. They thus recruited the first *apparat,* a most variegated body composed in many cases of people with a most dubious political and personal record.

There was, however, a distinction to be made between the parts of the country under Rumanian sovereignty and those still considered as 'zones of military operations'. In those regions of the country where the Soviet army had arrived in the course of what it considered to be military operations, as in Moldavia and in some parts of Transylvania, Dobruja, and Banat, it appointed whenever possible mayors, councillors, and local authorities of its own choosing.[5] At the same time the representatives of the hastily augmented Communist Party, and especially the newly-formed 'fighting patriotic units'[6] whenever available, were setting up local

[5] See T. Caraciuc, 'Aspects of the Rumanian CP's Struggle for a New State Machine in our Country', *Analele*, no. 6, Nov.-Dec. 1957. The author maintains that the transition was formed by the 'peasants' committees' set up by the party, which elected new mayors and prefects. Yet he acknowledges that the first such committees appeared in Northern Moldavia, a region separated from the rest of the country by the front and held by the Soviet army for almost five months (p. 55), and that 'a large number of the new prefects functioned without the approval of the central government' (p. 59). The first 'citizens' committees' and militia also appeared in Northern Moldavia, 'whence the local authorities had been evacuated before the arrival of the Soviet army' (pp. 60–61). In Northern Transylvania the problem of the state apparatus was linked with the struggle for the liberation of that province by the Soviet and Rumanian armies, which liquidated the old state apparatus (p. 62).

[6] Immediately after 23 Aug. 1944 the 'fighting patriotic units', organized into armed groups, were still for the most part limited, the great majority of them being formed by 'clandestines' and by former partisans of the detachments. They had rather the character of self-defence units. Through pressure on the government the historic parties tried to obtain the subordination of the fighting patriotic guards to the 'reactionary state apparatus'. 'At the meeting of the Council of

branches of the secret police, whose duties were to discover the 'saboteurs and spies' and to supply the Soviet army with the man-power and food supplies and other commodities it needed.

THE ARMISTICE, 12 SEPTEMBER 1944

The armistice convention was signed on 12 September 1944. The negotiations lasted for three days. Molotov conducted them with the ruthless stubborness which was to become legendary in other and more important international conferences. The two western ambassadors, Sir Archibald Clark-Kerr and Mr Averell Harriman, confined themselves to the rôle of silent observers. They sought above all to avoid any private interviews with the Rumanian delegation.

This delegation tried to define more closely some of the political and economic obligations drafted for their country. The Russians made it as clear as possible that the Rumanian delegation was there to sign a ready-made text and not to discuss it. Patrascanu shared many of his colleagues' anxieties as to the chances of a genuine collaboration, if from the start the Russian attitude was so intransigent. But obviously his greatest anxieties lay in another direction and were aroused by other prospects. He confided to at least one other member of the delegation that Rumania belonged exclusively to the Russian orbit and that the Russians were determined to bring the 'tough' elements of the Communist Party to power as quickly as possible. His nervousness and lack of communication with the leadership of the party during his stay in Moscow can also be seen in the statements he made to press correspondents in Moscow.

The convention, as it finally emerged, was to be used afterwards as a model for the armistice conventions of the other two former German satellites, Bulgaria and Hungary.[7] It imposed military obligations only on Rumania, although it was supposed to mark

Ministers of 17 Sept. 1944 Iuliu Maniu, Aldea, and Buzesti demanded that the Patriotic Guard should hand to the organs of the Ministry of the Interior a list with the names and addresses of the members of the organization; that they should be disarmed and should subordinate their activity to the gendarmerie and police, acting only on the orders of the latter (Gh. Tutiu & E. Cimponeriu, *Analele*, no. 3, Mar.-Apr. 1953).

[7] The Bulgarian was delayed until 28 Oct. 1944 because of the territorial and financial problems Bulgaria had to solve with Greece and Yugoslavia. The Hungarian, delayed by the military operations, was signed on 20 Jan. 1945. For Rumania, the convention was signed by Patrascanu, Gen. Damaceanu, Stirbey, and G. Popp. See text in Ciurea, *Le traité de paix avec la Roumanie* (1954). (Rumanian text published Buch., 1944.)

the beginning of Rumanian military collaboration with the Allies. And, although signed by representatives of all three powers, it channelled to the Soviet Union all damages to be paid and all services to be rendered by the country.

The territorial clauses acknowledged the Soviet annexation of Bessarabia and Northern Bukovina and annulled the Vienna award of Northern Transylvania to Hungary.

The political clauses established a direct collaboration between the Soviet High Command and the Rumanian Armistice Commission, created *ad hoc* to represent the Rumanian state in its dealings with the Allies. They also gave the Soviet High Command the right to censor newspapers and publications published in Rumania or imported from abroad.

The military clauses established the methods of the control of the territory and resources of Rumania by the Soviet army, thus crystallizing in an official text the *de facto* situation created by the presence of that army in the country. They also organized military collaboration against Germany and her allies. (Since 25 August sixteen Rumanian divisions had been fighting side by side with the Soviet army. In Hungary and Czechoslovakia, where they were well received, they liberated many villages and towns and took more than 100,000 prisoners. The Rumanian troops thus engaged lost nearly 170,000 men.[8] The military contribution of Rumania was unequalled by any other country which joined the Allies in the last phase of the war. From the point of troops lost in action in this short but violent campaign, Rumania comes fourth after the Soviet Union, Great Britain, and the United States.)

The principal economic clauses imposed on Rumania the obligation to pay for the Soviet occupation troops and grant them the use of various industrial and transport enterprises and services; to pay the Soviet Union over six years an indemnity of $300 million in goods (oil products, lumber, grain, &c) for Soviet losses caused by military operations and occupation; and to restitute all goods taken from Soviet territory during the war. The basis for regulating the indemnities (annex to Art. 11) was the American dollar at the date of the signature of the Convention (i.e. $35=1 oz. gold), but the prices for the deliveries were fixed by the Russians

[8] This figure is confirmed in 'Contribution of the Rumanian Army', *Analele*, no. 4, July-Aug. 1957, which shows that Rumanian troops were active in the liberation of Cluj, Oradea-Mare, and Bratislava. It mentions that in the 260 days of fighting, Rumanian units went from Mures to Bohemia, a distance of 1,000 km.

at the world prices of 1938, which were considerably lower than those of 1944. Thus, for example, the quantities of oil to be delivered were in fact doubled because the price per ton had risen from $15 in 1938 to $30 in 1945. A more detailed estimate of the cost to Rumania of calculating the payments on this basis was given by Mr Willard Thorp, a member of the American delegation to the Paris Peace Conference of 1946, to the Economic Commission for Finland and the Balkans in September 1946. According to this estimate, the actual cost of the indemnity of $300 million was 50 per cent above this figure by 1946,[9] and the cost must have gone up as the Rumanian currency depreciated.

'RUMANIA: 90 PER CENT'

At the beginning of October 1944 Mr Churchill and Mr Eden went to Moscow for yet another series of wartime talks with the Russians. For many historians of South-East Europe this meeting became the starting-point of a new phase in that region.

What happened has been told in detail by Sir Winston Churchill. In the sixth volume of his memoirs, *Triumph and Tragedy,* he recalls how, in his anxiety over the situation in Greece, he suggested to Stalin the extension and even the hardening of the agreement on spheres of influence of June that year. No one can describe better than Sir Winston the new agreement entered into with Stalin:

> The moment was apt for business, so I said, 'Let us settle about our affairs in the Balkans. Your armies are in Roumania and Bulgaria. We have interests, missions, and agents there. Don't let us get at cross-purposes in small ways. So far as Britain and Russia are concerned, how would it do for you to have ninety per cent predominance in Roumania, for us to have ninety per cent of the say in Greece, and go fifty-fifty about Yugoslavia? While this was being translated I wrote out on a half-sheet of paper:
>
> Roumania:
> Russia . . . 90%
> Others . . . 10%
> Greece
> Great Britain (in accord with U.S.A.) . 90%
> Russia 10%
> Yugoslavia . . 50–50%
> Hungary . . 50–50%

[9] See below, p. 137.

Bulgaria:

Russia . .	75%
The others	25%

I pushed this across to Stalin who had by then heard the translation. There was slight pause. Then he took his blue pencil and made a large tick upon it, and passed it back to us. It was all settled in no more time than it takes to set down.[10]

In Rumania's case the immediate effect of this arrangement was to usher in a much harsher and more stringent Soviet military control than previously. A political representative, I. V. Pavlov, later Soviet Ambassador in Paris, was dispatched at once to Bucharest and he made it clear that the 'contradictions' inherent in the policy and institutions of Rumania would soon have to be solved.

[10] Churchill, vi. 198.

4
Russia Refuses a *Modus Vivendi*, August 1944–March 1945

FROM the day on which King Michael dismissed Antonescu to that on which Soviet Russia imposed the Groza government on him, there were three Rumanian governments. All tried to solve the problem of genuine collaboration between an independent Rumania and Soviet Russia. The first two were under the presidency of General Sanatescu; the third under that of General Radescu. All three failed because of the direct and indirect refusals of Soviet Russia to deal with any but a communist-controlled government.

THE FIRST SANATESCU GOVERNMENT, 23 AUGUST–22 NOVEMBER 1944

General Sanatescu's first cabinet immediately restored the constitution of 1923 which had been suspended in 1938 by King Carol. Its main preoccupation was to try to come to terms and to find a lasting *modus vivendi* with the new dominant power of Eastern Europe.

This was a most difficult task, as at the beginning there was no official contact whatsoever between the Rumanian authorities and the Soviet troops pouring into the country. Nor was there any official contact after the armistice convention had established the procedure of contacts between the Soviet High Command and the Rumanian Armistice Commission. These contacts did not start to function until the end of October and were constantly ignored and over-stepped by the Russians. Sanatescu, a loyal and elegant cavalry officer, was unable to cope with his almost impossible task. Nor was his team of ministers able either to cope or to co-operate in such circumstances. The country was fighting a war and yet under occupation; responsible for deliveries and yet with its internal lines of communication cut; its own administration was hopelessly disorganized and yet it was under the pressure of a foreign administration which constantly interfered.

There were only two members of the first Sanatescu government who distinguished themselves. They were the youngest and had opposing ends in view—Lucretiu Patrascanu and Grigore Niculescu-Buzesti. All actions of Patrascanu, as representative of the Communist Party in the government and as Minister of Justice, were watched by the Communist Party and by Moscow. His impatience and anxiety under this pressure and dictation made him take some rash and irrevocable steps. He tried to rally round himself a popular movement to use against the self-appointed communist leaders of 4 April 1944. '*Patrascanu la putere*' (Patrascanu to power) was the slogan chanted in September and October 1944 at many communist-organized meetings.[1] Patrascanu believed that he would be helped in his plans by his friend Vasilichi, who was Dej's rival to the claim of being the leader of the communist workers. Vasilichi was very popular with the railwaymen, but having spent the war years in France he returned to Rumania too late to form a team with Patrascanu successfully to oppose the Dej–Bodnaras grouping. Patrascanu was probably inspired to this attempt at political action by a small group of genuinely revolutionary intellectuals, mostly young and of Jewish extraction, who, like him, were already sickened by the ease with which opportunists, politicians and intellectuals alike, were given full rights in the Communist Party under the new leadership.

Niculescu-Buzesti, the young career diplomat who had been promoted overnight from the position of counsellor at the Foreign Office to that of Minister of Foreign Affairs, was like Patrascanu surrounded by a small group of fervent young friends. These were mainly the young diplomats with whom he had co-operated in contacting the Allies in the last two years of the war. Like Patrascanu, Niculescu-Buzesti felt that he must act urgently. As Minister of Foreign Affairs in those weeks of chaos in which diplomatic relations with the powers were not as yet restored and external communications were cut, he had less to do than his impatience could brook. He was also convinced that to resist the communist attack from within was a more urgent task at that particular moment than to interest friendly powers from without.

[1] Especially at the great popular meeting of 8 Oct. 1944 at Anef, the huge stadium in Bucharest.

He therefore devoted himself to revitalizing the National Peasant Party, of which he was not a member, but which seemed to him to be the one genuine political and social force which could oppose subversion. Though handicapped by a fatal illness,[2] he wanted to help the aging Maniu in this formidable task which his forebodings told him must be accomplished as quickly as possible.

Maniu's decision not to assume the reins of government in August, when the whole country might have looked to him for guidance, can be better understood in the light of what has since happened than it could at the time. He had accepted on behalf of his party, and together with C. Bratianu and C. Titel Petrescu for the Liberal and Socialist Parties, the office of Minister without portfolio in a caretaker government until the elections. He insisted that the will of the people be freely expressed after so many years of dictatorship. The main point of the National Peasant Party was that elections should be held at once. But the communists and the Russians opposed this. Thus, although Maniu had also advised members of the National Peasant Party to accept office in the caretaker government, he did not want to accept the full responsibility of government before the dark cloud of Soviet intentions had been dispelled and before he himself was satisfied that Rumania enjoyed full sovereignty and sufficient freedom to order her own affairs. Once more he preferred to hold himself in readiness for tempering and reorganizing the party and perhaps for yet another stand in opposition, rather than to slide slowly and inevitably down the slopes of compromise and 'collaboration', in a Pétainist sense of the word.

COLLABORATION AND RESISTANCE

A comparison with Vichy and the atmosphere in France during the years of German occupation is not without relevance in a description of the political and moral climate in Rumania in 1944. As in the first phase of Vichy, there were added to the injuries of occupation the insults of ideological and doctrinal pretences. The inconveniences and humiliations of occupation were presented by the communists and their friends as a 'national revolution long awaited by the people'. The Rumanian people, it is true, had long been awaiting the overthrow of the pre-war and wartime dictator-

[2] He had leukaemia, of which he died in 1949 in New York.

ships. But they longed for democratic reforms, very different from those advocated by the teams from Moscow.

There is a second analogy. The possibilities of a short-cut to favour and privilege through political 'collaboration' for the few who were willing to accept this indignity created, as in the first phase of Vichy, a great moral cleavage in Rumanian society. Most people, tired of war, dictatorships, and the interference of politics in their private lives, were waiting for a reasonable peace and for a new, if uncomfortable start. Hope and anxiety were almost equally balanced in the thoughts of these simple people, three-quarters of whom were peasants. But they were prepared to show great patience and confidence.

The communists, however, under Ana Pauker's special supervision, were pressing on with their own 'recruiting campaign'. Hundreds of thousands of individuals received communist or affiliated party cards in the winter of 1944. They were disgruntled factory workers; a sizeable number of domestic servants; unemployed agricultural workers in the countryside; and in large numbers, the members of the discontented national minorities. (The official links between the Communist Party of Rumania and the Transylvanian sections of the Hungarian party were resumed as early as October 1944, that is almost six months before the administrative reintegration of Northern Transylvania. Thus on 22 October 1944 a communiqué appeared in the local press of Cluj announcing that the communist organization of Northern Transylvania had renewed its links with the central organization of the Rumanian Communist Party, which had been severed after the Vienna *Diktat*. The Hungarian organization handed over its cadres and members to the Rumanian one.)[3] There were also the numerous contingents of former prisoners of war, returning from Russia already indoctrinated or willing for other reasons to collaborate and finally some organizations and sections of the Iron Guard and of other fascist and semi-fascist parties.

The story of this recruitment was told in greater detail after Ana Pauker's fall, and indeed constituted one of the main accusations against her. She was held responsible for having imposed an indiscriminate and immoral policy of recruitment, accepting 'everyone from the streets' who would agree to add one more to

[3] M. Deheleanu and N. Kohn, 'The Struggle of the Workers of the Uneirea Factory, Cluj', *Analele*, Mar.–Apr. 1958.

the excessively meagre rank and file of the party.[4] She was accused especially of having deliberately accepted into the party not only members of the Iron Guard, then desperately trying to save their skins, but even whole organizations. At the plenary meeting of the Central Committee of December–January 1961 Draghici mentioned a formal pact between Teohari Georgescu, acting for Ana Pauker, and Nicolae Patrascu, a leader of the Iron Guard, whereby the latter brought into the party a sizeable sector of the membership of the fascist organization.[5]

The advantages of membership were obvious: jobs with wages and all other benefits attached to them in a country in dire straits. Moreover the recruitment was made with a dual purpose: that of swelling the volume of the rank and file and of finding the kind of people who would do the jobs the communists needed to have done for them at this stage of their penetration of the state machine. Many of these jobs were those of the informer and the 'tough'.

The communists were also engaged in more specialized recruitment. They quite soon attracted some members from the upper strata of Bucharest society. These included generals and commanding officers who bore heavy responsibility for certain actions in the war in Bessarabia, Transnistria, and the Ukraine, some Orthodox bishops, heads of Antonescu's police and especially of the secret police and intelligence,[6] writers, journalists, and university professors who had been on the mailing list—if not on closer terms—of the German Embassy, business men, bankers, and great industrialists confident that they could bribe their way in the coming dictatorship as they had done under previous ones. Finally, there were those politicians who, having already served in high posts under previous dictatorships, offered their services to yet another one. At lower levels and in the provinces the same pattern was reproduced and the same categories of people, probably also inspired by the example or advice of their like in the capital, were emerging invigorated from the communist and NKVD recruiting offices.

At the other extreme there were those who, either because of

[4] See speeches of Dej and Coliu at the Nov.–Dec. 1961 CC plenum (*Sc.*, 7 & 19 Dec. 1962).

[5] Ibid. 15 Dec. 1961.

[6] Eugen Cristescu, the head of Antonescu's secret police, testified against him at the trial and was allegedly put to work for Bodnaras, at once.

past political associations or simply because of disgust with the behaviour of the communists and of the Soviet troops in Rumania, saw no reason to believe that things could ever change for the better as long as the Russians held the upper hand in the country. These elements spoke openly of 'resistance'. Indeed, from the winter of 1944 rumour had it in Bucharest that resistance groups were being organized in the mountains.

In the communist determination to capture power they made use of four main 'front' organizations: the Union of Patriots, a loose group of National Peasants and Liberals who had defected from their party under the Carol–Antonescu dictatorship; Groza's Ploughmen's Front, which had a certain local membership in Hunedoara and in a few Transylvanian districts; the Patriotic Defence, which raised funds for wounded soldiers and commanded a militia of its own, its agents virtually extorting large contributions from all who could pay; and the society for friendship with the Soviet Union. In October 1944 the communists were able to engineer a split in the democratic opposition groups, when the National Peasants and National Liberals were excluded from the newly formed National Democratic Front (FND). This consisted of the communists and Social Democrats, together with the Union of Patriots, Ploughmen's Front, and united trade unions (in which Dej and Gheorghe Apostol were most active). All these 'parties', with the exception of the Social Democrats, were in dire need of members. The communists were arranging that some of the members they had recruited so quickly (many of the more unsavoury ones) should be distributed among these groups and at the same time they were continuing to infiltrate the Social Democrats on a large scale.

The National Democratic Front's political platform consisted of agrarian reform; making a contribution to the war effort as a result of which Northern Transylvania could be regained; promotion of workers' control; purge of war criminals and fascists from the administration; democratization of the army, &c. The platform of October 1944 also called for the nationalization of trade and industry, but this was dropped later.

THE SECOND SANATESCU GOVERNMENT, 4 NOVEMBER–2 DECEMBER, 1944

Sanatescu resigned on 2 November and was asked by the king

on the advice of the leaders of the democratic parties to form a new government on the same caretaker lines until elections could be held. The reshuffle had been made necessary for several reasons. The resumption of some relations at the level of 'political representatives' with the Allied powers and with the other western countries created embryonic possibilities for diplomatic activity. Niculescu-Buzesti resigned his post in favour of Constantin Visoianu, who inherited the mantle of Titulescu. Buzesti himself engaged more deeply in internal politics and in the arduous task of preparing the National Peasant Party for the elections. Indeed, and this was another reason for the reshuffle, the communist agitation was growing at such a pace in the country that only quickly held elections could dispel the threat of insurrection which the communists were clearly holding in reserve. N. Penescu, a National Peasant, was appointed Minister of the Interior, and thus controlled the police, the rural gendarmerie, and the appointment of local prefects and mayors. The communists not only remained entrenched in the government, but asked for and received more departments, the most important politically being the Ministry of Transport, which went to Gheorghiu-Dej, while Groza became vice-premier. But this did not in the slightest decrease their agitation against the government, which was more and more encouraged by the Russian authorities. This was also a result of the internal struggle within the party. The 'Muscovites' still reproached those who between April and August 1944 had taken the decisions in Bucharest for having been far too conciliatory, thus jeopardizing the chance of a swifter seizure of power. In his speech at the 30th anniversary of the party in May 1951, published in all official newspapers (a moment which coincided with the climax of the struggle between the Pauker and Dej wings of the party), Vasile Luca said that 'it still remains to be discovered how it was possible that, although the action was organized by the Communist Party while the Soviet army advanced like a whirlwind towards Bucharest, a para-military government was accepted without the large participation of the leadership of the Communist Party of Rumania'.

The agitation was now focused on the workers and peasants. In factories and industrial districts the agitators wished to create the nuclei of 'responsibles' who would see that 'everything would go to the front and for victory'. This was the slogan of the moment and it implied that the contribution of Rumania to the war against Hitler was being mishandled by the reactionary bourgeois elements, the heads of departments, and the employers and managers. This reproach came more and more frequently also in the Russian representations to the Rumanian government and authorities.

But the communists enforced the direct control of production by creating 'workers' production commissions'.[7] They demanded that the managements of factories and plants relinquish their powers of control and decision-making to these commissions, formed for this purpose and usually under the direction of persons unknown to the workers themselves. These were to report any cases of concealment of raw materials or of slowness of production. Another gambit designed to cause distrust between management and workers was the demand put forward by the communist trade unions that immediate collective contracts should be signed in all work plants. The communists also asked that the workers should be provided with consumer goods through co-operatives in the factories, although such goods were unavailable in a country bled white by the Russian troops for three months. They also instituted 'purging commissions' through the trade unions, discriminating between workers with good and bad records. Finally, the communists wanted the workers to co-operate also in the 'Economic Brigade against Speculation'. All these were ways of disrupting industrial production and embarrassing employers.

In the countryside the campaign was carried on by the 'Peasant Committees' which, pretending that they were helping the peasants to work the land of absentee or negligent landlords, were actually inciting them to dispossess the owners and share it out among themselves. The leaders of the 'Peasant Committees' assured the peasants that a new and total distribution of the land would be effected in the spring; they urged them to anticipate it and to seize their 'rights' before the reactionary governments could stop them. The 'Peasant Committees' had much less success than the communists could reasonably have expected. The only places in which they were joined by the peasants in agricultural work were the estates which had been abandoned by their owners —Saxons and Swabians who had left the country in the wake of

[7] Ervin Hutira, 'About the Workers' Control in Rumania, 1944–8', *Studii*, no. 3, 1957, p. 47.

the retreating Nazi armies and who had owned respectively large estates in Transylvania and Banat.[8]

The communists had no genuine popular support. The National Peasant Party, although still deprived of its powerful branches in Northern Transylvania and cut off from its contacts in Transylvania as a whole by the presence of the Soviet front line, showed a remarkable revival and once again staked its claim as the most popular party.[9] The peasants still rallied around it, in spite of the communist agitation among them for 'land reform'. There were surprisingly numerous applications for membership too from town workers, already suspicious of the intentions of the communist-appointed agitators and activists in the factories. (In February 1945 the National Peasants received the majority of the votes in the Malaxa works in Bucharest.) The arrival of a young generation of intellectuals and students, wishing for the resumption of normal democratic practices, swelled the ranks. The Liberals also showed signs of being popular with youth; and the Social Democrats grouped around Titel Petrescu made genuine progress in industrial constituencies.

Everywhere there was a great revival of political interest. Elections had come to be regarded as the only solution by all three democratic parties. Only the communists opposed them, thus showing their apprehensions. The tide was turning very much against them. Indeed, Ana Pauker, Vasile Luca, and Teohari Georgescu insisted that their task of gaining power would be made even more difficult once the traditional political institutions were functioning again.

But the Russians were not yet prepared to provide the means which such a 'revolution' would entail, nor were they interested in anything more than having their agents installed in the seat of power. Even for this limited move, they still needed a little more time. (Vyshinsky had visited Bucharest in mid-November and expressed publicly his satisfaction at the way things were going.)[10]

[8] See *Din lupta PCR pentru inchegarea aliantei clasei muncitoresti cu taranimea* (1955). See also Germany, Fed. R., *Dokumentation der Vertreibung der deutschen aus Ost-Mitteleuropa,* III: *Das Schicksal der Deutschen in Rumanien* (1957) for the question of the German estates.

[9] 'At this stage of the popular revolution the greatest danger for the revolution lay in the National Peasant Party, which influenced large numbers of the peasantry' (Boris Balteanu, 'The Fight of the RWP for the Establishment of the Régime of Popular Democracy, 23 Aug. 1944–6 Mar. 1945', *Analele,* July–Aug. 1957).

[10] He attended an official party in Bucharest on 14 Nov. and proposed a toast

Meanwhile they encouraged and advised 'rising revolutionary agitation' directed especially at the key Ministry of the Interior. 'Spontaneous demonstrations' were organized to shout 'Down with Penescu'. In one of these at the end of November troops were brought in by Penescu and a couple of workers were allegedly killed. Sanatescu, completely overwhelmed by events, reluctantly resigned. The king immediately appointed General Radescu, formerly Chief of Staff—whose candidature was approved by the Russians—to form a new cabinet on 2 December 1944. Radescu had a reputation for energy which Sanatescu lacked. He was personally known to several of the communist leaders as they had been inmates together in the same concentration camp to which Radescu had been sent by Antonescu for having written an outspoken letter to the German Ambassador.

THE RADESCU GOVERNMENT, DECEMBER 1944–MARCH 1945

Immediately on his appointment, however, Radescu, under pressure from the Russians, made an important concession to the communists. He appointed neither a National Peasant, Liberal, nor Socialist to the Ministry of the Interior which had been vacated by Penescu, now a main object of communist hatred. He placed this most coveted department 'above party politics' by keeping it for himself. But at the same time he appointed the communist Teohari Georgescu, a member of the Central Committee of the Communist Party, as Under-Secretary. This appointment was used by the communists to introduce into the police and security forces as many as possible of the agents trained in the 'patriotic guards' in the last three months by Bodnaras and the Soviet NKVD supervisors.[11] This obviously brought the party much nearer to the seat of power.

One of the greatest difficulties of the Radescu government was

to 'the health of the new democratic government of Rumania which thus enters the great family of democratic countries of the world'.

[11] The 'patriotic guards' were actually the recruiting cells of the personnel which was to become the militia. On 15 Jan. 1945 Radescu asked that the guards should be dissolved, but Teohari Georgescu refused. Communist historians recognize that 'the democratic forces led by the Rumanian CP used greatly to their advantage the positions they held in the central administration. Their ministers and deputy ministers eliminated reactionary elements and put in their place new men devoted to the masses of the people. The representatives of the popular forces in the Radescu government used their position in that government to rejuvenate the old state apparatus' (Caraciuc, in *Analele*, Nov.–Dec. 1957).

that it had no authority in Moldavia or northern Transylvania where, as has been seen, the Russians had installed their own nominees in positions of authority. In January 1945 Gheorghiu-Dej visited Moscow and apparently had orders to push the National Democratic Front programme. On 27 January 1945 the left leadership called for a new government, declaring Radescu a reactionary, and announced that only the FND had the confidence of the nation and could obtain the return of northern Transylvania. They also demanded immediate agrarian reform and, through their control of the printers' union, prevented publication of the National Peasant and National Liberal newspapers.

In the meanwhile Visoianu, the Minister for Foreign Affairs, and the members of the Foreign Office were making great efforts to convince the Russian mission of the disastrous political and economic consequences of the communist agitation. They also sought to explain to the newly arrived British and American missions the complexities, dilemmas, and dangers of the situation created during the previous weeks by the communist offensive. Both missions showed sympathy and understanding but they were helpless in face of the indifference with which their reports were received at home. Soon, however, any efforts by the members of these missions were made even more hopeless by an international conference which was to set the seal of Soviet dominance on the country. This was the Yalta Conference.

YALTA

The Yalta Conference of 4–11 February 1945, which dealt with all the great issues of the end of the war, also dealt with some related to the beginning of the peace. With regard to Eastern Europe, with the exception of Poland, which was rather a special case, the sentiments expressed were positive and laudable enough. But they were so vague as to be clearly capable of several interpretations. The Soviet Union, as the power on the spot, took good care to put its own interpretation on them.

Thus the declaration on liberated Europe committed the three powers and the Provisional Government of France to work together for the establishment of freedom in the liberated countries:

> The establishment of order in Europe and the rebuilding of the national economic life must be achieved by processes which will enable the peoples to destroy the last vestiges of Nazism and Fascism

and to create democratic institutions of their own choice. This is a promise of the Atlantic Charter—the right of all peoples to choose the form of government under which they will live—the restitution of sovereign rights and self-government to those peoples who have been forcibly deprived of them.[12]

In the context of the situation in Rumania at the time, the declaration seemed to provide the perfect answer to its problems; indeed, read by Rumanians in Rumania it sounded as though the Russians had adopted a more reasonable attitude. The declaration seemed to herald the end of the communist abuses and blackmail. Moreover when this text was connected with the news of the Greek communists' elimination from the political stage after their defeat early in 1945 by the British, the Rumanian people naïvely believed that 'the west' had regained the initiative and was intent on establishing peace through justice.[13]

THE VYSHINSKY COUP D'ÉTAT

Instead, only a fortnight after Yalta, the orders for final action by the FND in Bucharest were brought into execution.

On 24 February 1945 the National Democratic Front staged a great demonstration in the palace square in front of the Ministry of the Interior.[14] The crowds later marched towards the building of the Ministry. Radescu, who was in the building, called upon the army to disperse the demonstration. The troops did so firmly, proving once more their loyalty to the government and their ability to master any situation in which the Soviet army was not involved. During the demonstration, however, shots were fired from an unknown quarter, the bullets extracted from the victims not being of a type used by the Rumanian army. The bloodshed gave the communists the opportunity for which they had been waiting. Radescu, losing his temper, broadcast to the nation in order to free himself from the slur of being called a murderer, and in the course of his address he called Ana Pauker and Vasile Luca 'hyenas' and 'foreigners without God or country'. The communists demanded Radescu's arrest and were determined to settle accounts with him. Radescu was granted asylum in the British mission after almost a week of chaos.

[12] U.S. Dept of State, *The Conferences of Malta and Yalta, 1945* (1955), pp. 98–99.
[13] See R. Markham, *Rumania under the Soviet Yoke* (1949).
[14] See a good account in Wolff, p. 282.

At this juncture, on 27 February Vyshinsky arrived in Bucharest and insisted, in a stormy interview with the king, that Radescu should be dismissed and a National Democratic Front government under Groza should be installed. Next day, when the king temporized, Vyshinsky gave him a two-hour ultimatum, insisting that Groza was the only choice acceptable to the Soviet Union; otherwise Rumania might cease to exist as a sovereign state. At the same time the Soviet Command in Rumania was ordered to move Rumanian troops from Bucharest, which might have given the king the means of resisting the ultimatum, to the front, while the capital and palace were surrounded by Soviet tanks. Wisdom, recommended also by the American and British representatives, and the perennial hope that these governments would later redress this flagrant intervention by the Soviet Union prevailed, and the king, on 6 March 1945, bowed temporarily to the demand so formidably presented. Indeed, no representative of any foreign power had ever dared to behave in this way since Rumanian sovereignty had been established in 1877.

5
The 'Popular-Democratic' Régime March 1945–February 1947

'DUALITY OF POWER'

RUMANIAN communist historians and political theorists maintain that the advent to power of the Groza government on 6 March 1945 signified the installation of the 'popular democratic' régime. This in its turn was the first phase of the popular revolution in Rumania, the second being that of the dictatorship of the proletariat starting on 31 December 1947.

In terms of Marxist political philosophy the phase, which lasted from 1945 till 1949, is described as a 'duality of power'. During this phase, duly protected against foreign intervention by the presence of the Soviet army, the forms of the old state were maintained but they were filled from within with new revolutionary contents, which would make possible the 'qualitative change' from this provisional first stage to the second stage which was the 'stage of the dictatorship of the proletariat and the construction of socialism.[1] This, according to communist historians, was to occur on 30 December, 1947, when the monarchy fell and the new Republic was proclaimed. Moreover Vasile Luca himself declared that 6 March 1945 was far more important than 23 August 1944.

These historians made no attempt, up to 1959, to conceal the part played by the Soviets in the installation of this régime. Indeed, since 1948, the part played by the Soviet army in the establishment and the consolidation of the people's democracies has been stressed in the constitutional definition of all these states, with the exception of Yugoslavia. Thus official chroniclers of developments in Rumania show that even before the final coming to power of the Groza government the presence of the units of the Soviet army in Rumania constituted the decisive factor which

[1] Balteanu, in *Studii*, nos. 2 and 5, 1957.

doomed the plots of the bourgeoisie and landowners of Rumania, backed by the western imperialists.

The fact that Soviet Russia had obtained the upper hand in her relations with the United States and Great Britain when the time for action had come in Rumania is also acknowledged by them. Thus:

> Can we say that there existed at that moment the conditions for the revolutionary assumption of power by the democratic forces, headed by the Communist Party? The analysis of the factual situation which had emerged gives us a positive answer to this question. For first of all there had been created external conditions extremely favourable for a decisive defeat of the reactionary régime in Rumania. The gigantic successes of the Soviet Union had forced the imperialist circles of the United States and Great Britain to renounce their overtly hostile actions against the USSR and to more caution in their interference in the internal affairs of the countries which had been liberated by the Soviet Army.[2]

Furthermore 'in Rumania there were already stationed Soviet troops and their presence represented the guarantees that the Rumanian people would be quiet'. 'Under the leadership of the Communist Party, in the conditions created by the presence in our country of the Soviet army, it was possible to obtain the establishment of the democratic popular régime.'[3]

The importance of this first phase of the single continuous revolutionary process in Rumania is defined as consisting in its carrying out of the democratic tasks of the revolution whereas the second, socialist phase meant, on the one hand the hollowing-out or abolition of the old institutions of the Rumanian state and, on the other, 'the detachment of Rumania from an external point of view from the camp of the imperialist states'. This could be effected through the period of the 'duality of power' in which some institutions of the old state, above all the monarchy, were still respected.

The reason why this 'duality of power' phase could not be bypassed or even shortened lay in the fact that neither the international situation nor, even less, the internal one permitted more than was actually achieved on 6 March 1945. Thus

> The Communist Party had to take into consideration the fact that in the consciousness of a part of the masses of the people there

[2] Ibid. [3] Ibid.

were still rooted illusions with regard to the democratic spirit of the bourgeois-landowning parties. A part of the peasantry was still not convinced of the fact that the National Peasants are the enemies of the peasantry.[4]

This explained also the need for a coalition with certain bourgeois parties and individuals. In order to obtain this coalition certain important platform points such as the nationalization of industry had to be dropped.

Indeed the Groza government, formed under Vyshinsky's personal supervision, did contain, until the end of 1947, a 'part of the bourgeoisie'. It was represented by Tatarescu's wing of the Liberal Party which obtained four portfolios including the Foreign Office and vice-premiership for Tatarescu himself. It also contained three renegade National Peasants. But these were discredited politicians, Tatarescu himself being particularly notorious. No respected politician countenanced joining such a régime and the people were bewildered and sullen.

After 1959, however, the communist historians minimized the part of the Soviet army and presented the 'duality of power' as a far-sighted plan of the Rumanian Communist Party, which effected a smooth transition between the seizure of power and the final revolution.

GROZA'S FIRST ACT

Groza, with his jovial cynicism, was undismayed by the silence of the country which he had been set up to rule and even by the contempt of some Rumanian communist doctrinaires, among them Patrascanu. Knowing, as he put it, that 'the cat was in the bag', he happily installed himself in the old building of the presidency. In the same building, only in a more secluded suite, Emil Bodnaras was also installed. He and Pintilie Bodnarenko were in charge of all security and army operations and were the main contact men with the Russians and their team of advisers working on Rumanian affairs.[5] Gheorghiu-Dej was Minister of Communications and later of Economic Affairs. The immediate task now

[4] Ibid.

[5] There was actually no great difference between the ultimate status of some former Russian advisers, who now became Rumanian ministers, and that of the Soviet experts sent more recently in senior advisory capacities to the Rumanian CP and government. Many of the Rumanian communists were Soviet citizens and officers in the Soviet forces: Ana Pauker, Vasile Luca, Bodnarenko, probably Bodnaras.

was the 'liquidation of hostile forces' and the establishment of a reign of terror. This task was facilitated by the communists being in charge of the army and the Ministries of the Interior (Georgescu) and Justice (Patrascanu). The whole operation went very smoothly. Even the few arrests and detentions of the first months took the form of 'disappearances'. During this time party enemies such as Foris, 'war criminals' such as Eugen Cristescu, the former head of the secret police, and Clodius, the German expert on South-Eastern European economic problems, disappeared either from the prisons in which they were incarcerated or from their homes. Secret centres for investigation and re-education were busily at work in all parts of Bucharest and other cities.[6] Soon the rumour spread that the Antonescus had been brought back from Russia and were still being examined in order to prepare for their trial.

The public, however, had other topics of conversation. On 9 March, three days after the new government had been installed, it was announced with great flourish that Northern Transylvania had been restored to Rumania. This was merely a formal gesture, for Soviet troops were in complete control of the administration and communications there. But from a juridical point of view it did show that the armistice convention was held by the Russians to be as binding as a treaty. It also presented the western powers—the United States in particular—who were still pondering over a more sophisticated solution of this thorny problem, with a *fait accompli,* this time on the credit side of the ledger from the Rumanian point of view.

AGRARIAN REFORM

On 23 March 1945 another attempt to win more friends in the countryside was made with the publication of the bill for agrarian reform. This expropriated all farm properties of anyone who had collaborated with the Germans, of 'war criminals', and of those

[6] In many cases these centres were only halts on the way to Lublianka or other Russian prisons, where interrogation was spread over months and sometimes years. Persons thus 'displaced' either never returned or were brought back and tried and sentenced; or were simply sent back to the original place of detention and then released under pledge of total silence. 'During the night of 5–6 March the formations of fighting units arrested the most dangerous elements in the police. Immediately after 6 March many members of the formations were transformed into officers of the police or of the local leadership of the Security' (Tutiu & Cimponeriu, in *Analele*, no. 3, Mar.–Apr. 1958).

who held property of more than 10 hectares but had not worked it themselves during the previous seven years. It also expropriated all other property over 50 hectares in extent. Thenceforth privately-owned property was restricted to 50 hectares. This confiscation resulted in the expropriation of 143,219 individual holdings, totalling 1,143,911 hectares. A total of 1,057,674 hectares was distributed among the 796,129 beneficiaries who received on an average plots of 1.3 hectares.[7] (In the land reforms of 1919–21 4,312,920 hectares had been distributed to 1,036,367 peasants, each of whom received approximately 4 hectares.)[8]

The fact that the communists were fostering among the peasants the very land hunger which would later militate even more against collectivization did not deter them. They hoped that among the 700,000 peasants endowed with land some would vote communist or even join the party. In this they were following the Moscow schedule for the phases of revolution obligatory in all countries. That such a forcibly synchronized operation as the distribution of land had to be carried out at a stated interval after the seizure of power pointed to the existence of a uniform blueprint for the whole region. This seems true even though the texts of the reform bills in Poland and Hungary, where no substantial land reform had taken place before, differed in detail from those prepared for Rumania and Bulgaria, where they were unnecessary. This blueprint was in all probability a draft by the Comintern, refurbished during the war.

As it was, the agrarian reform in Rumania resulted in even greater numbers of economically unproductive plots of under 3 hectares. One of the after-effects of the main 1919–21 reform had been to show that a holding of under 5 hectares could not feed even the family which worked it. As a result, a natural regrouping of land ownership had taken place, the number of plots of between 5–10 and 10–50 hectors increasing, as those of under 5 hectares were sold.[9] The new reform simply upset the economi-

[7] The 'official' figures, but they are not necessarily reliable. See e.g. UN, *Econ. B. of Europe,* Nov. 1961.

[8] On the main agrarian reform, 1919–21, see Mitrany, *Land and Peasant in Rumania*; N. Cornateanu, *La réforme en Roumanie et ses conséquences* (Buch., 1937), and Roberts, *Rumania,* who provides both a thorough recapitulative examination of all aspects of the reform and a discussion of the differences between it and the communist reform of 1945.

[9] On this see M. Gormsen, *Short Introd. to Principal Structural Problems of Agric. in Rumania* (1945), a most lucid examination of productivity in relation to the size of properties.

cally more balanced situation which had gradually been created, as is shown by the following figures, in percentages of the total arable land :

Properties	*1927*	*1941*	*1948*
Under 5 ha.	47.29	33.3	57.7
5—10 ha.	18.77	26.0	23.0
10—50 ha.	16.26	21.4	16.3
Over 50 ha.	17.68	19.3	3.0

Sources: For 1927, see Mitrany; 1941: *Recensamantul agricol al Romaneie din 1941 date provisiorii* (1945); 1948: *Recensamantul agricol din RPR* (1948).

Moreover, from among the plots of land of under 5 hectares, those of under 3 hectares represented the great majority or, in the words of the preface of the census of 1949 'more than half of the agricultural exploitations of Rumania'.

ECONOMIC PENETRATION

On 8 May 1945, shortly after the land reform, a long-term economic agreement was signed in Moscow. This was distinct from the yearly trade agreements, the first of which was concluded on 16 January 1945. The long-term agreement consisted of four separate protocols, the most surprising and ingenious of which, from the Soviet point of view, was the last one. This established in Rumania a number of joint companies, the Sovroms. They were joint Soviet-Rumanian companies, to which each country was meant to contribute equally. There was a Sovrom for all the major branches of production, according to a plan which became evident in two years after the signature of the agreement. The most vital ones to the Soviet economy were brought into existence the moment the treaty was signed: Sovrompetrol on 7 July, Sovromtransport on 19 July, Sovrom-Lemn (timber) on 14 August, followed at greater intervals by Sovromgaz, Sovromasigurare (insurance), Sovromchim (chemicals), and Sovromcuart (uranium), which was not mentioned until it was handed back by the Russians after all the others.

These were the instruments whereby for several years the Soviet Government not only controlled but took possession of and exploited directly all the Rumanian sources of income. They signified Soviet Russia's determination to maintain, no matter how 'friendly' the existing government might be, a Soviet free zone within the Rumanian national economy and income and, as such, an extra-territorial right which could benefit only the occupier at the expense of the occupied. Indeed so extra-territorial was the right of ownership of the Soviet state in these joint companies that when the communist law nationalizing private ownership in industry was passed in 1947, it exempted from expropriation only the shares of the Soviet government in such companies.

In principle these companies were supposed to be set up with equal contributions from the two partners. But in practice the Rumanian part consisted of the plants, workshops, soil or natural resources, together with the necessary technical and financial capital, while the Russians, apart from their shares in German and Italian properties in Rumania, mostly contributed the installations and industrial equipment which the Red Army had seized during 1944. The directors and managers were Russians. The companies were exempted from taxation. Their products were shipped directly to Russia. (The main pipelines were already busily funnelling off Rumanian oil directly to Russian ports.) The Rumanian share in the profits, which should have been considerable, was subtracted directly from the armistice payments. In other words, 'the Russians first pillaged and then penetrated and took over the Rumanian economy.'[10]

This exploitation was so blatant that it soon became common knowledge, no matter how much the Rumanian communist press and radio tried to gloss over the fact.

THE ANTONESCU TRIAL, MAY 1945

Also in May 1945 the Groza government decided to bring the Antonescus to trial.[11] It might well have been that the government thought that by exposing all the mistakes and crimes committed during the Antonescu dictatorship they would enhance their own popularity. It was true that the nation resented Marshal Antonescu's action and rightly held him responsible for the war beyond the Dniester and its consequent tragedies. It is also true

[10] Wolff, p. 346.

[11] They had been spirited away immediately after their arrest in the palace on 23 Aug. 1944 by Bodnaras's Patriotic Guard and kept in secret in Rumania and in Russia. Ion Antonescu's testimony was made use of by the Soviet Prosecutor at the Nuremberg trials.

that in a free and democratic Rumania he would have had to answer for the decisions he had taken without consulting the will of the people. But by May 1946 it was already too late for the communists to try to appear in a better light than Marshal Antonescu. Even by then, the Groza government and the Rumanian communists were showing themselves far more subservient to Moscow than Antonescu had ever been to Berlin.

Antonescu's partial rehabilitation had also begun through revelations by German witnesses of the stand that he had made against Hitler's political, military, and economic demands.[12] Respect for him increased during the trial in which he showed, after long months of interrogation in Russian and Rumanian prisons, a hitherto unwonted serenity. In contrast to Mihai Antonescu, who had obviously broken under the strain, he was calm, more coherent than in the last years of power, and often convincing. In contrast to some of his former subordinates, who betrayed both their colleagues and their former actions, he maintained that his policy had been to defend Rumania against Soviet Russia, which he continued to describe as his country's main enemy. He accused no one and showed no bitterness towards the king or Maniu. The latter, having served as a witness in the trial, went over to the dock and shook him by the hand before leaving the court. Marshal Antonescu was sentenced to death on 17 May and met the firing squad with dignity and courage.

SOVEREIGN IN A NON-SOVEREIGN COUNTRY, AUGUST 1945–OCTOBER 1946

Before the installation of the Groza government, attempts to renew diplomatic relations between the three powers and Rumania had been ignored by Soviet Russia. But now that a government of Russia's choice was in power, she started to urge her two allies to recognize it as quickly as possible. It was around this further step in the consolidation of the communist régime that a new episode in the power game was to be played.[13]

[12] These were to be confirmed later by all major German witnesses of the talks between Hitler and Antonescu (e.g. Schmidt, Paul Otto, the interpreter), by all the official minutes of their conversations, and finally by Hitler's spontaneous remark on Antonescu in his *Tischgespräche*.

[13] See for this particular diplomatic phase Wolff, pp. 284–7, and B. Balteanu, 'The Failure of the Attempts of the Monarchy to Overthrow the Popular Democratic Régime', *Studii*, no. 6, 1957.

In 1945, soon after President Truman's inauguration, the State Department renewed its consultations with the British Foreign Office on the question of the attitude to be adopted towards Russian conduct both in Rumania after the Vyshinsky coup d'état and in Bulgaria. Public indignation was genuine and the fact that Stalin had elected to contravene so flagrantly the intentions of the three powers as expressed at Yalta was the obvious source of this switch in sympathy on the part of the man in the street. Yalta had very quickly acquired an ugly name, especially in the United States, where strong pressure was already being brought to bear upon the President to take a firm stand against the Russians.

At the Potsdam Conference, which was held between 17 July and 2 August 1945, the American delegation circulated a memorandum which, taking the Yalta declaration on liberated Europe as its basis, pointed out how different was the situation that had been created in Rumania and Bulgaria and asked for a change of government in both countries. The Russian delegation replied by demanding that all three powers should recognize the new and legal government of Rumania forthwith. They pointed out that in 1944 Russian representatives had not been allowed more rights in Italy than had the Americans and British in Rumania. They also recalled the British action in Greece. The Conference then went on to try to interpret such expressions as 'free elections' and 'broadly representative governmental authorities', 'democratic elements', and so forth, as contained in the Yalta declaration, with a view to deciding how they were to be applied in Rumania and Bulgaria; but were soon bogged down in trivial detail. In the final communiqué the two points of view were skilfully mixed. It was stated that the Council of Foreign Ministers had been asked to prepare the peace treaties with the four former enemy countries (Bulgaria, Finland, Hungary, and Rumania) but laid down that the peace treaties would be concluded with 'recognized democratic Governments'.[14]

But how wide was the difference of views between the powers could have been seen in their attitudes immediately after the Conference. On 9 August President Truman, reporting to the American people, stated that:

[14] U.S. Dept. of State, *The Conference of Berlin* (*The Potsdam Conference*) *1945* (1960), ii. doc. 1383, p. 1492.

At Yalta it was agreed, you will recall, that the three governments would assume a common responsibility in helping to re-establish in the liberated and satellite nations of Europe governments broadly representative of democratic elements in the population. That responsibility still stands. We all recognize it as a joint responsibility of the three governments. It was reaffirmed in the Berlin Declarations on Rumania, Bulgaria and Hungary. These nations are not to be spheres of influence of any one power.[15]

On 20 August the newly-appointed British Foreign Secretary, Ernest Bevin, made a similar statement, saying that 'the Governments which have been set up [in Bulgaria, Rumania and Hungary] do not, in our view, represent the majority of the people'.[16] But the Groza government was nevertheless recognized on 20 August by Moscow.

It was the young king who now decided to act. On 21 August, almost twelve months after he had declared the end of hostilities against the Allies, he summoned Groza and asked him to resign so that another government could be formed which would be acceptable to all three victors. After a brief consultation with the Soviet Ambassador, Groza returned with a blunt refusal. The king's answer to this unprecedented and unconstitutional attitude was a refusal to sign any laws, bills, or decrees of the cabinet or to receive any of its members. He addressed himself to the Allies, obtaining from the American government a clearly worded denial of the 'democratic and representative character of the Groza Government'. This same stand was maintained by Byrnes and Bevin at the London Conference of the three Foreign Ministers of 11 September to 3 October at which, in answer to Molotov's assertion that the régime in Rumania was both free and representative, the two western ministers reaffirmed the decision of their governments not to recognize it. Moreover, as a sequel to the argument with Molotov, Byrnes decided to send an independent American journalist, Mark Ethridge, to report on the situation.[17]

In Rumania the internal crisis was reaching a climax. The

[15] N. Ausubal, ed., *Voices of History, 1945-6* (N.Y., 1946), p. 428.

[16] H. C. Deb., vol. 413, col. 291.

[17] 'The report of the Ethridge mission was thus sharply critical of Soviet policy in the Balkans and its publication as originally planned would have been something of a shock to the prevailing view of American public opinion, which was still optimistic regarding the prospects of co-operation with the Soviet Union' (C. E. Black, *Negotiating with the Russians*, quoted by Cretzianu, *Lost Opportunity*, p. 160. The report was never published.)

administration, already weak and boycotted by the people, had come to a standstill when the king decided not to endorse its acts and deeds. The government could rely upon the Tudor Vladimirescu division, which had been hurried back from the front before any other regiment and was used by Bodnaras as the security armed force. In case of civil war it relied, as has been seen, upon the Soviet army. A sense of urgency and exasperation animated the Rumanians, who were not sure in whose favour time would play. The democratic parties, especially the National Peasants, whose members were openly persecuted and arrested in villages and towns, clung to the hope of elections being held as quickly as possible. But such hopes were already linked with 'superior external factors' which would help the king and the people to defend their rights. It was during this period of feverish expectation that the rise in listening to western radio stations took place, probably surpassing the numbers who had listened during the war, for it had become not only the most rapid source of information but also one of hope. The Rumanian services of the BBC and of the Voice of America were the authorities quoted in general conversations. The American and British missions in Bucharest could indeed try, as they earnestly did throughout this period, to remain as non-committal as possible in order to avoid antagonizing the Russians or giving to the Rumanians any ground for believing that behind the diplomatic fencing there was any firm intention or even possibility of helping them. The expression 'the Americans' or 'the British' in such context meant much more than anything the mission might say, or that the radios had said or had been understood to have said, by the anxious listeners.

THE FIRST COMMUNIST PARTY NATIONAL CONFERENCE

At this time the communists were taking steps to build up a well organized and disciplined party. The first National Conference of the party was summoned on 16 October 1945 to take stock of the situation which had arisen thanks to the huge, indiscriminate recruiting campaign, and to mould the party on orthodox lines. At this conference a Central Committee was elected and a Politburo set up. The Central Committee was composed of Gheorghe Apostol, Emil Bodnares, Constantin Campeanu, Nicolae Ceausescu, Iosif Chisinevschi, Miron Constantinescu, Dumitru Coliu, Constanta Craciun, Teohari Georgescu, Gheorge

Gheorghiu-Dej, Vasile Luca, Vasile Marza, Alexandru Moghioros, Andrei Neagu, Constantin Parvulescu, Lucretiu Patrascanu, Andrei Patrascu, Ana Pauker, Emil and Ilie Popa, Iosif Ranghet, Leontin Silaghi, Chivu Stoica, Elena Tudorache, Vasile Vaida, and Gheorghe Vasilichi. Many communists were still awaiting the return of more 'chiefs' from Moscow, especially the elusive Boris Stefanov.

The Politburo of the Central Committee was composed of Gheorghiu-Dej, Ana Pauker, Luca, Georgescu, Stoica, Vasilichi, and Constantinescu; the first four were also Central Committee secretaries, with Gheorghiu-Dej as Secretary-General. At the conference Gheorghiu-Dej read the political report while Ana Pauker presented the statutes. Thus the four who were to rule together until May 1952 from the first took the reins into their hands; and the man who was to emerge as Moscow's final choice was given the main position. But in 1961 he maintained that from the very first he was deprived of real power until 1952, when the party eliminated the other three secretaries who, he alleged, constantly overruled him on Moscow's orders. Dej and other speakers at the November 1961 plenary meeting said that until 1952 neither the Secretariat nor the Politburo nor even the Central Committee were allowed to do their work. For instance, the Central Committee and the Secretariat held only one meeting in 1947. Moreover Ceausescu threw more light on Dej's position by showing that from the first Vasile Luca demanded that while Gheorghiu-Dej should be the 'façade' Secretary-General, Ana Pauker should be the 'real' one; and Ana Pauker herself allotted to Dej the task of concentrating on the governmental work while she concentrated on the party work.[18]

The fact that Patrascanu was not elected to the Politburo shows that at no time after the formation of the new party did he carry any real political weight within it. He carried with him most of the intellectuals, especially the newly recruited ones, and with his oratory and more generous ideas could have inspired some of the young. But as an intellectual of considerable breadth of vision, he was suspect in the eyes of the leaders. A seat on the Central Committee and his governmental post as Minister of Justice may even have exceeded the limits to which the leaders were prepared to go. Otherwise the 1945 Central Committee represented fairly all the

[18] *Sc.*, 13 Dec. 1961.

internal groups of the party during the war with the exception of Foris.

The Conference also reported that the party now numbered almost 800,000 members, a tremendous increase from the thousand or so at the end of the war. Ana Pauker who, together with Miron Constantinescu, was responsible for recruitment between October 1944 and October 1945, and who had obviously made a success of it, was later accused of unorthodoxy and lack of discrimination. Indeed at the second plenum of the Central Committee, held in June 1948, the hasty recruitment carried out in 1945 was castigated in the main resolution, which stated that 'elements alien to the working class have infiltrated our ranks, elements which were active in the Iron Guard movement, various opportunists and careerists whose attitude is not in harmony with proletarian morality and who have no business in the party'. Moreover after Ana Pauker's fall *Scanteia,* on 14 December 1952, summed up this period by stating that much harm had been done to the party by the anti-Leninist line introduced by Ana Pauker after the party's emergence from illegality, by the policy of opening wide its doors to anyone and everyone. This accusation was repeated at the Second RWP Congress and still more fully at the Central Committee plenum of November 1961.

The early categories of members of the party have already been described. To them must be added roughly 100,000 peasants who received the card together with the land in 1945; some workers; and some young intellectuals. But the bulk of the membership was made up of those who, in common with the categories already mentioned, joined the party either before or after the seizure of power, in order to obtain or to keep their jobs, now at the mercy of the government. This, of course, had a decisive initial effect upon the quality of the new communists. The great majority were opportunists, transformed into officials, docile and indifferent and, for the most part, incompetent. A better layer was to be added in the next four or five years, formed by the younger men who had achieved some success in carrying out various aspects of the economic plans. Their political education, however, remained nominal. By order of the leadership, they received in 1945–6 eight-week courses. The first 'Communist University', the Stefan Gheorghiu Party School, was opened in February 1946 and then suspended in the following September in favour of the preparation for the elections of November 1946. The immediate post-war influx was therefore massive but of very low quality. 'The party-organs and organizations did not recall the Leninist principle that when the Communist Party is a party already seated in power, careerists from all classes and especially the middle class, rush towards it out of sheer opportunism', said the resolution of the enlarged plenary meeting of the Central Committee of August 1953.

A further opportunity to press home the communists' advantage was provided by the king's birthday, on 8 November 1945, when thousands of people, acting on a word-of-mouth suggestion which had been started by students, converged on the palace to cheer him. The communists sent trucks loaded with *agents provocateurs* to mingle with the crowd. This produced acts of violence; the trucks were overturned and burnt. The Tudor Vladimirescu regiment and police were sent to the Palace Square, and they fired on the demonstrators. Many arrests were made; there were fifteen dead and at least 100 wounded. That night and the following day the militia entered many houses and arrested leaders and members of the democratic parties on the pretext that they had helped the 'rebellion'. It was after the new wave of persecution thus started on 8 November that many young men decided to go into hiding, passing from one house to another or taking to the mountains where hopeless pockets of 'resistance' had already been formed by other young students and officers.

At the Moscow Conference in December, on the basis of the Ethridge report that the Rumanian and Bulgarian governments were authoritarian and excluded democratic elements, the United States proposed that the Groza government should be reorganized to include members of opposition parties, and that this government should undertake to respect 'basic freedoms' and hold free elections at an early date. Stalin made a limited concession to American wishes in the agreement signed on 26 December, in which the three Allied governments recommended that the Groza government should include one member each of the National Peasant and Liberal parties. An Allied Commission was to ascertain that these two members represented groups not already included in the government. The reorganized government was to give assurances regarding basic freedoms and free elections in which all parties would have the right to participate were to be held, after which the government would receive Anglo-American recognition. In so far as this new arrangement was tragically similar to that which had been made farcical by the Polish communists, and in so far as it was not backed by any further assurance or guarantee from the western powers, the Rumanians understood at once what this represented. Vyshinsky, Harriman, and Clark-Kerr arrived in Bucharest from Moscow on 31 December to implement the terms of the agreement, and met the king, who now again took up his duties. Harriman and Clark-Kerr then met the representatives of the opposition, who demanded certain guarantees before choosing members to participate in the government and also refused to commit their representatives to accepting responsibility for the cabinet's action when they were to be given only minor posts. They were advised to accept the assurances embodied in the agreement, and then nominated Mihalache and Bratianu. The Groza government rejected these nominations, and finally Emil Hatieganu and Mihail Romniceanu were included in the Cabinet to represent the National Peasants and Liberals respectively.

The Moscow agreement represented a Soviet victory, for the two opposition representatives were heavily outnumbered in the cabinet in which they held no portfolios, and moreover recognition of the Rumanian government was to precede the elections, so that the western Allies could exercise no pressure to try to ensure that the elections were free.

The king was preparing himself for as long a siege as possible in a country in which, although his authority had been grievously undermined, he thought it his duty to remain.

REAL AND LEGAL POWER, 1946

The United States and British governments recognized the Groza government in February 1946 on the conditions outlined in the Moscow agreement. But by the spring of that year it was clear that the Russians would not permit Groza to carry out the assurances he had given on the holding of free elections. Attempts by the National Peasant leaders to hold political meetings were frustrated and steps were taken to break up meetings by the historical parties and to curb their propaganda. Moreover the government made an organized attempt to gain support among other political parties, and in this they achieved considerable success at the Social Democrat Party Congress of 10 March 1946, when a large majority of the delegates voted to merge with the communists, thus splitting the party.

Collaboration between the socialists and communists had been hastily established in May 1944, within a loose organization called the United Workers' Front. This collaboration, however, convinced the Social Democrat rank and file and its genuine leaders, C. Titel Petrescu, Ilie Dumitriu, Ilie Mirescu, A. Dumitriu, and for a time Serban Voinea, that to continue in the conditions laid down for it would mean the annihilation of the party and its absorption by the much more dynamic and dangerous partner. But both the leadership and the rank and file were being continuously infiltrated by the communists and, while the sentiments of the party as a whole remained unchanged, its means of expressing them were being successfully stifled. After the installation of the Groza government, for the first time Petrescu suffered the experience of being outvoted in the Executive Committee. His pleas that socialists who had accepted portfolios in the government should resign were rejected, and Lotar Radaceanu and Stefan Voitec, the most important of these ministers and also leaders of the collaborationist wing, won their first victory. At the party conference of 1 December 1945 Petrescu was again victorious when the communist proposal to establish common electoral lists with the socialists was rejected. Yet from that moment in factories and workshops trade union representatives and foremen and engineers in charge of personnel began to discriminate between workers according to whether, when applying for ration or identity cards or for work, they described themselves as Petrescu or Radaceanu socialists. Supporters of Petrescu decided to allow the workers to declare themselves to be whatever was pleasing to the communists so that they would not be victimized, although the understanding was that they would vote with Petrescu at the elections. Although on the whole the workers remained faithful and kept their pledges at the elections of November 1946, the thinning out of the rank and file and the double allegiance did create a confusion to the advantage of the communists.

In the higher echelons the confusion was even greater and there crypto-communists were in real command of the party. More than half the members of the Central and Executive Committees were by 1946 secret members of the Communist Party.

Among them were three leading members of the Secretariat: Theodor Iordachescu, Barbu Solomon, and Mihai Leven. The Secretariat took care of the organization of the Congress of 10 March 1946. Invitations and credentials were refused or given according to the political allegiance of the participants. The official rapporteur of the Congress, Serban Voinea, opposed the alliance with the communists, but the communists and their Social Democrat supporters had left nothing to chance. Tudor Ionescu, always believed to be one of Petrescu's most trusted lieutenants, had been successfully suborned and read out forged letters allegedly addressed to Petrescu by Maniu and Bratianu. Thus the Congress ended in the party split, Petrescu and some right-wing party members walking out of the Congress and joining the other parties in opposition to the government bloc of democratic parties thus formed on 17 May 1946.

In the meanwhile the British and American governments continued to try to exert pressure to have the Moscow agreement implemented. Though most of their notes were ignored, they apparently had some effect, for on 14 July the king signed an electoral law providing for a unicameral legislature and granting the franchise to women while denying it to fascists, Iron Guardists, and those who had fought against the 'allies'. Elections were duly held in November, but all eye-witnesses, whether correspondents or diplomatic representatives of the two western powers whose duty it was to report on the observance of electoral freedom, were unanimous in agreeing that the conditions in which they were fought surpassed the gloomiest expectations. The following is an accurate description from a recent book:

But the Communists had apparently no intention of living up to the Moscow agreement. Although the Peasant and Liberal Parties were allowed to print their newspapers, there was much interference with the distribution, and it was often impossible to buy them outside the capital. Thugs invaded opposition political meetings and beat up those who attended; arrests multiplied. Protests from the United States and Britain were simply ignored. The government could not hold even a rigged election until it had intimidated and disrupted the opposition as much as possible.

The electoral law gave every advantage to the Communists. Polls were set up in factories and barracks where FND agents could bring direct pressure on workers and soldiers. Electoral lists were hastily compiled so that no real check could be made on inaccuracies. Women were enfranchised for the first time, and fascists, Iron Guardists, and those who of their own free will fought against the 'allies' were disfranchised. . . . On the eve of the elections, the western allies protested once more against these practices, but the Groza government rejected the protests, since the USSR had not joined in them, adding that the United States and Britain were guilty of unwarranted interference in Rumanian internal affairs. On November 19, 1946, the Rumanian people went to the polls in an election in which every fraudulent, violent, and unscrupulous device ever used in the Balkans was brought into full play.[19]

The results, block of democratic parties 347, National Peasants 33, and Liberals 3, were a foregone conclusion. Romniceanu and Hatieganu resigned from the now purely FND government, and the new Assembly first met on 1 December 1946.

What made the Rumanian communists and the Soviet government behave as they did during these elections in Rumania in 1946, when in Hungary, in 1945, they had permitted the people to vote more or less freely and thus to produce a result in which the communists were in a minority and the Smallholders, the Hungarian equivalent of the National-Peasants, in a majority? One answer lies precisely in this result. The Russians had seen the result of relatively free elections in Hungary. There the Communists had assured them that they had a fair chance of polling, in alliance with the Socialists, a majority sufficient to carry out the tasks of a coalition government. But having seen the Communists so decisively defeated in Hungary by the peasants, the Russians were not going to run a similar risk in Rumania.

The bitterness, anxiety, and anger in Rumania were unprecedented. Once more the people turned to the king who, they were sure, would refuse to open parliament. When he did so, his action was less well received than usual and criticisms were heard from those whose relatives and friends were already in prison or concentration camps, or in hiding. Indeed, after the elections and the consolidation of the communists in power, persecution took the form of organized terror which was steadily increasing. Tens of thousands of people were now reported as having 'disappeared', the great majority of them into gaols and camps; some into hiding in the mountains where rallying points were being formed; some

[19] Wolff, pp. 287–8.

abroad. It was natural that many should think of organizing some Rumanian activities abroad. Maniu himself refused to leave the country. Visoianu and Buzesti, on Maniu's advice, succeeded in escaping in December 1946. Mihalache and other members of the National Peasant Party were ambushed and arrested as they tried to escape.

6

1947: The Last Year of the Rumanian Kingdom

PEACE, 10 FEBRUARY 1947

THE last year of the Rumanian kingdom began with the signing, on 10 February, of the peace treaty. This had been awaited, for different reasons, by both the people and the government. The people still cherished the illusion that it would somehow be an opportunity of reintegrating Rumania into a world which they thought of as being free and just. The Groza government, on the contrary, knew that if Soviet Russia had allowed the satellite peace treaties to go through, it was because she was now assured that she could use them for diplomatic and political purposes. These could then supplement the military and economic advantages which the Soviet Union had derived from the armistice since the end of the war.

That time had worked in Russia's favour could be seen from the history of the signature of the treaties. At the Potsdam Conference in July and August 1945 it had been the American delegation that had raised the question of a more rapid conclusion of the treaties and had insisted on their urgent preparation by the Council of Foreign Ministers. Although relations between the western powers and Russia were by that time tense precisely because of the Eastern European and German controversies, it might still have been hoped that a quick settlement of the peace treaties would have eased Soviet economic pressure. But already at the Foreign Ministers' Conference of September 1945, although the situation in Eastern Europe and especially in Rumania and Bulgaria had become the main cause of discord, it was only one aspect of the growing conflict between the wartime Allies. When the Paris Conference met to discuss the treaties, on 29 July 1946, the situation had seriously deteriorated. The whole question of relations between the Soviet Union and the west was at stake and the situation in Eastern Europe had become simply a sector on a world-wide front.

Twenty-one nations participated in the Paris Conference.[1] They were: the United States, France, Great Britain, Soviet Russia, and China as members of the newly-enlarged Council of Foreign Ministers, and Australia, Belgium, Byelo-Russia, Brazil, Canada, Ethiopia, Greece, India, Norway, New Zealand, the Netherlands, Poland, Czechoslovakia, the Ukraine, the Union of South Africa, and Yugoslavia as countries which had contributed most towards the war against Hitler.

The Rumanian delegation was led by G. Tatarescu, Vice-Premier and Foreign Minister. Patrascanu, still Minister of Justice, was a member. The delegation contained a surprising number of diplomatic and economic experts of the old régime. This reflected the woeful lack of expertise in the party at that time, but at the same time the composition of the delegation had been carefully selected by the Groza government to try to convince the western delegations and governments that there was a certain continuity in Rumanian diplomatic affairs and that the delegation was not simply a mouthpiece of Moscow. During the meetings an informal delegation of Rumanian exiles was active in the corridors of the Palais de Luxembourg. They raised some special points and distributed various memoranda, which were necessary as the Rumanian governmental delegation could not fight for the interests of the country on any point which went against the Russian interests. The economic clauses provided an example of this contradiction. Not only the Rumanian exiles, but the American delegation too held, against the view of the official Rumanian delegation, that the 'reparations' paid to Soviet Russia far exceeded the sum specified in the treaty and acknowledged by the Rumanian government.

The project of the treaty with Rumania was first discussed on 13 August, when Tatarescu presented the observations of his government. The warm pleas put forward by Jan Masaryk on Rumania's behalf, in which he recalled Rumania's constant friendship and loyalty towards Czechoslovakia, as well as the essential part played by the Rumanian troops in the final liberation of his country from Hitler, made a striking impression.

[1] On this and many of the points covered in this chapter see Ciurea, *Traité de paix*, and J. C. Campbell, 'The European Territorial Settlement', *Foreign Affairs*, Oct. 1947, pp. 196–218.

When on 10 October the Rumanian treaty was discussed for the second time, the Danubian question of free navigation caused a sharp difference of opinion between the Anglo-American and Soviet-Yugoslav delegations. This seemed to be the most difficult obstacle in the way of concluding the treaty. The matter, however, was postponed. The Council of Foreign Ministers referred to it again at its New York meeting in November, when it was agreed that a Danube Conference should be arranged six months after the conclusion of the peace treaties to discuss the problem separately. This removed the stumbling-block from the negotiations then in progress, but led to the disastrous Belgrade Conference and its subsequent ordering of the Danube in accordance with communist wishes.[2] The Rumanian peace treaty was officially signed on 10 February 1947, at a formal meeting in Paris.

The text of the treaty[3] was in all essentials similar to those with Italy, Finland, Hungary, and Bulgaria, which were discussed and signed during the same meeting. Yet the signatories made their own distinctions, not always explicable. For instance, it was set down in the preamble that Rumania 'took an active part in the war against Germany' yet, as has been seen, in spite of the fact that Rumania had suffered heavier losses in the war against Germany and Hungary than any other country—apart from Soviet Russia, Great Britain, and the United States—and heavier by far than those of Italy, the signatories agreed to call the latter a 'co-belligerent' country but refused that title to Rumania.

Frontier problems were solved in an original way. Thus it was stated in Article 1 that Rumania's frontiers would remain those of 1 January 1941, with the exception of the border with Hungary, which Article 2 stated was to be re-established as it had been on 1 January 1938. The same article also repeated categorically the provision already written into the armistice convention, which declared the Vienna Award of 30 August 1940 to be null and void. This originated in a statement by the British government—which, at the time of the Vienna Award, was alone at war against Germany and Italy—to the effect that territorial changes made under duress would not be recognized by it at the end of the war. When the United States later came into the war, the State De-

[2] See J. C. Campbell, 'Diplomacy on the Danube', *Foreign Affairs*, Jan. 1949.

[3] World Peace Foundation, *European Peace Treaties after World War II* (1954), pp. 298-321.

partment on 27 July 1942 produced a similar statement, and Soviet Russia's first response to Rumania's intention of withdrawing from the war made on 2 April 1944 was that Northern Transylvania, or the major part of it, would be restored to her. This was actually put into effect through the peace treaty, with a minor dissension on the part of the American delegation, which took the position that by comparatively modest changes in the pre-war boundary a solution could be worked out which would be more satisfactory to the Hungarians.[4] The Rumanian delegation argued this point, stressing that it would also imply recognizing that acts perpetrated by Hitler and Mussolini at the height of their domination of Europe, and inspired by their doctrine of the New Order, could have produced lasting and useful effects. But the irony lay in the fact that when it came to the Russo-Rumanian frontier established by the Soviet ultimatum, helped and supported by Nazi Germany and fascist Italy, not only Soviet Russia but also the official Rumanian delegation found that it should remain as it had been on 1 January 1941. This attitude of the Rumanian delegation was castigated by foreign observers. 'From the prewar ethnic maps which Rumania submitted in order to show the Rumanian character of Transylvania, these lost provinces had been carefully expunged lest someone be reminded of the Rumanian character of the greater part of Bessarabia, now the Moldavian S.S.R.'[5]

The political clause contained in Article 3 was, to all intents and purposes, a new assurance that once given full recognition and international status, the new government of Rumania would not use its powers to initiate persecution and administrative discrimination. It pledged Rumania to take all the necessary steps to ensure to all its citizens, without distinction, the full enjoyment of human rights and fundamental freedoms, including freedom of opinion, of the press and of information, of worship and of public meetings. This, taken in conjunction with the clauses deal-

[4] 'Without pretending to advocate a fundamental solution of the Transylvanian problem, the United States believed that the return to Hungary of some solidly Magyar-populated cities and districts might provide a basis for better relations between the two countries. In London in September 1945 Mr Byrnes suggested that this possibility be studied, but 'neither the Soviets nor the British showed any enthusiasm. The latter felt that a change in the frontier would only exasperate Rumania without really satisfying Hungary and would harm rather than benefit Britain's position in Eastern Europe' (Campbell, in *For. Aff.*, Oct. 1947, p. 212).

[5] Ibid. p. 210.

ing with the right of the three powers to supervise the application of the treaty (Arts 37 and 38), led later, when the communist terror fell upon the people, to the ineffectual protests on 2 April 1949 made by the governments of Great Britain and the United States.[6]

The military clauses of the peace treaty limited the Rumanian armed forces to the following numbers: for ground forces, 120,000 men, including the frontier guards; for anti-aircraft defence, 15,000; for the navy, 5,000 men and 15,000 tons and for the air force, 8,000 men and 150 aircraft, of which only 100 were to be combat planes. The clauses also prohibited the possession, manufacture, or experimenting with atomic bombs, missiles, or submarines. But again, in 1950–1, when the Stalinist policy of rearmament was applied at top speed in the whole of Eastern Europe, it was already known that Rumania had overstepped these limits. On 4 February 1953 the British Foreign Office estimated Rumanian forces at 250,000 men, exclusive of the security forces.

Another military provision, which was potentially very significant, was that included under the heading 'Withdrawal of the Allied Forces' (Art. 21). Under this provision all the armed forces of the Allies, including those of Soviet Russia, were to be withdrawn from Rumania ninety days after the treaty had come into force, with the exception of such Soviet armed forces as Russia 'may need for the maintenance of the lines of communication of the Soviet Army with the Soviet zone of occupation Austria'. The same clause was also inserted in the Hungarian treaty.

The economic clauses repeated more or less the general dispositions of the armistice convention, but by the time of the signing of the peace treaty they had been outrageously distorted in at least two major respects. These concerned the total value of indemnities and reparations to be paid by Rumania to Soviet Russia and the abnegation, agreed to at the Potsdam Conference by Britain and the United States, of any claims upon German and Italian property in Rumania in favour of Soviet Russia, rights which later became the main basis of the Soviet-Rumanian joint companies known as Sovroms.

Despite its inconsistencies, the treaty could in more normal circumstances have fulfilled its obvious purpose of bringing

[6] See below, p. 195.

Rumania back into the European family of nations. But Europe was threatened by a permanent division and Rumania and Eastern Europe had been taken over by another power, bent on exploiting them. Thus, while undoubtedly effacing the abnormal changes imposed by Hitler, it presented no defence against the undermining policy of Russian imperialism.

THE ESTABLISHMENT OF STATE TERROR

From May 1947 reports of mass arrests of opponents of the régime began to come in as the Groza government with Soviet support proceeded to annihilate the opposition. In June the attack on the Peasant Party started, culminating in the arrest on 15 July of Maniu and Mihalache, after Mihalache, Penescu, Carandino, and others of their supporters had attempted to escape—with Maniu's approval—in a secretly chartered aeroplane from the airport of Tamadau. This persecution of the National Peasant Party more or less coincided with that of the other peasant parties in the Soviet bloc. In Bulgaria the Agrarian Petkov was brought to trial in July 1947. The Smallholders were endangered in Hungary from the August 1947 elections, which swept away any semblance of legality, and in Poland, from which Mikolajczyk and other leaders fled in October 1947. A synchronization of policy can clearly be assumed with the aim of breaking the strongest political resistance to the communists: the peasants.

The persecution of the Peasant Party leaders was accompanied by stark terror. The number of 'disappearances' which occurred after the beginning of 1947 can never be exactly computed, but it is believed that in 1946–7 some 60,000 people were executed. The terror fell alike upon old and young but naturally had a greater impact upon the young, as it directly influenced their way of behaviour and thinking. It transformed them into silent, sullen, and guarded individuals, impenetrable not only to foreign visitors but also to their teachers or parents, friends or foes. The percentage of people arrested in Hungary, Poland, and Rumania between 1947 and 1956 was lowest in the age-group of those under eighteen. This was partly because this group, apart from those of 'rotten social origin', had no incriminating record and partly because this category was more vigilant and better prepared to lie, cheat, and finally escape capture in the perpetual cat-and-mouse game which they rightly understood to be the relation between the individual and the totalitarian state machine.

In Rumania the National Peasant and National Liberal Parties were dissolved by decree in August 1947. Their headquarters were occupied, their newspapers suppressed. The rank and file of the Peasant Party in the countryside suffered less; it remained scattered in villages and hamlets, silent but active. Its opposition was apparent later in the social and economic struggle which the communists were to wage with the Rumanian peasantry. For here lies the main political difference between the Eastern European peasants and the Russian peasantry. The former had built, even if only for a short span between the wars, their own political parties and governments. This fact imbued them with a sense of political autonomy which the Russian peasants never had, and with a clear idea of their political, social, and economic relations with the state.

The supporters of the Liberal Party, the middle classes, never so numerous, dissolved socially and economically more rapidly than the peasantry. Yet part of them were to survive in the guise of the reformed intelligentsia. Only the Social Democratic Party remained for a further year in existence; but this was simply because the communists needed it for the 'fusion' in the monolithic Workers' Party which they were preparing.

To this systematic oppression there was no real possibility of organized resistance. There were many maquis pockets formed by fugitives in the mountains. In 1946–7 there was even some evidence that these were trying to unite under a common name, *sumanele negre* (the black jackets). They were made up mostly of scattered and more intransigent elements from the Iron Guard who had refused or failed either to leave the country with the German troops or to join the Communist Party; of young officers, priests, and civil servants, purged or uncompromising; of students and schoolboys; and of members of the cadres of the democratic parties proscribed by name after the elections. But these groups were more defensive than offensive, placing their hopes in an offensive from outside. The nearest they came to actual fighting was during the winter of 1949 and 1950 when they helped the peasants barricaded in the villages against the authorities and later troops who were sent to enforce collectivization in the villages. Together with 'kulak' and 'saboteur' peasant trials, the government had then to produce 'resistance' trials for those who had fought in this way.

As for the representatives of Free Rumania abroad, at the beginning of 1947 the only action was that of the 'diplomats' who had first become active in 1946 during the Paris Peace Conference. Hundreds of Rumanians, especially members of the wealthier middle class, were leaving Rumania clandestinely, 'helped' by individual Soviet and communist officials who, if paid highly enough, would transport them across Rumania, Hungary, and Austria to the western zone of occupation in Austria. These *émigrés* had a natural desire to 'help the country' by joining or forming a national movement in exile. The arrival of Radescu, Visoianu, and Buzesti was to give greater political weight to the exiles and the king's arrival at the beginning of 1948 gave a new impulse to such preoccupations.[7]

THE MANIU TRIAL

On 30 October 1947 Iuliu Maniu, Ion Mihalache, and seventeen others were brought to trial.[8] This trial was designed to be the great political watershed for its communist organizers. Yet during the trial, unlike that of Petkov in Sofia, only two of Maniu's co-defendants made forged allegations against him. Nor were these allegations political recantations. This was not an incidental failure in this particular communist trial in Rumania. Altogether, in no other Eastern European country have the communists been less eager to stage 'educative trials', in the sense that the accusations of the prosecutors and more particularly the confessions of the accused could be useful lessons to the people. This kind of rehearsed show did not take place in Rumania. None of the main communist leaders who were purged in Rumania—Foris, Patrascanu, Koffler, Ana Pauker, Vasile Luca, Teohari Georgescu, Chisinevschi, or Miron Constantinescu—has been tried in public. It is probable that from 1946 to 1956 the Rumanian communists rightly guessed that no ideological or even psychological subtle-

[7] Gafencu and Cretzianu were already there, one arriving from Switzerland and the other from Turkey. Visoianu and Buzesti arrived later. The Rumanian National Committee was founded in 1948. Radescu was its first President. Visoianu succeeded him in 1949.

[8] References in this section are mostly from the minutes of the trial as published in the Rumanian press (especially *Universul*) and from the RPR publication, *Trial of the Former National Peasant Party Leaders, Maniu, Mihalache, Penescu, Niculescu-Buzesti and Others*.

ties of the self-confessed anti-communist criminal could produce either anger or curiosity among the mass of the people, who opposed a solid front of hostile indifference to all kinds of variations on communist themes.

In the Maniu-Mihalache trial the Communist Party did not even speak directly through a public prosecutor, as it does, for example, in 'people's courts'. The court was a military one, thus perpetuating the method of political repression which had been used by Carol and by Antonescu and against which the National Peasant Party had always protested. Colonel Petrescu, the President of this court had been the prosecutor in the trial of Ana Pauker in 1936 and had presided, under Antonescu, in trials in Bessarabia and Transnistria. A further irony was that the Minister of Justice was Patrascanu, who had done more than anyone else to rally the support of the lawyers and intellectuals of the National Peasant Party for the defence of the communists in the military trials before the war. Patrascanu had also been Maniu's colleague in the preparation of the armistice and in the first post-war government.

No political dialogue was thus possible between the tribunal and the accused. On the contrary, the trial acquired a strange clarity of meaning as neither side hid its feelings or opinions. Unlike Cardinal Mindszenty, for instance, who confessed and later retracted and who was under obvious physical and moral strain, Maniu stated clearly and calmly his own views and acknowledged his own actions. So did all but two of the other accused.

The prosecution charged that there were three concentric 'rings' indicted in the same trial and plotting together against the security of the state. One was that of the democratic parties, or rather of the National Peasant Party, dramatically represented by no less than two of its leaders and founders. Maniu and his followers had conspired with two American intelligence officers to organize insurrection and set up American air bases in Rumania. The second 'ring' was that of the 'resistance abroad'. Visoianu, Buzesti, Cretzianu, and Gafencu had begun to denounce the new Rumanian government abroad, had set up organizations of exiles with certain funds transferred by Visoianu when Foreign Secretary, had asked foreign governments and institutions for help, and were in touch with the leaders of the National Peasant Party.

The third 'ring' was that of the 'rebellious civil service', represented in the trial by a small group of younger career diplomats, headed by Victor Radulescu-Pogoneanu. The Foreign Office, which in Rumania had always had the reputation of an élite corps, had enhanced this reputation by the smoothness and efficiency with which it had helped the king and Maniu in the negotiations with the Allies and the subsequent armistice.[9] This group was described as a ring of plotters which had maintained relations with their former leaders now abroad, with Maniu and the leaders of the democratic parties, and with the representatives of the American and British governments.

Several of the accused, in particular Maniu and Pogoneanu, the alleged heads of the two 'internal rings', defended themselves with great force. The debate fell back again and again on to one single point: the legality of their action or the legality of the restrictions which the government had imposed upon the normal political activities of the country. Thus: had Maniu authorized or even helped his colleagues in the projected flight abroad? Yes, he had. Why? Because he thought that since free opposition and legal criticism were prevented at home, the claims of the Rumanian people should be heard by the western democracies still responsible for the situation in the country. Why did he not go too? Because he thought that his place was with the people. Did he then intend to start a fight against the government in the country? He would continue his fight for the granting of free elections, genuine political liberty, the restoration of elementary human rights. By what means? By every means open to him. Did such means include plotting with the representatives of foreign powers, as he allegedly did during his conversations and contacts with American and British officials? The reply was that discussing the international and internal situation with diplomatic representatives was one of the usual duties of a statesman in any country. Had he maintained contacts with the Foreign Secretaries now abroad as exiles? Yes, they informed him of their useful activities and he advised them, whenever possible. Did he use unlawful channels of secret correspondence through the official of the Foreign Office accused with him? Yes, it was necessary to do so as the normal postal channels were closed.

[9] The entire Foreign Office had been purged in March 1946, when 105 ministers, counsellors, and secretaries were dismissed.

Did Pogoneanu recognize that he had been in touch with traitors abroad? Yes, Pogoneanu recognized that, but wanted to explain that they were not traitors but patriots whom he saluted from the dock. Why had he not gone too? Because he thought that his health might have made him a burden to them (Pogoneanu was crippled as a result of an early attack of sclerosis of the spine) and also because he wanted men better qualified than he, as for instance Visoianu, to go abroad and fight for the country.

This was the kind of dialogue of which the trial was mainly composed. It did a great deal to enhance still more the reputation of Maniu and to make that of Pogoneanu.

Maniu and Mihalache were sentenced to life imprisonment, the others to hard labour and solitary confinement for terms ranging from life to five years.

Maniu left the court as composed and courteous as he had been all his life and throughout the trial. He was seventy-four. This was the last time he was ever seen in public. In October 1956 it was announced that he had died in prison in 1952.[10] Only very scanty and unreliable reports had reached the outside world during the five years in which he allegedly still lived. But all had in common the description of him as being supremely serene, strengthened by a deep religious faith and a consciousness of sharing the suffering of the people he had served so faithfully.

A BANKRUPT COUNTRY

The introduction of state terror was soon accompanied by an economic bankruptcy which had been approaching since 1945.[11] In the summer of 1947 economic chaos had reached a scale unprecedented in the history of the Rumanian kingdom. There was hunger and dire need in many areas. From abroad, especially from the United States, food shipments were arriving. Inflation which had already shaken the weak Rumanian leu now went up in terrifying spirals. The pound sterling, which at the end of 1945 had been bought for the already high price of 30,000 lei, in the summer of 1947 could only be bought for 1 million lei. Rumania in the summer of 1947 was more reminiscent of the panic starva-

[10] In an interview given to Mr Jack Raymond of the *New York Times* by G. Tatarescu, the former Liberal Prime Minister, 14 Oct. 1955.

[11] See 'The Economic Field and Financial Policy', in Cretzianu, ed., *Captive Rumania* (1956).

tion and inflation in Germany and Hungary in 1919 than of any moment in her own history.

Four main causes lay at the root of this, and while each of them would have been enough to shake the structure of such a small country, their combination proved nearly disastrous. One was the aftermath of the war itself. The economy had been severely tried by collaboration with the Third Reich throughout the war, although from 1942 onwards Antonescu had succeeded in putting a stop to the ever increasing demands of the Germans.[12] The war on the side of the Allies was proportionately far more expensive in both men and money. No country could have undertaken two such successive military efforts without showing serious signs of strain.

The second and by far the most important cause was the pressure by Soviet Russia on the Rumanian economy, through the commitments of the armistice agreement and the plunder taken by the Red Army during the year of military collaboration and the two following years. As has been seen, by the terms of the armistice agreement, confirmed by the peace treaty, Rumania was to pay the USSR (1) a total of $300 million in goods in the form of an indemnity for Soviet losses by military operations and occupation; (2) the cost of the Soviet occupation troops (augmented by the prolongation of Soviet military occupation after the cessation of hostilities); and (3) the restitution of all property taken from Soviet territory during the war. But because the value of the first item was fixed, in terms of the 1944 dollar, at world prices prevailing in 1938, the actual cost to Rumania was estimated by Mr Willard Thorp in September 1946 at about 50 per cent above the $300 million total. Thus the $70 million already paid by Rumania in 1946 would have cost approximately $100 million in terms of current dollars, and the $230 million still payable would be liable to cost about $350 million. Thorp's estimate of the cost by September 1946 of maintaining occupation troops was about $325 million; of restitutions approximately $175 million, of other takings in goods and services approximately $425 million, and of several smaller items $25 million. Thus the total cost to Rumania by 1946 amounted to approximately $1,050 million.[13] This total

[12] See Hillgruber, pp. 200-8, on the final phase of the German–Rumanian economic relations.

[13] 'Remarks of Mr Willard Thorp, Representative for the U.S. at the Meeting of the Economic Commission for Finland and the Balkans', *Paris Conference, United States Delegation*, USD(PC) (PR) –24, 23 Sept. 1946', cited by Ciurea, pp. 126–7.

excluded direct war booty. Moreover since 1945 the various Sovroms had also been draining the country's wealth and resources.

The third cause was the communists' deliberate disorganization of production. There was constant political 'agitation' from the end of May 1944 until the spring of 1947. There were widespread arrests in villages and cities and ransacking of factories and workshops, involving the removal of technical installations and, in the country, of agricultural machinery. There was also serious interference in workers' activities in factories and the persecution and molestation of those who resisted them. At the Malaxa plant in 1946 Gheorghiu-Dej and Apostol came armed with machine-guns to break up the meeting at which the workers voted for the National Peasants. For all this the Communist Party was responsible. Finally, there occurred two consecutive droughts, in 1946 and 1947, among the worst ever experienced in Rumania.

While at the end of 1938 the total monetary circulation was 34.9 billion lei, in June 1944 it was 211.8 billion and on 14 August 1947 48.451 billion. While in August 1944 the cost-of-living index stood at 944 (August 1939=100), in April 1947 it stood at 440.869 and in July at 525.688.[14] The total industrial production had fallen by one-third from that of 1944. Oil production was 3.8 million tons as against 8.7 million in 1936. Agricultural production was less than half that of 1934–8. Budgetary expenditure in 1945–6 was respectively six and ten times higher than revenue. Any government in any country would have been forced to take immediate steps. The Groza government seemed to be content with preparing to adopt the currency reform, directed and personally supervised by Eugen Varga.

The currency reform was carried out by Varga on 15 August 1947, after having long been prepared in secret. The state paid the entire public debt with tons of paper-money it had itself printed. It then bought the whole cereal crop of the year, confiscated all the merchandise in stock in shops, workshops, and factories, paying for them in cash too, and finally purged a third of all state and private employees, paying them what they were owed in the same money. Then on 15 August the reform was announced, similar in its discriminatory methods and ultimate aims to those of the Soviet Union. Farmers and workers obtained a privileged

[14] Cretzianu, ed., *Captive Rumania,* p. 103.

exchange-rate, the rest of the population a markedly unfavourable one. The new leu was worth 6.60 mg. of gold and tied to the dollar at 150 to one. Communist institutions and banks and Soviet representatives were among the few to exchange all their reserves. Indeed, out of 48,500 million lei only 27,500 million were exchanged in the three days allowed for this purpose. The remaining 21,000 million represented, as a minimum, the Soviet-type of 'confiscation' thus operated by the state.

In common with the other satellites, the economic advantages for Rumania of the Marshall Plan offer of 5 June 1947 were obvious. But after the rejection of Marshall Aid by the Soviet Union on the grounds that it would constitute 'interference' by the United States in the internal affairs of the countries concerned, the satellite countries had no choice. Of the 22 other countries invited by the British and French governments to the Marshall Plan conference which began in Paris on 12 July, eight did not attend: Finland, Poland, Czechoslovakia, Hungary, Yugoslavia, Rumania, Bulgaria, and Albania. The Polish and Czechoslovak governments had shown that they were willing to participate in the Plan, and in June 1947 Tatarescu had issued a memorandum criticizing the government and its economic policy. But this was the period in which Soviet policy crystallized in an anti-western mould.

INTERNAL AND EXTERNAL NEGATIVISM, AUTUMN 1947

The Groza government had by now been in power for more than two years. So bad was its record and so unanimously discontented were all sections of the population that at this point, just before the winter of 1947, one may pause and consider why the Rumanian Communist Party was still more despised by its own subject people than were the other communist parties of Eastern Europe by theirs.

By this time it had become clear to the leaders of much stronger and more deeply-rooted European communist parties that they would soon have to choose between the maintenance of some of the popularity they, unlike the Rumanian Communist Party, had won during the war, and their loyalty to Stalin's Russia. The choice between these two paths was to be made rapidly by these parties. The Yugoslav Communist Party opted in 1948 for the break with Russia; the Czechoslovak for the break with freedom and democracy. But the Rumanian communists, who had no political capital, knew well that they had come to power and were maintained in power by the Soviet army. This party was indeed the most typical example of the new definition which Stalin was introducing for all the Eastern European democracies and had thus no choice or alternative from the very first. Such a party, and not the Yugoslav one, was closer to Stalin's wishes.

Although well aware of their unpopularity and difficulties, the communists made little effort to gain popular goodwill through a milder policy. Perhaps only Patrascanu was at this time putting forward some 'theses' in which a milder attitude towards the people could be discerned. He was allegedly recommending some positive and constructive action in collaboration with the democratic parties, but already in 1946, Gheorghiu-Dej had dealt severely with Patrascanu's deviations in his report to the Central Committee. The other and real leaders of the party were united in the opinion that the time for constructive government had not yet arrived. They thought that the Communist Party was still in a transition-administration in which, although they held the seats of power, they did not hold all of them, and especially the supreme one, from a formal point of view. They were still, according to their diagnosis, in the 'duality of power'. Consequently, they decided that as a revolutionary party they should continue to undermine the formal structure of the state and society and acquire ultimate and total power.

Gheorghiu-Dej, in his capacity as Minister of National Economy, was responsible for seeing that the deliveries to Russia were promptly dispatched and also for making an inventory of the national resources and wealth, in view of the coming nationalization. The fact that Teohari Georgescu, another party secretary, was Minister of the Interior had, of course, a greater and more apparent significance. He was there to answer to the party for the establishment of the necessary oppression and for smoothing the path for the further revolutionary steps.

The most significant of all political attitudes was, however, the restraint shown by the two other party secretaries, Ana Pauker and Vasile Luca, as well as by those leaders who, while not in the Secretariat, or in some cases not even on the list of the Politburo for 1945, were in charge of the most exclusive tasks of the party. These were Bodnaras, Parvulescu, Borila, Chisinevschi, and

Dumitru Coliu. They obviously refused to assume ministerial responsibilities. Had that important and Moscow-inspired wing of the party wanted to govern and had it felt that it was really in power, even in a coalition cabinet, it was Pauker, Luca, and Bodnaras who would have been delegated or even imposed upon the government rather than, for instance, Patrascanu. Instead, while the provisional governmental team was only marking time and clearing the way, the party was still concentrating on bringing the 'duality of power' to an end as quickly as possible.

During the Maniu trial an outcry against Tatarescu began on the grounds that the Ministry of Foreign Affairs and the diplomatic service were sheltering many opponents of the régime. Tatarescu's position worsened after the circulation of his June 1947 memorandum sharply criticizing the government. In September he was compelled to dismiss several hundred of the Foreign Office staff, and on 7 November he and the other Liberal cabinet members were removed from their posts, being replaced by Ana Pauker as Minister for Foreign Affairs and Vasile Luca as Minister of Finance, while in December Bodnaras became Minister of War. Ana Pauker with Gheorghiu-Dej and Chisinevschi had attended the conference held on 22–23 September at which the Cominform was founded. This event marked the slow beginning of active co-ordination with the Soviet bloc.[15] With Luca, Bodnaras, and Pauker in the government, the party embarked on what they thought would be the establishment of the dictatorship of the proletariat.

THE END OF THE RUMANIAN KINGDOM, 31 DECEMBER, 1947

The formation of the Cominform gave the signal for a new campaign of communist violence in Western Europe with the object of disrupting the economy of the countries which were to benefit from the Marshall Plan. This took place at the same time as the establishment of the water-tight isolation of the Eastern European people's democracies from the rest of the continent.

The continuation of the Rumanian kingdom within the heart

[15] This is what Prof. Hugh Seton-Watson in *The East European Revolution* describes as the phase of genuine coalition as against that of bogus coalition, for instance in Czechoslovakia. In Rumania, however, because of the local conditions coalition was from the beginning 'bogus' and had no chance to become genuine. The only difference was made by the acceptance by the communists of the king.

of the Soviet orbit was an anomaly even in 1945. The communists might publicly laugh at the 'anachronism' but to them it was one more important facet of the 'duality of power'. King Michael had of course been criticized by anti-communist Rumanians for some time, especially since he had opened Parliament after the trial of Maniu and Mihalache and accepted Ana Pauker, Luca, and Bodnaras as his ministers while tens of thousands of families were harried and ill treated by the communist authorities. Yet the people still had confidence in him. They knew that he was doing all that was left in his power to do.

On 12 November the king went to London for the marriage of Princess Elizabeth. He was surprised that the communist government made no move to prevent his going. The communist government were even more surprised, however, when, on 21 December, with the Queen Mother, he returned. Their hope, according to Groza in his last audience, that he would renounce the throne had not materialized. While abroad he had become engaged to Princess Anne de Bourbon Parma, but this had not weakened his determination to stay among his people to the end. The problem of his marriage had already been brutally dealt with by the communist government, which bluntly stated that 'Rumania could not afford it'.

Nine days after his return, Groza and Gheorghiu-Dej asked the king to come back from his country retreat at Sinaia for urgent reasons. He arrived on 30 December and received them in audience, in the presence of the Queen Mother. They asked him to abdicate. Each adopted a different line. Groza, with his usual vulgarity, made it sound like a good bargain, which he, an honest broker, was promoting. Dej evoked with fanaticism the future of a Rumania of the people. He also confessed that the king was an 'unsettling influence' and that while he remained in Rumania 'there would always be trouble'. He conjured up the evidence from the Maniu trial which could be used to make it seem that the king was plotting with the Americans and the British.[16] They presented him with a ready-made abdication instrument which he was to sign on the spot. When he refused, they gave him half an hour to think it over. Meanwhile he learnt that the palace telephones had been cut and that the palace itself was surrounded by communist troops. When he returned to the audience room

[16] A. Gould Lee, *Crown against Sickle*, p. 167.

and again refused to sign, Groza stated that the government would strike. 'There will be bloodshed, civil war perhaps, but the responsibility will be yours.'[17] He signed. On the same day the government announced the creation of the Rumanian People's Republic and prepared the draft of a new constitution.

Thus ended the rule of a young man who had twice been king of Rumania and yet, apart from the few months between 23 August 1944, when he led Rumania out of the war and of Nazi domination, and 6 March 1945, when he saw it fall under Soviet domination, he had never had the opportunity of being the constitutional, modern, and devoted monarch the Rumanian people knew him to be. Thus ended also the Rumanian kingdom, whose seventy years of existence had coincided with those of the country's full sovereignty.

[17] Ibid. p. 173.

Part II

THE TOTALITARIAN STATE, JANUARY 1948–FEBRUARY 1956

7
Final Touches to the Blueprint

THE Republic had been proclaimed and Professor I. C. Parhon was appointed head of the new state. Parhon was a distinguished endocrinologist who, in the days of anti-fascism, had been one of the Communist Party's star fellow-travellers, and during the war had made himself useful to it by signing communist-inspired letters and manifestoes and persuading other scientists and professors to do the same.

What kind of a republic was it to be? Hardly any Rumanian in January 1948 knew the answer to this question. It is now known that the Rumanian Communist Party was divided between various solutions. At the two extremes were, on the one side the Gheorghiu-Dej group with the idea of continuing something between a communist and a parliamentary state, possibly linked with the other Eastern European communist states through a federation which would extend from the Baltic to the Mediterranean. On the other there was the Luca group, suggesting that the Rumanian People's Republic should be a Soviet republic, one of the federated states of the Soviet Union. The latter solution, the final or absolute one, was feared to be imminent by many in Rumania and the West,[1] but it was averted. Co-ordination with the Soviet Union, however, was almost complete.

THE TREATY WITH RUSSIA, 4 FEBRUARY 1948

In January Petre Groza as Prime Minister, Ana Pauker as Foreign Minister, Gheorghiu-Dej as Minister of Industry, and Vasile Luca as Minister of Finance went to Moscow as the leaders of a vast delegation of experts and officials. On 4 February 1948 Groza for the RPR and Molotov for the Soviet Union signed a treaty of friendship, co-operation, and mutual assistance between the two countries. This was the first such treaty signed with one of

[1] *New York Times*, 10 May & 2 July and *The Times*, 13 August 1948, carrying an official denial by the London Embassy of the RPR on this subject.

the states which had waged war against the Soviet Union: Hungary followed on 18 February and Bulgaria on 18 March. With Czechoslovakia the treaty had been signed on 12 December 1943, and with Yugoslavia and Poland on 12 and 21 April 1945 respectively.

All six treaties were based on the idea of common defence against Germany.[2] But this was rather a matter of interpretation according to the background and circumstances in which each of the treaties had been signed. Leaving on one side the Czechoslovak-Soviet treaty, which resembled the Anglo-Soviet one of 1942 and as such was a wartime alliance, the other five were almost identical, with some minor differences between the two signed in 1945 and the three in 1948. But 'Germany' had a different meaning in each of them. When the signatories agreed in 1948 'to take all joint action in their power to obviate any threat of renewed aggression by Germany or any other Power which might be associated with Germany either directly or in any other way' (Art. 1), this statement, as Molotov himself said, 'becomes especially important now when the fomentors of a new war from the imperialist camp are endeavouring to knock together military and political blocks directed against the democratic states'.[3] The treaties were directed for the most part against the western powers,[4] including the future Western Germany, and aimed at the military and diplomatic strengthening of the European Soviet bloc of which the Cominform, already strongly on the offensive, was to be the political guardian.

But the uniformity of treatment thus imposed by the Soviet Union on all the Eastern European countries under her direct control becomes more evident when the text of the treaties is compared with that signed between the Soviet Union and Finland on 6 April 1948.[5] Here the problem of sovereignty of the minor partner, after having been hotly debated, was finally solved in its favour in the text. In it, Finland committed itself only 'to carry out its duty as a sovereign State' and 'to direct all the forces at its disposal towards defending the integrity of its territory . . . with

[2] Art. 1, Soviet-Rumanian Treaty (U.N. Treaty Series, vol. 48, 1950).

[3] *Moscow News*, 7 Feb. 1948.

[4] *Pravda* linked the signature of the Soviet-Rumanian treaty with 'a charge that American imperialists were transforming Western Germany into a base for military operations' (*Christian Science Monitor*, 7 Feb. 1948).

[5] U.N. Treaty Series, vol. 48, pp. 149–61.

the help, if necessary, of the Soviet Union or together with the Soviet Union' (Art. 1). Finland also asked and obtained that there should be consultations between the two parties on the point of whether and when there was 'a threat of the military aggression referred to in Article 1'. Stalin himself delivered a speech on the occasion of its signature in which he said:

> Soviet people hold that each nation—whether big or small—has its own qualitative peculiarities, its specific nature, which belong only to it and which other nations lack. These peculiar features form the contribution which each nation makes to the common treasury of world culture and which supplements and enriches it. In this sense all nations—big and small—are in a similar position, and each nation is equivalent to every other nation.[6]

None of these clear affirmations of sovereignty was to be found in the treaties signed with the countries under direct communist control or in the speeches of the Soviet leaders delivered on the occasion of their signature. These countries merely committed themselves to act together with the Soviet Union at any time against any aggressor,[7] and were treated by the Soviet Union as diplomatic and military subordinates.

THE FOUNDATION OF THE RUMANIAN WORKERS' PARTY (RWP)

Four days after the first (Warsaw) meeting of the Cominform, the Central Committee of the Rumanian Social Democrat Party and Politburo of the Communist Party issued a joint communiqué expressing their desire to collaborate in a Rumanian Workers' Party. This merger had been resisted by Petrescu and his followers in the independent Social Democrat Party but had the backing of the last Congress of the official Social Democrat Party on 5 October 1947, which was attended by delegations of socialists from abroad as well as by an imposing phalanx of the Rumanian Communist Party headed by Dej, Ana Pauker, Vasilichi, and others, among them, of course, Groza. The resolution on fusion was carried with acclamation. At that time, according to figures given by Barbu Solomon in his speech to the Congress, published

[6] *Soviet News*, 14 Apr. 1948.

[7] There was also a difference in duration: the Soviet-Rumanian treaty was for 20 years, the Soviet-Finnish for 10 years, with an automatic extension of respectively 5 and 1 years.

in *Scanteia,* the Social Democrat Party numbered 560,201 members, of whom 155,303 were workers, 30,346 craftsmen, 45,097 civil servants, 17,083 clerks, 13,903 professional workers, 8,663 salesmen, 253,803 farmers, and 46,003 others. To these must be added another 193,011 members of youth and women's organizations. The report also mentioned that among the members were 19,457 village teachers, 2,940 secondary school teachers, and 341 university professors.

On 12 November 1947 the Central Committee of the Social Democrat Party adopted the principle that the two parties should be united, and the new Rumanian Workers' Party had its First Congress on 21–23 February 1948. The final resolution[8] of this Congress announced that the party based its activity on 'the teachings of Marx, Engels, Lenin, and Stalin' and heralded reforms that would be made to establish a popular democratic régime. It announced that a new constitution would be drawn up which would reflect changes in the social and economic structure of the state, including the creation of people's councils, the reorganization of justice, education, culture, and worship, and economic measures to transform Rumania into an advanced industrial-agrarian country. The working class was described as the leader of the new society and the RWP as the vanguard and guide of the workers. In foreign policy the resolution emphasized Rumania's allegiance to the anti-imperialist camp led by the Soviet Union, and the importance of the Soviet-Rumanian treaty.

A new Central Committee headed by Dej, Luca, Pauker, had among its full members: Augustin Alexa, G. Apostol, E. Bodnaras, Petre Borila, Pintilie Bodnarenko, I. and Liuba Chisinevschi, Miron Constantinescu, Constanta Craciun, I. Vinte, Dumitru Coliu, Mihai Dalea,[9] A. Draghici, Gheorghe Florescu, Tudor Iordachescu, Misha Leven, Constantin Mateescu, Mihai Moraru, Ion Pas, Emil Popa, Iosif Ranghet, Leonte Rautu, Leontin Salajan[10] (Silaghi), Lotar and Eugenia Radaceanu, Nicolae Radavonici, Avram Serban, Barbu Solomon, William Suder, Chivu Stoica, Zaharia Tanase, Olimpia Tenescu, Vasile Vaida, Gheorghe Vasilichi, and Stefan Voitec.

The full list was a comprehensive Who's Who of the party's personalities before the rise of the new generation. The newly

[8] Resolution of 23 Feb. 1948, in *Rezolutii,* i.
[9] See below, p. 353. [10] See below, p. 357.

elected Secretariat was again in the hands of the initial four, with Lotar Radaceanu as Fifth Secretary for a brief period. Gheorghiu-Dej remained the Secretary-General, though he was not yet in a position to assert his supremacy over the other three. Apostol, with Chivu Stoica as number two, was in charge of the trade unions. Chisinevschi was supported by Rautu at the Agitprop (an office which was incidentally to become more important by the transfer of the Cominform Journal and headquarters to Bucharest). Moghioros controlled the Orgburo; Vasilichi, Youth Affairs; Ranghet (who died soon afterwards) cadres; Vasile Vaida the Peasant Commission; Constanta Craciun the Women's Commission; Pintilie Bodnarenko the administration; and Parvulescu the Control Commission. The communists were in full charge of the ministries of the interior, justice, foreign affairs, defence, economy and finance, and so controlled the entire state machine.

The Congress also changed the old National Democratic Front into a Popular Democratic Front, including the RWP, Ploughmen's Front, National Popular Party (formerly Union of Patriots), and the Hungarian People's Union (Madosz),[11] which like the Confederation of Trade Unions, the Union of Workers' Youth, and Union of Democratic Women, were front organizations. On 28 March the Popular Democratic Front obtained 92 per cent of the votes in elections for a new assembly to vote on the constitution, and the government obtained 405 of the 414 seats.

WAS PATRASCANU A POTENTIAL TITO?

One of the focal points of the RWP Congress of February 1948 was the attack launched publicly upon Patrascanu, in his presence. This had the immediate effect of his exclusion from the new Central Committee. Eventually it led to his disgrace and execution in 1954, after a trial *in camera*. How far, however, his case can be thought of as the purge of a 'pre-Titoist', that is to say the victim of an anti-Tito purge even before the excommunication of Tito himself, is still a moot point.

The man chosen to denounce him on 22 February was Georgescu, allegedly one of the victims of Foris's and Patrascanu's dealing with the *Siguranta* during the war. Georgescu told the Congress, with his victim sitting near-by, silent and seemingly

[11] The National Popular Party disbanded in 1949; the Ploughmen's Front and the Hungarian People's Union became front organizations.

indifferent, that Patrascanu had 'fallen under the influence of the bourgeoisie', had 'become an exponent of bourgeois ideology', and had constantly and voluntarily 'over-estimated the forces of the enemy', that is of the class-enemy, potentially helped by the western imperialist powers'.[12]

In the resolution of the Central Committee plenary meeting of 10–11 June 1948, these charges were more clearly outlined. It averred that:

A typical example of the renunciation of the policy of the class struggle against the exploiters and of the urging of collaboration with the exploiting classes is to be found in the political position of Patrascanu. Several weeks before March 1945 Patrascanu, in complete contradiction to the party line, resuscitated the slogan of collaboration with the whole bourgeoisie or with an important part of it. In 1946 he defended the thesis of an alliance with the whole peasantry including the exploiting elements, hostile to the working peasantry. Falsifying the history of the heroic struggle of the workers in Rumania, he wrote in a slanderous manner about the 'lack of influence and the inability to influence the proletariat and of the sporadic activity, lacking in continuity and depth of the party'. Patrascanu tried to deny the leading part of the proletariat and attributed their rôle to the bourgeoisie. In his practical activity he followed the policy of appeasement towards the exponents of bourgeois-landlord reaction when the party was fully engaged in the struggle against reaction. He followed the line of nationalist-chauvinist policy. As regards economics, he preached the bourgeois policy of freedom of trade and, after the currency reform, he asked for the leu to return to the chaos of inflation and thus helped to the strengthening of the economic position of the capitalists. In this way Patrascanu became the mouthpiece of bourgeois ideology and interests in the ranks of our party. The party resolutely rejected his counter-revolutionary theories which were inspired by the ideology and interest of the class enemy. It must be considered a mistake that these 'theories' were not unmasked sufficiently and in time.[13]

These strictures on Patrascanu's political action and thinking since the Communist Party's return to legality were in fact distorted half-truths. (The crude accusations of police collaboration and treasonable activities in association with Foris during and before the war were published only briefly before his summary 'trial' in 1954.) Some of the charges, however, were true and, if

[12] *Rezolutii*, i. [13] Ibid.

anything, to his credit. In the immediate post-war situation his policy might have given the party some popularity and would almost certainly have proved to be sounder economically than the official party policy. But seen from the point of view of people like Vasile Luca, who was obviously the leader of the attack on Patrascanu, his theses bore an old-fashioned pre-Fifth Congress (1932) flavour. In the vastly changed circumstances of 1948 these seemed to them not only out of date but clearly treasonable.

Thus the accusation of having 'resuscitated' the slogan of collaboration with the entire bourgeoisie, or with important segments of it, could mean two things. One was that just before the Vyshinsky coup d'état Patrascanu had advocated the continuation of a policy of collaboration with the National Peasants if they changed their leadership—an attitude similar to that taken by the party towards the Social Democratic Party. He had many reasons for this. He had realized, at least since the reorganization of the Secretariat and Politburo in May 1944 and October 1945, that he was now on his way out of the leadership of the party. But in a coalition with the National Peasants he might have regarded himself as the natural leader. He would thus emerge as a national leader, imposed by the masses and by circumstances upon the party. Such a plan might be feasible for democratic politicians in conflict with democratic parties in free countries; but it had little chance in an occupied country with a monolithic party, with no life of its own except that lent to it by the Russian party. And it was very late in the day for such a game. For the Rumanian Communist Party and its Russian supporters the aim was to control the country. Thus the difference between the position of Tito and Patrascanu between 1945 and 1948 can be summarized in this double distinction: while the former was in control of the party which was in control of the country, the latter was slipping out of the party which was only then attempting, by means of Soviet intervention, to reach the sources of power.

The other meaning of the expression 'resuscitated' in the context of the Central Committee resolution carried echoes of an even older feud between Patrascanu and the party. The accusation that he had often libelled the impotence of the proletariat and the sporadic and superficial activity of the party, which surrendered the leading rôle to the bourgeoisie, evoked the pre-1932 ideological schism in the party between the Old Kingdom wing—intellectuals and workers—and the Bessarabian wing, which together with the workers' groups was to take control of the party at the Fifth Congress. Here again there is very little to be found in common with Tito's straight revolutionary policy.

But in two ideological respects there were certain analogies between the accusations against Patrascanu and those which the Soviet Central Committee was at the same time making against Tito. When the Rumanian resolution stressed that Patrascanu wished in 1945 to collaborate with 'the whole peasantry, including exploiting elements hostile to the working peasantry', this was an almost identical accusation with that directed against the Yugoslav Communist Party, that it had rated the peasants above the working class and had also failed to distinguish between kulaks and other peasants. It must not be forgotten that at the time the Rumanian Workers' Party was preparing to shape the new 'people's democracy', which entailed wholesale nationalization, industrialization, and collectivization. Patrascanu, weary of the useless lies in which the party had already entangled itself, called for more realism. To antagonize even larger segments of the population, to destroy even further the economy for the sake of 'ideological advances' on paper seemed to him to be unrealistic. Especially with regard to the peasants he had every reason to view the prospect of forcible collectivization with scepticism.

The other analogy may be found in the allusion made to his line of 'nationalist-chauvinist policy'. In the context of 1948 this may have sounded similar to the alleged anti-Russian attitude of Tito, Kostov, Rajk, and Gomulka. Actually, however, this accusation in Patrascanu's case more likely referred to his anti-Hungarian attitude from 1944 to 1947 (the year of the peace treaty) on the Transylvanian problem. In another section of the June 1948 resolution, dealing separately with the problem of nationalities in the RPR, it is again mentioned that the 'fight against the anti-Marxist nationalist-chauvinist attitude of Patrascanu has helped towards the establishment of fraternal relations of the Rumanian people with the other nationalities living on the same territory'. In July 1946 Gheorghiu-Dej had already dealt with this deviation of Patrascanu in his report to the Central Committee on 'the position of the RPR regarding chauvinistic and revisionist trends'. Hence the hint in the 1948 resolution that it had taken such a long time to condemn his theories.

Finally, the question of whether Patrascanu was involved at the end of 1947 and the beginning of 1948 in direct diplomatic dealings and contacts between South Eastern European communists with a view to forming a Balkan federation must be examined. This diplomatic episode shook the confidence of the Russian Communist Party in certain of the East European leaders.[14] It probably accentuated their distrust of Tito and hastened the final decision to expel Yugoslavia from the Cominform.

Dimitrov was forced to retract his over-optimistic statement about a coming Balkan federation, made on 17 January 1948, in Bucharest, after a violent attack by *Pravda* on 28 January. Soon afterwards, already ailing, he was summoned to Moscow where he died. The whole incident may also have reflected upon Patrascanu. Tito had been in Bucharest from 17 to 20 December 1947 for the signing of the Yugoslav-Rumanian treaty. Whether the Russians were informed of some further plans for a Balkan federation made by Tito and Patrascanu remains unknown. The fact remains that the Yugoslav press and party were silent about Patrascanu's case. Only at the height of its continuous attack on the Soviet-dominated communist parties on 4 March 1950[15] did *Borba* publish a news item reporting that Patrascanu was shortly to be tried, together with certain Yugoslav citizens, for a pro-Tito conspiracy.

When Patrascanu was tried, between 6 and 14 April 1954, his co-defendants were a mixed group of personal friends ranging from the former Marshal of the Palace, Ion Mocsony-Stircea, to Lena Constante, the artist,[16] and the published charges were of having headed a group of spies and plotters with links leading to the 'traitors', Foris and Koffler. The military court was presided over by Colonel Ilie Moisescu. Patrascanu and Remus Koffler were sentenced to death, H. Zilber, A. Stefanescu, and E.

[14] See 'The Evolution of the Cominform, 1947–50', *World Today,* May 1950.

[15] *New York Times,* 5 March 1950.

[16] Some links of personal friendship did exist between certain of the accused: for example, between Patrascanu and his wife and Belu Silber, the typical Eastern European philosopher-economist of Jewish origin who, already attracted to the Communist Party in the later 1920s, violently reacted against its discipline and drabness; Harry Brauner, a brilliant musician and folklorist; his life-long friend Lena Constante, outstanding painter of Byzantine ikons and churches; E. Calmanovici, a successful engineer and builder in search of intellectual companionship; and H. Torosian, the Armenian businessman, formerly communist consul in Paris, where he acquired a large hotel; and Koffler, Foris's greatest friend in the CC of the war years. But this was not a political group.

Calmanovici received life sentences; Moscony-Stircea and H. Torosian were sentenced to fifteen years' hard labour; H. Brauner and Lena Constante to twelve years'; others to lesser terms.[17]

THE RPR'S FIRST CONSTITUTION, APRIL 1948

The National Assembly as 'elected' on 3 March met on 6 April. On 8 April it started discussing the draft of the constitution; this had been published on 6 March and was approved unanimously on 13 April.[18] The reasons which led the communists to its quick adoption were obvious. The 'duality of power' had come to an end. The shape of the state had been entirely and violently altered, the former basic institutions destroyed; different 'structures, super- and infra-structures' were allegedly taking shape beneath these changes. Rumania was, with Czechoslovakia, the last of the communist-bloc countries without a Soviet-type constitution. This does not mean that all the constitutions of the six satellites were entirely aligned to that of the USSR. The Polish and Czechoslovak constitutions were not based on the principle of 'government by the Assembly'; in both, the President of the Republic had political prerogatives of his own. Besides, all six of them differed from that of the USSR in that they did not formally acknowledge the guiding rôle of the Communist Party. Nor did they extend the principle of nationalization of the means of production to all sectors and branches of their economy. Private

[17] According to an eye-witness account published in *Vocea libertati* (Athens), May 1958, certain communists were instructed to make specific accusations at the trial. For example, one of the witnesses was Ecaterina Borila (wife of the present member of the Politburo), who testified that Patrascanu had made certain statements from which it appeared that he was plotting to win power and eliminate others from the CC; he had also made declarations of a nationalist character. Another witness was Ilka Wassermann, director of *Cartea rusa*, who said that Patrascanu had connexions with imperialist agents, that he was a nationalist and anti-Semite and a former agent of the *Siguranta*. Although there was no evidence to support these allegations, she was considered one of the main figures of the prosecution. Another witness was Gheorghe Tatarescu, who was to prove that during his stay in Paris the defendant had contacts with western governments with a view to bringing Rumania into the western orbit, but when Tatarescu had barely begun to speak, Patrascanu rose furiously, exclaiming: 'Such scum of history are brought to this trial as witnesses against me, who am a communist. If such an individual has to prove that I am not a communist, it is only a proof of the low level of the Rumanian Communist Party which needs such elements, as well as evidence of the total lack of proof in this odious trial, so that it has been necessary to resort to such a witness.' Patrascanu interrupted and contradicted Tatarescu so many times that finally the prosecution gave up this witness.

[18] Text in A. J. Peaslee, ed., *Constitutions of Nations* (1950, iii. 37. See on the constitution A. Gyorgy, *Governments of Danubian Europe* (N.Y., 1949); H. G. Fabre, *Théorie des démocraties populaires* (1950).

property was still accepted. But they were all republics; they were all based on communist constitutional principles, of the national sovereignty embodied in people's councils and of the non-separation of powers in the state.

The 1948 RPR constitution went straight to the most advanced position held in the sphere by any people's democracy. Like the Yugoslav, Albanian, Bulgarian, and Hungarian constitutions, it adopted from the beginning the principle that 'the whole power of the state is derived from the people and belongs to the people', through the Grand National Assembly, and below through people's councils (soviets). These had not yet been established,[19] but were described in detail as 'the representative organs of the masses in local administration'. They were to 'rely on the initiative and extensive participation of the popular masses' and the basic power lay with them. The Grand National Assembly was 'the supreme organ of state authority'. It made laws, declared war, and concluded peace. The Presidium and the Council of Ministers were responsible solely to the Assembly. The Presidium, composed of a President and three vice-presidents, a secretary, and fourteen members, was elected for a period of four years. The Council of Ministers was the supreme executive and administrative organ, but not an organ of state authority.

Civil rights were lavishly granted, but with ominously restrictive interpretations. Article 32 will serve as an example: 'The citizens have the right of association and organization, if the aims pursued are not directed against the democratic order established by the Constitution'. This, in a police state, was enough. Indeed, this part of the constitution was void of any meaning in the conditions of intense political and social persecution carried on 'for the sharpening of the class struggle' as decided in the party's resolutions and orders.

Articles 5–15 dealt with the economic and social structure of the state. Private ownership of land and of industrial and commercial establishments was recognized (Arts. 5–6, 8–9, 11, 13–14), but Article 11 envisaged the possibility of nationalizing privately owned means of industrial production, banks and insurance companies 'if demanded by the general interest'. This aligned the

[19] The Law on People's Councils was adopted only on 15 Jan. 1949, and the first provisional committees of people's councils were set up on 18 April in some towns and villages. See below, pp. 170 ff.

constitution with the Soviet one, in which the economic powers of the state were among the most important provisions.

By and large, this first constitution marked the fact that Rumania was in a state of transition from capitalism to socialism. For communists a constitution is in any case only the expression of a certain moment in the class struggle in the revolutionary society. But in Rumania the two fundamental elements of the economic and political structure of a communist society, the nationalization of the means of production and the domination of the soviets, had to be effected after the constitution had heralded them. Without them, and all the other changes and steps which they entailed, there could be no proper control by the state of production and of all other activities, as required in a Marxist society. The point for the Rumanian communists was not whether they wanted or not to attain a higher status in the hierarchy of communist states and societies. Their problem was whether they could accomplish even the basic two points: for both, an overall planned economy and establishment of soviets, presented very serious difficulties.

Yet by the time it was set down on paper that Rumania was to be another people's democracy, the meaning of this term had already changed in Russian political theory. In the light of the ideological struggle with Yugoslavia, the concept of the people's democracy underwent fundamental revision. For the RPR a double time-lag had thus been created, since it was already behind the requirements of its constitution. That was why this constitution was to last only four years.

ALLEGIANCE TO THE SOVIET UNION

The Cominform–Yugoslav dispute led to the hasty addition of one more essential criterion for a people's democracy: a built-in assurance of allegiance to the Soviet Union. It is useful from this point of view to compare two definitions of a people's democracy given by Georgi Dimitrov, the Bulgarian communist leader and Comintern head, first in 1946, prior to the referendum on the question of abolishing the monarchy (quoted by Chervenkov at the first meeting of the Cominform in September 1947), and then in December 1948, at the Fifth Congress of the Bulgarian Communist Party. The first read:

Bulgaria will not be a Soviet republic; it will be a people's republic in which the leading rôle will be played by the overwhelming majority of the people . . . [It] will be a people's republic in which private property, acquired by labour, will be protected by the state authorities . . . but in which big capitalist profiteering private property will not be allowed to doom the laboring people . . . to hunger and poverty . . . [It] will leave no open door for the return of the shameful past—monarchism, fascism and the Greater Bulgarian chauvinism. . . . Bulgaria will be a . . . free and independent state with its national and state sovereignty.[20]

This was the image of the quasi-dictatorship of the proletariat within an entirely independent national state, the 1945–8 version.

The second, produced two years later and six months after the Yugoslav-Cominform split, read:

The people's democracy and the people's democratic state . . . were made possible . . . as a result of the historic victory of the Soviet Union in World War II and of the struggle of the masses under the leadership of the working class for national freedom and independence. The people's democratic state represents the rule of the toiling people—of the overwhelming majority of the people under the leadership of the working class. . . . The people's democratic state is a state in the transitional period, destined to ensure the development of the country along the road to Socialism . . . [It] is built in cooperation and friendship with the Soviet Union, the land of Socialism . . . [It] belongs to the democratic anti-imperialist camp. . . . Under the conditions of the military collapse of the Fascist aggressor states . . . and of the immense strengthening of the might of the Soviet Union and the existing close cooperation with the USSR and the new democracies, our country and the other new democracies were enabled to bring about the transition from capitalism to Socialism, without the establishment of a Soviet system, through the system of people's democracy, on condition that this system is consolidated and developed, and leans on the support of the USSR and the new democracies.[21]

The two salient points in the comparison of these two definitions are, first the emphasis in 1948 on the dictatorship of the proletariat, and secondly the great stress then laid on the recognition of Russia's right to guide the people's democracies, her own creation. The new Soviet thesis, as summarized in the Cominform Journal, was that 'the attitude to the Soviet Union is the keystone

[20] Cominform Journal, 15 Dec. 1947.
[21] Ibid. 1 Jan. 1949.

of genuine proletarian internationalism for all Communists . . . Nationalism today is the main danger to the successful construction of the new state system.'[22] Ultimately these two points, linked together, were expressed as: 'Our force, the force of our Party and the working class, was multiplied by the fact that the Soviet Union and the Soviet Army were always there to support us with their assistance. . . . Thanks to the fact that we can rely upon the Soviet Union and so be spared from a civil war, the foremost function of our dictatorship of the proletariat is a task of economic and cultural construction.'[23]

Thus the Rumanian Workers' Party had learnt very soon after passing the first constitution that they were expected to perform the double 'dialectical task' of establishing a communist state which on the one hand would have the political and economic structure of a general employer, organizer, and controller of society and, on the other, would pay due political and financial tribute to the suzerain power through whose help this state had been brought into being.

[22] Cited in 'The Evolution of the Cominform', *World Today*, May 1950.
[23] Cited ibid. pp. 146 & 150.

8

The Scaffolding, 1948–50

NATIONALIZATION OF INDUSTRY, JUNE 1948

On 11 June 1948 the Grand National Assembly passed a bill nationalizing industrial, banking, insurance, mining, and transportation enterprises.

In pre-communist Rumania many major public services and enterprises had either been nationalized or had been state owned from their inception. The railways, the postal and telegraphic services, tobacco and other monopolies were all owned or controlled directly by the state and there were a state printing house, state forests, and state fisheries. The state too had important shares and rights of control in heavy industrial concerns dealing with armaments and aviation. The sector of the economy thus owned or controlled by the state was relatively large and corresponded to the growing need for state intervention and state capital if the country was to go farther with the industrialization of its resources than was possible with the help of private capital, whether domestic or foreign.

For the communists, wholesale nationalization of industry had been a cardinal point in their pre-war programme, a point which they held in common with the Social Democrats, the other Marxist party. Since the war, however, they had sometimes for tactical reasons played down this demand. While at the National Conference of 1945 it was stressed vigorously,[1] it had been dropped from the 1946 platform. But although it may have been played down as a public demand, the groundwork for state control was being laid through direct revolutionary action at the local level or by preparatory governmental measures. In many districts the Communist Party had succeeded in setting up active economic commissions of the trade union councils and economic co-opera-

[1] 'The entire industrial potential of the country, state owned and owned by private capital, must form a whole from now on' (Gheorghiu-Dej, *Articole si cuvantari* (1951)).

M

tives of the workers with the task of restoring enterprises either destroyed by bombing or abandoned by their owners, the administration of the restored enterprises being entirely in the hands of the workers.[2] The preparatory governmental measures had begun in December 1945 when the Ministry of Industry had fallen to the communists, and especially after July 1947, when a ministerial commission for economic rehabilitation was set up. Between these dates a number of steps were taken with the final intention of the overall nationalization of industry. The two most important were the nationalization of the National Bank of Rumania, through a law of 28 December 1946, which entailed the direct control and ownership of all national credit institutions;[3] and the publication of a 'census' of centres of private industrial, commercial and transport enterprises of 13 October 1947, which provided as complete an inventory as possible for the coming requisition.

The 1948 law expropriated five main categories of industrial enterprises. They were: those of national economic importance, which included oil, textiles, timber, railways; those of regional importance, by which was meant especially the large consumer goods and food industry enterprises; any metallurgical plants employing over 100 workers; all enterprises with a capacity of over 10–30–50 h.p. according to the kind of industry; and practically all banks and trade and insurance companies. It also included plants and factories specifically listed in the text of the law itself. This list of 687 enterprises duplicated in many respects the generic categories thus defined. The shares and rights of ownership previously held by private owners passed to the state but the new owner refused to acknowledge the debts and unpaid loans of the confiscated companies. The law provided for the indemnification of owners or stockholders, and a body was set up under the Finance Ministry which was supposed to issue bonds, but all stipulations were valueless as the government did not respect the law.

Roughly 1,060 such enterprises were nationalized up to 1950, that is 90 per cent of the total industrial production, but although there had been long preparatory measures, the actual take-over was carried out very inefficiently. The law itself, for instance,

[2] See, e.g., S. Kovacs & F. Grun, 'Lupta organizatiilor locale de partid pentru nationalizarea inteprinderilor industriale din Judetul Mures', *Analele*, no. 3, May-June 1957.

[3] The Soviet-Rumanian Bank was exempted.

covered any omissions by stating that enterprises nominally designated even 'if their names and addresses were partially inaccurate or if they had been changed' could be taken over by the state representatives, subject to further corrections. This blanket clause became a source of major complaints and recriminations. Although businessmen and big industrialists were well aware that the axe would sooner or later fall on them, the government kept its decision secret until the last moment to prevent the owners and directors from sabotaging the plants or misappropriating the funds. This added in part to the confusion. The small businesses, in particular, were taken by surprise. In some districts the party formed 'nationalization committees', the members being told only on 10 June the purpose for which they had been called.

In the same districts many of the initial new directors were recruited from among the workers, members of the nationalization committees. From the beginning they were faced with the impossible task of 'producing at once', although they were without any prior knowledge of technical management, and without raw materials and supplies of the necessary goods. But in general, the provisions of the law that 'the nationalized industries shall be administered by those ministries in whose spheres they operate' or of 'the local communal authorities' meant in practical terms the immediate appointment of former state engineers or civil servants, in the great majority non-party men who had been hastily 're-educated'. Centralization was from the first excessive and the sincerity and the competence of the new managerial team appointed by the ministries very doubtful.

For the doctrinaires of the party (both communist and former socialist) the act of 11 June 1948 represented the main revolutionary action and has subsequently been presented as the real dialectical moment, the 'threshold' at which the backbone of the old society was broken. The resolution announcing it stressed that nationalization would liquidate the contradiction created by the fact that the 'working class' had already assumed political control of the country but was not in control of the economy. It would hasten the advance towards socialism, thus strengthening the country's political and economic independence, and put an end to state capitalism.[4] It would abolish private capitalist profit and

[4] Communist economic historians for whom the nationalization of June 1948 was the moment of revolutionary achievement and the beginning of the road to

thus place at the disposal of the country more wealth and resources. But, above all, it would remove the last obstacle in the way of future economic planning which could alone lead to economic progress and to the liquidation of underdevelopment and economic backwardness. With nationalization, the ground had been cleared for the new communist economic policy.

One of the great claims for nationalization was that it ended foreign exploitation. But the nationalization law left a loophole for the most blatant foreign exploitation. It exempted from expropriation 'the capital of those enterprises which had been assigned to a member state of the United Nations as a result of the fulfilment of the peace treaty or of war reparations'. This provision was very soon to make the Soviet government the only large industrial capitalist owner in the RPR. This was effected through the notorious Sovroms. At the time of the nationalization there were already four of these in being: Sovrompetrol, Sovromtransport, Sovromlemn, and Sovrombank. Between nationalization and the beginning of the first one-year economic plan, six other Sovroms were established: for natural gas, insurance, the chemical, building, and metallurgical industries, and tractors. They all enjoyed extra-territorial privileges, exemption from stamp duties and taxes, and all had Soviet managers and controllers, both before and after nationalization. Their income and capital were free of any national or economic restrictions. In the case of the oil industry, moreover, an even stranger relation was created by nationalization between the semi-capitalist Sovrom and the rest of the industry. In the place of all the individual oil companies now expropriated, two large state companies, 'Moldova' and 'Muntenia', were set up. These were to produce 66 per cent of

socialism have recently added a new interpretation of it, which is worth considering. This is that it marked the end of 'state capitalism' (Simion Pop, 'Capitalismul de stat in Romania in perioada regimului democrat-popular', *Probleme economice,* no. 1, 1958). According to this theory, state capitalism flourished between the seizure of power in March 1945 and the nationalization of 1948; by state capitalism is implied all the corrective and controlling measures taken by the Economic Department during that period. According to this interpretation, after nationalization state capitalism existed only in agriculture, that is to say in the contracting and purchasing by the state from the private owners of farms. The expression existed in communist terminology previously, but was then used merely to describe the sector of the economy owned by the state in a non-communist country. ('In our country there coexist the small producer, private capitalism, the sector of state capitalism and the socialist elements in different economic sectors', Gheorghiu-Dej, Political Report at the CC of the RWP Congress, Feb. 1948, in *Articole si cuvantari*). Ten years later, however, its meaning was changed in order to include transactions between the socialist state and the capitalist elements in it.

the country's oil. It would have been natural for the new RWP government to favour these new state enterprises. On the contrary, they were mercilessly subjected to competition by Sovrompetrol, with the result that they both had to be liquidated on 1 September 1950 and were soon afterwards absorbed by Sovrompetrol.[5]

THE BEGINNING OF STATE PLANNING, JULY 1948

The first act towards raising the scaffolding on which the new structure was to be based was the decree of 18 July 1948 establishing a State Planning Commission. Its duties were to submit reports to the government on the general economic situation, pointing out any existing discrepancies in production, to elaborate a general plan of the national economy, to co-ordinate all economic sectors in the national economic plan, and to carry out economic planning. It comprised six departments: planning; plan co-ordination; checking of execution of the plan; research and statistics; accountancy; and press and public relations. Similar planning commissions appeared at about the same time in Bulgaria and Hungary. Indeed, the setting up throughout the Soviet bloc of these commissions heralded the formation in January 1949 of the Council of Mutual Economic Assistance (Comecon), which was designed as an overall economic commission for all the Cominform countries, with the exception of the Soviet Union which had retained its hegemony. In Rumania the inaugural chairman of the State Planning Commission was Gheorghiu-Dej himself, First Secretary of the party and Minister of National Economy.[6] Vasile Luca, Minister of Finance, was one of its most influential members.

It was later made known that here too the two antagonists clashed constantly, Luca allegedly sabotaging all the major plans by refusing the financial aid necessary for their fulfilment.[7] Dej relinquished this post on 23 April 1949, when Miron Constantinescu, the youngest member of the Politburo, was appointed to it. Constantinescu saw an opportunity to put his doctrinaire concept of the state into practice. He quickly gained ascendancy in all state activities through his control of and influence in the Planning Commission, the cadres of which he filled with specialists

[5] C. N. Jordan, *The Rumanian Oil Industry* (1955).
[6] See speech by Gaston Marin at the CC meeting of Nov. 1961 (*Sc.*, 12 Dec. 1961).
[7] Ibid.

and technicians. Moreover the Planning Commission was to have its own services, established in all central organs as well as in the more important local ones, to see that planning was effective and the plans carried out. This created yet another administrative network, supervising and directing the other main administrative network, already subordinated to the pressures of the party echelons. When Constantinescu was removed from all his posts in 1957, one of the charges levelled against him was that his leadership of the Planning Commission had been unrealistic, based on violent means of achieving his goals and on false statistical results designed to conceal the failures.[8]

But here precisely lay the main problem of the new régime in 1948–9, when economic planning was due to begin and when the state was to become the totalitarian employer as in the Leninist definition of a dictatorship of the proletariat. This problem was where to find the capital needed for investment, the vast supplies of raw materials for industrialization and, most pressingly, the technical and managerial personnel for all the posts on which would depend the functioning of the entire state economic machine. Other Soviet satellites had begun to grapple with the problem earlier than the RPR. As from 1946 (Poland) and 1947 (Czechoslovakia, Bulgaria and Hungary), all the other people's democracies had already had their experience of planning. Even if their first two- or three-year plans were called 'reconstruction' and did not fully express the idea of abolishing underdevelopment through rapid industrialization, the mechanism in itself and the more specialized personnel it necessitated had already been in operation before the major industrialization plans came into being. In the RPR the first one-year economic plan was to start only in 1949 and only as a timid rehearsal. It suffered from a woeful lack of experts, technicians, and managers; it also lacked the skilled manpower necessary to begin large-scale industrialization.

In the resolution of the Central Committee introducing nationalization, the party leadership had shown its awareness of the manpower problem. It asked the party organizations to ensure 'the best mobilization of the working class for the new tasks which face it in the promotion of the national economy'.[9] It urged them to concentrate especially on the raising of cadres for the economic posts of command, on the help to be given to the new directors in

[8] Ibid. [9] *Rezolutii*, i.

the reorganization of the nationalized enterprises, and on the training of technicians and workers in the efforts to create industry.

As far as the creation of cadres is concerned, it was decided to adopt the three ways already tried not only in the Soviet Union in 1928–9 but also in the other people's democracies during the reconstruction plans of 1946–9. These were: (*a*) giving the workers a direct share in the conduct of the state; (*b*) transforming workers into intellectuals through education; and (*c*) using and re-educating the specialists taken over from the past.[10] These three methods of producing technicians were the only rapid ones open to the party and government. The technical training and education of the young generation obviously needed more time. The first technical schools and courses were set up only in 1949 in the hope that they would fill some of the positions needed in the Five-Year Plan scheduled to begin in 1951.[11] But it was impossible that they should produce quickly enough the vast numbers required even for the first one-year plan. Yet the list of the responsible posts as issued in a Decision of 17 January 1953 was as follows:

(*a*) Heads of institutions and of state and co-operative economic organizations and enterprises.
(*b*) Directors-general, directors, and heads of independent departments of ministries, institutions, and enterprises, of co-operatives and public organizations and functions similar to them.
(*c*) Technical managers and chief engineers.
(*d*) Chief and principal accountants.
(*e*) Chiefs of working sites or production sections.
(*f*) Judges, prosecutors, and state arbiters.
(*g*) Leaders and responsible heads of administration in scientific, educational, literary and artistic institutions.
(*h*) Inspectors of national and regional competence attached to the units specified under paragraph (*a*) above.

[10] I. Lorincz, 'Role of Soviet Experience in the Creation of a New-Type State Apparatus', *Justitia noua*, no. 5, Nov. 1954.

[11] In the Soviet Union such 'responsible posts' have certainly existed in the past, for both the civil and criminal codes refer to them under the name of *dolzhonostnoye litso*; they probably still exist. Although a number of western writers on Soviet state structure (notably the American scholar J. Barrington Moore) have dealt at length with this institution, so far no list of such key posts in the Soviet Union has come to light. It is not unlikely that the RPR list given here is either a translation of or an adaptation of a hitherto unpublished Soviet original. (See G. Ionescu in Cretzianu, ed., *Captive Rumania*.)

(*i*) Regional delegates of the State Committee for the Collection of Agricultural Products.
(*j*) Heads of departments attached to the executive committees of regional, city, and district People's Councils.
(*k*) Legal advisers of ministries and other central agencies of the state administration and heads of legal departments.
(*l*) Chief editors, deputy chief editors, and chief departmental editors.
(*m*) Secretaries-general of newspaper offices.
(*n*) Heads of health units.
(*o*) Administrators of pharmacies.
(*p*) Elected employees who exercise functions paid by the organizations that elected them.
(*q*) Secretaries of the offices of ministers and deputy ministers.
(*r*) Station masters of the principal railway stations.
(*s*) Commanders of vessels of the merchant navy.
(*t*) Heads, administrators, and leaders of economic sections, departments, and similar units, of canteens, workshops, and all other sub-units organized on the principle of independent management, even if they are not actually corporate bodies.
(*u*) Heads of state stores and of co-operative commercial enterprises.
(*v*) Heads of security and fire brigade sections.
(*w*) Deputies or legal substitutes for persons having the duties listed above.[12]

These posts covered both the industrial-economic posts required by the plans and the political-administrative ones required by the people's councils. Their creation could not be further delayed and was actually announced only fifteen days after the launching of the first One-Year Plan. The total number of people needed for this double operation can still not be calculated accurately. The only way of doing so would be to multiply at least some of the twenty-four categories by the tens of thousands of central and local units requiring such specialists in the whole country. How these posts were filled in the first year it is difficult to imagine. According to a later pronouncement (1950) of the party, 'in the responsible posts of the state-apparatus, the percentage of workers had grown from 24.2 to 40 per cent'.[13] This would confirm the

[12] RPR Council of Ministers Decision no. 139, 17 Jan. 1953.
[13] Resolution of the plenary meeting of the CC of the RWP concerning results of verification of party members, July 1950 (*Rezolutii*, i).

impression that up to the first Five-Year Plan less than half of the managerial and responsible posts were in the hands of workers either brought directly into management or after a brief training. The other and greater part were either given to former technicians or were left vacant. The system of 'nomenclatura' was also initiated then and has remained operative, as in the Soviet Union, ever since. It provides the most efficient method of establishing party control over the appointments in all kinds of jobs and at all levels.

The problem of the necessary manpower and especially of skilled workers for the period 1949–51 was solved in the same way as that of the 'cadres', that is to say the emphasis fell on those workers already employed in industry.[14] Until new contingents of skilled workers could emerge from the technical schools which were only just beginning to function, the productivity and discipline of those workers already employed in industry should rise by virtue of the fact that a fundamental change had taken place in their relations with the 'employer'. A new rule was assigned to the trade unions in this respect. The resolution of the plenary meeting of the Central Committee of 22–24 December 1948 on trade union problems defined the new régime as 'a form of the dictatorship of the proletariat'. It stated that within it, the trade unions 'represented the mass of the proletariat'.[15] But their task was changed. In the state enterprises, which were now the common property of the working people, the unions were called upon to organize the efforts of the working class for the fulfilment of the plan. They must fight against the old attitudes of the workers towards work. They should raise production. They should create and organize socialist competition in production. They should see that all enterprises adopted the collective contract 'by which better links should be formed between the general interest of the state and those of the workers', which has since become the general contract for all nationalized enterprises.[16] At the same time the system of payment by piece-work, more easily controlled by norms of production, was everywhere substituted for the old

[14] 'The rapid training of tens of thousands of skilled workers is accomplished not only by training new personnel but also by re-training old workers' (*Rumanian News*, 3 June 1953, quoted by N. Spulber, *The Economics of Communist Eastern Europe* (1957)).

[15] *Rezolutii*, i.

[16] Ibid. no. 31 (res. of 22-24 Dec. 1948).

system. Trade unions were asked to control the working in future of both the collective contracts and norms of production.

The first One-Year Plan was voted by the Grand National Assembly on 27 December 1948. It came into force on 1 January 1949. Little is known of its original provisions. It was designed to bring about an increase of 40 per cent over the general production of 1948. The investments planned for it were 82,000 million lei. On 2 March 1949 a Labour Manpower Office was created. It was to co-ordinate all the requirements of all factories, plants, or offices for filling vacancies for new or old positions, and to affix its mandatory rubber stamp on any appointment or dismissal of any employee.[17]

PEOPLE'S COUNCILS AND THE REORGANIZATION OF JUSTICE

The contradiction between the existence of people's councils in the constitution and their non-existence in the code of laws (not to speak of their actual existence) was solved by the passing of the Law on People's Councils of 15 January 1949. The law carefully failed to define the power of the people's councils in the state. This was done by both constitutions, that which preceded the law and that which followed it in July 1952.[18] In the latter the fiction was still maintained (Art. 2) that the people's councils were 'the political base of the RPR', but while the Grand National Assembly was 'the highest organ of state power' (Art. 22), the people's councils were 'the organs of state power in regions, districts, towns, and rural localities' (Art. 51). They were thus the local administration as opposed to the central administration, to which they were categorically subordinated. Article 66 of the Law on People's Councils proclaimed: 'The Grand National Assembly, the Presidium and higher people's councils exercise control over the activities of subordinate people's councils. The Cabinet, the competent central administrative agencies and the Higher Executive Committee exercise control over the activities of subordinate executive committees.'

The duties of the people's councils were: the realization of the principles of socialist order in local life; to mobilize, and organize direct participation of the masses in the administration of their interests; to carry out the local plans and participate in the realization of the state economic plan; to strengthen brotherhood among

[17] Decree on Labour Manpower Office, no. 86, 5 Mar. 1949.
[18] See below, p. 215.

the workers, regardless of race, language, and religion; to raise the cultural and political level of the masses; to protect public health; to organize the provisioning of the workers and to put down sabotage and speculation; to promote equality between men and women and establish maternity wards and schools; to supervise the citizens in the carrying out of their legal obligations. According to Article 19, these deliberately unspecified duties were to be carried out by guiding and controlling the 'social, cultural and economic activities of the institutions . . . within the jurisdiction of the people's councils', which must set up and carry out the local plans and budgets, examine problems of a general nature, and so forth. In addition, various decrees and special laws added to the duties of the people's councils. These duties ranged far and wide. They included setting up 'architectural sections', increasing cotton cultivation and crops, taking a census of children between the ages of 1 and 14, transporting lumber products, keeping communal agricultural registers, organizing sales co-operatives and agricultural associations, taking steps to control disease in pigs, organizing the public guard, supervising markets and fairs, securing the payment of state and local taxes, and so on. The people's councils were also in charge of all the national drives and campaigns for various purposes. All this had to be done with incompetent and scanty personnel and with grossly insufficient financial means; in the 1954 budget their entire allocation was still some 5 million lei, compared with the 32 million assigned to the central administration.

County, district, urban, and rural people's councils were set up under the law, there being originally sixteen for the regions, including the city of Bucharest. After various administrative reorganizations and following the 1952 constitution, there were eighteen regions. Members were to be elected by the people, but initially, in April 1949, they were in all cases appointed by the government and took office in July of that year. In September 1950 a law prescribing the methods of election was passed, and in October the old front organization was revived for the elections, and voting on a single-list principle took place on 3 December. Decree No. 391 of 24 September 1953 introduced supplementary restrictions on those eligible to vote for the councils, but it was already known that the lists had to be approved by the Minister of the Interior (People's Security Division) and by the party. The party also controlled the appointment of the officers of the executive committees which ran the councils—a president, one to three vice-presidents, and a secretary. From the start a great effort was made to give the councils a working-class composition; sixty-two of the presidents of the provisional people's councils set up in April 1949 were skilled workers as against four intellectuals, and in the rural councils a similar effort was made to integrate the 'working peasants'. From 1953 there was a greater emphasis on the smaller regions—communes—which were given proportionally more representatives in the regional councils.

But the Rumanian people's councils, like those in the Soviet Union, have never acquired power of decision or leadership in the state. Their functions have oscillated between being a representative institution, part of the constitutional set-up, and a harassed local administration, overburdened and despised. If only because of their existence, however, they did alter the old administrative structure of Rumania. As Teohari Georgescu said, in introducing the bill establishing the people's councils, 'a kind of dictatorship of the proletariat was taking shape'.

The establishment of people's councils was paralelled by the introduction of a system of justice modelled on that of the Soviet Union, the main features of which may be summarized as a repudiation of the separation of judicial and executive powers, the subservience of judges to state and party policy, and the setting up of military and other special courts to try persons deemed socially dangerous. In Rumania the death penalty for treason and economic sabotage was introduced on 12 January 1949, Rumania being the first Eastern European country to extend the death penalty so widely. A law for the organization of justice of 2 April of that year was framed on the principle of defending the social and economic structure of the state and entrenching people's democracy. It provided for the 'election' of people's assessors, who were in fact nominated by the party, people's councils, or other mass organizations. Decree no. 187 of 1949 abolished the penal code of 1937 and incidentally made provision for the punishment of 'acts considered as dangerous to society' even if these were 'not specifically provided for in the law as crimes'.[19] By Decree no. 79 of 31 March 1950 the judiciary was

[19] Free Europe Committee, *Penal Law and Justice in the Communist Regime of Rumania* (N.Y., 1952).

in effect collectivized, private legal practice being abolished and a system of lawyers' co-operatives—known as the State Notariate—being created, sharing fees with the Ministry of Justice. A special law of 12 August 1950 imposed the death penalty for crimes against order and domestic freedom, against national independence and sovereignty; it applied to 'negligence by workers leading to public disaster', theft and destruction of military equipment, and plotting against the state, spying and economic sabotage. The subordination of the organs of justice to the operation of such state objectives of policy as the execution of the Five-Year Plan was completed and elaborated in 1952.[20]

Many institutional forms of the old Rumanian state were rapidly being changed to mould them into patterns which might fit into a dictatorship of the proletariat. Education, religion, the administration of minorities and of the security forces were all submitted to thorough reforms between August 1948 and March 1949. At the same time the intellectuals were being made to conform to the party line.

EDUCATION

The reform of education mainly aimed at changing the curriculum within the existing school system. The decree of 3 August 1948 embodying the reform[21] preserved the four traditional phases of Rumanian schooling—kindergarten, elementary, medium, and secondary. Kindergarten for children between 3 and 7 remained optional. Elementary schooling was to last for seven years but free compulsory schooling was limited to four years. This was linked with elementary courses for illiterates of any age lasting for one to two years. Here the communist régime wished to make a special effort to reduce illiteracy in order to 'raise the cultural level of the people'. Medium schooling was to last four years and was divided into four types of school: lycées, teacher training schools, technical schools, and professional (trade) schools. Here again it was in the number of units granted to each category and in the advantages open to pupils in certain schools as compared with others that the main distinction lay. Thus the lycée, the old mainstay of higher education in Rumania, was

[20] See below, p. 218.

[21] Law for the Reform of Education, 3 Aug. 1948, published in the Official Gazette of the same date.

considered by the new law as a theoretical school, with inevitably more limited prospects for the pupils because technical education was regarded as more valuable. Secondary education comprised universities and polytechnics, and institutes for higher learning (these last were set up in various industrial, mining, and agricultural centres and other localities).

Technical schools flourished. On them the régime depended for a quick flow of new technicians and experts to cover the growing needs of state planning. However, disappointment was to come soon enough; as early as 1953 the whole system of quick technical training had to be slowed down and changed. But in 1948 great hope was placed in these schools. They came under the direct supervision of the various economic or social ministries which, in consultation with the State Planning Commission, decided on the number of graduates they were to produce. There were schools for the various industries, for agriculture, finance, administration, public health, plastic and other arts, gymnastics and sports, and so on. Trade schools too were given a great impetus, but they differed from those of pre-war Rumania. They were open to youths of between 14 and 16 years of age who had already passed through the four years of compulsory education. The courses lasted for two to three years and were again under the direct supervision of the appropriate economic or social ministries. Finally, there were schools for unskilled workers of between 18 and 25, with courses lasting for six months to a year and designed only to pass them into the category of skilled workers.

In the universities and polytechnics courses lasted four to six years and in institutes of higher learning three to four years. Here again the latter, under the supervision of the economic and social ministries, fared better at the beginning than the old universities under the traditional supervision of the Ministry of Education. Their goal was to 'form experts needed in state production'. Institutes were set up for agriculture, the oil industry, forestry, public health, &c. Workers' faculties also were instituted, with a two-year course, the graduates of which could then apply for studies at the universities or institutes of higher learning to which they were attached. These were open almost exclusively to industrial and agricultural workers who had already obtained a four-year school certificate and who had distinguished themselves in production.

Class distinctions among the candidates to universities were less sharp. According to a decision of the Inter-University Council of 7 October 1948, candidates of any social origin could be admitted to practical faculties (polytechnic, medicine, textiles) up to a quota of 70 per cent of the total. But 30 per cent had to be recruited exclusively from sons of workers and of peasants owning less than 3 hectares of land, and according to their academic marks. In theoretical faculties (arts, law, economics) the respective percentages were to be 80 and 20 per cent. The sons of workers were required to bring certificates from the factories or plants where their fathers worked, the sons of poor peasants from the communal authorities, later the people's councils.

The essential change in education lay in the substitution of Stalinist propaganda and indoctrination for the objective teaching of various subjects. From the kindergarten, said Gheorghe Vasilichi, then Minister of Education, when presenting the law, the children must be trained for communal life.[22] In schools, the teaching of religion was banned; but that of Marxism-Leninism was made compulsory for all classes. The Russian language was introduced as a compulsory subject in the fourth year. Textbooks of grammar, history, and sciences were hastily rewritten in order to belittle and distort the Rumanian tradition, while putting the Soviet Union on a pedestal. Slav influence was stressed in every field of Rumanian culture.

THE RUMANIAN INTELLECTUALS

The Rumanian, like the Czechoslovak, intellectuals have shown a much more passive attitude under communism than their Polish, Hungarian, or even their Bulgarian counterparts. As far as the Rumanian intellectuals are concerned, there are two main reasons for this. First, there was no bridge or even positive contact between the great majority of the intellectuals of Rumania and the régime. In general, the Rumanian intellectuals, mostly of democratic or right-wing political inclination, adopted and maintained after 1944 an attitude of either non-co-operation or downright hostility towards the government. At the time too, the party dominated by the 'workers' group', carried out with an almost

[22] Cited by Ciurea, *Captive Rumania*, p. 211.

obsessive distrust and suspicion a deliberate policy of discrimination against and persecution of the intellectuals. Secondly, what left-wing intellectuals there were—the group of academics and the few veteran writers who had sympathized with or actively supported the party—were, even if the party had encouraged them, not numerous enough to act as a real intermediary between the rest of the intellectuals and the régime, let alone between the régime and the country. As it was, many of these intellectual sympathizers became estranged after the fall of Patrascanu. In addition, the purge of Ana Pauker in 1952, with its inevitable anti-Semitic undertones, alienated the Jewish left-wing intelligentsia, which had also to suffer in the general campaign against 'Zionism'.

In its prejudice against intellectuals, however, the régime drew a distinction between the technical and the creative intelligentsia. Towards the technocrats, the attitude of the party was quite different. Ever since the first of the economic plans in 1949, the need for specialists became very acute. After 1949, therefore, a partial truce was called in the persecution of the former bourgeois architects, agronomists, engineers, scientists, doctors, and all kinds of technicians. Some of them were released from prison, quickly rehabilitated, and quickly given jobs of responsibility. At the same time, after 1949 the party was doing its utmost to pump new contingents of young specialists, directly earmarked for immediate employment, from the newly-created technical universities.

The creative intelligentsia, however, was never considered indispensable by the leadership, and especially by Gheorghiu-Dej. Patrascanu or even Ana Pauker would have been more inclined to think that the writers and artists of a communist régime are in a way its symbol or the measure of its vitality. Dej and his workers' group could never bring themselves to think of them as anything more than a luxury which all communist states must apparently have. Artists of all kinds in a dictatorship of the proletariat were only justified in so far as they sang and pictured the efforts and success of the working class in this dictatorship. Dej's principles in this matter were simple and obstinately held. His determination to hammer them home was unabated. Since his accession to the leadership, and especially since 1956, he had attended in person practically all the writers' congresses and had tried forcefully to persuade them directly of the principles of the infallibility of the party in artistic guidance and of those of a strict and stern socialist realism. The working class should inspire the artists' work and not vice versa.

The first echelons of the Agitprop of the Rumanian Workers' Party called to direct and organize the works of the creative intelligentsia have, in some respects, reflected during the last fifteen years the worst features of both the 'Muscovite' and the 'native' groups in the party. From the 'Muscovites' they adopted the distrust of the Rumanian mind and its western orientation: they wanted the intelligentsia to seek inspiration only from Russian sources and to acknowledge the dominant influence of Russian culture in the past and of Soviet culture for the present. From the 'native' workers they took over the suspicion that the intelligentsia as a social group was indelibly marked by instinctive anarchic tendencies or by petit-bourgeois liberal instincts. Thus the team of Chisinevschi, Rautu, and Roller, which was in control of Agitprop between 1946 and 1953, clamped down ruthlessly on any creative expression which did not conform completely with the narrow straight-jacket they imposed. They removed from public and intellectual life practically all intellectuals with pre-communist reputations and saw to it that the sons and daughters of these people were similarly victimized. They mechanically transplanted Zhdanovist socialist-realism without flexibility or even imagination. From their hack writers and artists they demanded an undeviating example of humble and stern discipline.

Those writers and artists who consented to the rôle which Chisinevschi and his associates demanded were for the most part very meagre in talent. But one or two were very able indeed. Of the latter the name of Mihail Sadoveanu springs most readily to mind. Sadoveanu had had a deservedly great reputation for a quarter of a century. Politically he had always been left wing, though he had been made much of by all the previous régimes and governments in Rumania. When the communists took power, he rather surprisingly consented to be designated by them as the official grand old man of socialist literature and ideology in Rumania and, more surprisingly, consented to have his novels purged of strong nationalistic and occasionally anti-Russian sentiments. The case of George Calinescu, a most important Rumanian critic, was in some ways similar. So was that of a body of university professors who, like Sadoveanu, had been grouped around

Viata romaneasca and who had rendered fellow-travelling services to the party in opposition. The group was headed by Parhon, Stoilov, Traian Savulescu, Iordan and George Oprescu who, with many of their assistants and students, were accorded great honour at the price of toeing the party line. The same applied to a group of former surrealist artists and writers, who, together with the western surrealists, whose doyen, Tristan Tzara,[23] was a Rumanian, joined the communist ranks in the late 1930's. (Tristan Tzara himself was a member of the French Communist Party.) Geo Bogza, Aurel Baranga, and the painter Jules Perahim were the natural leaders of this group; they were also acknowledged by the party and declared themselves willing to serve. Other writers who had also served the previous régime, such as Victor Eftimiu, Zaharia Stancu, and Maria Banus, added their well-known names to the list. There was as well a group of intellectuals and artists gravitating around Patrascanu: Belu Silber, Lena Constante, Harry Brauner, Marcel Breslasu were among the most brilliant and were soon scattered.

Even men who had served prominently under the royal dictatorship were taken up provided they would comply. The party hired them and fully employed them. Two important novelists with the same surname, Cezar and Camil Petrescu, headed this strange group. The first had a great reputation as a novelist, but had always been associated with right-wing political and ideological groups and had been the director of King Carol's party newspaper at a time when flattery to Hitler's régime was the keynote of Rumanian official propaganda. Poets such as Cicerone Teodorescu, Eugen Jebeleanu, Radu Boureanu, and many others with little reputation were also hired.

Most of these belonged to the older group of writers with prewar reputations who expressed their willingness to serve. By doing so even the greatest of them tarnished their professional reputations, and although in some cases the motives which prompted them were not necessarily dishonourable, they achieved nothing for creative culture, saw many of their respected colleagues languish in prison, and changed in no degree the brutal attitude of a régime which basically despised them.

In addition to this older group there was a younger generation

[23] Even his *nom-de-plume* was based on a pun in the Rumanian language: *Trist in tara* (sad in the country.)

which Chisinevschi, Rautu, and Roller nurtured and from which they hoped much. But this group did not turn out as the Agitprop expected, nor was it what the public, even the new public of young workers, technicians, and administrators, would have liked. The leaders were the poet Mihai Beniuc, A. E. Baconski, Labis, the novelists Petre Dumitriu, Dan Desliu, Eugen Barbu, and Marin Preda. Among critics there was Ovid Crohmalniceanu, Paul Georgescu, Silviu Iosifescu, Ion Vinte, and among playwrights Horia Lovinescu, Ana Novak, and Aurel Baranga.[24]

Some of these writers were not without ability but they turned out works of crudest propaganda nature, ridiculing the previous régimes and glorifying the present, denigrating the capitalist west and adulating the Soviet east. (Here mention must be made of the particularly tendentious work of falsifying Rumanian history and replacing the standard histories and history textbooks by the revised historical determinism version in which the determining factor was always Russia.)[25] But even so the régime was not satisfied. The works of the new writers, according to the party, did not show enough interest in the realities and achievements of the new socialist state. The party was continually having to pressure them in their choice of themes. The pressure was greater than the party had expected it would have to bring to bear on 'the sons of the revolution'. Like their elders, the young writers submitted manuscripts which either questioned in a Mayakovskian way the finalities of the revolution or were inclined to choose themes which contained nothing of present-day Rumanian life. They were historical reconstructions or abstract digressions. The specific fight which the party had to wage with the older writers was thus to continue with the younger ones. It was a matter of evasion. The writers would collaborate with the party, produce books and works, toe the ideological party line in public meetings, collective resolutions or messages, and in individual articles or studies, but their works—that is to say the work that they maintained that

[24] See a report by Petre Dumitriu himself in *Ost-Europa*, Dec. 1960.

[25] A very authoritative survey of this subject is: Michael Rura, *Reinterpretation of History as a Method of furthering Communism in Rumania* (1961). It deals especially with what may be described as the 'Roller period', 1947–54. During these years Roller was in charge of revising Rumanian historiography in general and history textbooks in particular. In 1948 he published the first new *History of Rumania* changed in 1952 to *History of the RPR*, which for some years remained the only authorized histories. These, 'besides bearing little resemblance to history as represented by standard pre-war classroom texts', are largely compilations of selected data which are ideologically treated.

they should write, if their books were to be sold and so fulfil their function of contact with the 'masses', would have very little to do with this kind of 'building of socialism'. Resolution after resolution of the Rumanian Workers' Party and of the leadership of the Writers' Union selected by the party stressed almost with despair the need, indeed, the moral obligation of the writers to go down to 'the field' and to see with new eyes and describe with new enthusiasm the achievements of the communist régime. But as the next resolution would show, the writers failed to do so. Either they had once more evaded the issue or, if forced to accept it, they had shown a yawning indifference towards it which was easily detectable in the lack of naturalness and in the boring effect of the work on its readers.

Oddly enough, the party had greater difficulty in 'educating' the new group than in 're-educating' the old. These young people were inclined to believe in the socialist ideas, even if they understood that their realization in the Soviet bloc and especially in the RPR was only a deformed and probably wrong example of what they should be. The party tried to wring from them the works they wanted by a mixture of criticism and cajolery. The latter took the form of the most blatant feather-bedding. They were given special treatment and the most extravagant financial rewards. The earnings of Rumanian writers published by the communist régime were considerably higher than those of their Polish colleagues or indeed of those of any of the other people's democracies. Some Polish writers were quoted as telling a group of Rumanian writers that while the communist government in the RPR fed their writers better, the communists in Poland allowed their writers to bark freely.[26] In spite of that, however, the attitude of the writers towards their mentors in the Agitprop remained sceptical: the goose failed to lay the golden egg.

RELIGION

The day after the education decree appeared on 4 August 1948, a decree on religious cults was published. The election of a new Orthodox Church Patriarch, Justinian Marina, a member of the Communist Party, had been secured on 24 May 1948. Justinian was forty-five years old and was then almost completely un-

[26] A Rumanian communist writer who 'chose freedom' in 1960 told the author of this conversation with a Polish writer in Warsaw.

known.[27] With the new decree the state, which in Rumania had always controlled the Orthodox Church in certain respects (the clergy was paid by the state), entirely took over the direction of ecclesiastical affairs. All estates and funds belonging to the Church were nationalized, and hence its need for the direct support of the state became more acute. By selecting the Patriarch and the majority of the members of the Holy Synod, of the National Church Council, and of the administration of the partiarchate from Communist Party members, and by subjecting the entire organism to the direct financial control of its ministries, the government took over and transformed the Orthodox Church into another of its branches. As in the Soviet Union, the Church was relegated to an ancillary rôle in the communist state.[28] This did not mean that the whole Orthodox Church in Rumania was corrupted. As will be seen, Rumanian priests formed one of the most numerous categories of political prisoners or detainees in the labour camps. Nor does it mean that the religious or spiritual life of Rumania was to be destroyed, or that the Church ceased to be the focal point of this life. But as a political operation, the seizure of the Orthodox Church was successfully effected in 1948.

With the Roman Catholic and Greek Catholic (Uniate) Churches of Rumania the matter of control was not so simple and brutality had to be used to bring these institutions, with their close links with the west, to heel. The status of the Roman Catholic Church was governed by the Concordat of 10 May 1927, which recognized the separation between that Church and the state. This status began to be violently attacked in the press and by the leaders of the Rumanian Workers' Party during the first months of 1948. During this period, Catholic priests and higher clergy were arrested in great numbers.[29] On 17 July 1948 the government unilaterally abrogated the Concordat.[30] Catholic

[27] As a village priest he had hidden Gheorghiu-Dej, in August 1944, in his house for a few days.

[28] 'Our clergy has before it the example of the Orthodox clergy of the Soviet Union' (*Sc.*, 22 Feb. 1948).

[29] In a note of protest of 2 October 1948 to the Ministry of Foreign Affairs of the RPR the Apostolic Nuncio mentioned that in many instances the priests were brought by force to the local prefectures. In the offices of the *Siguranta* (state security police) they were intimidated, threatened with imprisonment, with separation from their families, with deportation and even with death. Those who resisted the initial acts of violence were thrown into underground cells, ill treated, subjected to exhausting questioning and finally set free only when, broken by the inhuman treatment of their gaolers, they agreed to sign.

[30] Decree No. 358 of the Grand National Assembly.

schools were taken over by the state. Catholic priests were dismissed and arrested. A decree of 18 September 1948 reduced the number of Roman Catholic sees from six to two. The two remaining bishops were arrested on 20 and 26 June 1949. An attempt by the government to substitute a Catholic hierarchy friendly towards it met with a violent reaction from the Vatican. The Roman Catholic Church remained in a state of total opposition to the régime.

The Greek Catholic Church (Uniate) was dealt with, if such comparisons are relevant, more in the way in which the Social Democratic Party was forced to 'merge' with the Communist Party. After a long campaign of false promises and invitations by the Orthodox Church to 're-enter the bosom of the Mother Church', a congress was summoned in Cluj on 1 October 1948, designed for precisely that purpose. Thirty-eight delegates and 423 priests signed an act confirming their passage to Orthodoxy. The Greek Catholic hierarchy excommunicated them almost immediately. The government reacted by arresting a great many priests and by depriving, on 8 November 1948, all four Greek Catholic bishops of their bishoprics. On 1 December 1949 all dioceses and religious communities of the Greek Catholic Church were abolished; their property passed to the state with the exception of that taken over by the Orthodox Church.

The same choice, suppression or collaboration, was offered simultaneously to the other religious denominations in the RPR: Protestants, Jews, Moslems. But as these denominations were formed by specific national groups, their relations with the new state of the RPR forms rather part of the latter's policy towards minorities.

MINORITIES

The Politburo of the Central Committee of the Rumanian Workers' Party in December 1948 issued a resolution on the 'national question'.[31] It reiterated Stalin's thesis of equality in diversity among nationalities liberated from the class yoke; and also quoted a passage from his speech on the signature of the Soviet-Finnish treaty of friendship of 6 April 1948, in which he spoke of equal sovereignties. It denounced the 'nationalities of the treasonable clique among the leadership of the Yugoslav Com-

[31] *Rezolutii*; American Jewish Committee, *The Jews in the Soviet Satellites* (N.Y. 1953).

munist Party'. It recalled the firm stand taken by the Rumanian Communist Party against suppression or persecution of minorities and its efforts since the end of the war to establish friendly relations within the new Rumania between the Rumanians and other peoples living in the same territory: Hungarians, Jews, Russians, Ukrainians, Bulgarians, Greeks, Albanians, Germans, and Serbs. It castigated once more Patrascanu's chauvinistic attitude towards certain minorities. It drew the attention of the party organizations to the fact that there was still ample evidence that not enough effort was being devoted to the fight against chauvinism, especially at a moment when the class enemy was attempting to spread anti-Sovietism in the country.

This did not mean, continued the resolution, that the Politburo was ignorant of the chauvinistic anti-Rumanian tendencies among the national minorities themselves. In the Magyar Popular Union, for instance, the old leaders who had only recently been superseded had, in the face of the class enemies, held on to the wheel far too long with the help of the pernicious slogan of 'Magyar unity'. The same problem had occurred also among the Germans in Transylvania (Saxons) and the Banat (Swabians) who, in spite of the great advantages they had drawn from the new régime, were firmly holding to the attitude of 'German unity', in this aggravated by the fact that even youth was infected by Nazi ideas. Even among the Russian and Ukrainian populations in the country, continued the resolution, the 'kulaks' were active; more literature in Russian must be produced for them. The Albanian, Bulgarian, Greek, and Serbian minorities were also chauvinistically inclined. The Serbs were particularly dangerous since Tito's estrangement from the communist fraternity. But the main thrust of the resolution was directed against Zionism, which formed 'a nationalist, reactionary political movement of the Jewish bourgoisie', which tried to isolate the Jewish working population from the people among whom they lived and continually tried to sabotage the Democratic Jewish Committee.

This attack on Zionism coincided with the anti-Zionist, anti-Israeli policy adopted by the Soviet Communist Party from September 1948, and was also a consequence of the elimination of the Jewish opposition in Rumania. The Democratic Jewish Committee, which emerged in June 1945, represented the attempt to conscript the Jews in a common front; it was based on an alliance of Jewish communists, Social Democrats, and others, and was opposed in the main by the Union of Rumanian Jews and the Jewish Party. At a conference held in Bucharest in December 1947, the Democratic Jewish Committee had demanded the elimination of this Jewish opposition, in consequence of which the Jewish Party voluntarily dissolved itself that same month, while the Union of Rumanian Jews was disbanded in November 1948. But as the political and economic plight of the Jewish community worsened, so demands to emigrate increased: by June 1947 150,000 Rumanian Jews had registered for emigration to Palestine, compared with 70,000 at the end of 1944. The Democratic Jewish Committee then began a campaign against clandestine emigrants; with the co-operation of the Hungarian and Czech authorities, emigrants were returned to Rumania where they were arrested and given prison sentences; from December 1947 they were also deprived of citizenship and their properties were confiscated. In 1949 Zionist leaders were imprisoned and tried, with wide publicity, and in April of that year the welfare institutions of the Jewish communities were taken over by the state. Anti-Zionism reached a new climax in the autumn, with reports of the trial of Rajk and his Jewish co-defendants, and in March 1950 a new conference of the Democratic Committee expelled six prominent Jewish leaders for not fighting Zionism with sufficient energy.

Jewish religious observances were regulated not under the decree on religious cults of 1948 but under a statute published in the Official Gazette of 12 July 1949, according to which only one Jewish community could exist in each town, each to belong to the Federation of Jewish Communities. A Supreme Rabbinical Council of twelve was appointed by the Minister of Religion on the recommendation of the Federation. The merger of the various communities was effected in July 1949 and the Council appointed in September, when Grand Rabbi Moses Rosen was appointed its president. Rosen, who had assisted the Federation to toe the party line, was appointed Grand Rabbi after Grand Rabbi Alexander Safran fled to Switzerland in December 1947. At the 1950 conference of the Democratic Committee he broadened the basis of the attack on Zionism by including in the denunciation such 'warmongers' as Morgenthau, Baruch, and Benjamin Cohen.[32]

[32] 'Rumania', by N. Sylvain, in American Jewish Committee, *The Jews in the Soviet Satellites*.

The expected persecution of the Serbian minority began in earnest only in May and June 1951. Ten to fifteen thousand Serbs from the Banat, living on the shores of the Danube up to a depth of 50 kilometres, were brutally 'evacuated' and deported to the Baragan plains. The measure coincided with the active military preparations then being taken on the Rumanian-Yugoslav frontier in the cold war against Tito. Similar treatment was meted out to the Turkish minority in the Dobruja, the scattered remnants of which were evacuated from that province during 1951 and 1952 and deported in terrible conditions.

The reorganization of the Magyar Popular Union was a quite different and largely a political matter. Here a new and younger group of the strong Hungarian wing within the Rumanian party, with strong industrial affiliations, took the lead and thus influenced the decision. Alexandru Moghioros was asserting his ascendancy at the expense of Vasile Luca, already suspected of being a 'Magyar chauvinist'. A new leadership was appointed to the Union which pledged itself to collaborate with the new state. It was, however, strongly in favour of 'decentralization', which was eventually to be achieved by the creation of the Autonomous Magyar Union by the 1952 constitution. These changes did not materially affect relations between the state and the Reformed Calvinist and Unitarian Churches, with their entirely Hungarian congregations. But the widespread persecution of the Catholic Church affected many Hungarian priests and laymen.

POLICE AND SECURITY FORCES

In terms of establishing the dictatorship of the proletariat the creation of the militia on 22 January 1949 and the dissolution of the old rural and urban police were considerably overdue. Since 1945 the police had been entirely restaffed, but the militia had not yet been brought into existence, although this institution was now working in nearly all the other people's democracies and was considered as 'a symbol of the dictatorship of the proletariat'. It was supposed to protect the rights and liberties of the working people as well as the property of the state. It issued and checked identity and ration cards for every person living in the RPR. Itself a branch of the Ministry of the Interior, it had as many branches as there were new regions, including one for the city of Bucharest, divided into eight commands for each of its districts. It employed roughly 40,000 people.

In the RPR, however, its influence remained relatively small compared with that of the security forces.[33] These numbered some 165,000 men who carried out joint police and army operations. Among them were included the crack elements of the Guards of Patriotic Defence, set up by Bodnaras between April and August 1944 and subsequently continuously strengthened, and the People's Security (*Directoratul General al Sigurantei Poporului*), the real and almost omnipotent secret police. The secret police was divided into eight sections: information, operations, research, counter-espionage, discovery of hostile elements, technical, cadres, and secretariat. It controlled the activities of all departments as well as those of the party. It has played and is still playing a decisive rôle in the state and in the maintenance of the régime in control and power. The co-ordination of the security forces with the army was brought about in 1948, when the 'People's Army' was also reorganized so that it might correspond to the needs of the people's democracy. The 'Higher Political Directorate of the Army' (*Directia Superioara Politica a Armatei*) was founded on 28 March 1948.

Thus the legal, cultural, and political framework of the dictatorship was almost entirely completed.

COLLECTIVIZATION, MARCH 1949

In the first five days of March 1949 the government and party approved three measures affecting agriculture. On 2 March the last 'land reform' was passed, the state expropriating all agricultural property over 50 hectares.[34] The victims were mostly genuine farmers who could not be reproached with 'absentee-landlordism' and most of their farms were, indeed, highly mechanized and modernized. The owners were evicted overnight and deported to unknown destinations by the militia. Their houses were occupied at once. Scenes of horror were widespread. This procedure was different from that accompanying the agrarian reforms of 1945 when expropriation had not been accompanied by persecution of the owners. Now, however—and this was the other big difference—there was no mention of the land being distributed

[33] See H. S. Aronovici, *National Security in Rumania* (N.Y., 1956).
[34] Law of 2 Mar. 1949.

to those who tilled it. This time the state took possession, and either handed it directly to those state farms which already existed or else turned the adequately equipped ones into collective farms. Almost 1 million hectares thus seized went to increase the surface of the 'socialist sector of agriculture'.

Then in the course of a meeting which lasted two days the Central Committee decided on the fundamental 'tasks of the party in the fight for the strengthening of the alliance of the working class with the working peasantry and for the socialist transformation of agriculture'.[35]

In the wake of both these moves there came the setting up without any further delay of collective farms wherever possible. By the end of the year there were already fifty-six such farms in existence. Their growth was at first slow, but in 1950 it was to gain momentum.

The Central Committee resolution of 3–5 March 1949 was and has remained the basic text on collectivization : it is still the clearest statement on Rumanian communist agricultural policy. The solution of the peasant problem, it stated, was the main and most difficult task facing the dictatorship of the proletariat and the construction of socialism. In practice this was true, because if there was to be any socialist planning at all, then the problem of integrating agricultural production within the national income could be solved only by increasing the socialist sector of agriculture and thus directing it, through socialist trade and socialist finance, towards the main centre of execution of the plan. Moreover, if there was to be any social progress in a people's democracy it should appear in the reduction of the endemic poverty in the countryside.

The party, as stated in the resolution, found there were five non-socialist categories of agriculture in the countryside. There was first the 'agricultural proletariat', landless peasants, a mass of about 256,000 families, who worked for the kulaks. Their situation was different from that of other agricultural wage-earners, working for the state. Their aim, and the aim of the new state, would be to absorb the 'proletariat' in the brigades of the collective farms.

The great majority of the agricultural holdings were in the hands of the poor peasants who formed the second category. Most of these possessed plots of up to 3 hectares of land which formed

[35] *Rezolutii*, i.

57 per cent of the total area of all holdings. This claim in the resolution was true only in the exaggerated interpretation of the basic statistics published by the Rumanian communists at the time and must be accepted only with reservations. Thus the general breakdown of the size of the individual holdings in 1948 was:

Size of individual holdings	*Per cent of total area in 1948*	
Less than 1 hectare	7.1	
1–3 hectares	26.2	
3–5 hectares	24·4	
		57·7
5–10 hectares	23.0	
10–20 hectares	10.6	
		33·6
20–50 hectares	5·7	
Over 50 hectares	3·0	
	100.00	

Source: *Probleme economice*, Sept.–Oct. 1948

The owners of less than 3 hectares were just over half (33 per cent as against the 24 per cent) of those owning between 3–5 hectares. The resolution stressed that all these plots were unproductive and in many instances scattered over more than one lot. These 'poor peasants' would thus undoubtedly prefer a different form of production.

The 'middle peasants'—a third category—were, according to the resolution, producers of three-fifths of the entire agricultural production and represented almost 34 per cent of the number of holdings (the 33.6 per cent made up by the category of those owning between 5 and 20 hectares). Only after 1947 had it been decided that the 'middle peasants' should include also those owning between 10–20 hectares. (The first calculation, which some leaders of the Communist Party as well as some socialists still adhered to in 1947, was that the middle peasants could not own more than 10 hectares. Thus in his report to the 1947 Congress of the Socialist Democatic Party Barbu Solomon had stated that the agricultural proletariat held up to 5 hectares and the middle peasants up to 10 hectares, respectively 3,321,468 and 453,715 heads of families).[36] The 'middle peasants', stated the 1949 resolution, were the main allies of the working class in the countryside.

[36] *Libertatea*, 8 Oct. 1947.

They were to be attracted into the work of building socialism, which was also common sense, for the larger and better equipped the farms, the easier was the formation of a state-controlled co-operative around them.

The fourth category was formed by the kulaks (*chiaburi*), who were not defined in terms of land owned but by the fact that they use hired labour on their farms. The fifth had been the remnants of the landowning class, whose property, however, had just been 'completely liquidated by the state'.

In the socialist sector the state farms, because of the elimination of the landowning remnants, had been extended to 500,000 hectares or 43 per cent of the arable surface of the country. The resolution stated that the village co-operatives must be reorganized and play an important part in the future. Machine-tractor stations (MTS) were also to be set up.

The party then repeated its basic Leninist principle that socialism cannot be built only in towns, and that it was inextricably linked with the socialist transformation of agriculture. It recalled Lenin's dictum that individual private ownership 'produces capitalism and bourgeoisie constantly, spontaneously and in mass proportions'. The only answer to the peasants' land hunger and the need for building socialism was the collective farm. Here the resolution attacked the Yugoslavs for having ignored the fundamental laws of collectivization.

The policy to be adopted, therefore, could be summed up by the old slogan : to lean on the poor peasants, strengthen the alliance with the middle peasants, and wage a ruthless war on the kulaks. Those party members and organizations who had confused kulaks and middle peasants were reproached by the resolution. So were those who had antagonized the latter and thrown them into a state of unnecessary solidarity with the kulaks. Against the latter special discriminatory measures were decreed. These applied in their relations with the other peasants, in fiscal policy, in the delivery of quotas and credit facilities, and in preventing them from acquiring more land. They were to be contained and only liquidated in the end.

Co-operation was presented as a necessary institution for the future, but from the context it was obvious that it was the trade and distribution co-operatives, as the main link between the agricultural producers, which were being considered. Mention was made too of peasant 'associations in work', especially for the purpose of making use of the state tractors. The usefulness of such associations lay especially in the fact that they brought about the amalgamation of small, unproductive patches of land. The state farms were to progress through mechanization and through drawing on the experience of Soviet agronomy.

Above all, continued the resolution, the collective farms would set the seal on the socialist transformation of agriculture. A model statute was to be drafted at once for all of them which should include the principles that no kulaks be permitted to join, that the former owners could keep a plot of land near their house, and that there should be equal distribution of products. They should be set up only with the approval or orders of the Central Committee of the party and of the government. It was the duty of the party to control and to foster this action directly and through the people's councils, 'which must carry out a class policy'.

Compared, therefore, with the doctrine of the 15th Congress of the Russian Communist Party in 1927, which afterwards became the basis of Stalin's collectivization in 1929, the agricultural policy of Rumania (as of other Cominform Eastern European countries) differed in that it did not proclaim the liquidation of the kulaks but only their containment, and did not urge immediate and total collectivization but rather a progressive and well-prepared action. When compared with Tito's policy, it differed in utterly rejecting the idea of allowing the middle peasants (and the kulaks) to join production co-operatives while retaining their property rights over individual plots of land or farms.

INDUSTRIALIZATION, DECEMBER 1950

The chairman of the Planning Commission, Miron Constantinescu, advised by a considerable team of Rumanian economists, Soviet experts from the Gosplan, and Eastern European colleagues from Comecon, could only prepare the directives of the first Five-Year Plan in time for the meeting of the Politburo of 13 April 1950. This meeting drafted the principles and directives of the 1951–5 plan. The directives became law on 16 December 1950, when they were adopted by the Grand National Assembly, only two weeks before they were due to come into force. This unusually short interval—the directives of the Five-Year Plan are usually published some six to twelve months before their enforcement—

suggested the difficulties with which the documents had been drawn up. Consultations with individual enterprises had been reduced to a minimum; basic statistical data were in many cases based on wishful-thinking. The 'balance estimates'[37] were arbitrary; many of the accompanying documents were incomplete.[38]

Yet this was a most ambitious and rigidly conceived plan.[39] Moreover it was soon accompanied by the supplementary slogan, which lasted for over two years, of 'Let us fulfil the Five-Year Plan in four years'.

Investments during the five years were to total 1,330,000 million lei (calculated at 1950 prices; at the official rate of exchange equivalent to £3,160 million), and were to be allocated as follows:

	Per cent	
Industry, of which:	*51*	
Capital goods:		
Oil	9·7	
Natural gas	0.9	
Electricity	11.0	
Coal	2.0	
Metal & engineering	12.9	
Other	5.6	42.1
Consumer goods	9·3	9·3
Agriculture & forestry	10.0	
Transport & communications	16.2	
Building, distribution, social, cultural, administration, &c.	22.4	48.6
	100.0	100.0

Source: As for note 39 below.

The machine-building industry, 'the pivot of industrial development of the national economy . . . which will produce the necessary equipment for the oil and mining industries, the tractors and

[37] A term which in communist economic terminology describes the balance sheets of raw materials, manpower, and investment on one side and distribution between branches and factories on the other.

[38] These are, or should be: (1) global statistics; (2) production programme; (3) technical development programme; (4) investment and building programme; (5) raising of the people's standard of living programme; (6) wages and employment programme; (7) cost of production plan; (8) financial programme; (9) the national economy estimates; (10) regional breakdown of the plan; (11) estimate of income and expenditure of socialist economy; (12) norms for using raw materials and fuels; (13) bill of goods for essential products; (14) foreign trade plan. On the problem of planning in Eastern Europe see Jan Marczewski, *Planification et croissance économique de démocraties populaires* (1956) and sect. 3 of Spulber, himself indebted to Marczewski for earlier research.

[39] *Law for the Five-Year Plan of Development of National Economy of the RPR for the years 1951-5* (Buch., 16 Dec. 1950).

agricultural machinery, &c' was given great emphasis. The plan also provided for the productivity of labour to be raised by 57 per cent. Planned production for 1955 of principal commodities was as follows:

Production Targets of Principal Commodities, 1955

Crude oil	10.0	million metric tons
Coal	8.5	,, ,, ,,
Natural gas	3.9	million cu. metres
Cement	2.9	million tons
Lumber	3.5	million cu. metres
Electric power	4.7	million kwh
Steel	1,252	thousand metric tons
Pig iron	800	,, ,, ,,
Iron ore	740	,, ,, ,,
Rolled steel	828	,, ,, ,,

The stress laid on the production of electric power was usual in communist planning. Production in Rumania had hitherto been small. The planned increase was to be based partly on hydro-electric developments, partly on the wider use of lignite. The target for crude oil was 'ambitious and optimistic',[40] having regard to the decline in output since the peak year of 1936. Despite the fact that the main purpose of the plan was to convert Rumania 'into a country with a developed socialist industry and with a mainly mechanized socialist agriculture', the target for tractors was only 5,000, for tractor ploughs 6.3 thousand, for reapers and binders 2.5 thousand. Production of textiles (in sq. metres) was to amount to 267 for cotton cloth, 39 for woollen cloth, and 42 for silk fabrics; for footwear the target was 20.7 million pairs.[41]

It was also announced that the standard of living of the 'working masses' would constantly improve, so that by 1955 it would be '80 per cent higher than in 1950'. By that date there would also be approximately 3 million workers, technicians, and office workers in the 'national economy', representing an increase of 38 per cent over 1950. The working class was expected to increase by 570,000 men and women. In 1955 the population would receive, through state trade and co-operatives, 1,235,000 tons of bread, 165,000 tons of sugar, as well as the textiles and footwear specified above.

[40] *Petroleum Press Service*, Apr. 1951.
[41] *Vneshniaia torgovla*, no. 2, 1951.

The Rumanian plan represented, therefore, still an elementary plan of all-round development and industrialization. Like the Yugoslav, Czech, or Bulgarian long-term plans, it essentially reproduced the pre-war Soviet plans of industrialization and development on a Rumanian scale. It, however, overlooked completely the fact that the various Soviet five-year plans had themselves suffered many failures, while their successes were mainly due to the enormous resources of land, raw materials, and manpower upon which Russia could draw. Nor did the plan take into consideration the fact that the iron ores necessary for heavy industrialization could be provided, in default of trade with the west and now with Yugoslavia, only by Soviet Russia. This was expensive both because of the distance and because of the unfavourable rate of exchange of any Soviet products bought in Rumania in roubles. Last but not least, the plan partly overlooked the question of financial or technical equipment for the investment plan and contingents of technical cadres and skilled workers.

The main Rumanian architect of this plan, Miron Constantinescu, was an odd combination of two differing and opposing trends. He was a rigid doctrinaire in economic planning, following faithfully the Stalinist line of absolute control and centralization. From a national point of view, however, he was inclined to oppose the tremendous Soviet economic demands on Rumania.[42] In this he had something in common with the Yugoslavs, whose purely economic policy he none the less deplored. His position was therefore diametrically opposed to that of his main foe in the party, the Hungarian Vasile Luca. Luca shared with the Yugoslavs the more pragmatic and realistic approach to running the economy and the finances of the country for more immediate purposes, such as getting food and consumer goods to the workers from the reluctant, ultimate source, the peasants. But Luca was an old Comintern-type communist for whom everything that was done by any Communist Party was only for the glory of the Soviet Union, to whose ultimate purposes all their action should be subordinated.

The plan was linked even before its application to two other projects. One was a ten-year plan for the electrification of

[42] He signed the first agreements for the dissolution of the Sovroms in Moscow in May 1954, and was given the credit for having brought about this improvement in Soviet-Rumanian economic relations.

Rumania.[43] This, appearing about a year or so after the law for the people's councils, strikingly recalled Lenin's principle: 'Soviets plus electrification equals Communism.' Although divided into two five-year plans, so that it would be repeated in the provisions of the general plans, the electrification plan was to be considered as a separate undertaking.

The other and earlier project was the construction of a Danube–Black Sea Canal.[44] This was decided on by the Politburo on 25 May 1949, and at once transformed into law, although it was not even mentioned in the first two one-year plans. In the preamble of the law it was, moreover, specifically mentioned that the project had been 'undertaken' on the initiative of Comecon. Certain authors as, for instance, Jan Marczewski, are inclined to believe that this project was part of the massive one of building an 'Eastern Ruhr' to which Soviet iron ores and coke would have been indispensable. Transportation would have been assured through a double canal: Black Sea–Danube and Danube–Oder–Rhine.[45] These authors acknowledge that the project received the instant approval and financial backing of the Soviet Union which otherwise was refused to the main Rumanian projects embodied in the national plans. This would seem to confirm the other interpretation, namely that the canal answered to certain urgent military plans of Stalin, the most likely being that of sending as many small Soviet vessels as possible up the Danube in the event of an aggravation of western-Soviet relations about Yugoslavia.[46]

In Rumania's case, whatever the ultimate economic or strategic purposes of the Black Sea–Danube Canal may have been, this project had quickly become a monstrous agglomeration of labour camps. Directed to work on it, as on many other similar 'project sites', were every kind of arrested or detained victims of the régime. They included members of the former democratic parties,

[43] 15 November 1950. It forecast the following:

	1950	*1960*
Installed power	740,000 kw.	2,600,000 kw.
Available power	600,000 kw.	2,500,000 kw.
of which:		
Thermic	550,000 kw.	1,665,000 kw.
Hydraulic	50,000 kw.	853,000 kw.
Power per sq. km.	2.53 kw/sq. km.	10 kw/sq. m.
Power per head	37.5 w/head	150 w/head.

[44] Decision of 25 May 1949 (*Rezolutii*, i).

[45] *Planification*.

[46] The abandonment of this project at the very beginning of the 'peaceful' Malenkov-Khrushchev era would also seem to confirm this.

members of the middle classes, recalcitrant members of the intelligentsia, 'kulaks', farmers dispossessed of their land, 'saboteurs' or 'idle workers', Catholics, Orthodox priests and laity, Zionist leaders and rank and file, the Yugoslav population from the shores of the Danube, Saxon farmers from Transylvania, Turks from the Dobruja—all these categories came under one law or another of the dictatorship of the proletariat and, as such, were shuttled ceaselessly between prisons and re-education camps. The situation was similar in Bulgaria and Hungary where, however, 'deportation' was the most common feature.

WESTERN PROTESTS

The many flagrant violations of human rights occurring in the East European states gave rise to energetic protests by the western governments and the United Nations. On 2 April 1949 Great Britain and the United States, as guarantors, with the Soviet Union, of the peace treaties with the three former German satellite countries, sent the Rumanian, Hungarian, and Bulgarian governments sharply and in the main identically worded notes. These notes recalled the long series of violations of the undertakings on human rights these governments had assumed through the peace treaties and asked that they immediately stop the inhuman acts which accompanied their political and economic 'reforms'.[47] On 11 July 1949 the Soviet government informed the British and American governments that it considered their action to be an interference in the affairs of the three countries. In September of that year the two western governments asked the fourth session of the General Assembly of the United Nations to take the matter up. The Assembly referred this demand to the International Court for advice. The Court stated on 30 March 1950 that in its opinion there was a breach of the peace treaties and that the governments concerned should appoint an arbitration commission to investigate the situation. All three communist governments refused to do so. On 3 November 1950 the General Assembly issued a resolution sharply condemning these governments. The practical effect, however, was nil. Full information of the steps taken by the western

[47] 'The disregard shown by the Rumanian Government for the rights and liberties of persons under its jurisdiction . . . has indeed become so notorious as to evoke the condemnation of free peoples everywhere' (U.S. Note; see *Interpretation of Peace Treaties with Bulgaria, Hungary and Romania,* International Court of Justice, *Pleadings,* &c.: Advisory Opinions of March 30th and July 18th 1950, p. 28).

governments was given to the people of Rumania, Hungary, and Bulgaria for the purpose of maintaining their morale through the broadcasting services of western stations. In Rumania the maquis gathered strength and were in some places linked to spontaneous resistance to collectivization by the peasants, of which more will be said later.

9

The Stalinist Apex, 1950–2

THE years 1950–2 may be described as those of the culmination of Stalinism; they were also years during which in Rumania, as in the other satellite countries, the economic and political strains of government were the most severe. The prime ministers and their colleagues of states which were theoretically sovereign but in practice closely controlled by the Soviet Union have been described aptly as 'hated by the people, mistrustful of each other and regarded in Moscow as expendable'.[1] Hence the wave of cabinet changes, purges, and dismissals in all the countries of Eastern Europe. Before describing the fundamental political shake-up in Rumania, which culminated in the 1952 purge of the top leadership, it is necessary to give a brief outline of the features which made the régime the object of a general loathing and execration which was intensified by severe economic hardship.[2] These features were above all the ruthless mobilization and control of labour in the attempt to fulfil the industrialization programme, the enforcement of agricultural collectivization, and a marked worsening of the economic situation caused by policies imposed by the Soviet Union.

THE MOBILIZATION AND CONTROL OF LABOUR

Although great numbers of individual industrial workers were absorbed into the state apparatus, at no time was there a crystallization of the will to leadership in industry and other fields of production of the workers as workers, either through the trade unions or through workers' councils. Control of management was from the first denied to them. The technical intelligentsia both old and new, and especially the party, saw to it that no 'workers' opposition would endanger appointments to the key posts in industry of individuals intent upon the immediate problems of production.

[1] RIIA, *Survey 1952*, p. 165.
[2] Exacerbated by the currency reform described on pp. 203-4 below.

There was no time or inclination for groups of uninstructed workers.

In the RPR the status and conditions of the workers were decided not by the workers themselves but by two organizations, both of them creations and servants of the new state. One was the ineffectual General Confederation of Labour. The other was the Labour Manpower Office, established in March 1949, later to be taken over by the Central Office of Labour Reserves, established in May 1951 and directly responsible to the Council of Ministers. The Manpower Office, in collaboration with the Central Planning Commission, listed the jobs to be filled and controlled all appointments and vacancies within the framework of the economic plan, which affected all factories and plants. The Directorate of Manpower Reserves 'distributed any available skilled or non-skilled labour reserves in rural or urban areas, in accordance with the requirements of the national economy' and supervised also the annual drafting and training of 45,000 to 55,000 'young workers', as authorized by a special decree of 8 May 1951. The local people's councils were put in charge of drafting the requisite numbers into these reserves.

The most important of various decrees and laws regulating labour conditions was the labour code of 8 June 1950. Designed to implement the Five-Year Plan, this regulated collective agreement and employment, norms, wages and salaries, hours of work and rest, &c. Under it the main rôle of the trade unions was to negotiate the collective agreement, which was signed by a union official indirectly appointed by the party and the head of the enterprise (usually state), whereby the workers 'assumed' obligations to fulfil and exceed norms of production. The collective agreement and the norms were the pivots of the entire system of employment.[3] While provision was made for discussion of the agreement by the workers with the union committee of the enterprise, the usual purpose of the discussion was to increase the production target set by the Ministry. Failure to live up to the obligations undertaken in this way was punishable under the 1948 penal code and its later amendments, while a law of 1949 imposed the

[3] Art. 27 of the labour code laid down that 'The respective Ministries, in agreement with the respective trade unions, will establish working norms for all production branches, functions and specialities, fixing the quantity and quality of production or of operations which wage and salary earners are bound to perform during a definite time, under normal working conditions.'

death penalty for crimes endangering the security of the state or the development of the national economy. Two other decrees made the dependence of the employees even more complete. The first[4] stated that all workers must have work-cards punched and kept up to date by the employers. The second[5] prohibited manual workers, clerks and technicians of state enterprises and agencies, construction projects and mass organizations, from leaving their employment without the prior consent of the head of their work unit, and the re-employment of any person not legally released from his previous job. At the same time absenteeism and strikes (theoretically impossible under a system of ownership of enterprises by the people) were also punishable under the penal code.

A chief means of paying minimum real wages was the extension of the piece-work system, which proved a potent means of raising production norms. This was reinforced by a Stakhanovite movement, which gained momentum after a decree of October 1951 under which Stakhanovites began to become a privileged class, and by the use of 'voluntary brigades' for unskilled work. A decree of 1950 made such work a compulsory part of the school curriculum. Through these means as well as through 'social competitions' the state employer could keep real wages down to a very low level.

In addition, forced labour became a more and more marked feature of the régime. It was introduced by Article 111 of the labour code, which affirmed the right of the Council of Ministers to call upon the citizens of the RPR to carry out certain types of temporary labour service. It soon assumed the character of enormous punitive-economic camps to which all charged with sabotage, of deliberately non-fulfilling production norms, or with absenteeism were sent for 're-education'. The ranks of forced labour were also swelled by victims of mass deportations undertaken to reduce overcrowding in cities as a result of industrialization. The Danube–Black Sea Canal project became notorious, as also the camps of Galati, Craiova, Vlahita, and Ialimota and the sites of the hydroelectric installations at Stejar-Bicaz. It is believed that the permanent population of the camps reached 180,000 persons, and the Canal project alone, divided into eight separate camps, used 40,000 prisoners, to which were added 20,000 so-called free

[4] Decree no. 41 of 31 May 1950 for issuing work cards.
[5] Decree no. 207 of 13 Nov. 1951.

workers. The system was officially recognized in all satellite countries as a means of 'socialist construction'.

FORCIBLE COLLECTIVIZATION

The depth of the opposition of the farmers to the policy of collectivization may best be gauged by the fact that the administration was compelled to modify its policy in September 1951. As late as March of that year the party had still been boasting of its successes; it was then stated that 1,029 collective farms had been set up in 1950, with 65,974 families of poor and middle peasants and comprising 265,640 hectares; 853 of these farms had been set up during the summer of 1950 alone. At the time there was no criticism of the methods employed for this speedy achievement, which was represented as a matter of self-congratulation. Those responsible for agriculture during the period were still Ana Pauker in the Secretariat and, to some extent, the Minister of Finance, Vasile Luca. The real situation behind the façade was that at the beginning of 1950 there were only 56 collective farms; the March 1951 total had been achieved in direct defiance of the principle of the free consent of the working peasants. The Russians were shown a façade of effective and persuasive collectivization being carried on at a pace comparable with that in Bulgaria and more recently in Hungary.

It was Pauker, Luca, and Georgescu who were later held responsible for 'combining a right-wing deviation with a leftist adventurist line' in 'treading under foot the principle of voluntary participation of the peasants in the socialist transformation of agriculture'.[6] In the winter of 1949 and throughout 1950 the peasants resolutely opposed the teams of collectivizers sent from the cities to expropriate their land and to organize them into brigades. The militia and even the army were brought in against the villagers. Long sieges were laid against entire regions, and with the help of some 'partisan groups' the peasants fought pitched battles against the forces of the government. The regions Dolj, Arges, Bihor, Bucharest, Timisoara, Vlasca, Hunedoara, and the part of Western Transylvania populated by Moti were the scenes of such events. Many summary trials of 'saboteur kulaks' took place during these years, sometimes ending in death sentences which sent

[6] Dej report to 2nd RWP Congress, 23–28 Dec. 1955 (Cominform Journal, 30 Dec. 1955, p. 7).

villagers with Rumanian, Hungarian, and Saxon names alike to the firing squads. One of the shocking revelations made by Dej at the plenary meeting of the Central Committee of November–December 1961 was that, allegedly on orders from Ana Pauker and Teohari Georgescu, mass arrests of peasants 'accused of failure to discharge their obligations towards the state' were carried out all over the country.

> In the name of the struggle against the kulaks [he said] more than 80,000 peasants, most of them working peasants, were sent for trial; more than 30,000 of these peasants were tried in public which provoked great concern among the peasant masses brought to attend these infamous frame-ups.[7]

The result was the expropriation of land for the setting up of the thousand or so collective farms. The farms were mainly concentrated in four regions, two of which had in common the fact that they contained large units of the Soviet army, controlling the shores of the Black Sea or the Danube, the other two the fact that they had previously been cleared of large numbers of former landowners. The great differences in methods of collectivization between a small country, entirely cultivated and with agrarian overpopulation, and the vast spaces of Russia were obvious. There was no 'virgin land' to which the peasants could be deported, thus fulfilling a dual practical purpose. Moreover the balance observed by Stalin between progress in collectivization and in mechanization had been totally overlooked by the Rumanian Stalinists. At the beginning of 1950 there were 102 Machine Tractor Stations (MTS) to 56 collective farms; in 1951 138 to 1,027. It must also be pointed out that most of the families which made up the early brigades were 'landless' or 'poor' peasants. They thus brought to the farms only their labour and their unproductive and scattered plots. All these factors made for an unpromising start for the collective farms, and the immediate general effects were shortages of food and agricultural products both for the internal market and for the export orders of the Russians.

Hence the modification in policy. In the summer of 1951 orders were issued that forcible collectivization was to cease. The provision that 'no collective farm should be set up without the prior approval of the Council of Ministers' meant a drastic reduction in

[7] Dej Report (*Sc.*, 7 Dec. 1961; *Agerpres Inf. Bull.*, 10 Dec. 1961).

numbers. Only 62 were set up in the whole of 1951. More attention was paid to mechanization; 5,000 more personnel were added to the annual number of 27,520 persons employed by the MTS. The activity of the stations was concentrated more exclusively on the land of the collective farms: by 1952 half the surface serviced by the MTS belonged to the collective farms.

More important, the Central Committee resolution of 18 September 1951 criticizing 'errors' in the policy of the socialist transformation of agriculture provided for a retreat from the full collective in stressing the importance of agricultural associations, i.e. voluntary productive associations in which each peasant retained his property but worked for mutual profit. The new associations were defined as

> agricultural associations known in the Soviet Union under the name of Toz [which] represent an inferior form of agricultural production co-operatives in which the land, the cattle, and the means of production are not collectivized, but remain the property of the associated peasants; in which the associated peasants by removing field boundaries pool together their plots of land for the purpose of raising agricultural production through the application of agro-technical means and the use of tractors and farm machinery in which the associated peasants work the land in common and solve in common all administrative problems.

This was an unexpected step for a régime which had taken its stand on the impossibility of building 'socialism in the countryside while maintaining private ownership'. It afforded a striking demonstration of the failure of collectivization in its Soviet form.

On 18 March 1952, that is when Luca and Pauker were already out of the inner leadership, the general introduction of a system of agricultural quotas to be handed over to the state by the owners of agricultural land was decided. It established a wide range of quotas by which 'all owners and cultivators of agricultural land were obliged to hand over agricultural products to the state at established prices'. All individual and collective farms were included, with the exception of those under half an acre in size. Compulsory quotas were fixed per hectare—for 'middle' peasants 300–350 kg per hectare, for kulaks between 590 and 825 kg per hectare. This amounted to a tax on production of between 20-60 per cent per hectare of the crop. To this were added the fiscal taxes, themselves also scaled on a discriminatory social tariff, and the fees to the MTS if and when their help was available. The quotas of kulaks could be increased by 25 per cent while those of collective farms in their first year could be reduced by 25 per cent. This seemingly more orderly system of obtaining crops from the producers was designed to replace the Pauker–Luca dual system of confiscating the crops whenever possible. The system of compulsory quotas remained in force until 1955, when the quotas were abolished and a system of 'contracting and purchasing' was introduced.

THE 1952 CURRENCY REFORM

The deterioration in the economic situation in Rumania during 1950–2 mentioned at the beginning of this chapter was in the main caused by the combination of the industrialization programme, Soviet exactions, and in addition the imposition of the satellite rearmament programme which was the Soviet riposte to the signature of the North Atlantic Treaty Organization. Even in the manipulated budgets produced by the RPR government, defence expenditure represented 17 per cent in 1950, 20 per cent in 1951, and 17 per cent in 1952 and 1953. Moreover one of the reasons advanced for the emphasis on heavy industry in the industrialization programme was the need for the increased production of armaments. Such an effort could not be made without straining even more the already meagre and exhausted resources of the country, and reducing even further the chance of 'financing' the non-defence industrialization projects of the plans. Chronic shortages of industrial and consumer goods inevitably made for renewed inflation, rising prices, and hoarding by the peasants who had anyway been antagonized by collectivization. A further lowering of the average standard of living of the industrial workers was also inevitable. In these circumstances the administration resorted for a second time to currency reform. The effects of the first currency reform had disappeared long since. Prices of staple foods were three times higher while wages had increased nominally only by 50 per cent. The second currency reform, decreed on 28 January 1952, established a new leu based on the ruble instead of the dollar, whose external value was fixed at 2.80 to 1 ruble. Internal rates for the exchange of old for new leu varied: for state enterprises, Sovroms, collectives, and other favoured classes the rate was 20 : 1; for private deposits 50 : 1 on the first 1,000 lei,

100 : 1 on the next 2,000, and 200 : 1 to 3,000 or over. For cash sums the rate was 100 : 1 for the first thousand, 200 : 1 for the second, and over that 400 : 1. Decrees issued at the same time fixed wages and prices at one-twentieth of their former level and reduced some postal and railway charges. Broadly speaking, the currency reform reduced purchasing power by more than two-thirds, with the state gaining what the population lost, although according to direct sources corruption at high level made the operation less fruitful than the reform of 1947. But the measure entirely failed to cope with inflation, for the peasants once more succeeded in amassing substantial cash balances by selling on the free market, while at the same time the plight of the industrial workers was greatly aggravated. Discontent flared into open strikes. Although in fact the reform had been prepared by Soviet experts, it was the Rumanian official in charge, the Minister of Finance, Vasile Luca, who was held to blame for its failure and for other economic ills. He was not to be the only scapegoat for Moscow's realization that detestation of all that is associated with Stalinism had reached a dangerous climax.

THE PARTY BEFORE THE PURGE

Before matters had come to this pass, a thorough overhaul of the party machine had been undertaken. This 'verification' of the party membership was undertaken as the result of a Central Committee decision of November 1948 aimed at eliminating 'careerist and opportunist' elements which threatened to sabotage the proletarian section of the party, as the result of mass admittance.[8] The investigation had lasted for eighteen months, from November 1948 to May 1950. It had probed deeply into each basic organization. A total of 200,000 investigators had been working, in the strange expression of the resolution, as a 'non-party *aktiv*', which means that they probably included members of the militia security police, the Ministry of Justice, and especially the armed forces. At the top, that is to say at the Central Committee level, the work of these investigators was co-ordinated and sifted by a triumvirate formed by Ranghet and Moghioros and headed by the old watch-dog of the party, the austere Constantin Parvulescu, president of the party Control Commission.

[8] See Dej's article, 'For Purity of the Party Ranks', Cominform Journal, 23 June 1950.

Before discussing the results of this 'verification' it is necessary to discuss just whom the party comprised before those 'verified' and found wanting were purged.

The first layer of members, recruited in 1945, was made up of the unattached (non-Social Democrat, non-National Peasant) workers, and of some workers from among the younger Iron Guardists. They had been admitted without any difficulty and at once had been offered responsible positions in factories and trade unions. A category of workers assiduously courted by the communists at the same period were domestic servants, who were particularly useful in reporting upon the houses where they worked. In the countryside recruiting among the peasants was, significantly enough, both scarce and for the most part clandestine. In as many villages as possible the communists tried to form action committees, in which four or five villagers could be relied upon to organize and to incite the others prior to events such as the agrarian reform.

To this category of socially privileged members, there was added during 1946 and 1947 the whole mass of troops of the Tudor Vladimirescu and other divisions. These divisions had been formed at first by prisoners of war in the USSR. Later they were augmented by large numbers of soldiers from the former Rumanian regiments fighting alongside the Soviet divisions against the Germans and of groups formed among administrative personnel engaged by the Soviet army in the provinces of Rumania in which it was operating. Also included at this time were professional and clerical staffs in state or private enterprises, seized either by the communists or by the Soviet army during the first year of occupation.

After the merging with the dissident Social Democrats in 1948 and the creation of the Rumanian Workers' Party, a third layer of membership was formed. Party ranks were swollen by the accession of part of the left-wing Social Democrats, by members of other smaller political organizations which were engulfed by the communists, and by some non-party members of the General Confederation of Labour.

The fourth layer was made up of those who had been invited since 1948 to join the new party on the basis of their success in any sector of the newly established administrative apparatus. They undoubtedly formed a very mixed group. Most of them, however, were young and the great majority considered party membership as essential to their careers. Skilled workers turned out by the two-year technical courses; peasants who had joined collective and state farms; students in elementary training schools or universities and institutes; the newly-formed administrative personnel of the people's councils: all these joined the RWP and were given a special place as being the product of party education. The older men of this last layer, who had known other dictatorships, considered their affiliation merely as another phase of necessary opportunism. With the younger ones the case was more complicated. Trained in their formative years by a communist state, they were unaware of any other political way of life. But apart from a small minority who went directly into jobs as activists, organizers, and secretaries, the rank and file's first duty towards the party was general administrative work; agricultural campaigns, fulfilment of industrial plans, general and local elections, and other overt activities were their main tasks. These operations were launched with the enthusiastic resolutions of the Central Committee and government, resolutions written like battle orders with every organization having its duty to perform.

Thus the party had become from the beginning mainly a machine for supervising difficult economic and administrative work. From a political point of view it lacked a unified sense of purpose. The rank and file were apathetic and insincere, the cadres inferior to their tasks. In the words of the resolution of July 1950 on the organization of the party as a result of the 'verification', 'the unwarranted attitude of the party organs which, faced with the increasing needs of the state apparatus, have not borne in mind the need to have powerful party cadres, has caused a great fluctuation of the party cadres'.[9]

That the cadres were still ill-equipped and inferior even in 1950 is best shown by the fact that from 1949 half of the party members had still to go through some urgent form of elementary training.

It was decided that the number of members of the party to be taught Marxism-Leninism would in 1950–1 be 323,862 as against 249,125 in 1949–50.[10] This presented enormous training problems. Of these, only about 20,000 would be able to attend the

[9] Rezolutia sedintei plenare a CC al RMP cu privire la resultatele verificarii membrilor de partid si la primirea nouilor membri in partid, July 1950 (*Rezolutii*, i).

[10] Decision of the CC of the RWP on the results of the school year 1949–50 and on the preparation of the school year 1950–1 in the party teaching (ibid).

party schools or universities already in being; 250 students were assigned to the A. A. Zhdanov higher school of social sciences, 200 to the Stefan Gheorghiu University,[11] and some 1,900 to the evening universities of Marxism-Leninism at Bucharest, Iasi, Cluj, Timisoara, and Targu-Mures. The remainder, the vast majority, were assigned to hastily improved schools with courses lasting three to six months, study circles on the Soviet Communist Party, and various evening courses in villages and towns. Those party members earmarked for full-time courses were given leave of absence from their everyday work. It can be seen from such a system that very few would get a real education.

The problem of education was interlocked with the still unresolved problem of youth in general. Since the end of 1948 the party leadership had shown a grave concern about the state of the party youth.[12] It was felt that a great mistake had been made in dissolving the Union of Communist Youth (UTC) on the ground that it was 'too narrow' and that what was needed was a new youth organization 'without class character'. Thus the UTC had been replaced by the 'Progressive Youth' based on the idea, now branded as mistaken, of 'uniting all youth' without distinction of class. The result was a heterogeneous, purposeless mass. This was again a crime to be laid to the door of Ana Pauker, Teohari Georgescu, Miron Constantinescu, and Patrascanu. In 1946 a Union of Working Youth (UTM) had been formed but simultaneously with a Young Villagers' Union, a Students' Union, a School Pupils' Union, a Young Magyars' Union, all of which pursued separate and often highly eccentric courses. At its plenary

[11] The A. A. Zhdanov school prepared ideological and political cadres—the future professors, political advisers, and newspaper editors. The Stefan Gheorghiu school prepared the leading cadres in the party organizations and the 'organizers, activists, secretaries and Agitprop personnel' (see article by Chisinevschi in *Pravda*, reproduced in *Sc.*, 26 Jan. 1952 & 4 Jan. 1953: 'The Future Cadres of the Intellectuals of the Party'). The curriculum of the first year at the Zhdanov school included the history of the CP of the USSR, political economy, dialectics and historical materialism, structure of the socialist state and of the RWP, history of Rumania, Russian language, and contemporary international politics. In the second year philosophy since Hegel was added to the course. The selection of students was based on the rule that no candidate could have had any previous political affiliation with the Rumanian CP during the war—an odd echo of Foris's leadership. Both schools were and are still under the supervision of the Agitprop and of the college of the Control Commission, which functions with the Bucharest organization. At the time of the purge and reorganization of the party, they thus came under Chisinevschi and Parvulescu.

[12] Resolution of plenary meeting of CC of RWP of 22–24 Dec. 1948 on the activity of the party among youth (*Rezolutii*, i).

meeting of December 1948 the Central Committee abolished all youth organizations apart from the UTM. The main ideological task of the UTM was to fight against the '*avant garde* spirit of youth'.[13]

The party was also having great difficulty with its organizational work. On 23–24 January 1950, before the 'verification' findings had been made public, it had been decided to set up an Orgburo again.[14] The Orgburo was made responsible for the general supervision of the organizational work, and made decisions on behalf of the Central Committee. It was to adjust the social composition of the party, which was described again as the source of the main evils. It was to streamline the bureaucracy and to cut red tape. It was also decided that the party Control Commission was to take a stronger stand and to punish those who infringed the programme, statutes, and discipline of the party. The agencies of the Control Commission were the party colleges, functioning within the orbit of the party district (regional) committees. The Control Commission was to have as many sections as its work required. To the three directorates—administration, cadres, and Agitprop—and four main commissions—workers, peasants, youth and women—there were to be added those dealing with industry, transportation, trade, supply, and other matters. It was again decided that the local leading organs would be organized on a territorial principle while the basic organizations would be created and function in factories, institutions, MTS, and collective farms. They were to number between 3 and 300 members and their main task was the mobilization of workers for the fulfilment of the Plan.

THE PURGE OF ANA PAUKER AND HER RECRUITS

The 'verification' resulted in a purge which eventually eliminated from the party 192,000 'exploiting and hostile elements'. This was more than 20 per cent of the total membership before the 'verification'. The undesirables had had a bad effect on the entire party; their influence had made itself felt in the work of all the organizations. They had been indiscriminately accepted, or rather entered on the books of the party, in 1945–6. Half of them, accord-

[13] 'In a series of organs of the Union of Working Youth there still exist rightist tendencies' (resolution of August 1953, ibid. ii).

[14] Decision of plenary meeting of CC of RWP of 23–24 Jan. 1950 on the tasks of the party in organizational work (ibid. i).

ing to the resolution which announced the results, had not even allowed themselves to be verified, either because they did not want to have the past investigated or because they had been only formally entered on the books. They were largely 'elements alien to the working class, morally corrupted people, careerists . . . fascists, bourgeois nationalists, exploiters, etc'.[15] As has been seen, they had been granted party membership by Ana Pauker when she was in charge of the huge and rapid mass recruitment.[16] Later, in July 1957 when Miron Constantinescu was also purged, but as a 'Stalinist' in the wake of the Malenkov–Molotov purge in Russia, he was found guilty of sharing the same errors in 1945, when he and Pauker were both in charge of the operation.

The massive purge, and in particular the implication of Ana Pauker, seemed to indicate that a struggle for power was going on in the party leadership. Moreover purges in the Jewish Democratic Committee, and especially an investigation into the affairs of the Jewish Union, which the party and judiciary had been carrying out since 1949, affected Pauker's relatives. An investigation into the Hungarian Committee similarly affected Vasile Luca. On 13 March 1951 a new step was taken in the party reshuffle. Elections to its leading organs were held throughout the nation and at every level. The operation was carried out swiftly. Suggesting that the party was to be 'rumanianized' (anti-Semitism was spreading in all the East European parties) and claiming that the best candidates would be 'workers who had already shown their mettle in responsible work', the Gheorghiu-Dej group succeeded in having elected to the party organs workers, technicians, intellectuals, and army officers who had been working in the state apparatus. The 'roots' of Ana Pauker's party were thus severed. Then in May 1951 came the celebration of the thirtieth anniversary of the party. Dej paid lip-service to her and Vasile Luca, when he mentioned them as the only two still in the party who had been in the leadership since the foundation, but they, in turn, acknowledged him as the sole leader. So did the whole party. From that moment Dej was supreme. He quickly began to consolidate his supremacy, and in this he was undoubtedly aided by the fact that he suited Moscow's requirements as an unquestionably orthodox communist but one who had the reputation of being less unpopular than those who were to be made the scape-

[15] Dej in Cominform Journal, 23 June 1950. [16] See above, p. 119.

goats for policy failures. Moreover Gheorghiu-Dej was a Rumanian, whereas Luca was Hungarian by origin and Pauker Jewish.

While the degree of responsibility as between Soviet pressures and between an internal struggle for power must remain a matter for speculation, between March and June fundamental changes in the Rumanian party leadership and a far-reaching reorganization of the government and party occurred. The first step was taken at a Central Committee plenary meeting held on 29 February–1 March 1952, when, after the uncovering of grave 'mistakes' and 'frauds' in the application of the currency reform of January committed by the Finance Ministry and the National Bank, both under Vasile Luca's control, he was invited to apologize. He then confessed the grave mistake he had made in discovering his right-wing deviation so late. At the same meeting it was found that Ana Pauker and Teohari Georgescu had shielded Luca by adopting a 'conciliatory line', and a letter was sent to the party members and organizations informing them. But according to the official account, after this meeting Luca rebelled against the decision of the plenum and held separate discussions with Georgescu and Pauker, with a view to taking concerted action against the decision.[17] Then, at a meeting held on 13 March of a Commission set up by the Central Committee to deal with the case of the three victims, Luca retracted his acknowledgement of his mistakes and was supported by Georgescu and Pauker. The explanation is probably that at the Central Committee plenum the three thought that they might get away with some compromise formula, but that later, seeing exactly what was contained in the letter to the party members and organizations, they realized that they were doomed and decided to put up a fight. During the same month Luca and those associated with him, the assistant Finance Minister and president of the State Bank, as well as Georgescu (Minister of the Interior) and the deputy Minister of Foreign Trade were dismissed. Then, at a second plenary meeting held on 26–27 May, the Central Committee, taking into consideration the fact that Luca had retracted his confession, had broken his pledge not to follow the party line unswervingly, had rebelled against the party decisions and had tried to drag other members of the Central Committee on the same course, unanimously decided to expel him from the party and to send him to be examined by the

[17] *Sc.*, 3 June 1952.

Control Commission. He was accused of directly sabotaging the currency reform, undermining the development of individual and collective farms, and protecting capitalist trade. At the same time Ana Pauker was severely criticized and refused re-election to the Politburo and Secretariat because she had 'helped and encouraged the rightist deviations of Luca and Georgescu', but since she had 'acknowledged some of her errors', for the time being she remained a member of the Orgburo and retained her government post as Foreign Secretary. Georgescu's 'conciliatory attitude' had masked 'an opportunist right-wing spirit', and he had taken no measures against speculators. The deviations of all three were linked with their living on a 'slope of aristocracy', having broken away from the masses. Pauker had earlier opposed collectivization and favoured private farmers; all three had contributed to increasing the cost of living, and at the time of the currency reform they had 'retained the wages of many workers and employees' because of their opposition to that measure.[18] The report of the plenum announced that Vasile Vaida, Minister of Agriculture, and Lotar Radaceanu, Minister of Labour and Social Welfare, had been dismissed, the latter also being dropped from the party organs.

This radical purge was accompanied by a reorganization whereby the Politburo was reduced from 13 to 9 members, the Orgburo from 17 to 11, and the Secretariat from 7 to 5. The new Politburo (elected at the same CC plenum) consisted of Gh. Gheorghiu-Dej, A. Moghioros, I. Chisinevschi, M. Constantinescu, G. Apostol, Chivu Stoica, E. Bodnaras, P. Borila, and C. Parvulescu. The candidate members were Dumitru Coliu, N. Ceausescu, and A. Draghici. The new Orgburo consisted of Moghioros, Apostol, Borila, Stoica, Pauker, Rautu, Florescu, S. Toma, L. Chisinevschi, and N. Ceausescu. The Secretariat was composed of the five first-listed members of the Politburo. Moghioros was in charge of the cadres, I. Chisinevschi of doctrine and ideology, Constantinescu of planning, and Apostol of questions concerning the workers and peasants. No new list of the Central Committee was published.

The new party leadership was certainly more cohesive than the old. Dej was now dominant; three strong personalities had been removed. But the leadership was more cohesive than the party as

[18] Ibid. 3 June 1952.

a whole. Within the new large ruling caste many pockets of vested interest had quickly and inevitably grown, each engaged in a covert or overt struggle for its own aims. There were also groups who, so to speak, enjoyed 'extra-territorial' privileges. These were the people who worked for the Russians in the Sovroms, the Soviet trade agencies, or even the Soviet forces, whose loyalty was not to the Rumanian régime but whose material privileges often exceeded those of the ruling communists.

Some of the divisions within the party were reflected within the new Politburo where, while Dej, Apostol, and Stoica represented the 'native group', Moghioros represented the Hungarian wing, Petre Borila and Chisinevschi the Bessarabian, while Bodnaras remained the representative of the armed forces and security service, being still Moscow's trusted agent. Constantinescu stood for the new intelligentsia. It was not that these men were identified with different ideologies, nor did they represent centrifugal forces. But they did represent interests which had to be taken into account.

On 2 June 1952 Gheorghe Gheorghiu Dej was appointed President of the Council of Ministers (premier). He combined this with his post of Secretary-General which he had held since the national conference of October 1945. This was an honour which he had long coveted. All five of his counterparts, the party leaders of the 'loyal' people's democracies, were also either presidents or premiers Gottwald and Bierut were heads of state of the Polish and Czechoslovak Republics,[19] Rakosi in Hungary, Chervenkov in Bulgaria, and Hoxha in Albania were presidents of the Council of Ministers. Thus Dej, albeit belatedly, joined the company of the 'little Stalins'. On 29 June he further elaborated on the dismissals of Luca, Pauker, and Georgescu in a speech which clearly revealed the failure of the industrialization programme. Thus Luca was blamed for 'retarding the development of heavy industry' and for holding up capital investments; 'hostile elements' in the financial-banking apparatus and the mining industry had resulted in under-fulfilment of the 1951 Plan. Luca had also encouraged kulak and other capitalists: 'tens of thousands' of kulaks were masked as middle peasants and even exempted from taxation; he had fixed speculative prices on the

[19] On 2 June 1952 Petru Groza replaced Prof. Parhon in this titular post in the RPR.

open market and encouraged capitalist trade and profiteering. He had bitterly resisted the currency reform. Pauker and Georgescu had pursued the same policy of opposition to the party line, and Pauker had obstructed the state purchase of agricultural products, held up the organization of more co-operatives, tolerated kulak penetration into collective farms, etc. Georgescu had lost 'militancy and class sense', which enabled such activities by hostile elements to take place.[20] Though the attack on Pauker could hardly be interpreted as anti-Semitism, because of the elevation of the Chisinevschis at the same time as her downfall, she was suspected of contact with the 'outside world', i.e. with foreign intelligence services, through Israel, where her father had died on 31 March 1952. His funeral had been delayed so that his son Solomon (who in an interview with the London *Daily Herald* on 2 November 1949 had denounced his sister for Jewish persecution) could return from Rumania, where he was his sister's guest. The continued contacts between the members of this strange family surprised many observers at the time. Rumours that Ana Pauker also held personal deposits in foreign banks made her still more vulnerable. The security services in Rumania and the Soviet Union were eager to stress 'ambiguities' in her conduct. A strong case could, therefore, be made against her, and on 5 July she was dismissed as Foreign Minister, being succeeded by S. Bughici. It was not, however, till 12 September that she was stripped of her last remaining post as vice-premier of the Council of Ministers. But Pauker was not formally tried, whereas Luca on 10 October 1954 was sentenced to death by a military court, although on appeal the sentence was commuted to life imprisonment.

Gheorghiu-Dej's version of this episode, as given at the Central Committee Plenum of November–December 1961, was that it was a landmark both in his own career and in the evolution of the party. He said that Ana Pauker and Luca, using their positions, controlled the party over the heads of the Politburo and the Central Committee and even of the First Secretary, who was overruled by them. 'It may be stated that throughout this period from September 1944 until their removal in May 1952 the Leninist standards were seriously infringed in the Party leadership.'[21] While it is true that Dej and the native group considerably

[20] RIIA, *Documents, 1952*, p. 267–9; Cominform Journal 29 June 1952.
[21] *Sc.*, 7 Dec. 1961; *Agerpres Inf. Bull.*, 10 Dec. 1961.

strengthened their position, and from that time assumed official control of the party, it must be remembered that what made this change possible was the shift of the Bessarabian wing. Borila, Rautu, Coliu, the perennial Bodnarenko, Bodnaras and, at the time, probably even the Chisinevschis, influenced as ever by the Ukrainian wing of the Russian Communist Party, which itself during the last years of Stalin was influenced by Khrushchev, preferred to back the more 'national' group of the party. Thus Dej was in fact exchanging for his previous alliance with Pauker, Luca, Bodnarenko, and Bodnaras an alliance with Borila, Rautu, Bodnarenko, and Bodnaras. That this change did not mean much from a basic political point of view, or especially from that of whether it could be thought of as 'destalinization', can be clearly seen both from the situation at the time and even better from the situation after Stalin's death. At the time of the purge, Stalin could have had no reasons for opposing it, for it was he who had appointed Dej as First Secretary in 1944, and the tight Soviet grip over Rumanian affairs was not jeopardized by the new coalition. Indeed, after Stalin's death the Rumanian party remained one of the most conservative and most reluctant to join in the destalinization practised by the Russian, Polish, Hungarian, or even Bulgarian parties. The Rumanian purge was thus intended to make the party less unpopular through a change of personnel without any substantial change of ideology or methods. The positive continuity was obvious in the fact that with the exception of the three main protagonists and later of Chisinevschi, the top echelon of the party remained unchanged. The negative continuity was shown by the rash decision to have Patrascanu, who had allegedly been persecuted by Luca and Pauker, shot in 1954 after a summary trial, thus removing the one man who might seriously have thought in terms of liberalization and destalinization. Preventive action was going to be taken later against Miron Constantinescu, another Rumanian intellectual suspected of liberalism.

All this being said, it remains to note that in spite of the cumulative power which Dej had assumed in the summer of 1952 as the First Secretary, allegedly in full control of the party, and as prime minister in full control of the administration, he skilfully avoided falling too soon into the trap of making himself known as Rumania's 'little Stalin' (as, for example, his Bulgarian colleague

Chervenkov). Perhaps on the one hand this was not in his nature: his approach was always more oblique, his attitude shrewder, and his preference for not over-playing the hand that had been dealt. But on the other, the writing on the wall was already plainly giving warning of the need for caution. From Moscow came increasing rumours of Stalin's decline. His death in 1953 was to be followed by changes in doctrine and policy by his successors. From the communist countries of Eastern Europe, including Rumania, came frequent reports of growing discontent and the dangers of open revolt, which indeed flared up with unexpected violence in the East German rising of 17 June 1953.

THE 'SUPERSTRUCTURE OF THE STATE'

On 8 July, a little over a month after Gheorghiu-Dej assumed the premiership, the new genuinely Marxist–Leninist draft constitution was published. The Rumanian People's Republic had always been defined as a people's democracy. It was placed in category 3 (*b*) of the four forms of states within the Communist orbit acknowledged and described by communist doctrinaires.[22] These were: (1) the Soviet state; (2) the Soviet Socialist Republics within the USSR; (3) the people's republics or the people's democracies, divided into (*a*) the Chinese People's Republic and (*b*) the smaller people's republics of Poland, Rumania, Outer Mongolia, &c; (4) the democratic republics such as North Korea, Eastern Germany, North Vietnam, truncated parts of a former unitary state. The Rumanian People's Republic, like all others in its class 'accomplished the functions of a dictatorship of the proletariat'.

What were these functions and how were they put into practice? In the first years of the existence of the RPR they were defined as follows:[23] to crush the exploiting classes, to defend the country against aggression from without, and to build up the economic-organizational and cultural-educational structure of the new

[22] See especially article by Silviu Brucan in *Sc.*, 25 May 1954.

[23] The doctrine of the communist state and implicitly of the popular democratic states has fluctuated noticeably since Stalin's death, fragmenting into different national theories: Poland, Yugoslavia, Rumania, etc. In the Rumanian state doctrine, since 1955 there have been controversial, if only tentative interpretations. It was therefore preferred to use here the version of the Stalinist period given by an authorized expert, L. Rautu, Deputy Director of the RWP Agitprop and close collaborator with Chisinevschi's and Yudin's Cominform Journal when it was published in Bucharest. The text of his long study, 'The State of People's Democracy and its Functions', appeared in *Sc.*, 29 Dec. 1951.

society. These were functions characteristic of the dictatorship of the proletariat in the first stage of its existence.

This first function of the people's democracy was very important because in Rumania there were still remnants of the crushed exploiting classes, particularly in the countryside. It was also important because the chief organizers of conspiracies against the RPR were abroad in the capitals of the imperialist states, especially in the United States. The second function of the state, the defence of the country against aggression, was crucial at that moment when the war preparations of the imperialists were mounting.

The third function arose from the dual definition given by Stalin of the functions of a dictatorship of the proletariat, that is: 'to use the state power of the proletariat in order to separate the working classes from the bourgeoisie' and 'to use the state power of the proletariat for the organization of socialism, for the abolition of classes'. In spite of the existence of a considerable non-socialist sector in agriculture and in trade, economic life in its essence was directed by the state economic plan. The economy no longer developed haphazardly, but in accordance with the policy of the party and of the government. The economic-organizational and cultural functions were a specific feature of the dictatorship of the proletariat. The capitalist state could never have such a function. The rôle of the state thus defined made it imperative for the party to consolidate the state. The party was the vital basis of the régime of the people's democracy.

These principles appeared as new provisions in the constitution finally approved on 24 September 1952.[24]

The first paragraph of the introductory chapter of the new charter announced that the RPR 'is a State of working people of town and country'. The second stated that this state came into being 'as a result of the historic victory of the Soviet Union over German fascism and of Rumania's liberation by the glorious Soviet Army'. The allegiance thus expressed to the Soviet Union confirmed in such a context the *de facto* relinquishment of sovereignty into hands of a foreign power, which had been refused by Yugoslavia. Article 86 defined the main internal changes which had taken place since the approval of the 1948 constitution: 'The Rumanian Workers' Party is the leading force of organizations of

[24] A. J. Peaslee, ed., *Constitutions of Nations*, 2nd ed. (1956).

the working people as well as of the state organs and institutions. All organizations of the working people in the Rumanian People's Republic rally round it.'

The dictatorship of the proletariat was most completely expressed in Article 2: 'The foundation of people's power in the Rumanian People's Republic is the alliance of the working class with the working peasantry, an alliance in which the leading rôle is held by the working class.' The soviets, or people's councils, as the main instrument of government in this dictatorship were acknowledged in Article 4, paragraph 2: 'The People's Councils are the political foundation of the Rumanian People's Republic.' Finally, the changes effected in the economic and social structure of the country since nationalization and other measures were expressed in Article 5, which stated that there were three social-economic forms: the socialist, the small-scale production of commodities, and the private capitalist. The latter, according to Article 11, still comprised 'kulak holdings, private commercial enterprises, small non-nationalized industrial enterprises'.

As in the 1948 constitution, there was no separation of legislative, executive, and judicial powers in the state. The Grand National Assembly was the unique expression of the will of the people in all its manifestations.

One innovation brought about by the 1952 constitution, and imported directly from Soviet law, was the *Procuratura*. This was vested with 'supreme supervisory power to ensure the observance of the law by the Ministries and other central organs, by the local organs of State power and administration, as well as by officials and other citizens'. It was divided into twelve directorates, staffed by well-trained agents and informers, tightly controlled by the party itself.

The constitution also announced the formation of a Magyar Autonomous Region, included in the list of administrative-territorial divisions given in Article 18.[25] Article 19 described this region as consisting of 'the territory inhabited by the compact Magyar Szekely population'.[26] By Article 20 the autonomy

[25] There were 18 regions established by a decree of September 1950: Arad, Baia-Mare, Barlad, Bucharest, Cluj, Constanta, Craiova, Galati, Hunedoara, Iasi, Oradea, Pitesti, Ploesti, Stalin (Brasov), Suceava, Timisoara, and the Magyar Autonomous Region. In 1956 a new reform reduced them to 16, abolishing Arad and Barlad. Bucharest city is considered a region.

[26] At the time of the census of 21 Feb. 1956 it had a population of 731,361, of whom 567,509 were Magyars and 145,718 Rumanians (*An. Stat. 1957*). The region

granted to the new region was defined in so far as the 'laws of the RPR and the decisions and directives of the central organs of the State are compulsory in the territory of the Magyar Autonomous Region'. There was thus no problem as to whether sovereignty was impaired or whether the region was to be transformed into some sub-federal unit. Later developments and subsequent rewording of the basic laws confirmed this point.

Law and Justice

The provisions of the new constitution regarding the judiciary (Ch. 6) were supplemented by a new law for the organization of justice of 2 June 1952, which set up a hierarchical system comprising a Supreme People's Court, regional courts, and people's courts for regions, cities, and districts. The Supreme Court was elected by the Grand National Assembly for a five-year term, while the judges of lower courts and special courts were appointed by the Minister of Justice, the 'people's assessors' being 'elected' as before. Article 64 of the constitution made provision for the creation of special courts, i.e. the setting up of special jurisdictions for a particular civil or criminal case, the most widely used being courts martial. According to Article 1 of the law of 2 June, their express purpose was 'to defend the social and state order of the RPR, to fight mercilessly against the enemies of the working people, as well as to strengthen the discipline and fighting capacity of the RPR armed forces'.[27] Article 2 of the same law explicitly laid upon the judiciary the task of education and propaganda; the courts were to 'educate the citizens of the RPR in the spirit of devotion to the fatherland, of socialist construction, of the exact fulfilment of RPR laws, of particular care for socialist property, of labor discipline', &c. Hence the all too familiar spectacle of highly publicized trials, admissions of guilt, and sentences of a severity calculated to intimidate and warn any disposed to non-conformity.

includes the sectors Ciuc, Gheorgheni, Odorhei, Reghin, Sangeorgiu de Padure, Sfantu Gheorghe, Targu-Mures, Targu Secuesc, and Toplita. Targu-Mures is the capital and administrative centre.

[27] Cited by V. Veniamin, 'The Judiciary', in Cretzianu, ed., *Captive Rumania*, p. 303.

10

The Need for Relaxation, March 1953–February 1956

At the time of Stalin's death the whole Soviet bloc, including the Soviet Union, was in the throes of an economic crisis, itself the result of Stalinist policies. This was mainly characterized by an acute shortage of essential supplies, often combined with an overproduction of the wrong kind of goods, in all the countries of the bloc. This economic crisis in turn aggravated the resentment at Soviet hegemony and exploitation, to an extent that threatened to undermine the whole system. Throughout the spring and summer of 1953 the leaders of the Eastern European countries had been openly voicing their difficulties, and simultaneous statements, almost identical in content, had demonstrated the gravity of the reactions. During Stalin's lifetime such criticisms were dismissed as examples of deviationism or counter-revolutionary activity, but with Stalin's death his successors were compelled to make a change and even to admit political and economic errors. As before, the policy-makers in Moscow set the course for all the satellite states. Hence throughout the bloc the 'new economic policy' and the emphasis on 'consumer goods' and on agriculture. The 'consumers', who were primarily the workers and the intelligentsia, were to be given more satisfaction, while 'consumer goods', ranging from food to clothing, were to be produced and delivered. Official attention was switched to the producers of food and raw materials for the town markets, the peasants. Thus agricultural problems came once again into the foreground, together with the fundamental question of the rate of development of industrialization and the practicability of concentrating on heavy industry.

By the end of the summer of 1953 changes had taken place everywhere. Malenkov's and Khrushchev's promises immediately after Stalin's death helped towards the first experiment in concession by the East German government, which led to the violent reaction of its population on 17 June 1953 and the hurried self-indictment of the new Hungarian government on 4 July. These were closely followed by similar statements by Bierut on 21 July, Gheorghiu-Dej on 28 August, Vilem Siroky on 7 September, and Valko Chervenkov on 9 September, all revealing faults in the plans of their respective countries. They culminated in Malenkov's statement of 8 August and Khrushchev's agricultural directive of 7 September, thus beginning the assault on the previous economic policy.

The structural problem of the Eastern European economies was in theory still the conflict between industrialization and agricultural production, and the terms in which their spokesmen described their difficulties were similar to those of the Soviet directive on agriculture. Yet the differences between Soviet Russia and the satellite countries were great. In general these differences may be grouped under three main headings. First, differences in cause. While the announcement from above of the new economic policy in Russia took place at the same time as the change in government and leadership, in the satellite countries it coincided with and was heralded by popular unrest and economic collapse but there was no change in leadership. Secondly, there were differences in emphasis and in the general presentation of the problem. The Russians were told that owing to, and following upon a long and successful phase of industrialization, a new phase could begin in which the needs of agriculture and light industry could, to some extent, be met. But the satellite régimes had to admit the failure of their industrial plans and had to reduce or emasculate them, immediately introducing new interim plans on an emergency basis. Thirdly, Russia had benefited from the trade and economic exchanges which had impoverished the satellites. This impoverishment was aggravated by the intensive economic-military collaboration of 1951–2 which, as has been seen, placed upon the overburdened economies the impossible new tasks of urgent defence preparations and rearmament.[1]

Before Stalin's death, in the spring of 1952, the Eastern European administrations were forced to the conclusion that they were opposed by that section of the population which they looked upon

[1] See ECE, *Economic Survey of Europe, 1954* (1955). Ana Pauker herself declared on 1 Dec. 1950 'we have concentrated on heavy industry primarily because we wanted to strengthen the defence of our country'.

as their main buttress, the industrial workers. The vicious circle created by the impossible production norms and the scarcity of necessities exasperated the proletariat. But by May and June 1953 the situation had become more serious, culminating in the riots of 17 June in East Berlin and accompanied by a wave of unrest throughout Eastern Germany, Czechoslovakia, Poland, and to a lesser extent Bulgaria and Rumania. The new economic policy which attempted to improve the supply of goods on the domestic markets by providing farmers and retailers with incentives ended in the hostile action of the German workers against privileges granted to other sections of the community. The economic machine therefore seized up: the villages refused to send more food to the towns and the factory workers refused to work unless they were provided with more and cheaper goods and food. The strikes in their turn paralysed the execution of the plans. Finally, when a further attempt at relaxation was made, the two apparently hostile groups of producers, the agricultural and the industrial workers, united and, on 17 June, exploded.

Thus the Eastern European Communist Parties' reactions between July and September 1953 provided a clear example of the merging of two different trends into one political move. From their East German colleagues they caught a sense of panic and of the imminence of their own economic disaster, but they wrapped this up in the terminology and line of reasoning that was being discussed in Moscow and which came into the open with the Malenkov–Khrushchev speeches.

THE SOVIET 'NEW COURSE' UNTIL THE TWENTIETH PARTY CONGRESS

What has been named the 'New Course' can, in Eastern Europe, be described briefly as the period of two or three years between Stalin's death and the Twentieth Congress when the new Soviet leaders, engaged on their own internal struggle for power, advocated a policy based on the principles of collective leadership, a higher standard of living for the people, and a desire for a *détente* with the West.

The application of the New Course varied greatly throughout the bloc. In the Soviet Union there were great changes in social, political, and economic policy, many of which have been retained and have probably become a permanent part of Soviet society.

In Poland and Hungary the New Course gave a tremendous impetus to the groundswell of discontent which eventually led to revolution. In the rest of the bloc, including Rumania, the impact was more superficial. The changes were beneficial but many of them proved to be only temporary and, in retrospect, some proved to have been little more than gestures. In these countries the New Course was never allowed to assume the character of a general debate in the economic, political, and social fields. Their régimes felt the new breeze blowing from Moscow but were chary of it, knowing that if they let it gather momentum it would become a whirlwind. Indeed, it was not the intention of the Soviet leaders to permit each satellite government to adapt the New Course to its own estimate of the economic and social needs of the country. Amendments, corrections, concessions could indeed be proposed and accepted, but not to the extent of impairing either of the two fundamental laws for the people's democracies: that of the growth of socialism and that of collaboration with the Soviet Union, their sole political and ideological guide.

SELF-CRITICISM IN RUMANIA

After less than a year as Prime Minister, it fell to Gheorghiu-Dej to undertake the reassessment of policy that involved sharp criticism of what had gone before. In Rumania this was a slightly more delicate task than, say, in Russia, where Stalin could be saddled with the blame for the past, or in Hungary, where the Workers' Party through Imre Nagy criticized Rakosi, both implicitly and explicitly, for errors in leadership. Gheorghiu-Dej had the task of criticizing the party and himself. This took place at the enlarged plenum of the Central Committee held on 19–20 August 1953,[2] which published an informative communiqué and an overall resolution, ranging from the necessity to establish collective leadership to the reorganization of agricultural production. Then on the ninth anniversary of the liberation, on 22 August 1953, Dej summarized for the Rumanian people the bitter findings and sharp decisions of the plenum, sandwiched between the usual reasons for rejoicing over the régime's achievements.[3] The criticism

[2] 'Decision of the enlarged plenum of the CC of the RWP of 19–20 Aug. 1953 with regard to the tasks of the party in the field of the development of the national economy and of the steady raising of the material and cultural standard of the working man', *Rezolutii*, ii.

[3] RIIA, *Documents, 1953*, p. 190.

of basic policies was concerned especially with the difficulties of industrialization and its effect on the working class, and the lack of progress on the part of the party in establishing broader contacts with the people. It is possible that the past was too recent to make the three fallen leaders, Pauker, Luca, and Teohari Georgescu, responsible for all the evils of the Stalinist period. While immediately after their fall they were widely and publicly criticized for their nefarious influence on state affairs, Dej and the new leadership of the party were seemingly more reluctant to make public, even to the party rank and file, the question of whether the party itself had been ruled from without through the Moscow-controlled security forces, of whether the First Secretary and Central Committee had been free to take decisions or whether all this time they had been virtual prisoners of a group of 'foreigners' backed by Moscow. The full disclosure of the rôle of the Pauker group was only made after the Twenty-Second Soviet Congress.

The resolution of the enlarged Central Committee Plenum of 19–20 August 1953, while confessing shortcomings in fulfilling the industrialization programme, acknowledged that 'first of all the rate of industrialization, particularly in the sphere of heavy industry, was excessively accelerated'. Moreover the slogan of the fulfilment of the Five-Year Plan in four years had been adopted without sufficient preliminary study. The resolution linked these failures with a mistaken policy of investment.[4] The volume of investment planned for heavy industry was excessive in relation to national income and, as such, put too great a strain upon the economy and upon the people. The ratio between the accumulation fund and the consumption fund was also incorrect. This resulted in an unsatisfactory rise in the standard of living of the working people. Plants and enterprises which were not actually needed had been financed lavishly, funds allocated to agriculture and consumer needs had been niggardly. This had caused serious irregularities in the development of the economy.

The investment policy as drafted in the plan was a mistaken one both in itself and especially in terms of the economy to which it was applied. It was a mistake from the beginning to allocate only 10 per cent of the investment to agriculture and forestry, the

[4] 50 per cent of the 1951 budget expenditures were devoted to the financing of the national economy. The other sources were the state and Council of Ministers reserves, bank deposits, public loans, or, for that matter, the currency reforms and the initial funds of the enterprises themselves.

sector which employed more than two-thirds of the working population and contributed more than half of the national income, while allocating 51.4 per cent to industry, including 42.1 per cent to the producer goods industry and 9.3 per cent to that of consumer goods. The result of such a policy would inevitably be that the new industries would not expand enough, the national income would show no adequate increase, while in the meanwhile the agricultural base would be gravely damaged.

Moreover Rumania's financial resources and national income between 1950 and 1953 were in no way favourable for massive investments over such a long period. In 1953 the three main sources of the national income, as taken in the Marxist economic sense (i.e. comprising only goods and services) were as follows in the RPR: investment 32 per cent; private consumption 52 per cent; public consumption 16 per cent. In the inter-war period, on average, the investment was between 7 and 9 per cent and private consumption roughly 70 per cent. This may be contrasted with figures published by the UN Economic Commission for Europe showing that for the year 1954 the RPR's target of investment was the highest of all the people's democracies, the next being Czechoslovakia with 27 per cent, and the lowest East Germany with 13 per cent.

The recognition that the national income had been gravely affected during the first years of the plan amounted to the recognition in Marxist terms that the ratio of investment could not be maintained. There is no evidence that the Soviet Union gave any substantial assistance towards the investments needed by the plans. Its investments in the Sovroms between 1946 and 1952 (which will be discussed later) were outside the state-controlled economy. Thus the sources of investment had to be found exclusively internally, mostly in the state budget's expenditure.

The operation of financing the plan, meaning the allocation of the gross investments required for the new constructions and plants and at the same time paying the wages of the necessary manpower and providing the market with consumer goods and food, was to have been Vasile Luca's main responsibility for the duration of the plan. As has been seen, in the thicket of accusations against him in 1952 three main charges emerged.[5] The first was that he

[5] Plenary meeting of the CC of the RWP, 26–27 May 1952 (*Rezolutii*, ii). See also 'Rumania in 1952', *World Today*, July 1952, and art. in *Sc.*, 3 June 1952.

had undermined the socialist sector of agriculture and at the same time had not fulfilled the programme for the collection of agricultural supplies for the state central fund. The second was that he had failed to provide the necessary funds for the adequate financing of the national economy. The third that he had opposed and sabotaged the currency reform. The first of these accusations will be discussed below. The two others could hardly have been the fault of any one man. They sprang from the entire conception of economic policy. The problem was how to cover the three different main expenditures assumed by the satellite states. These were the expenditures of the normal budget, those for the industrialization and socialization of the country, and the new heavy expenditure on defence and rearmament. All these were to be met out of budgetary incomes, of which in Rumania one-half was appropriated by Soviet Russia.[6] The residue, entered under one form or another, of the reparations' account, the loss in foreign trade by the fact that it was entirely controlled by the Soviet Union, and the drain on the national income caused by the Sovroms were primarily responsible for the serious reduction in the national income. The measures adopted of currency reform and stringent depression of wages through the piece-work system and Stakhanovism were, as has been seen, not enough to ensure the continuation of the industrialization projected by the Five-Year Plan. A further blow fell in 1952 when deliveries of iron ore from Russia were virtually stopped. In 1950 Rumania had imported approximately 250,000 tons of ore, mostly from Krivoi Rog, and in 1951 some 300,000 tons.[7] But in 1953, with the drop in supplies, pig-iron production fell by about 60 per cent below the provisions of the plan for that year. Thus the metallurgical industry, the key to heavy industry in the plan, stagnated in 1953. This too adversely affected relations between the party and the workers, because lack of progress in industrialization caused unemployment.

The resolution of 20 August severely criticized the trade unions for not having conveyed more frankly the wishes and criticisms of the workers and for not functioning properly as a 'transmission

[6] In the last budget with accurate figures published in Rumania, that of 1947–8, the heading 'International obligations' represented 46.6 per cent of the total expenditure. The entire column was made up of the various accounts to be paid to Russia.

[7] UN, *Econ. Bull. for Europe*, May 1955.

belt'. It also criticized as severely the party itself as a collective body.

FAILURE OF THE PARTY AND FRONT ORGANIZATIONS

As in the case of the speeches of other satellite leaders acknowledging 'errors' in the management of the party, the Rumanian criticisms did not attack the system itself. The resolution referred to the 'criminal traitor Beria' as an agent of western imperialism; no reference was made to the abuses of the secret police. It was pointed out that in the end the party would control the administration of the armed forces and the police, but this was not the sequel to any criticism; indeed, the mainstay of the régime was not the party but the secret police, to whom the entire Politburo was more indebted than to the party. To weaken the only strong wing of the entire shaky edifice would only have made the régime weaker still.

The party was found wanting in its ability to forge links with the masses.[8] The party and government were cut off from the people,[9] the only bridge between them being the constant flow of orders and rubber-stamped circulars issued from the various headquarters of the entrenched bureaucracy.[10] All sections and front organizations of the party had a share in the responsibility for not having established a proper party discipline and especially for not having forged links with the masses. To start with, the *apparat* of the Central Committee itself had not satisfactorily checked the fulfilment of the decisions of the Committee and had not called the Committee's attention quickly enough to the mistakes committed by the lower echelons. The regional organizations had especially shown a constant tendency to stifle or to ignore the criticisms and opinions expressed by the cadres. In the Bucharest organization this was particularly marked.[11] The First Secretary of the City

[8] Decision of enlarged Plenum of CC of RWP concerning the correction of the work of the party and of the strengthening of the ties of the party with the masses, 19–20 Aug. 1953 (*Rezolutii,* ii).

[9] 'Serious failings are noticeable in the activity of the organs and organizations of the party as well as in that of the state organs with regard to the strengthening of the ties with the masses' (ibid).

[10] 'It is necessary to put an end as quickly as possible to the tendency to replace the live work of educating and organizing men in the field of work by bureacratic methods in party work (abuse of circulars, instructions, telephone orders, excessive number of meetings, &c) (ibid).

[11] The Bucharest organization was coming into question not for the first and by no means for the last time. Because of its numerical and political importance it was decided in 1950 to organize it separately with a number of sections analagous to those of the Central Committee and divided into territorial regions.

Committee Bureau had taken all the decisions himself and had not consulted the other members. The special criticism of the work of the Central Committee and of the Bucharest organization again pointed towards Ana Pauker. Later it was recalled that she and Vasile Luca had ignored the Central Committee and even the Politburo and taken decisions by themselves; and Pauker was in direct control of the Bucharest organization, which was by far the most powerful and important of all of them. Bucharest, however, was not the only city castigated by the resolution; Arad and Oradea, other industrial centres, although second to Bucharest in the number of industrial workers, were mentioned in the same connexion.

Also in this connexion the responsibilities of the trade unions, the Union of Working Youth, and certain ministries and departments were singled out by the resolution. The trade unions and General Council had not succeeded in establishing themselves as a bridge between the industrial workers and the management, government, and party. The trade union organs, headed by their Central Council, did not show enough care for the workers and their standard of living; they did not fulfil their mission to see that workers' rights were being respected and that the labour code and the collective contracts were implemented. But when the trade unions did sometimes raise their voices for the workers, 'their demands were often rejected with abuse by some ministries and departmental direction, without even analysing the possibilities of solving them'.[12] The Ministries of Agriculture, of Collective Farms, of Food Industry, and of Light Industry were those most responsible for this; but obviously these departments were under fire for the lack of food and consumer goods on the market in the first years of the plan.

As for the Union of Working Youth, it had showed superficiality in its general task of educating the youth in a proper Bolshevik discipline, and it did not keep a proper link with the masses of young workers and with the bulk of the students. But what was worse was the fact that the Marxist–Leninist education of the cadres of the Youth Union was extremely poor and that as a consequence, lacking in political vigilance, they allowed 'many organs of the Workers' Youth to produce leftist manifestations'. This was not the first time that 'leftist manifestations' had been

[12] Decision of 19–20 Aug. 1953 (*Rezolutii*, ii).

spotted by the party in its own hierarchy in the youth organization nor was it the last, for a storm with youth was to come at the time of the Polish and Hungarian uprisings of 1956.

The failure of the party and of its organizations was even worse in the countryside. The party had underestimated its duty to foster its links with the masses of the working peasants. The needs and justifiable demands of the working peasants were ignored; no efforts were made to exercise a proper control over the way in which state organs applied their tax and collection policy or to avoid the abuses perpetrated by the state in its dealings with the peasants. Politically the party had failed to 'transform' the newly set up people's councils into mass organizations of workers. The party had forgotten the basic Leninist principle that only by building the alliance between the working class and the working peasantry could the new society be constructed. Instead, in many instances, the working peasantry had been so seriously antagonized by the party and government that ultimately this 'threw them into the arms of the kulaks'. Thus the two principal classes of the dictatorship of the proletariat had been ill treated and antagonized by the party. (There was also a reminder that the party organization should make a greater effort to rally intellectuals.) The party had once more to be reorganized and corrected.

With this in mind, it was decided that from then on all regional committees should hold conferences every two years and elect new committees, while all regional and urban conferences should be summoned annually. Moreover the Central Committee resolved to convene a Congress of the party itself in March 1954.[13] The Congress (which was in fact repeatedly postponed) had, among other points on its agenda, the adoption of new statutes. The Orgburo, which had been reconstituted in 1951, was dissolved.[14] The Politburo and Secretariat were again to share its functions as defined in 1951. Also a perfunctory appeal was made to all organizations and branches of the party to respect the principle of collective leadership. The Central Committee as well as the basic organizations were reminded of the importance of

[13] This was the statutory term; it was also statutory that the holding of the Congress should be anounced a year in advance. But ultimately the Congress was adjourned *sine die* in 1954 and held only at the very end of 1955 (see below, p. 240).

[14] Ana Pauker's elimination from this body has never been announced, but it is probable that the entire Orgburo ceased to function normally after she and Luca were purged in 1952.

discipline. But the emphasis of the entire resolution was still anxiety about the party itself and its structural weaknesses.

From this point of view, the most important feature of the resolution was the injunction that 'in the shortest time possible' there should be set up a 'party *Aktiv* of between 80,000–100,000 comrades'; they were to be recruited from among the best party members in factories and institutions, state and collective farms, and front organizations. The *Aktiv* should collaborate with the leading party organs. This injunction came as a surprise even to sceptical observers of the party. It seemed hardly credible that a party with a membership of 600,000 could not produce 80,000 satisfactory 'activists', but it was a fact; and it was a long time before the party set up its own, fully loyal *Aktiv*.

These negative criticisms were accompanied by some positive concessions and changes, which may best be considered under the headings of relations with the Soviet Union, relations with the workers, and relations with the peasants.

RELATIONS WITH THE SOVIET UNION

Two important economic concessions were made by the Soviet Union. The first was the dissolution of the Sovroms; the second a relaxation, albeit a slight one, of the Soviet stranglehold on foreign trade.

In the case of the Sovroms, two Soviet-Rumanian agreements of 31 March and 18 September 1954 (signed for Rumania by Miron Constantinescu) provided for the sale and transfer to Rumania of the Soviet shares in all but two (Sovrompetrol and Sovromcvart) of the joint companies; Rumania was to pay back their value in instalments over a number of years.[15] Similar agreements were made with the other people's democracies, but it was Rumania and Hungary which stood to gain most, as the joint-stock companies were most numerous in these two countries. As Spulber points out, however, these countries had to purchase, for unspecified sums, both the former German assets and the new contributions.[16] The two remaining Rumanian companies were dissolved in 1955 and November 1956 respectively, and after the Hungarian revolution the Russians cancelled the debts of all the

[15] *Soviet News*, 29 Sept. 1954.
[16] Spulber, p. 204.

ex-enemy countries. It was then stated that the total for Rumania alone was over $700 million.

The question of Rumanian foreign trade is dealt with at greater length elsewhere (pp. 301 ff). Here it is sufficient to say that by 1953 the value of Rumanian imports from non-communist countries had risen to $57.5 million compared with 35.4 million in 1951. Although the value dropped somewhat in 1954, it continued well above the 1951 level.

Of greater significance was the adjustment of diplomatic and strategic relations between the two countries. Similar adjustments were being made by the Soviet Union with all the people's democracies and were made necessary by the changes which were occurring in the international situation. These changes were to lead to the signing of the Austrian peace treaty and the Soviet rapprochement with Belgrade in 1955.

The Austrian peace treaty was signed on 15 May 1955. It marked the end of a long and painful road of negotiations. It has remained also the single European achievement of the 'Geneva spirit' even though in reality it antedated the Summit Conference of July 1955. Under the treaty, Austria pledged herself not to join any military alliance and not to permit the establishment of bases on her territory by any foreign power. Russia, in turn, pledged herself to evacuate her zone of occupation by 31 December 1955 at the latest.

It was, of course, the last provision which was of most interest and concern to Hungary and Rumania. If Soviet troops withdrew from Austria, the stationing of Soviet troops on the former supply and communications routes in these two countries would no longer be necessary. Yet the presence of Soviet troops in these two countries was a safeguard against trouble from the local population. Thus the Soviet Union had to seek some other means of 'legalizing' the stationing of troops on foreign soil. This was under discussion when the Warsaw Pact was born.

Ostensibly to counter the establishment of Western European Union by the Paris agreements of October 1954, the Soviet Union summoned its satellites to Warsaw on 11 May 1955. Since this was officially a state and not a party matter, the meeting was attended by the premiers and foreign and defence ministers of the states. The Warsaw Treaty[17] was signed on 14 May, the operative

[17] RIIA, *Documents, 1955*, p. 193.

article being Article 5, which created a 'unified command of the armed forces, which, according to the agreement, will all be put henceforward under the orders of the command'. The Soviet Marshal Koniev was appointed commander-in-chief of this command. The treaty was enough to ensure the continuity of Soviet control over Rumania and Hungary because it gave a legal basis for the continued stationing of troops in these countries.

Thus for the time being Soviet troops stayed in Rumania. In an interview given in August 1955 to a western newspaper, Gheorghiu-Dej cited NATO as the reason. He did not, of course, mention that at that time the presence of Soviet troops was still considered both by himself and by Moscow as an essential bolster to his régime or the fact that economically (the oil and uranium deposits) and strategically Rumania was considered important enough for their presence. The exact number of Soviet troops in Rumania had never been ascertained. There were probably never more than 100,000 in the country, for the most part stationed in Moldavia and Southern Bukovina, Constanta and the elbow of the Danube, on the common frontier between Rumania, Hungary, and Yugoslavia. The Soviet air force, however, was another matter. It is believed that in 1953 there were four Soviet jet plane air divisions at Buznau, Ianca, Craiova, and Arad, with no less than 86 aerodromes. By the terms of the Warsaw Treaty, these bases and aerodromes were considered part of the unified command and therefore were to remain in any circumstances.

In view of this, it seems that the presence of the Soviet forces was needed mainly for psychological purposes. In 1958, two years after the weathering of the storm caused by the Hungarian revolt, and because of the need for concessions to the satellites, it was decided to remove them altogether, that is back beyond the Pruth, or still within easy striking distance of every part of the country.[19]

PARTY REORGANIZATION

In the Soviet Union the ascendancy of Khrushchev in 1954 was accompanied by a reassertion of the rule of the party as against that of the government, with a separation of functions between

[18] The text was released on 12 Aug. by the official RPR news agency Agerpress. It included a short introductory notice to the effect that 'as a sequel to the withdrawal of the Soviet troops from Austria some Western newspapers have published a news item according to which the Soviet troops stationed in Rumania will withdraw from Rumania by October 1st.'

[19] See below, p. 288.

the two, and a similar division of functions occurred in the satellite régimes. In Rumania this took effect on 19 April 1954 at a plenary session of the Central Committee, when it was decided to abolish the post of Secretary-General and substitute a Secretariat of four members, headed by a First Secretary. The members of the Secretariat would concern themselves only with party matters and would not hold any government posts. Gheorghe Apostol was elected as First Secretary, resigning as vice-premier and Minister of Agriculture, while Gheorghiu-Dej gave up the post of Secretary-General. The Orgburo was again abolished. While these changes were exactly paralleled in the other bloc countries (for example, in Poland the chairman of the Central Committee, Bierut, resigned the premiership, and in Bulgaria Chervenkov resigned as Secretary-General), it was noteworthy that the Rumanian Central Committee meeting took place only five days after Patrascanu's condemnation and execution on 14 April. Thus the main possibility of genuine opposition and difference of views within the party had been ruthlessly eliminated before any 'liberalization' took place. The following shows the composition of the Secretariat before and after the changes of April 1954:

Before 19 April 1954	*From 19 April 1954–5 October 1955*
Secretary-General	*First Secretary*
Gheorghe Gheorghiu-Dej	Gheorghe Apostol
Secretariat	*Secretaries*
Gheorghe Gheorghiu-Dej	Nicolae Ceausescu
Iosif Chisinevschi	Mihai Dalea
Alexandru Moghioros	Ianos Fazekas[20]
Miron Constantinescu	
Gheorghe Apostol	

The Politburo remained unchanged except for the addition of two candidate members, N. Ceausescu and A. Draghici.

While it was apparent that Gheorghiu-Dej retained his supremacy uncontested, it was at the same time clear that behind the scenes profound disturbances were taking place in the party, since the Rumanian was the only East European Communist Party not to hold a New Course party Congress by the end of 1954. As has been seen, the Second RWP Congress was due to take place in March 1954, was first postponed until the end of

[20] See below, p. 352.

October, but then put off again in mid-October on the pretext that the party organs needed to devote their full attention to autumn sowing. But as late as February 1955 no definite date had been fixed, although by the party statutes the Congress should have been held in 1954. In the opinion of many observers, the leadership's inability to organize a Congress, as well as other party activities such as a campaign to appease minorities, indicated that the New Course measures had not been successful and had themselves caused new disruptions. It was not until September 1955 that it was finally announced that the Congress would be held in December, almost four years overdue. On the eve of the Congress, on 5 October, Dej resumed the position of First Secretary, resigning the premiership, which was now held by Chivu Stoica, his staunchest ally.

RELATIONS WITH THE WORKERS

During the New Course period and before the Second Congress, the régime had to take some steps in the industrial sphere to reduce the tensions built up in the Stalinist period.

First of all, they decided to close the biggest and best-known labour camps. Some reduction of forced labour was noticeable in the first half of 1953; in 1954 the Danube–Black Sea Canal was abandoned (probably because of the new Soviet government's lack of interest in this Stalinist strategic project) and the labour camps on this site were closed, as were some other big camps. The government, however, continued and still continues to make use of forced labour, although no longer in a widespread and systematic way but rather under the pretext of 're-education' in civic duties. For instance, between 1955 and 1960 a project for utilizing the reeds of the Danube delta was one of the enterprises to which groups of 'delinquents' were sent to work out their sentences or even without being sentenced. But throughout the communist bloc, from Russia to Czechoslovakia, forced labour activities were substantially reduced at the start of the New Course and huge labour camps were closed in all the countries.

Then something had to be done to lessen the growing discontent of the industrial workers and to overcome apathy in industry. Absenteeism and industrial migration had increased from 1951, and assumed enormous proportions between 1954 and 1955. In

1954 alone absenteeism had cost the state 9 million working days.[21] The new wages decreed at the same time as the currency reform of January 1952 did not improve matters. The Five-Year Plan results for 1954 were even more unsatisfactory than for any previous year. Hardly any branch of industry had fulfilled its targets. The railways and artisan co-operatives exceeded their plans, but the results for metallurgy and machines, oil, electric power, and the food industry all fell below the target set, the most disappointing being the construction industry where only 87·3 per cent was fulfilled.

On 24 November 1953 a new wage law was enacted with the object of improving workers' wages and boosting industrial output.[22] Workers in the food, textile, oil, and light industries were given considerably higher rates of contract pay. A more thorough piece-work system was introduced with a supplementary system of bonuses for the over-fulfilment of production norms. The wages of workers on a piece-work system were to be 10–15 per cent higher than those of contract workers; such workers would also receive a bonus, to increase progressively and equally with the quality and quantity of work produced above the basic norm.

On 27 December 1954,[23] in another concessionary move, the government announced the derationing of the main consumer goods and the abolition of rationing. This was, of course, meant to be a popular move. But in reality, although the prices of the goods were reduced, the general effect was to allow unofficial market prices to take over from the rationed prices.

Yet the category for which the government continued to show most concern was the technical intelligentsia, even though the new wage law was designed to increase wages of all workers and employees. The preamble to this decree stated that the basic rates in force since 1949, which divided all workers indiscriminately into general categories of employment, had been found unsuitable. It had not differentiated enough, especially between managerial and technical personnel, for which fifteen categories had been created.

[21] Report to Second Congress, 1955 (*Sc.*, 24 Dec. 1955). Of the 9 million working days lost, 5.7 million were due to unauthorized absences and 2.3 million to authorized leave.

[22] Decision of Council of Ministers concerning the improvement of the system of wages, the encouragement of qualifications for workers, and the raising of productivity (*Sc.*, 24 Dec. 1953).

[23] Resolution of the CC of the RWP and of the Council of Ministers on the abolition of the system of supply by ration cards and rations (ibid. 27 Dec. 1954).

It had not taken into account the fact that the managerial and technical personnel were more important to the national economy when working in the field, and had thus encouraged the 'bureaucratization' of such personnel. The wedge between the managerial and technical personnel on the one hand, and the manual workers on the other, was thus driven even more deeply. The intelligentsia was to be removed from the categories of general workers in which it had been up to that moment. Article 7 announced that the entire system of wage payment was to be changed for managerial personnel, engineers, technicians, specialists, clerks, and minor administrative employees. From then on they would be paid according to the functions which they exercised in the hierarchy of the production apparatus. Later it was announced that the average monthly wage of a specialist would be 800 lei, to which another 500 would be added to those with doctorates. Moreover income-tax reductions decreed on 27 November 1953 were a further concession to the intelligentsia and civil servants. They reduced in particular taxes on wages over 500 lei, which were among the highest wages of manual workers. For salaries of 150 lei monthly the tax was 7.6 per cent; for those of 2,500 lei and over, 16 per cent was the ceiling. In contrast with the wages of the intelligentsia, those of the manual workers remained at the average of 350 lei monthly.

	1950	*1953*	*1956*
Total personnel	809	1027.7	1,101.1
Socialist industry	743.9	918.3	972.1
State industry	65.3	109.4	129.1
Co-operatives			
Total workers	627.3	847.6	916.8
State industry	569.7	750.1	803.1
Co-operatives	57.6	97.5	113.7
Persons occupied in private sector	188.9	86.3	129.0

Source: Ann. Stat., 1957

The discrepancy of treatment given to the technical intelligentsia and the industrial workers was paralleled in that between the growth of the industrial workers and of the bureaucracy during the years of the first Five-Year Plan, which in more ways than one moulded the economic and social structure of Rumania under communism. In seeking to discover the figure for genuine 'workers' in the official labour statistics of the régime for 1950–3 and 1956, one finds the data shown in the table above.

Thus compared with the figure of roughly 750,000 workers in Rumanian industry in 1936, the absolute increase by 1956 must have been between 200,000 and 250,000. In contradistinction to this, the number of technical personnel and bureaucrats had increased more rapidly. From the figures given in the above table, it appeared that in 1956 there was almost one non-manual worker to almost every four workers in industry (respectively 1,101,100 minus 917,000 workers: 184,000 non-manual workers). This swelling of the administrative apparatus is, of course, a feature characteristic of all communist economies and is the origin of the 'new class'. But it has especially bedevilled underdeveloped economies such as the Rumanian, where the inherent tendencies towards bureaucratization have always necessitated a fight against it. This fight had not yet been won.

RELATIONS WITH THE PEASANTS

The retreat from full collectivization which the government had been compelled to initiate in September 1951[24] proved to be a wise move. The agricultural associations (Toz) met with a much less obstinate response from the peasants than the dreaded collective farms. Their numbers showed a steady increase from 1952 to 1958. This development had been reversed in Soviet Russia. There too in the first years of 'voluntary collectivization' (1927–30), the Toz associations had been much more popular than the collective farms, but the moment Stalin began his drive for genuine collectivization, the Toz were rapidly closed down and their importance in the 'socialist sector' faded to nothing in three years.[25] In the RPR, on the contrary, three years after the strenuous efforts to establish a doctrinally correct collectivization, Ana Pauker was criticized for delay in the organization of 'the association for the joint tilling of the land (Toz type)'.[26]

[24] See above, p. 201

[25] See N. Jasny, *The Socialized Agriculture of the USSR* (Stanford UP, 1950).

[26] Moghioros's speech at the CC plenum of Nov.–Dec. 1961.

Undoubtedly the communists could present this 'inferior' form as a first and easier step in the process of collectivization. Since 1951 the party press and reviews had been full of arguments showing that all co-operatives and associations are only transitional forms to the final stage of *kolkhozes*. But the growing success of the co-operatives, based on the principle of ownership of the land, gave these arguments between 1955 and 1958 a rather remote character. On the contrary, what did happen was that by allowing and encouraging this kind of co-operative to flourish, the Rumanian party could afterwards present impressive statistics for the progress made in the 'socialist sector' of agriculture. By considering all these forms of association as socialist forms, the agrarian policy of the RWP could be represented as an unbroken advance towards its goal. When the term 'co-operativization' replaced that of collectivization, the substitution of one kind of socialization of the land by another, which had previously been condemned as merely 'engendering capitalism', was for a time endorsed. This was the personal success of Moghioros, who had taken over the responsibility in the Politburo for agricultural affairs.[27]

On 5 September 1953 a measure to give tax relief to agricultural producers was announced. Debts and undelivered quotas from the previous year were cancelled. Some taxes and delivery quotas for milk, meat, and wool were reduced. A new system of advance sales for cattle and animal produce, industrial raw materials, fruit and vegetables was instituted. Also the taxes on the sale of surplus farm produce (commodities which the farmer had left over after having delivered his quotas) were halved on the condition that these surpluses were to be sold to the state.

These concessions were, of course, welcome but they were within the framework of a system which was distinctly unwelcome. It is true that most of the peasants in 1953 and even in 1956 were still uncollectivized. But the fear of collectivization was in itself a deterrent to increased effort. The effect on production,

[27] In his speech at the CC plenum of Nov.–Dec. 1961 Moghioros recalled how, although the basic resolution of March 1949 had specifically recommended the setting up of Toz-type associations, which would make easier the transition to collective farms, Ana Pauker had delayed its implementation by asserting that if such associations were set up, the peasants would leave the existing collective farms and join the associations. 'It thus became necessary for other comrades to carry out this task set by the party.'

therefore, was very disappointing. The following table shows the average yields per hectare in the main crops:

	1934	*1948*	*1953*	*1954*	*1955*	*1956*
Wheat	10.3	9.4	14.4	8.7	10.2	8.4
Maize	10.4	6.2	11.2	15.0	18.0	11.0
Barley	9.4	7.6	12.2	38.7	10.6	7.9
Rice	25.6	14.4	27.2	32.3	18.6	21.8
Flax	20.6	17.1	11.1	11.6	18.2	17.5

Source: Ann. Stat., 1957

It will be noticed that, generally, 1953 was a good year for average yields. This was mainly thanks to the good weather. But although the concessions, coming as they did late in the year, could not in themselves have materially affected the results, the fact that since Stalin's death in March concessions had been in the air may well have partially accounted for the increases.

The total volume of production (in '000 tons) for the same period was as follows:

	1934–8	*1948*	*1953*	*1954*	*1955*	*1956*
Cereals	8,016	5,428	8,621	8,064	9,956	7,139
Wheat	2,630	2,397	3,964	2,140	3,006	2,436
Maize	4,055	2,260	3,225	4,953	5,877	3,931
Barley	165	85	262	169	211	136
Rice	1	11	55	50	35	36

Source: Ann. Stat., 1957

Any comparison with the pre-war period is pointless because of the loss by Rumania of her most fertile areas during and after the war. But in average yields per hectare comparisons are still valid, and on this basis the small peasant farming of the pre-war years, which was in itself far from efficient, shows up quite favourably.

The slowness of the collectivization was revealed by Gheorghiu-Dej at the Second Party Congress in December 1955. The whole socialist sector (state farms, state land, collective farms, and agricultural associations) covered only 26.5 per cent of the country's arable land, which totalled about 9,700,000 hectares. Within this the co-operatives covered only 8.3 per cent of the arable land, the state farms and state land—of which the former royal estates had formed the nucleus—covered 13.7 per cent. This slow progress—or to put it in another way, the prudence of the régime in not rushing collectivization as, for example, was done in Bulgaria—was even more strikingly reflected in Dej's report in the figures showing the social structure of the countryside. After ten years of communist rule it was as follows:

		Per cent
Members of collective farms		5.5
Members of agricultural associations		5.8
Agricultural workers	under	1.0
Peasants with smallholdings		45.2
Peasants with medium holdings		40.5
Kulaks		22.0

Source: Sc., 25 Dec. 1955

Apart from their political significance, these figures also revealed important socio-economic trends. One notable trend was the drastic thinning out of the agricultural proletariat. There were probably three main reasons for this. First, the peasant in the state farm brigades and the workers on the MTS were now considered not as landless peasants but as 'a new detachment of the working class in the villages'. Second, the agricultural proletariat had also lost many members as a result of the agrarian reform in 1945. Third, many landless peasants had been absorbed in the industrialization drive.

But the most significant trend was the growth of medium-sized landholdings. While the percentage of smallholdings had decreased from 57 per cent of the arable area in 1948 to 42.4 per cent in 1955, medium holdings had risen from 34 to 40 per cent and were still growing. 'This shows', said Gheorghiu-Dej in his report, 'that the middle peasant is increasingly becoming the pivot of the village and that his importance as a producer of agricultural goods is also increasing.'[28] According to figures released at the end of 1956, the small and medium holdings together were still producing 75 per cent of the entire crop of cereals and vegetables of the country. By communist definition a smallholding is one up to 5 hectares, a medium holding one between 5 and 20 hectares.

The growth of the medium-sized holdings continued a process

[28] *Sc.*, 25 Dec. 1955; *Agerpres Inf. Bull.*, 10 Jan. 1956.

which had been going on between the wars. But it was surprising that the middle peasants had the means to extend their holdings and thus consolidate their social and economic position in the villages. This suggested that the peasant class, in spite of persecution, compulsory quotas, exorbitant taxes, and exaggerated prices for the use of the services of the MTS, had been able to resist collectivization and to maintain its traditional position in the economy of the country. However, the final show of strength was still to come.

For the time being the main objective of agricultural policy was to see 60–70 per cent of the entire agricultural output coming from the 'socialist sector' by the end of the second Five-Year Plan. The socialist transformation of agriculture, Dej said in his report, was 'an objective necessity' for achieving higher socialist production in the national economy as a whole and for the harmonious development of agriculture. The chief tasks of the party during the plan period were to step up work for the more rapid formation of new agricultural associations and collective farms, but on the basis of 'strict adherence to the principle of free consent'; to strengthen and develop existing collectives and agricultural associations, with a view to guiding the peasants towards joining 'higher forms of agricultural producer co-operatives; to increase yields and productivity, extend the cultivated area, and cut down production costs.'[29] Thus in the years of discontent and tensions, the Rumanian communists were more concerned with output and with supplying the towns than with ideological aspect of collectivization.

THE SECOND RWP CONGRESS

The Second Congress, so many times postponed, was finally held on 23–28 December 1955 and was attended by delegates from thirty-three Communist Parties.[30] Its deliberations were held in an atmosphere of forced enthusiasm from first to last. Two last-minute announcements, however, did cheer the rank and file. The more important one was the news of Rumania's admission to the

[29] Ibid.

[30] The CPSU delegation was led by Alexei Kirichenko, member of the Presidium and First Secretary of the CC of the Ukraine CP. This was another occasion on which the Ukrainians showed their special interest in Rumanian affairs.

United Nations,[31] which was released to the press a few days before the Congress and was afterwards referred to in many of the main speeches. The second and minor one was the purchase by the Rumanian government of Sovrompetrol. The Congress agenda included the report of the Central Committee by Gheorghiu-Dej,[32] and reports on the Central Revision (finance) Committee by N. Guina (a member of the Central Committee and Ambassador to Yugoslavia), on the directives of the second Five-Year Plan by Chivu Stoica, on the adoption of new party statutes by N. Ceausescu, and the election of the new leadership.

This last resulted in the election of a new Central Committee consisting of 56 members and 34 candidates, some of the new members being regional party First Secretaries. Among the casualties were, of course, the principal victims of the 1952 purge and Gheorghe Florescu (a former youth leader and one of the Rumanian communists in France during the war). Ion Gheorghe Maurer, subsequently to become president of the Presidium and later premier, and Gheorghe Vasilichi (Patrascanu's friend among the railway workers, who had also spent the war years in France) were demoted to the rank of candidate members. The new Politburo was identical with the old one but for the addition of three members: P. Borila, A. Draghici, and N. Ceausescu. Draghici continued also to be Minister of the Interior, having under him all the security forces except those dependent upon the army. The order of precedence in the new Politburo differed from that of April 1954 in that Stoica now moved up to second place, followed by Chisinevschi, Apostol, Moghioros, Bodnaras, Constantinescu, Parvulescu, Borila, Draghici, and Ceausescu. The candidate members were Dumitru Coliu, Leontin Salajan, Leonte Rautu, and Stefan Voitec. Gheorghiu-Dej remained First Secretary, the other secretaries being Chisinevschi, Ceausescu, Ion Fazekas, and I. Cozma. The Control Commission was headed by Parvulescu, with Liuba Chisinevschi and Ion Vinte as vice-presidents.

The Party

Although Dej once more showed that he had a clear lead over all

[31] By the 'package deal' of 14 Dec. 1955 whereby sixteen nations were admitted, among them the communist bloc countries, although Bulgaria, Hungary and Rumania had been 'branded' by the UN in 1950 (see above, p. 195). Italy, Spain and Finland were the most important admissions gained by the West in this bargain.

[32] *Sc.*, & *Agerpres Inf. Bull.*, 10 Jan. 1956.

his rivals, the section of his report to the Congress dealing with the party gave a further indication of why it had not been possible to convene the Congress sooner. His statement 'that every deviation from the Party line jeopardizes the very existence of the Party and that the fight for the purity of its ranks, for its monolithic unity is the supreme duty of all the members' seemed to point to the behind-the-scenes struggle in the leadership since the 1952 purge and the difficulties encountered in dealing with the followers of Pauker, Luca, and Georgescu. As has been seen, it was at this Congress that Dej again attacked the three former leaders for indiscriminate party recruitment, for forcible collectivization, and for trying 'to prevent the Party from exercising control over those important state sectors that had fallen into their hands'.

His report also contained fairly complete data on the size and depth of the party. It stated that it numbered 595,398 members and candidates, of which 56,583 were candidates. The total number of members was smaller than at the 1948 Congress. The reasons given for this were the 1950 purge and the fact that during 1948–52 it had accepted no new members. After 1952 the party had, however, formed 8,000 new basic organizations among which, while many of the participants were redistributed from 'territorial' to 'factory' organizations, there must also have been a fair number of new members selected from the new (young) administrative personnel. A total of 29,393 'basic' organizations in factories, works, and agricultural units, as well as in territorial districts, had been formed; 76,000 members worked in the offices of these organizations. The party had altogether 19 regional organizations, 190 district organizations, and 159 city organizations. In the committees of these organizations 11,000 cadres were at work. It was also reported that the task given to the Central Committee by the plenum of 13 August 1953, to create a party *Aktiv* of 80,000–100,000 members, had been carried out. The *Aktiv* was at work, with new members faithful to Dej.

Although complete figures were not revealed as to the strength of each organization within the party and of the order of their importance, it can be deduced from the report of the Credentials Commission that Bucharest city remained by far the strongest. It had 115 delegates. As each delegate to the Congress represented 700 members, Bucharest city must have had nearly 80,000 members, followed by the regional organizations of Ploesti, with 76 delegates (roughly 50,000 members), and of Cluj, with 64 delegates (46,000 members).

While it is true to say that there may be a great difference between the structure of the delegations and that of the party in general (a delegate must have been longer in the party), the following figures of the Credential Commission's report[33] shed some light indirectly upon the social strata in the party. Thus 10.85 per cent of the delegates had belonged to the party since its illegal days, 40.51 per cent since 1944–5, 25.84 per cent since 1946, 22.21 per cent since 1947, and only 0.58 per cent since 1948 onwards. These figures show that, in spite of the purge, the group of members recruited by Ana Pauker and Miron Constantinescu in 1945 and 1946–7 remained by far the greatest, forming roughly 88 per cent of the groups from which the delegates had been elected. But these were, as has been seen, the most unreliable, the members then recruited being composed mainly, if not exclusively, of opportunists of all kinds anxious to obtain through their membership either a job or pardon for some involvement during the pro-Nazi era. The age composition of the delegates was: 37.21 per cent up to the age of 35; 17.31 per cent between 36 and 40; 33.08 per cent between 41 and 50, and 12.4 per cent over 50; 79.2 per cent were ethnic Rumanians; the rest were 'recruited from the ranks of the national minorities'.

The social composition of the party must still have been giving the leaders cause for concern. The task given to the Central Committee in 1950 to raise the numbers of workers from 37.2 to 60 per cent had not been fulfilled. The percentage of workers at the end of 1955 was only 42.61 per cent, and even among the candidates being considered and trained the percentage of workers was only 47.93 per cent. There was a sense of alarm in the appeal made by Gheorghiu-Dej when he again insisted that 'we must ensure in our party an increase in the number of workers, especially from the main industries, who are actually manual workers, so that the working-class element can become the preponderant element in our party'.[34] The distinction thus drawn between the actual manual workers and the loosely defined statistical category of workers was relevant here. According to figures given at the Congress, there were 2,600,000 'workers'. But they included techni-

[33] *Sc.*, 15 Dec. 1955. [34] Ibid.

cians, agricultural workers, and many other categories more or less definable as 'in the field of production'. This being the case it meant that 42.61 per cent, that is roughly 200,000 men and women, represented less than 10 per cent of those who had been described as 'workers' by Apostol.

The report on the training and education of the party was also concluded in the usual terms of dissatisfaction. From Rautu's speech it was learnt that only 65 per cent of the total number of members and candidates had been or were being passed through the various elementary schools or party courses. More than one-third of the members had not received any form of instruction or training. This reflected the same hurried and indiscriminate approach to the recruitment of members for which Ana Pauker had been criticized. The only difference was that, while before 1949 any kind of member had been welcome, after the establishment of the 'dictatorship of the proletariat' stress was laid upon attracting to the rank and file those elements who had shown efficiency and skill in production, either industrial or agricultural, with a definite bias in favour of the former category. But from an ideological point of view, the new category was still as weak as the former one.

This weakness was mainly due to the fact that the party had in reality always stressed the need for practical ability to solve current practical tasks. The main reproach against party education was not that members had failed to absorb a sufficient dose of Marxism–Leninism or had shown an insufficient revolutionary consciousness. It was that it had lagged behind with the problems of daily life and of the necessities of the practical activity of the party.

> More than ever before, this is a moment in which the scholarly approach to the internal propaganda work of the Party must be abandoned. The internal Party propaganda must be indissolubly linked to the practical aspects of the construction of socialism and especially to the problems of the economy. The principal shortcoming in the content of the Party propaganda and ideological work in general is dogmatism, its learning by heart, uncreatively, of Marxist-Leninist teaching.[35]

Another worrying problem was the prevailing absence of any

[35] Dej report, previously cited.

effective 'transmission belts' between the party and people. This sprang partly from the weaknesses in the practical type of education and partly from the fact that in social composition the party was certainly not broadly based. The most obvious lack of contact was in the countryside where the private peasants were still in a large majority. In the towns contacts with industrial workers and youth were admitted to be unsatisfactory. For this the party blamed the weakness of trade union work and the fact that activity among youth had failed to get down to the really local level but had mainly confined itself to the regional, district, or city committee level. The party, it was admitted, had failed to remember that what characterized youth was its dynamic energy and its need to serve a cause. Its oral and written propaganda had not paid sufficient attention to the 'fight against bourgeois ideological influence and to the theoretical confusion to be found in many newspapers and periodical articles, in books and pamphlets, in university courses and public lectures'. It was clear that since the end of 1955 the party had been aware of the obduracy with which Rumanian youth had resisted communist teaching and doctrine, and that the continuing strength of their attachment to national and traditional values caused a wide gap between it and the tentative and uncertain attempts of the UTM to forge some links with the mass of young people.

This was true in general also of the people's councils, with the difference that these were more recent and more complex organizations than the trade unions and the UTM. Here too the party organs had failed to see how the councils could help towards 'uniting the Workers' Party with the peasant and working masses'. The party had sought to dominate them almost exclusively; it had not given them the chance of operating even as semi-independent local units. This attitude had 'frustrated the councils, depriving them of any initiative, lessened their responsibility and prevented them from playing their effective part as organs of administrative leadership'. But no remedy for this shortcoming was at hand, as the shortage of cadres and the isolation of the party within the country meant that trusted party personnel had to be employed in state assignments. The confusion created at the top, where party, government, army, and in particular security jobs had always been done practically by the same people, was being carried right down to the lowest echelons. Here too the tasks 'in the field' were so urgent and so arduous that the people who actually had the power of decision could not really spend the time and means in trying to influence without coercing and to persuade without overriding. Jobs had to be done; and were being done with great difficulty, by the people initially chosen on the grounds of security and willingness.

One of the deeper moves which perhaps could be detected in the reorganization of the party at the Second Congress was in the steady influx of younger people, especially of new First Secretaries adopted by the widely enlarged Central Committee as members or candidate members. These were younger men recruited from the field of production and then quickly passed through the party schools. They represented a new layer of managerial party leaders who have been found since 1951 at all levels of the party machine.

The other moves were reflected in some of the amendments to the party statutes. A new article freed the Central Committee from the obligation of holding a National Conference. This, of course, weakened even the illusion of party democracy. At the same time, new regulations made it clear to the party organizations that they had no right to control the ministries and central and state organizations. They could merely report their observations and misgivings. But the main purpose of the amendments was to secure a better social composition of the rank and file. New and longer terms and new and stricter conditions were set for the admission of members and candidates. Men under twenty were not to be accepted as candidates unless they were members of the UTM. Also the stage of candidature was prolonged from six months to one year, eighteen months, or two years, according to the social and professional qualifications of the candidate. In only one case could the organizations reduce the duration to the six months previously demanded and that was for industrial workers who had been in production for at least five years. This provision was doubly relevant as on the one hand it pointed to the category of men who had been active in the first Five-Year Plan and who had shown their mettle within it; and it disclosed that this category seemed to be reluctant to join the party.

These, then, were the main features of the party as revealed by the Second Congress. The party had gained some stability at the top, but as a whole it still fell far short of a purposeful vanguard of socialism. Quantitatively and qualitatively it left much to be desired. Its popular basis was narrow and it was failing to influence the country as a whole, especially the young. Its power, of course, was unchallenged but its still prevailing weaknesses often left it with repression as its only instrument of policy.

The State of Industry

The principal economic report to the Second Congress was delivered by Dej. It was announced that the first Five-Year Plan, in terms of total industrial production, had been fulfilled the previous month. The volume of industrial production was 2.9 times as high as in 1938 and 3.4 times as high as in 1944. The output of producer goods was roughly 3.9 times what it was in 1949 and that of consumer goods had grown 2.9 times compared with 1944.

Planned and Actual Increases in Industrial Output, 1950–5
(m. tons and percentages)

Commodity	Plan		Actual
	Absolute increase		*Per cent increase*
Electric power (b.kwh)	2.6	2.2	104
Hard & brown coal	4.6	2.3	59
Crude oil	5.0	5.5	110
Iron ore	0.4	0.2	53
Pig iron	0.5	0.3	80
Crude steel	0.7	0.2	38
Rolled steel	0.4	0.1	24
Sulphuric acid	91	40	78
Cement	1.8	1.0	56

Source: UN, *Econ. Survey of Europe in 1955*, table 107.

However, Dej had to admit that the plan had not been fulfilled in the whole range of industrial goods. These included steel, coal, cement, cellulose, textiles, leather goods, sugar, dairy and fish products.

In investments, 67 per cent of the entire total had been absorbed by the oil industry, the development of electric power, the machine-building and chemical industries. The fuel and power industries alone had absorbed 34 per cent of the total investments. But the investment plan itself had not been entirely fulfilled. A breakdown of planned and achieved investments follows.

Planned and Actual Gross Fixed Investment, 1951–5

('000 m. pre-reform lei at 1950 prices)

	Plan (published 1950)	Actual
Heavy industry	586	695
Light industry	124	93
All industry	710	788
Agriculture	133	131
Transport & communications	215	141
Trade	29	32
Housing	43	48
Schools, hospitals, public bldgs, &c.	163	120
Other	37	
Total	1,330	1,260

Source: UN, *Econ. Survey of Europe, 1955,* table 112.

Gheorghiu-Dej reported that during the period of the plan over 100 new factories or other enterprises had been opened. In 1955 there were 2,223 industrial enterprises in the socialist sector of industry. They were divided as follows, according to the administrative sphere to which they belonged and to their percentage contribution to the total output of socialist industry:

Total Socialist Industry

	No.	Per cent output
State industry:	1,598	93
Nationally directed	(1,306)	(86)
Locally directed	(292)	(7)
Co-operatives	625	7
Total	2,223	100

Source: Dej report to 2nd RWP Congress

The number of workers in the nationally-directed state industries had risen from 548,481 in 1950 to 700,522 in 1955. There were seven enterprises employing more than 5,000 workers, 13 employing between 3,000 and 5,000, and 116 between 1,000 and 3,000. It was significant that it was the building and construction industry which employed the greatest number of workers—400,000 against only 175,000 in 1950. The other basic industries, such as fuel and power, mining, metallurgy, chemicals, and building materials between them employed most of the remaining labour force.

Despite the failure of many industrial plans there had obviously been a considerable quantitative growth in industry, especially heavy industry. Yet the entire output of industry represented only 47.5 per cent of the national income, which was considerably less than in Czechoslovakia and East Germany and even in Bulgaria. The adverse comparison with Bulgaria was all the more striking because before the war the reverse had been the case. Finally, the national income had been planned to be 2.6 times as great as in 1950. But even according to a rather favourable estimate,[36] it was only 1.87 times greater, that is to say 72 per cent of the target.

Progress had obviously been made, but in terms of the plan the results had been far from satisfactory. Nor had progress been made at a steady rate. It had been the result of a great last-ditch effort in 1954, when the plan had already been brought back to its initial duration of five instead of four years. The entire schedule had then been more carefully organized and massive imports of the most needed raw materials ordered. Many technicians came specially from Soviet Russia, and the labour force was augmented by using some of the prisoners and inmates of labour camps. All these factors made their presence felt.

The Second Five-Year Plan, 1956–60

The report on the directives for the second Five-Year Plan, 1956–60, was delivered by Chivu Stoica, Chairman of the Council of Ministers.[37] The directives[38] reflected the new economic trends which had been developing since 1953 when the Council for Mutual Economic Assistance (Comecon) began work on harmonizing future economic plans throughout Eastern Europe. Rumania was assigned special tasks. While continuing to build up her heavy industrial base, which meant emphasizing the machine-building, metallurgical, mining, and fuel and power industries, Rumania was to concentrate especially on expanding the production of chemicals obtained as by-products of the petroleum and

[36] UN, *Econ. Survey of Europe, 1955,* table 113.
[37] *Agerpress Inf. Bull.,* 10 Jan. 1956.
[38] See *Probleme economice,* no. 1, Jan. 1956.

natural gas industry and those based on salt. The growth of the chemical industry, because of the tremendous investments in oil, had brought an increase in oil production and justified Rumania looking forward to 'having an important petro-chemical industry in a few years'. On this point the directives gave details. By 1960 oil production was to have risen by 28 per cent, methane gas by 26 per cent. Output in the chemical industry as a whole was to increase fivefold by 1960. New plants for the production of synthetic rubber, plastics, tyres, mineral fertilizers, and sulphuric acid were to be built and commissioned as soon as possible. An entirely new scheme for the development of the cellulose industry through the use of reeds and sedge from the Danube was outlined; it was to produce 50,000 tons of cellulose annually.[39] Uranium production and the building and construction industry were to receive special attention.

But although the whole plan was ambitious, and though the relative emphasis continued to be on the basic 'Sector A' industries, the planned pace of development was considerably less than in the first Five-Year Plan. The United Nations, basing its figures on official RPR sources, gave the following comparison between actual and planned national income and industrial production for 1950–5 and 1955–60.

National income			*Industrial production*		
Percentage increase over period		*Percentage decline in rate of growth*	*Percentage increase over period*		*Percentage decline in rate of growth*
1950–5 Actual	*1955–60 Plan*		*1950–5 Actual*	*1955–60 Plan*	
93	50	46	116	60–65	44–48

Source: UN, *Econ. Survey of Europe, 1956*, table 3.

These modifications in the character and pace of planning were undoubtedly a reflection of the Soviet approach to economic plan-

[39] This became one of the most commented upon features of the new plan. On the one hand it was the source of new recruitment of forced labour in 1957–8, when all 'undesirable elements' were sent to work there. On the other it was one of the most advertised Comecon projects of regional collaboration, as Czechoslovakia, East Germany, and Poland shared in the project. See 'Communists Pool Resources for Big Cellulose Plant', *The Times*, 28 May 1958.

ning of the bloc through the vehicle of Comecon. At the Twentieth Soviet Congress Khrushchev himself remarked that today every socialist country did not have to develop all branches of heavy industry. He later amplified his remarks in an interview given to a group of Hungarian journalists who were visiting the Soviet Union.

> It is impossible [said Khrushchev] to have developed everything everywhere simultaneously. Unfortunately, we have often spoken in vain. Hungarians, Poles, Rumanians and also others have tried to build up everything by themselves. . . . The sooner and the better we develop the division of labour between our countries, the greater will our economies be. Each socialist country has to succeed in producing a great part of its production in large quantities and at low cost.[40]

Rumania could, on paper, still build up her heavy industry and so lay the economic foundation for socialism, but within this general framework she was apparently to specialize in oil, methane gas, cellulose, timber, and the chemical industry, as well as in more specialized types of production such as equipment, tractors, and lorries.

A great deal of stress was laid on the need for much greater industrial efficiency, for the raising of productivity and the lowering of production costs. The directives envisaged that productivity must have increased by 1960 by 45–50 per cent in industry and 50–55 per cent in construction. Costs were to be lowered by 15–20 per cent in industry as a whole. The theory of the 'real wage' was given even greater attention so as to justify the freezing of the nominal wage and a recalculation of production norms. This was a depressing prospect for the working population, and one which was not brightened by the plans for consumer goods.

In this respect, the new plan showed that the promises of the first years of the New Course were again forgotten. The main allocations for investments were as follows: 56 per cent for industry, of which only 6 per cent was for consumer goods; 2.5 per cent for construction; 12.5 per cent for agriculture and forestry; and 17.5 per cent for social and cultural activities. Thus, while many of the industrial targets were by previous standards reasonable, there was to be no attempt to produce more consumer goods

[40] Quoted from *Nepszabadsag*, 21 July 1957, UN, *Econ. Survey of Europe 1957*, ch. vi, p. 31 n. 46.

or to increase wages. The new plan also held out little hope that the small benefits which the New Course had conferred on the workers would be continued. In fact it confronted them with the two rather ominous slogans of raising productivity and lowering production costs. There was, therefore, no reason for the workers to wax enthusiastic over it, and the year 1956 opened with them in a particularly discontented mood, since the plan seemed to have set back any hope of real improvement for at least another five years.

But that year was to produce a radical change in the situation throughout Eastern Europe. Discontent was widespread throughout the bloc and it was, ironically, the new breeze which blew from Moscow which fanned the flames. In February, at the Twentieth CPSU Congress, Khrushchev made his secret speech denouncing Stalin. Though the speech was never published by Soviet sources, its substance and spirit soon made themselves felt throughout the bloc and had the effect of releasing the safety-valve on the mounting discontent. The Poznan riots were the first explosive sign of industrial unrest, but they were accompanied by a whole series of political changes in several of the countries which gave impetus to the irresistible demand for change. They culminated in the 'events' (as they were named) of October and November in Poland and Hungary.

Part III

BETWEEN THE TWENTIETH AND TWENTY-SECOND CPSU CONGRESSES

11

After the Twentieth Congress, 1956–7

THE profound effects of Khrushchev's secret speech denouncing Stalin at the Twentieth CPSU Congress in 1956 necessarily made a deeper impression on public opinion than his report of the Central Committee on the work of the party since the preceding Congress in 1952. But on a longer-term view, the confirmation, in that report, of the policies most closely associated with Khrushchev's advent to power was more important in shaping satellite policies, in particular economic policies. In general these policies confirmed the post-Stalin New Course; in particular, in domestic policy, the announcement of the principle of 'collective leadership' in Mikoyan's speech was more fundamental than the attack on Stalin. This principle was to mean broadening powers at all levels in the central and local party and government administration. In conformity with it, Khrushchev criticized the top-heavy bureaucracy and announced the intention of stimulating initiative, which meant that steps had to be taken to prevent the abuse or authority by the police and administrative organs. There was to be greater scope in intellectual life and less dogmatic rigidity. The main object of foreign policy was to be 'peaceful coexistence', or peaceful economic competition with capitalism. The essential basis of this policy was, in Khrushchev's words, that 'armed interference' was unnecessary, since the economies of the Soviet Union and the people's democracies were advancing so steadily, while that of the capitalist countries was developing so unevenly, that the victory of communism was assured.

As is well known, when the delegates from the Eastern European countries who had attended the Congress returned to report to their national parties, it immediately became apparent that the dethronement of Stalin above all provoked a ferment that was to lead at the end of 1956 to the Polish and Hungarian revolutions. The upheaval in Eastern Europe in turn brought about a sharp change in Khrushchev's position in the Soviet presidium, which was intensified by the realization that the overstrain in the Soviet economy in 1955 was recurring in 1956. These factors combined to bring about some modification of Khrushchev's main policies in 1956 and, of course, some important concessions had to be made to the satellite countries, including agreements on the stationing of troops, modification of the terms of trade, and the provision of loans and credits; more important, modifications in the economic plans of the entire bloc had to be made. By the summer of 1957, however, unrest in the satellites had been controlled, and Khrushchev had reasserted his supremacy in the Soviet presidium, but in July that year the strength of the internal opposition to his policies became apparent with the announcement of the purge (at a meeting of the Central Committee held from 22 to 29 June) of Molotov, Kaganovich, Malenkov, and Shepilov, shortly to be followed by the dismissal of Zhukov. From this time onward Khrushchev's main policies, in particular those of decentralization and peaceful coexistence, which had received a setback in December 1956, were to be paramount, although it proved impossible to reimpose theoretical unity, and practice was allowed to differ in such important respects as agricultural policy, where some countries retained collective farms while in others they had virtually disappeared. On the other hand the Soviet leadership, and in step with it the leadership of the satellite countries, became increasingly concerned with 'anti-revisionism', especially in the intellectual field. The new spirit was exemplified in the joint Bulgarian–Soviet statement of February 1957 announcing an 'unbending determination to fight against any attempts at revising Marxism–Leninism, against any vacillation or retreat from it, against the attempts to create ideological confusion'. But if 'the thaw' was, ostensibly, put into reverse in the countries of Eastern Europe, Khrushchev's main tenets, especially that of 'peaceful coexistence', were to cause a more profound division in the Soviet world than those caused by destalinization in Poland and Hungary—the Sino-Soviet split.

In the economic field the most important policy of Khrushchev's régime was the attempt to bring about the economic co-ordination of the people's democracies through Comecon. The need for greater economic co-operation and integration through the co-ordination of national economic plans, the joint development of resources, specialization of production, &c, was emphasized in the programme of the Twentieth Congress, where Khrushchev announced that the basis for co-ordination was the dovetailing of the new five-year plans of the people's democracies with the sixth Soviet five-year plan. In the co-ordination of economic planning Comecon undoubtedly made considerable progress from 1956, but the aim of economic specialization clashed with national interests and was seen as a threat to national industries in the satellite countries; consequently in this respect Comecon achieved only a more modest success. From early 1959 the Soviet leaders continued to urge that the cost of developing the more backward bloc economies (of Rumania and Bulgaria in particular) should be discussed. This was one of the themes of the Twenty-First CPSU Congress, but here again resistance was encountered. The reconstruction of Comecon to make it a more effective organ of policy and Rumania's strenuous opposition to the rôle assigned to it belong to a later section of this book.

THE SECRET SPEECH: POLAND AND HUNGARY

Of all the Eastern European governments, the Rumanian was the least affected by the convulsions of destalinization. The calm in Rumania was from one point of view proof of the Rumanian Workers' Party's weakness and apathy. Had it had some direct roots in the people, were it at all responsive to currents of opinion, had it fought its own battle with genuine ideas for specific national problems, it would certainly have been more obviously affected. But because of its weakness, its lack of ideological or national tradition and men of outstanding stature, the party concerned itself with only one thing—staying in power.

In Poland there were three main sources for the movement for liberalization. First, the continuous action of the Polish intelligentsia, which justified the reputation it soon won as the most courageous and patriotic in Eastern Europe. Secondly, the anti-communist, anti-Russian stand of all strata of Polish society, from the peasants stubbornly resisting collectivization to the workers, increasingly dissatisfied with their lot in the 'dictatorship of the proletariat'.

'Bread and freedom', the slogan of the Poznán strike which triggered off the revolution, expressed the demand for better conditions for all classes and the claim for political, national, and religious freedom; indeed, the Church had constantly been the rallying point of the Polish quest for basic freedoms. The third source was the party itself which, through the surviving leader of the opposition, Wladislaw Gomulka, saw in the Twentieth Congress the removal of the main stumbling blocks imposed by the Stalinist leadership on the 'Polish way to socialism'. On 20 October 1956, after the departure of the Soviet delegation to the eighth Polish plenum, the Soviet-Polish communiqué was published which confirmed that Poland had been liberated from direct Soviet control. Collectivization was abandoned; the workers were given better conditions and more trade union freedom and managerial co-partnership; intellectuals were allowed to express their opinions and to write as they wished; a satisfactory *modus vivendi* was established with the Catholic Church; some political and electoral freedom was restored at once.

In Hungary too the uprising began in intellectual circles. When the Twentieth Congress gave them the opportunity to speak up, they did so, at a meeting of the Petöfi Circle on 27 June 1956, with so concentrated an attack on the Stalinist leadership, and especially on Rakosi himself, that it directly contributed to his 'voluntary' resignation. By September the pressure in the party for the rehabilitation of Imre Nagy resulted in his reinstatement on 13 October. On 23 October he was appointed Chairman of the Council of Ministers in confused circumstances, as revolutionary bands were already attacking public buildings in Budapest. But Nagy was not Gomulka, and the Hungarian party did not have the flexibility or depth of the Polish one. On 24 October Gerö had already asked for Soviet military assistance, and this exacerbated the Hungarian people, already united in the will to end Soviet domination of their country. As in Poland, collective farms were abandoned at once; workers' councils were set up; Nagy was brought to power. His first radio address to the people, on 25 October 1956, announced that the Hungarian government would begin negotiations with the Soviet Union, among other things on the withdrawal of Soviet troops in Hungary, on the basis of 'equality between Communist Parties and socialist countries'.[1] On 3 November the Hungarian people forced Nagy to declare Hungary's neutrality, but next day Soviet troops and tanks moved in to crush the revolution.

[1] P. E. Zinner, ed., *National Communism and Popular Revolt in Eastern Europe* (1956), p. 417.

Shortlived as it was, it was the Hungarian revolution that made more impact on Rumania than the Polish one. Events in Poland could have taught a useful lesson to the Rumanian party. At the time it ignored them. But the revolution of the Hungarian people fired the imagination of the Rumanians who, like the Hungarians, based their political judgement on the premise that only Soviet armed might maintained the communists in power and who, again like the Hungarians, believed that the communists were too weak to offer a solution of their own. The Rumanian government was as much afraid of Hungarian developments as the people were hopeful; and the Rumanian Workers' Party, highly aware of both the Polish and Hungarian examples, tried now to forestall any new outbursts of anti-Soviet feeling in order to concentrate upon the dangers of anti-Stalinist opposition within the party.

THE RWP AND THE TWENTIETH CONGRESS

Between 23 and 25 March 1956 the Central Committee of the Rumanian Workers' Party held an enlarged plenum to discuss the Twentieth Soviet Congress.

Gheorghiu-Dej presented the report of the delegation which had gone to the Congress and which was composed of himself, Chisinevschi, Constantinescu, and Borila. The report[2] contained a first part in which Stalin was generally criticized, stress being laid on the personality cult. Credit was given to him for the main achievements of his rule, but it was somewhat regretfully admitted that towards the end he had spoiled many of the results as well as his reputation by indulging in the personality cult and by allowing some of the state organs, especially the security forces, to use terroristic and brutal methods. Nothing was said of the secret speech, and the whole part of the speech dealing with the Soviet Union was a muted version of Khrushchev's public speech.

When it came to the part dealing with the impact of Stalinism on his own party, Dej spoke of the Stalinists in the party without giving their names. He said that a part of the leadership had used non-Leninist methods and had been able to get away with such methods until 1952. It was obvious to everyone that it was Ana Pauker, Luca, and Georgescu to whom he was referring.

[2] 'Report of the Delegation of the RWP concerning the 20th Congress of the CPSU', *Sc.*, 29 Mar. 1956.

Since these leaders had been dismissed, Dej said, the party had taken decisive steps to extirpate such methods. He quoted the plenary meeting of August 1953 and especially the Second Congress of December 1955 as the beginning of the new phase, of the new mentality, and of the new methods by which collective leadership and internal democracy were reintroduced in the life of the party. He pledged the party leadership to 're-examine some decisions of the Central Committee, and some speeches of the state and party leaders, so as to put an end to the ugliness of the personality cult' as well as to 'strengthen the collective character of the leadership' and continually develop the internal democracy of the party. About the relations with the peasants, he made another veiled reference. He said that one bad effect of Stalin's influence on the Rumanian party was seen in the relations between the workers and the peasants, because of the theory that the more the building of socialism progresses, the more the class struggle sharpens. He said that this had alienated the peasant class, an indirect reference to Ana Pauker's attempts to impose forcible collectivization in 1949–51. (A second reference to this action was to be made at the discussion of the Twentieth Congress at a meeting of the party *Aktiv* of the Stalin district of Bucharest on 22 May 1956, when Dej said that without the knowledge of the rest of the Central Committee the 'deviationists' had taken many provocative measures, staging mass arrests and trials of working peasants.) As far as relations with the security forces were concerned, Dej said that although they had accomplished many good things, especially in uncovering imperialist spies in the RPR, the security organs had overstepped the limits of legality. He asked that the control of the party over all activities in the RPR should be ensured and strengthened.

In contrast with the Central Committee plenum of 1961 held to discuss the Soviet Twenty-Second Congress,[3] Dej's speech to the 1956 plenum was the only one published. The reason for this may have been one that was not disclosed until July 1957 (and more clearly still in November 1961), that two other members of the Rumanian delegation to the Twentieth Congress, Miron Constantinescu and Chisinevschi, attacked Dej during the plenum, accusing him of responsibility for the Stalinist principles and methods of the party. They were probably both acting for

[3] See below, p. 333.

different reasons and were united only in common opposition to Dej. As both had been to Moscow, both had found in the electric atmosphere of the Twentieth Congress their own reasons for launching their attack on Dej, whom they considered to be the real Stalinist culprit, on their return.

Chisinevschi was indeed a genuine Stalinist, friend and devotee of Ana Pauker, who tried to defend her against the accusations hurled at her by the First Secretary, by the same man who had been First Secretary since 1944 and who was now trying to escape so lightly by incriminating her and Vasile Luca. But Constantinescu, according to one interpretative theory, appears to have been trying to exploit the circumstances and a momentary alliance with Chisinevschi to provide an opportunity for discussion on the genuine need for liberalization in the party and country. Inspired by the new atmosphere in the communist world, the theory ran, he rose against the entire Stalinist leadership and demanded that the need for real reforms should be accepted and that a proper cleansing from the top should be initiated. In this he took a personal risk, because he too was deeply associated with the leadership and had silently shared in their deeds since 1944. But on the other hand his friends would stress that he was remote from having any direct responsibility for the worst forms of repression; and the description of him by Ceausescu in 1961[4] as a man initially opposed to the party, who year after year swallowed great doses of bitterness while eagerly awaiting his opportunity, may have been an accurate one.

Although Dej's victory was assured, the top-level conflict seems to have continued until the crushing of the Hungarian revolution. It was only then that the stand taken by Constantinescu and Chisinevschi failed and they were punished accordingly.

After the March plenum the party leadership went down to the regions, each important member of the Politburo and Secretariat visiting one region to discuss the documents of the Twentieth Congress.

In Bucharest Dej, taking Constantinescu with him, went to the various district meetings in the capital. The meeting in the Stalin district on 22 May was by far the stormiest.[5] Here two important segments were involved: the Bucharest organization and the

[4] Speech at CC plenum, 30 Nov.–5 Dec. 1961.
[5] *Sc.*, 23 May 1956.

writers. It was clear that the ferment was spreading rapidly among the latter.

THE WRITERS

The opposition of the writers and artists to the incompetent and stubborn Agitprop had been growing. Without the impetus of the movement of the Polish or Hungarian writers, it spread more, and more quickly than the leadership of the party had reason to expect. The two main centres were in Bucharest and Cluj, where a new group around the review *Steaua* had the distinction of being a homogeneous one, although it was formed of both Hungarian and Rumanian writers. They were all animated by sincere socialist ideals, but wanted to have the freedom to express them as they wished. The group was also better informed about liberalization movement through their knowledge of the Hungarian situation and of the publications and debates of the Petöfi circle. In Bucharest, on the other hand, the sources of inspiration were numerous and confused and there was no active solidarity between the various individuals who felt that the moment had come for a proper discussion of the basic conditions of artistic and cultural activities in a people's democracy. They were simply individuals, hesitant of discussing such problems even with a colleague. The fact that the Bucharest writers had not yet had time to crystallize into a group or alliance helped the party to crush their restiveness much more easily.

When the first clash between the writers and the party took place on 22 May 1956,[6] one cannot even be sure whether it was or not something of a trap set by the party to catch one or two individuals and warn all the others through their punishment. On that date a meeting of the party *Aktiv* of the district committee of the RWP in the Stalin district of Bucharest was held. This district party *Aktiv* had among its members an unusual number of writers and artists. It was already known that discussions among the writers on how their activities might be liberalized were coming into the open. It was therefore to be expected that on such an occasion discussions might flare up. This was probably the reason why so minor and routine a meeting was attended by Gheorghiu-Dej, Miron Constantinescu, and Leonte Rautu, the second in

[6] 'For a High Level of Ideological Work'; the debate of the party *Aktiv* of the district committee of the RWP, IV Stalin, Bucharest (*Sc.*, 23 May 1956).

command at Agitprop. The writer who had the courage to criticize the Stalinist methods of the party and voice the need for liberalization was Alexander Jar. Jar was a lonely, unattractive, and violent man of Jewish origin, who had suffered greatly in German concentration camps where part of his family had met a terrible end.[7] His novels were not of a high literary standard but his descriptions of Nazi horrors had an authentic and gripping quality. At the same time, according to the party,[8] he had 'strong nationalistic tendencies', that is to say he did not always show the Russians in their most pristine light and preferred always to emphasize specific Rumanian behaviour and attitudes. In the first months of 1956 he had made himself better known by some bold appeals for more liberalization in the party literary review, and especially in an interview published in *Gazeta Literara,* where he had gone as far as to say that 'in our country police measures are used against some writers'. This was a challenge which could not go unheeded in a police state. At the May meeting in the Stalin district he was evidently inspired by the presence of Gheorghiu-Dej. According to the official version of the proceedings, he displayed an anti-party attitude. He said that he, like so many other writers, had lived for the past years a double life between his conscience and what he had been asked to do, between what he wanted to write and what he published. He claimed that this was true not only of the writers but of all party members and of all communists; 'Party members think less and less', he averred. He described the process of self-blinding and of sterilization of thought through which all party members have to go if they are to obey the rules and to follow the suffocating discipline of the party. He contested the right of the party to interfere to such an extent in the private life and thoughts of its members. After this sharp and unpredented criticism, he made an ardent plea that the party should at least now start on 'another path'. This was the path of liberalization which had been already taken in the Soviet Union and which was being followed by so many other parties. Why should only the leadership of the Rumanian Workers' Party put up such a stubborn resistance against this inevitable and salutary trend?

[7] His wife, a Rumanian communist, was savagely murdered by the Gestapo in France. See also a study on Jar by Wolfgang Oberleitner in *Die Presse* (Vienna), 31 May 1962.

[8] All quotations from Jar's speech reproduced here are from the *Scintea* article quoted in n. 6 above.

Indeed, he said, this was the last chance, for 'during the period of the building of socialism, literary and artistic creation were led by the party to total disaster'. He was seconded, albeit much more timidly, by the playwright Davidoglu and the critic Ion Vintner, who both advocated a new liberal trend in the ideological and intellectual affairs of the party. But these were indeed lonely and weak voices against the torrent of protests which arose from the compact ranks of the members who had been specially dragooned into coming, and from Dej himself who rejected the allegations and treated the pleas of the three writers as a clear case of treason. But the party press took the unprecedented step of quoting, together and indiscriminately, what Dej, Miron Constantinescu, and Rautu had said during the meeting.[9] Among their utterances were much sharper criticisms of the past than were made at the Central Committee plenum of the previous March, and it is probable that Constantinescu tried to carry his fight for liberalization a step farther at this meeting.

But now there were the beginnings of an open revolt. The party was obviously aware of the example of the Polish student paper *Po Prostu* and the Hungarian Petöfi circle. It was also aware that Jar had no real following or even friends. A full-scale counter-offensive was, therefore both necessary and possible. On 1 June 1956 *Scinteia* published a full-page verbatim report of the previous day's meeting of the basic party organization of the writers of Bucharest.[10] This was a typical Stalinist kind of meeting in which everyone attacked the main villain and if necessary confessed his own mistakes or faults. Not a single voice, as recorded by the report, defended Jar. He was expelled from the party, and Davidoglu and Vintner were severely castigated.

In spite of this, the preparations for the congress of the Writers' Union continued in a troubled atmosphere. It must be noticed in this connexion that apart from the electric atmosphere which had been felt in Bucharest since the Twentieth Congress, this period coincided with two important visits. Kozlov had stayed in Bucharest in the last weeks of May. Tito had passed through it on 1 June and was returning on a state visit on 24 June, the very day when the writers' congress ended after a week of meetings.

[9] Ibid.
[10] 'Against Deviations from the Party Spirit', *Sc.*, 1 June 1956.

This congress[11] was a more animated affair than the previous one. Many individual writers made strong pleas that dogmatism and dogmatic control should be curbed. Mihai Novicov, O. Crohmalniceanu, Paul Georgescu, Petre Dumitriu, and especially A. E. Baconsky and Titus Popovici expressed in different, and often opposing ways, their opposition to dogmatism. Popovici, for instance, spoke mainly of the deleterious impact of the dogmatic theory of socialist-realism. He said that there were bureaucratic elements in the publishing houses and cultural institutions who reduced everything to their limited criteria. 'Our era', he said, 'denounced the policy of the ostrich towards the problems which it raises : these problems exist even if we are asked to ignore them.' But at the end Mihai Beniuc, a young communist Transylvanian poet turned *politruk,* was again elected to the highest office. The congress ended on a note of almost total reconciliation between the writers and the party over Jar's demise.

Nevertheless some changes were taking place. Chisinevschi had already been taken out of Agitprop activities. Rautu was appointed temporarily and it was being pondered whether Constantinescu should not become the head and thus responsible for all intellectual activities. Rautu, also a Bessarabian Jew, like Chisinevschi, was however of better quality than his colleague and predecessor. Even people who hated him recognized that his methods were different, more perfidious perhaps but also less crude. His Stalinism was better covered by a cloak of intellectual agility. Furthermore, either on orders from the Politburo or through his own convictions, he believed in the advantages of quality in literary and artistic production.

These, then, were the months in which old writers, professors, historians, scientists, and artists were taken out of prison and rehabilitated. They were given jobs, sometimes even their old jobs back. Tudor Arghezi, the greatest Rumanian poet, reappeared, aged and tired, as did many other figures of whom the Rumanian public had not heard since the communists came to power. The changes were also visible at the Academy. Roller disappeared and the institutes and sections were now filled with people known for their work and ability. Mihai Ralea, A. Rossetti, and especially Atanasie Joja, under the benevolent aegis of the old Sadoveanu took over the active direction. The young writer Petre Dumitriu

[11] Held from 18 to 24 June 1956. Speeches and reports are summarized from *Sc.*

had been appointed, with Constantinescu's help, director of the State Publishing House. Soon translations from American, French, and British writers began to be published. The best books of the Rumanian writers under communism were also published in these years: Eugen Barbu's *The Grave*; Titus Popovici's *The Stranger* and *The Thirst*. Here the influence of Camus was not only in the titles. Marin Preda's *Moronetzi* was probably the most original novel produced under the present régime, a strange Dostoyevskian study of characters without any relevance to the themes of socialist-realism. Dumitriu himself published *Family Chronicle*, a brilliant satire on the past régime which rapidly became a best-seller, partly because, as the author himself acknowledged,[12] the public preferred to read about the past than about the present. There was also Calinescu's *The Poor Ioanide*, a novel banned because its indictment of the Iron Guard and the fascist movement were so clearly directed against all totalitarian régimes. In poetry the works of Baconsky and Labis were obviously directed against their environment. In drama the plays of Ana Novak and Aurel Baranga probed more deeply than socialist-realism would countenance. At the Historical Institute a new generation of historians were exploring subjects which had been forbidden till then: the history of the peasant revolts and movements in Rumania; Rumania between the wars and Titulescu's fight for peace; a new history of Rumania. The old professors were consulted and admitted into the seminars and the Roller-type of exclusive Russian interpretation of anything Rumanian was much toned down. If the aims were not substantially changed, the means were different and better. The party had proceeded dialectically. It had faced the open revolt openly; and it had, without saying so, accepted the necessity to improve its methods.

Had the Hungarian revolt succeeded even partially, these salutary developments in Rumania might have continued and broadened very fast. But even defeated it had its immediate and national impact on Rumanian intellectual life.

[12] In a conversation with the author.

12

The Impact of Poland and Hungary

DURING the rising in Poland an important Rumanian delegation left for Yugoslavia, where it arrived on 19 October 1956. Its chief members were Dej, Stoica, Borila, Rautu, and Grigore Preoteasa, Minister of Foreign Affairs. The Rumanian press played down the political or ideological importance of this visit as much as possible, presenting it rather as an official contact between two neighbouring governments. At the same time, and even more significantly, the press adopted a very non-committal attitude towards Gomulka's emergence as the leader of the Polish party and government. It did, however, reproduce *Pravda's* article criticizing the Polish press and intelligentsia. Gheorghiu-Dej's statement, upon arriving in Belgrade, stressed that the Rumanian Workers' Party sincerely rejoiced in the re-establishment of friendly relations between the Yugoslav and other parties.[1] As for events in Hungary, the RPR refrained from mentioning them until 25 October. On 26 October they were stigmatized as the work of capitalist agents. It is still a moot point whether Dej was not acting as Khrushchev's emissary to discuss with Tito the deteriorating situation in Hungary and its possible repercussions on neighbouring countries such as Yugoslavia and Rumania, which might be faced with a free, anti-communist and western-integrated Hungary.

On 27 October there were demonstrations in Bucharest, Iasi, Cluj, and Timisoara. These were mostly student demonstrations and one of the demands most frequently heard at them was for the abolition of the teaching of Russian in schools and universities.[2] But especially in Bucharest, Iasi, and Timisoara, the workers were also active. Unrest was particularly marked at the head-

[1] *Pravda*, 10 Nov. 1956.

[2] *New York Times*, 30 Oct. & 3 Nov. 1956; *Daily Mail*, 2 Nov. 1956. The only western correspondent then in Rumania, Wells Hangen of the *New York Times*, was expelled on 4 Nov. 1956.

quarters of the railwaymen in Bucharest;[3] and in Iasi, near the Soviet frontier, where many Soviet troops were stationed, street demonstrations took a defiant form.

On 28 October Gheorghiu-Dej and the Rumanian delegation hurriedly left Yugoslavia, although their talks were by no means ended. Before leaving, however, Dej, who had arrived brimming with Soviet orthodoxy, agreed a sentence in the final communiqué advocating the inadvisability of foreign intervention in the affairs of other countries.

Back in Rumania Dej, and more particularly Bodnaras, who was responsible for the preparedness of the armed forces, had at once to take urgent measures. Some were aimed at easing the passage of the Soviet troops needed for operations in Hungary. From the beginning of October 1956, that is since the danger of revolutionary movements in Hungary and Poland had been apparent, the Soviet forces in Rumania had been increased to many more than the two divisions at which they had allegedly stood since 1948. For the passage of the units to Hungary new forces were massed in Rumania, especially on the Hungarian frontier. The old wartime communication line with the front was once more established. At the same time the increase of Soviet strength in Rumania was a source of strength to the Rumanian government, which was bending all its efforts to stemming rising unrest in that country too.

The second series of government measures was designed to re-establish order. Widespread arrests were made, up to 1,200 in towns alone during the first days, according to the British and American press.[4] Police patrols and guards were reinforced. On 30 October the Timisoara, Oradea, and Iasi regions were placed under special military jurisdiction and no foreigners were allowed to enter either Moldavia or Transylvania. A military parade, due on 7 November, was cancelled at short notice; and a medical congress to which foreign guests had been invited was also postponed. Nevertheless on 1 November, when the new armoured divisions entered Hungary, more demonstrations took place in Moldavia and in the stronghold of the railwaymen, Grivita, near Bucharest. In ministries and official circles the atmosphere was noticeably tense.

[3] *New York Times*, 30 Oct. & 3 Nov. 1956.
[4] *New York Times*, 30 Oct. & 3 Nov. 1956; *Daily Mail*, 2 Nov. 1956.

Steps were also taken to placate the anger of the more excited sections of the population, the workers and students, with immediate promises. The waves of popular unrest did not reach the peasants quickly; as in Hungary, they were the last to hear the news. But some unrest was registered in the villages, although it in no way approached that in the industrial and university towns. Here political discontent was coupled with acute economic distress because of one of the worst harvests since the communists took power. Queues for food and even for bread had been a feature of life in Bucharest and other cities since August. The black market flourished again and prices on it soared. The peasants in the villages were more than ever reluctant to bring any of their produce to town. Exasperated housewives pressed the workers, who in turn pressed the managements and trade unions. As in Poznan, the slogan 'bread and liberty' began to be repeated at workers' meetings. On the other hand the slogans of the students were mainly anti-Russian. Secretly prepared meetings were held: the biggest took place in one of the main squares of Bucharest. As an urgent concessionary move, the government announced on 29 October that the minimum wage of all workers would be raised and that supplementary allowances would be made for children. Special attention was given to the railwaymen who, on 1 November, were granted paid holidays and free travel, to start at once. On 2 November Gheorghe Apostol unexpectedly attended a large meeting called by the railwaymen. He stressed the difficulties they had with their wages and standard of living and promised governmental help. It was noticeable that Dej, the railway workers' 'hero', stayed away.

With youth too developments in November added to the rising discontent voiced in universities and schools. On 22 June 1956 the Politburo had published a new decision[5] concerning political and educational work among students. It spoke frankly of the 'unhealthy attitude' of the students who 'despise the cultural and technical achievements of our country and of the other countries of the socialist camp' and show 'a total servitude towards the cultural and scientific achievements of the capitalist countries'. The students were criticized for being 'mystical' and for indulging in constant 'manifestations of nationalism'. In July it was reported that many arrests had been made among students in all the uni-

[5] *Sc.* same date.

versity towns. On 18 August a country-wide meeting of students was called in order to form a new association of all the students of the RPR, but by the beginning of November, when a second wave of unrest swept the universities, nothing had been heard of this organization. On 5 November 1956 Miron Constantinescu addressed a student meeting in Cluj and promised that the government would put an end to the teaching of Russian and would improve their standard of living. On 18 November he was appointed Minister of Education.

A third centre of unrest during November was the Hungarian population of Transylvania, especially among the Hungarian intelligentsia. The confessions made afterwards by a group of Hungarian professors and scholars of 'national feeling of solidarity' which they had expressed with the Hungarian people before the Soviet intervention are a proof of the depth of the feeling. Some of the most unruly and most widely attended meetings of workers and students took place in Transylvania and in the Autonomous Magyar Region. The greatest concentration of Soviet troops was in these regions, thus serving the purpose of being nearer to the Hungarian frontier but also no doubt to the most explosive spot in the country. It must be stressed, however, that this was by no means the only trouble spot. The situation was equally dangerous in Bucharest, although the communist administration at present prefers to acknowledge only unrest among the Hungarian population, as a reminder to the Rumanians of the 'chauvinist and irredentist ultimate aims of the Hungarian fascists and reactionaries'; and to make the recurrent insinuation that an overthrow of the communist (Rakosi or Kadar) régime in Hungary would have meant the emergence of an aggressive Hungary on the Rumanian border, with immediate claims upon Transylvania.

Finally, steps had to be taken towards strengthening and reorganizing the army, whose loyalty had been so uncertain at the end of October. The behaviour of the Hungarian army during the revolution or, again, the immediate anti-Russian reaction of the Polish army, could not but convince the Russian and the Rumanian authorities of the need to remodel the RPR forces. This movement was carried out in depth with great thoroughness. New cadres of officers took over. When the Soviet troops left Rumania in the summer of 1958, they left behind entirely remodelled Rumanian army and security forces. After the storm had been weathered the Rumanian régime was called upon to supply some immediate help to the Kadar government. On 21 November an important Rumanian delegation went to Budapest, led by Gheorghiu-Dej and Bodnaras. Like the Czechoslovak visit which preceded it, the purpose of the Rumanian visit was to supply the food and drugs so urgently needed.[6] But it was also to help towards the reorganization of the security forces which had been practically destroyed during the revolution. Many Hungarian refugees have testified that the reorganization of the Hungarian AVRO was made possible through the massive importation of Hungarian-speaking Rumanians and Slovaks. The presence of Bodnaras and his longer stay in Budapest would seem to confirm this. This visit also explains the 'exile' of Imre Nagy and his colleagues in Rumania.

These, then, were the main reactions in Rumania during and after the Hungarian revolution. They were certainly short-lived, superficial, and sporadic. But still Rumania was the country in which solidarity with Hungary was more openly and more strongly expressed than in any other satellite, with the exception, of course, of Poland. Everything consistently pointed towards a similarity of the Rumanian and Hungarian attitudes to the régimes imposed upon them by Soviet Russia. Yet the absence of an open frontier with the west (as had Hungary after the evacuation of Soviet troops from Austria in the autumn of 1955), the lack of a permanent rallying body and guidance such as that given by the Catholic Church to the Hungarians and Poles, and the caution of the régime in not allowing the intellectuals and workers' councils to take a definite lead in public affairs made any larger scale reaction improbable.

In fact the Hungarian revolution produced a situation in Rumania which might have erupted if that revolution had not been crushed. It was the first days of November 1956 that were dangerous for the Rumanian régime. As Khrushchev himself significantly remarked on 8 November 1956, when addressing the Moscow Komsomol, there were 'some unhealthy moods' among students 'in one of the educational establishments in Rumania', and he congratulated the Rumanian party on having taken the

[6] On 7 Dec. Parvulescu announced in his speech on the anniversary of the Russian Revolution that the RPR was already sending food and medicaments worth 13 million lei to Hungary (*Sc.*, 8 Nov. 1956).

necessary steps to deal with them quickly and effectively.[7] It is probable that the fact that Khrushchev allowed the Rumanian party to escape with only perfunctory lip-service to destalinization, without offering any victims to it, was also an indication of his appreciation of the Rumanian calm, which was evidently also appreciated by Tito for his own reasons. When Tito visited Moscow on 1 June 1956 he passed through Rumania and on his return on 24 June paid an official visit to the country. This came as a surprise at the time to those who knew that one of the main objects of his visit to Russia was to discuss relations between Yugoslavia and the other European communist countries, especially the neighbouring ones. Of these, one of the most virulent in the campaign against Titoism had been Rumania, which had sheltered anti-Tito refugees, originated anti-Tito broadcasts beamed to Yugoslavia, and whose leading personality, Gheorghiu-Dej, had been the rapporteur of the first Cominform denunciations of Yugoslavia. Yet Tito preferred to pass through Rumania rather than Hungary. 'When I went to Moscow', he said, 'there was great surprise that I did not travel via Hungary. It was precisely because of Rakosi that I did not want to do so. I said that I would rather not go through Hungary even if it would have meant making the journey three times shorter.'[8] Moreover at the end of his visit, in a statement to the foreign press, he wondered why Rumania was described in the West as a satellite régime. No doubt during his visit to Moscow he accepted the Soviet leaders' estimate of Dej, which was presumably similar to the argument they had used (but which Tito had not accepted) in Rakosi's case, that 'he was prudent, that he was going to succeed, and that they knew of no one else whom they could rely upon in that country'.[9] Tito's information about unrest in Rumania probably confirmed the apprehensions of the Soviet and Rumanian leaders. As was seen from his attitude during the Hungarian revolution, he was opposed to any attempt to bring a non-communist régime to power in a neighbouring country. Finally, it might well be that he considered Ana Pauker and Vasile Luca as the Rakosis of Rumania. (This analogy has repeatedly been made by the Rumanian communist leaders, who spoke not only of the similarity of methods and prin-

[7] *Pravda*, 10 Nov. 1956.
[8] Address to meeting of Yugoslav League of Communists, Pula, 11 Nov. 1956 (in Zinner, p. 524).
[9] Ibid.

ciples of Rakosi and Pauker but also of their direct contact both with each other and with Stalin and Molotov.[10] Their dismissal in 1952 may well have been explained to him as the removal of the really anti-Titoist elements in a party which otherwise, had it not been under strict Stalinist orders, would have preferred to follow some of the Yugoslav experiments.

Thus throughout the period of destalinization the same Rumanian communist team as before carried on as usual and served up the same mixture as before—domestic repression tempered by some moderation, an unconditional loyalty to the Soviet Union in foreign policy, coupled with a firm ideological anti-revisionism and dogmatism. But then Dej showed himself the Kremlinist par excellence, and perhaps the best description of Rumania during the period was that given by a Rumanian official to a Western press correspondent in 1962 when he said: 'There has been no revisionism, no Titoism, no relaxation, no tightening'.[11]

RUMANIAN-SOVIET RELATIONS

As has been mentioned, among concessions that the Soviet Union was compelled to make after the Polish and Hungarian uprisings were new agreements on the stationing of troops and on the provision of economic assistance.

On 26 November 1956 the Rumanian Prime Minister, Chivu Stoica, led an economic delegation to Moscow. On 3 December a joint statement was released by Tass.[12] It is worth comparing this statement with that released after the Polish-Soviet talks which had immediately preceded those with the Rumanians.[13] Both statements pledged co-operation on the principle of complete equality of rights and non-interference in the internal affairs of each country. Both made the point that the stationing of Soviet troops on Polish or Rumanian territory was by agreement, and only with the consent of the governments concerned. In the case of Rumania, 'the temporary stationing' of Soviet armed forces there, 'as provided for under the Warsaw Treaty', was deemed to be necessary because of 'the aggressive military bloc in Western Europe', the remilitarization of Germany, and United States and

[10] See espec. Dej report to CC plenum of Nov.–Dec. 1961 (*Sc.*, 7 Dec. 1961).
[11] Paul Underwood in *Sunday New York Times*, 15 Apr. 1962.
[12] *Soviet News*, 4 Dec. 1956.
[13] BBC, Summary of World Broadcasts, pt. IIA, no. 779, 21 Nov. 1956.

NATO bases 'near the socialist countries'. But the agreement on the presence of Soviet troops in Poland was far more specific and hedged with limitations dealing with numbers, disposition, movements, jurisdiction, &c.

The texts differed also in their main economic provisions. The Polish-Soviet text spoke of the determination of the two governments 'to develop and consolidate economic co-operation between the two countries on the basis of equal rights, mutual advantage and mutual fraternal assistance'. The Rumanian-Soviet text mentioned that questions relating to economic co-operation were discussed, and that it had been agreed that deliveries should be made of certain goods especially needed 'to ensure the operation of industry and the improvement of the population's standards of living'. The Poles won the concession that all Polish 'debts' arising from the credits between 1946 and 1953 should be considered settled, and they also obtained a long-term credit of 700 million rubles to cover goods delivered by the Soviet Union to Poland. The Rumanians obtained a promise that the Soviet Union would supply them with iron ore, metallurgical coke, and pipes and other commodities, without which further plants and indeed whole departments of heavy industry would have had to be closed down. Also, because of the bad harvest in Rumania in 1956, the Soviet government agreed to 'lend' the RPR 450,000 tons of wheat and 60,000 tons of fodder grain, to be paid for under the trade agreement. It also pledged itself to supply plant and installations on credit to the value of 270 million rubles for the building of chemical industrial works. The RPR government was to 'repay' this credit by delivering chemicals produced at these works. This part of the agreement was reminiscent, but in different conditions and for a limited operation, of the agreements which Germany had imposed upon Rumania before and during the war and which had amounted to an export of capital in order to manufacture and deliver to the foreign partner the finished product from the raw materials either obtainable in the country or imported from abroad. Finally, the Soviet Union agreed to postpone for four years the repayment of the credits granted to the RPR between 1949 and 1955. This too was a far cry from the cancellation of the Polish debts. As one British newspaper commented, the communiqué gave 'the appearance of having been signed between two equal partners but it is clear from its terms that the Rumanians are less equal than the Poles'.[14]

ECONOMIC ADJUSTMENTS

After calm had been restored following the Hungarian revolution, the régime genuinely set about trying to mitigate some of the discontent which had produced the storm. A plenum of the Central Committee of 27–29 December 1956[15] reduced investments for the second Five-Year Plan so as to 'improve the proportion between the accumulation fund and the consumption fund of the population'. State capital investments for 1957 were fixed at 12.7 billion lei as against 14.8 in 1956, or a total reduction of 15 per cent. The plenum authorized that the increase of industrial production, which in 1956 had been set at 10–12 per cent, should be reduced to 3.8 per cent in 1957. The target for producer goods was to suffer the most drastic cut: the increase, set at 13.6 per cent in 1956, was to be only 5.4 per cent in 1957. As for future capital investment, the man responsible for the operation described it as aimed only at completing and putting into operation the working sites already opened and at limiting the opening of new sites to a 'very restricted number of industrial objectives of high profitability and economic efficiency'. Thus the Five-Year Plan directives which had themselves set out to limit industrialization to the main industries, for which Rumania could supply her own raw materials, were reduced further in scope by the decisions of the December plenum.

At the same time the workers were promised some immediate increase in their cash payments and a higher basic tariff wage. On 24 January 1957 a plenum of the Central Committee of the trade unions met to consider the decisions of the party Central Committee plenum of December. The agenda ranged from the problems of the share of the workers in industrial management to that of the new wage system. As for the first, the demand for the active participation of the workers in the organization and leadership of production (as the agenda called it) was the result of frequent claims for the establishment of workers' councils. The answer of the leaders of the party was firstly to try to inject new life into the still-born 'production meetings', and secondly to effect some de-

[14] *Manchester Guardian*, 4 Dec. 1956.
[15] Report by Gheorghiu-Dej, *Sc.*, 30 Dec. 1956; *Agerpres Inf. Bull.*, 10 Jan. 1957.

centralization in the economic administration. In his report to the plenum, Apostol[16] took the usual 'dialectical line' of communist leaders in periods of stress. He asked the workers to be more co-operative with the management and economic authorities, but at the same time he criticized the latter for not having paid enough attention to the constructive proposals of the workers' agencies. With great emphasis he revived the idea, hitherto kept in the background, of production meetings. He promised that within the framework of these meetings, which embody the collective experience of the workers, engineers, technicians, and economic leaders, 'all problems were to be discussed'. It was decided that at these meetings decisions could be taken concerning production problems the solution of which depended exclusively on the respective team or department. One year later, however, it was disclosed that the production meetings had been more successful in larger concerns or plants than in the small and medium ones. This suggests that the setting up of such meetings still depends on the initiative of the officials rather than on that of the workers themselves. Otherwise it would be more natural to see spontaneous meetings taking place in small and medium enterprises where the control and presence of the party officials are less overwhelming than in the large ones. One may surmise, therefore, that these meetings are probably still without real power. The state and party would like to make more use of them, in order to integrate the workers more actively into the productive processes and to take the edge off any discontent.

On 15 March 1957 a further concession was promised. It was announced that enterprises which could show a profit above the estimate of the plan could afterwards transform 65 per cent of this profit into an 'enterprise fund', which could in turn be used directly by the management to reward the best workers and to increase the social-service expenditure of the enterprise. But the total amount that could be drawn from the fund was to be calculated proportionally not only to the general output but also to the quality of goods produced and to their production costs. The amount to be drawn thus varied from 15 to 65 per cent.

These two measures were the first tentative steps towards the establishment of some kind of workers' management in the RPR. Neither of them, however, re-established a direct right of decision

[16] *Sc.*, 30 Dec. 1956.

by the workers, as in both the initial decision was taken by the management, which limited the sphere of production meetings and the amount of the 'enterprise fund' according to instructions from the central authorities.

At the same time some measures towards economic decentralization were taken. The number of ministries was reduced from 25 to 16 on 16 March 1957.[17] Consequently, through various minor decrees and decisions, the personnel in the state administration in local and central economic bodies and even in the party were reduced. On 19 March the premier, Chivu Stoica, announced that the people's councils were to be given the funds with which to carry out some of the functions allocated to them. Their budget was doubled (to 200 million lei), and 4,000 small and medium industrial enterprises were put under their direct supervision. As in the case of the enterprises, the people's councils also had the right to use supplementary profits as they thought fit, without the prior approval of the central administration. It seems, however, that all these measures were applicable only to the fringe of the real economic activity, which remains concentrated in the 'top enterprises' in the great towns, and as such comes under the direct supervision, control and guidance of the central organs of the government, party, and trade unions.

The reform of the wage system announced in the resolution of the December 1956 Central Committee plenum aimed at an immediate 15 per cent increase in wage rates. The standard wage once more became the decisive element in the workers' earnings. The 15 per cent increase, applied proportionately and according to the scale, could lead to a 36 per cent increase in the total wage. Piece-work earnings (which since November 1953 had been the essential part of the workers' earnings) were to be reduced, directly through the lowering of premiums for the fulfilment or overfulfilment of norms, and indirectly by having the latter recalculated and readjusted in accordance with the technical level of the enterprises and with the output of the most successful factories or workshops.

Here the authorities suspected—and in many cases with justice—that the control of the managers and even of the economic departments of the government had allowed the workers to get

[17] The communiqué on the 14 March meeting of the Politburo of the CC spoke of the need to 'liquidate excessive centralism' (*Sc.*, 17 Mar. 1957).

away with a far too low scale of norms. This had raised costs of production and diminished real productivity. Hence, through a decree modifying some of the articles of the labour code, it was decided that Article 27, which had previously dealt with the establishment of norms of production, should be changed and 'working norms' should be established on the basis of the investigation of working conditions and of the technological factors of the entire field of production.

A new article (27a) was introduced which permitted the central organs of the administration and the executive committee of the regional people's councils, in collaboration with the management, to increase working norms whenever the new technical means provided had in reality reduced the time needed for the production of goods; or whenever technical mistakes had been made in the assessment of the norms. The central economic authorities were thus given wide powers to raise the norms and so to control more rigidly the factories and plants in which, during the last year of the first Five-Year Plan and the first of the second one, a tacit conspiracy between the workers and the technical managers had led to the slackening of the entire pace of production. The fear of the state employer that the workers would react to the new measure with the weapons of absenteeism or leaving their jobs had become less acute by 1957–8. By then, there was some unemployment and the workers had reasons to fear for their jobs. A resolution of 24 February 1957 struck at the category of 'peasant workers', i.e. villagers seasonally employed in some industries, especially in the timber industry, which formed a permanent sector of the RPR manpower; and the right of the factories to terminate the contracts of individual workers was subsequently enlarged through various administrative decrees or measures. Also, as the United Nations' *Economic Survey of Europe* for 1957 rightly pointed out, 'recent changes of pension laws in Bulgaria, Hungary and Rumania, in striking contrast with past policies, have expressly aimed at the curtailment of labour supply'.

It can be seen, therefore, that these post-November measures were a mixed blessing for the workers. But by 1958, directly through increases in wages and indirectly through a much more rational approach to planning, their position was considerably better than before the Hungarian revolution.

AGRICULTURAL POLICY AFTER NOVEMBER 1956

The upheavals in Poland and Hungary caused the virtual abandonment of the collective system of agriculture in both these countries. In Rumania there was no need for any drastic concession, but the régime did decide on one significant move to quell discontent in the country's still mainly privately-owned agriculture. It dismantled, earlier and more completely than in Poland, the system of compulsory quota deliveries for the private producers. On 1 January 1957 it was announced that compulsory deliveries of grain, oilseed, pulses, potatoes, and milk were being abolished. Farms with less than 1 hectare and the private plots of members of co-operative farms were also exempted from compulsory deliveries of meat. For other farms compulsory deliveries of meat remained, but it was promised that they would be terminated in the future.

There were two reasons for the move. Apart from trying to ease the farmer's lot and, by giving him more incentives, increase the food supply to the towns, it was generally felt throughout the bloc that the quota-deliveries system had come to the point of diminishing returns. According to the United Nations' *Economic Survey of Europe* for 1956, there were three main official grounds for criticism of the system which were especially relevant in Rumania. First, the quotas were generally too high, not leaving room for any adjustments due to local or temporary conditions. The farmers' debts towards the state accumulated from one year to the next. Secondly, the quotas were too 'steeply progressive', corresponding to the size of the farm. This, of course, particularly antagonized the middle farmers, who were now the 'pivot' of agricultural production. Thirdly, the high quotas could be borne only by kulaks, who with the means at their disposal could produce on their farms more than the middle farmer, who was obliged to work the land himself, or pay the exorbitant fees of the MTS.

More important than this concession was the continuation of the New Course policy of modified collectivization. There was no question of the dissolution of any collectives. In fact the existing farms were bolstered by large donations of state land, more technical capital, and concessionary fiscal capital. But there was no insistence on a very unpopular policy which might have disturbed the delicate equilibrium.

In 1957 there were 2,564 collective farms with a surface of 1,301,000 hectares, of which 1,179,800 hectares were arable land. By regions, Constanta came first, where 69.4 per cent of the entire arable surface had passed into the socialist sector.[18] (Later in the year, it was announced that socialization of the land in this region had been 100 per cent effective.) It was followed by the region of Galati, where 45.6 per cent was co-operativized, and Timisoara with 29.9 per cent. The first two regions were characteristically enough those in which the Soviet army and navy had important quarters and bases and which, at least in the harbour areas, had been cordoned off since 1944. Constanta had always been a region of vast estates and state farms; and many Bulgarians in 1940 and Turks in 1948 had left their estates and returned to their homelands. In Timisoara many Swabian landowners had also left their very efficiently run farms after the German military debacle of 1944. The remaining regions made up the general percentage of 20 per cent of the arable and 17.4 per cent of the agricultural land.

The land apportioned to the collective farms since the end of forcible collectivization in 1952 came from two sources: from the peasants themselves and from the state. The percentages of land used by the collective farms was as follows in 1952–6:

	1952	*1956*
Total	100.0	100.0
Given by the state	16.9	24.0
Contributed by owners	83.1	76.0
of which:		
(a) poor peasants	(24.1)	(25.0)
(b) middle peasants	(59.0)	(51.0)

Source: N. Belli, 'Socialist Ownership in the RPR Agriculture; *Probleme economice,* 12 Dec. 1957.

The table shows that the proportion of land given by the state had increased while that contributed by the middle farmers had decreased. Yet it is precisely this category of peasant owners that the régime wanted to attract to the collective farms, as their plots were bigger and more compact and as they brought with them also the means of production. In this respect it must be noted that on the one hand the average size of a collective holding had

[18] *An. Stat. 1957.*

grown from 258 hectares in 1948 to 439 hectares. On the other, what is called the 'basic' means of production, that is the fixed investment of each holding in tools and machines, &c, had increased by almost three times as much; this total can be divided as follows according to its origins:

	1951	*1955*
Total	100.0	100.0
Through collectivization	36.3	19.8
Through donations	31.8	14.8
Through formation of common fund	13.3	35.2
Through state loans or investment	18.6	30.2

Source: As for table above.

During the same period the value of the 'indivisible fund' of the collective farms, which according to the state is the indivisible property of the unit and theoretically is the hard core of socialist ownership, increased four times, from 143,887,000 lei in 1951 to 676,105,000.

The greater part of the 'indivisible fund' came from the value of the work of the collective farmers themselves, i.e. was deducted from their income. But some also came from state loans. In 1956 the state granted hurried loans to the collective farms of a sum of roughly 200 million lei, more than one-third of the entire amount of loans granted to them since they began in 1949. This shows the great efforts made in the years 1955–8 to encourage the formation of new units, as well as to maintain the older ones in existence. Among these efforts was also the attempt to improve the quota-income of the members and especially to pay more regularly and more honestly their earnings for 'work-days'; the improvement in collaboration between the collective farms and the MTS; and the reduction of any kind of taxes, quotas, and expenses for repairs and maintenance. According to Gheorghiu-Dej, the net income of a collectivized farmer in 1956 should have been double that of a private farmer.

Nevertheless none of these concessions convinced the Rumanian farmers of the advisability of joining the collectives at the time, and since force was not now applied, they stayed away. On the other hand the agricultural associations made considerable progress. They were to become the transition belt, used extensively by the government, for progress from private ownership to collectivization.

YOUTH AND STUDENTS

The régime's policy on youth and education has always been determined by two main factors—the conditions under which the communists seized power and the tasks which were subsequently assigned to the national economy.

As has been seen, on coming to power the communists had great difficulties in finding even the minimum number of intellectuals who could become the first layer of 'technocrats' needed by the state employer. Thus the creation of a new class of intellectuals, emanating from the ranks of the people and devoted to the régime, seemed to the communist leaders the only possible way of solving not only the economic problem but the problem of building up the new Rumanian People's Republic. One of the main agents in the régime's policy of transformation was to have been the communist youth movement.

The Union of Rumanian Communist Youth was founded in 1924, but in the first two decades of its existence, until 1944, it never succeeded in attracting even a small minority of the young people of Rumania. It failed to establish cells in the army, schools or universities, in many branches of industry or in the villages.

The lessons of this inter-war period were not lost on the communist leaders. Having failed in this period to attract youth with slogans such as 'the sacred right of vacations', the seven-hour working day and student autonomy, the party realized that a policy of compulsion had to be instituted. The youth had to acquire a communist mentality and had to be submitted to all means of verification to ensure their reliability; and it had to be professionally trained according to the dictates and requirements of state policy.

The Union of Working Youth (UTM, set up in March 1949) in Rumania, like the Komsomol organization, had and has a vital rôle to play in both aspects of this policy. Open to all young people between the ages of 14 and 26, in 1960 it numbered about 1,800,000. It was and is meant to remain a mass organization, the real militancy of which was supplied by its local committees, most of whose secretaries and members were Communist Party members. These committees have many tasks. As the party's main agent in the schools, colleges, and universities, the UTM checks on the behaviour of both teachers and students, the enthusiasm and competence with which a subject is either taught or learnt, and the academic and ideological progress of the students.

This means, of course, interference in schoolroom activities, where one would normally expect the teacher to be in charge. That the UTM is actually encouraged to poach on the teacher's domain was shown by the instructions given to its members by the seventh plenum of its Central Committee as late as October 1959. Local branches were ordered to keep an eye on those students with such decadent habits as failing to do their homework, whispering or talking during class, or truancy.

Where the UTM has attempted to assume direct control of the minds and often the bodies of Rumanian youth is outside the schoolrooms or the factories. At all levels of education, the UTM is virtually the dictator of all types of extra-curricular activity. These activities range from the organization of summer holiday camps, international youth events, sporting events, &c, to the much more sinister organization of atheistic so-called 'naturalist societies', the discussion group on Marxism–Leninism, the specially summoned demonstrations of youth to support some aspect of the régime's policy or to register disgust against western policy.

The establishment in March 1957[19] of Student Associations has led some observers to question whether the UTM would remain as active in the universities as it had been. The Associations were founded only a few months after the Hungarian revolution, which had had serious repercussions among Rumanian youth. They were obviously intended as some sort of concession. But there is no doubt that they were firmly under the control of the UTM, which in turn was controlled by the party. No private students' clubs were allowed. Nevertheless it is with the students that the régime has had the greatest difficulty. In Bucharest, Iasi, and Cluj universities the students are kept as isolated from outside contacts as possible. In 1960, during the celebration of the centenary of Iasi University, visiting western scholars and others were not able even to look in at a student ball.

The other great problem, that of producing politically reliable cadres, of moulding the communist man, seems as far away as

[19] National Conference of the Student Associations', *Sc.*, 9–11 Mar. 1957.

ever from solution. The attitude of Rumanian youth during the period of the Hungarian revolution clearly showed the serious failure of the régime's attempts at indoctrination. Since 1956 and the disillusionment which all idealistic youth underwent at that time, active opposition seems in most cases to have lapsed into a sullen passivity, an evasiveness, or a scepticism in the face of all attempts at party indoctrination. Reliable information speaks of the complete indifference of higher school students towards learning Russian and towards courses in Marxism–Leninism. The same applies to the extra-curricular political meetings which the UTM is constantly drumming up. The apathy and even cynicism in the higher levels of education is more striking because educational opportunities are now restricted almost entirely to the classes on which the party was obviously basing its hope—the children of the proletariat and peasantry. Some 90 per cent of the places in higher educational institutions are now filled by sons and daughters of workers and peasants.

ANTI-REVISIONISM IN THE SECOND HALF OF 1957

On 4 July 1957 it was announced that the Soviet Central Committee in plenary session together with the Central Revision Commission from 22–29 June had deprived the 'anti-party' group of Malenkov, Kaganovich, Molotov, and Shepilov of their posts. This purge was the culmination of their opposition to Khrushchev's policies, which they had openly attacked at a meeting of the Soviet presidium on 18 June 1957. The domestic measures they opposed included destalinization, decentralization—especially in agriculture—and reduction of the bureaucracy, the improvement of incentives to peasants, including the abolition, as from the end of 1957, of compulsory quotas from private plots of collective farmers. In foreign policy they opposed 'peaceful coexistence', in particular rapprochement with Yugoslavia, the theory of different roads to socialism, and the doctrine that war was no longer inevitable. The defeat of the 'anti-party' group meant the paramountcy of the policies for which Khrushchev stood, including a set of 'theses' on industrialization he had put forward at a Central Committee meeting in February 1957, and which had been embodied in a law in May. Under this law most of the central industrial ministries of the USSR were dismantled and the administration of industry was instead put in the hands of local economic councils, which were to be appointed by local party organizations. Thus the main lines of bloc policy were firmly set.

Before the announcement of the Soviet purge the Rumanian party Central Committee held a plenum on 1–3 February and 28–29 June to discuss the tasks assigned by the Second Congress and conclusions to be drawn from international events and from the Twentieth CPSU Congress. At the June session of this plenum Chisinevschi and Constantinescu were removed from their posts, although this was not announced (by *Scintea* and Agerpres) until 4 July, after another Central Committee meeting held on 1–3 July. Both men were accused of plotting against the leadership of the party, of trying to slander the leading party and state organs and influence discussion on the lessons of the Twentieth Congress. The resolution published by Agerpres stated that Chisinevschi had 'worked closely' with Ana Pauker and had 'helped to glorify and build a personality cult about her'; Constantinescu had in particular 'exactly applied, without critical judgement, the directives and orders of Ana Pauker'.

This Rumanian purge, which could only have been linked with the Russian one if news of the Russian purge had leaked out before the *Pravda* announcement of 4 July, may well have represented an attempt to take more positive action on destalinization, but there may also have been a special need to get rid of these two powerful figures, and in particular Miron Constantinescu, since 1944 the chief editor of *Scinteia* and secretary of the Central Committee, later in charge of the organization and direction of that committee.

While Chisinevschi, a Bessarabian Jew and a Muscovite by inclination and experience, was a communist genuinely in the Pauker spirit, unlike Pauker, his attempts had little imagination or verve. He was not without ability, but his attempt to transplant mechanically Soviet methods and experience led to complete failure. With Constantinescu, however, the case was otherwise. At least since March 1956 he had been considered a possible liberalizer. Although he was still deep in the leadership of the party and did not show any signs of opposing it, at that time his name began in intellectual circles to exercise the attraction which Patrascanu's had at the start of communist rule. Like Patrascanu, Constantinescu was an intellectual, and his interest in cultural matters revived partly because he was under growing official criticism for his mistakes at the Planning Commission. At the Second Congress he had been openly criticized by the man who was obviously earmarked as his successor: Gaston Marin.[20] When in 1956 he lost his Planning Commission job and was given the Ministry of Education, this appointment was partly justified by his new reputation among the intellectuals. How much was also heard and known of growing differences of opinion between him and the party leadership and, immediately after 23 March 1956, of his open attacks on Dej, is a matter for conjecture. But Bucharest has always been a city where rumour ran like wildfire, and there is some evidence that for sudden reasons his popularity rapidly rose among the writers in the spring of that year. He too, however, appears to have been a casualty of the events of October–November 1956. Although at the June–July 1957 plenum he was represented only as a brutal and incompetent Stalinist, and although Dej maintained this at the November–December 1961 meeting, other speakers, and very influential ones, gave different stories.

Thus Petre Borila,[21] the old Bessarabian, said that after the Twentieth Congress Chisinevschi and Constantinescu, in order to make people forget their own Stalinist errors, tried to direct the party on a path of anarchic 'liberalization' which would open the gates to all the petit-bourgeois ghosts. They would meet separately, trying to form a faction, and carry on anti-party discussions. 'And all this', he exclaimed, 'happened in 1956, in the year during which the events in Poland and Hungary took place'. He also stated clearly that the object of their attacks was Gheorghiu-Dej personally. In a matter of a few days these former Stalinists had contrived to take a line diametrically opposed to that of Gheorghiu-Dej, 'assuming the white colour of innocence'. As has been seen, Ceausescu, Dej's loyal young assistant at the same meeting described Constantinescu as a man with a background alien to the party, who was awaiting the opportunity to strike a blow at its leadership and unity. 'This moment he and Chisinevschi thought had come in 1956'. Finally, Gheorghe Apostol, the permanent heir-apparent of the party, stressed that the two had tried to introduce into the party the 'theory' of the possibility of an exchange of opinions outside the party. They rose against the democratic centralism of the party. They wanted the party to

[20] See below, p. 353. [21] *Sc.*, 7 Dec. 1961.

have more groups and wings, each to have the freedom to discuss the problems of the party within them. He too referred to the plenary meeting of March 1956 in which Constantinescu and Chisinevschi had mounted an offensive against Gheorghiu-Dej and in which in the troubled atmosphere of that year they had almost carried the day: it took the whole development of the Hungarian revolution and its final defeat for Dej to be able to reinstate himself and to lead, in the summer of 1957, the final counter-offensive against the two factionalists. There is little evidence to indicate how much support either of the two men had. There were probably many in the party who sympathized with what Chisinevschi stood for. But the tide was obviously against this trend of opinion and, in any case, Chisinevschi was hardly the man to rally any significant following. With Constantinescu it was different. He had personality and stature; he seemed to stand for something which many fervently desired and he seemed to be thoroughly in keeping with the spirit of 'the thaw'. Support for him therefore may well have assumed dangerous dimensions. The only other man whom the party has since incriminated is Constantin Parvulescu who, at the November–December 1961 plenum, was accused of joining in secret meetings with Chisinevschi and Constantinescu. This was certainly the reason for his expulsion from the Politburo and Central Committee at the Third Party Congress in June 1960.

After June 1957 the only purge of note was in the summer of the following year when Constantin Doncea, one of the old Grivita heroes, lost his last foothold of power by being dropped, along with three others, from his position as Central Committee candidate. Doncea had apparently been at the centre of an old workers' group which was strongly critical of the extravagant living and lack of communist idealism of the present leadership.

13
The Opportunities for Coexistence, 1958–60

The period between 1958 and 1960 saw the implementation of the main tenets of Khrushchev's policies by the countries of the bloc, which in general attempted to carry out the precept of approaching communism 'approximately at the same time' announced by Khrushchev in January 1959. This objective embraced, in the economic field, a rapid acceleration of agricultural collectivization, which was speedily stepped up in Albania, Bulgaria, Eastern Germany, and Hungary, and a year later in Rumania; at the same time the targets for industry, especially heavy industry, were raised in order to build the necessary 'economic base' for socialism. If the whole bloc was to approach communism more or less simultaneously, then countries like Rumania obviously had to hurry. At the same time 'peaceful coexistence' opened the door to further contacts with the outside world, and this policy in Rumania, together with rising industrial production, led to the extension of trade with Afro-Asian countries and to some extent with Latin America and Western Europe, as well as cultural exchanges with various European and non-European nations, with all the dangers inherent in such exchanges. There was in consequence a stiffening of official policy towards intellectuals, and any tendencies towards liberalization in literature and the arts were stunted. As Gheorghiu-Dej expressed it at the Third RWP Congress in 1960, it was necessary 'tirelessly to combat manifestations of liberalism, bourgeois objectivism, nationalism and chauvinism'.

THE WITHDRAWAL OF SOVIET TROOPS

Perhaps the most dramatic single event in Rumanian–Soviet relations since the Hungarian revolution was the withdrawal of Soviet troops from Rumania in the summer of 1958. A Warsaw

Pact conference held in Moscow in May 1958 ended with a communiqué signed on 24 May announcing the withdrawal in the near future.[1] It was also announced that a further division would withdraw from Hungary, and that the Warsaw Pact countries would begin a systematic reduction of their armed forces, including a 55,000-man cut for Rumania.

This withdrawal was based on considerations of diplomacy and propaganda. It was designed to show that Khrushchev's promise to withdraw troops from European countries could be carried out were it not for the alleged danger of the NATO forces in Europe, which threatened the integrity and peace of the socialist countries. Rumania was in a less vulnerable strategic position than the other countries of the bloc, having no open frontier with a non-socialist country. Soviet troops could therefore be withdrawn from Rumania, but not from countries more immediately threatened. Diplomatically, the move aimed *inter alia* at furthering and making more convincing the Rumanian peace offensive in the Balkans. How could Rumania be the spokesman for such a move, while Soviet troops were openly and publicly garrisoned on her soil? Indeed, in several statements made either by the RPR government in memoranda addressed especially to the Greek and Turkish governments or by its spokesmen at the United Nations, the *leit-motif* of Rumania having been freed from all foreign troops and bases was constantly heard.

In reality, the move did not entail any risk for either the Rumanian or the Soviet governments. Rumania's only 'open' frontier is with Yugoslavia, all the others being with Warsaw Pact countries. Soviet divisions in Bessarabia and the Southern Ukraine could roll back at once in any emergency. Soviet air and naval bases still remained on Rumanian soil. Since November 1956 the entire RPR army had been remodelled; some of the high command were former Soviet citizens; new Soviet officers had been brought under false names and identities into the army and security forces. The only risk was that the Rumanian people themselves, although aware of the futility of such a move, might attempt a direct challenge to the puppet government.

The people did not do so, but the régime left nothing to chance. It showed its nervousness by a series of legal enactments which were perhaps the most draconian ever known in the satellites.

[1] *New York Times*, 28 Mar. 1956.

The most notorious of these was Decree No. 318 of 21 July 1958 which amended the penal code. Under this decree new crimes and punishments were established and the death penalty was imposed for a wide variety of infringements.

Among the new crimes, most of them punishable by death, some originated from the régime's concern over the political behaviour of the people and the possibility of their trying to express their dissatisfaction more clearly than before. Thus Article 9 of the new code imposed the death penalty for any Rumanian citizen dealing with foreigners for the purpose of engaging the state in a declaration of neutrality. This, of course, was an obvious aftermath of the demand during the Hungarian revolution for neutrality and implicitly for Hungary's withdrawal from the Warsaw Pact. In order that such a policy should not be thought feasible by the Rumanians as well, the government decided to treat it as a criminal matter even in the case of an individual. Another crime punishable by death was the revealing to any foreigner where the archives and collections of the RPR were to be found. A series of articles dealing with insults to representatives, insignia or symbols of friendly foreign powers, or of the Rumanian government, army, and administration showed the régime's concern over possible outbursts against Soviet Russia or itself. Youth was a particular target of the new amendment; so-called 'hooligan' offences by juveniles received a much broader definition. The other categories of new crimes were connected with the régime's economic difficulties. The definitions of theft, embezzlement, and bribery were extended to include all forms of 'economic sabotage' perpetrated either by the fast-growing economic bureaucracy of the state or by the citizens' refusal to comply with further measures of confiscation, expropriation, or compulsory work. The administration's concern over the non-fulfilment of targets in so many areas and with the catastrophic harvest was indeed great in 1958. By the autumn the first death sentences for the new crimes were applied. Also at the same time the sending of people 'to the reeds' was enormously increased as a result of the new penal measures. The clearing of the marshy region of the Delta for new projects, among them the great cellulose enterprise financed jointly by Poland, Czechoslovakia, East Germany, and the RPR, was the cause of this new kind of forced labour. All delinquents with minor sentences or even people only detained were sent 'to the reeds'.

Finally, another decree authorized the government to purge from office such people as: former officers of the royal army; former landowners; persons who had been sentenced in the past for political crimes; and the children of persons in the above categories.

The severity of these measures was obvious. But their sinister character was enhanced by their never being made public in the press or on the radio. They were simply printed in the *Official Bulletin*, which is published by the Presidium of the Grand National Assembly and has a very limited circulation. They were later reprinted in the official *Collection of Laws, Decrees, and Decisions*. To have made them public would, of course, have been a tremendous self-inflicted propaganda defeat for the régime. The fact that they were withheld gave a Byzantine character of uncertainty to the legislation.

FOREIGN POLICY

Before examining the main aspects of internal policy during this period, it is worth briefly surveying first the Rumanian contribution to the Soviet peace offensive from 1958 to 1960. This contribution was mainly confined to an initiative in the Balkans, first for a general *détente* in the area and secondly for a nuclear free zone.

The Rumanian proposals have become linked with the name of the former premier, Chivu Stoica. The first was made on 10 September 1957 when notes were circulated to Albania, Bulgaria, Greece, Turkey, and Yugoslavia, proposing a conference of premiers to discuss differences and pave the way for a general *détente* in the area.[2] Bulgaria and Albania, of course, accepted immediately. Yugoslavia accepted in principle, but with the reservation that all Balkan countries should agree to participate. Greece and Turkey rejected the proposal, the Greeks stating that it was inopportune for the time being.[3] This setback, however, did not daunt the Rumanian government, which has persisted with its proposal ever since, although the sharp deterioration in party relations with Yugoslavia which followed the Seventh Yugoslav Congress at Ljubljana in April 1958 and the growing acrimony with Greece and Turkey over the question of rocket bases seriously diminished whatever chances it may have had of being accepted.

[2] Radio Bucharest, 10 Sept. 1957. [3] *Sc.*, 23 Sept. 1957.

It was the Turkish and Greek acceptance in principle of NATO rocket bases on their territories that caused the second Bucharest move in the Balkans. On 8 June 1959 the government reissued an invitation to a Balkan summit conference to discuss the setting up of a peace zone in the Balkans under a great-power guarantee. This new proposal obviously resulted from Khrushchev's visit to Albania in May and early June where he condemned the establishment of American missile bases in Italy and gave warning of Soviet retaliation if Greece accepted them. Khrushchev promptly welcomed the renewed Rumanian initiative, and Albania and Bulgaria again enthusiastically greeted it. Tito, understandably uneasy about being surrounded by rocket-bearing nations, repeated his acceptance of the proposal in principle. Greece rejected the proposal and Turkey ignored it. Subsequently Greece, in particular, became the object of an intense propaganda barrage from both Rumania and Bulgaria, which was at least partly designed to play on the natural anxieties of the Greek population over the question of nuclear warfare.

This propaganda barrage continued until the end of 1960 and up to now has been a signal failure. Much of the Rumanian effort to win over Greece has been vitiated by the fact of Bulgaria being her ally. The mutual antipathy between the Greeks and the Bulgarians has shown little sign of abating; talks between the two governments which began in December 1960 broke down with bitter recriminations, after which relations became even more embittered. But it would be unwise to dismiss the Rumanian offensive as permanently ineffectual.

In its relations with Yugoslavia, the RPR has followed the Khrushchev precept of hostility on the party level and cordiality on the state level. But since 1956 its hostility on the party level has been very restrained. The contrast here with the attitude of Albania and Bulgaria, with whom Yugoslavia has traditional and territorial disputes, is striking. Even after the Hungarian revolution Rumania was slow to condemn Tito, and when the condemnation did come, in March 1957, it was carefully worded and cautious. Nor did Rumania quickly or loudly join in the chorus of bloc protest over the Ljubljana programme of April 1958. Gheorghiu-Dej held back his own personal criticism for almost a year. He did not speak out until the Soviet party's Twenty-first Congress in January 1959, at the Third Rumanian

Party Congress in June 1960. Then his remarks were the most critical ever made by a Rumanian leader against Titoist revisionism, or indeed against any revisionism. As by then Rumania was already striving within the Soviet bloc for her own industrial 'leap forward' and because of the Sino-Soviet conflict, Dej could propose his own variations on dogmatist themes.

State relations with Yugoslavia have been very correct, if not close. There have been constant exchanges of visits of various kinds, although all of these have been on a relatively low level. The fact, of course, that Belgrade has very often supported Moscow-inspired initiative in foreign policy has naturally facilitated good state relations. An incident, however, in trade relations did lead to mild recrimination of a diplomatic nature. The annual commercial agreement for 1957 provided for a contraction rather than an expansion of trade, but the real trouble occurred over the Rumanian refusal to supply crude oil. This, according to the Yugoslavs, was in contravention of the Brioni agreement of 1956. The Rumanians replied that their move was a retaliation against a Yugoslav refusal to supply them with raw copper, because it might be seen as exporting strategic materials. In 1960 the trade agreement was again renewed and provided for a 20 per cent increase in the total volume of trade; again, however, there was no mention of any exchange of crude oil for raw copper. This petty wrangle was the only jolt to otherwise cordial state and economic relations. Collaboration on the gigantic Iron Gates' project on the Danube has been continued over these two years, increasing in pace at the beginning of 1962.

POLICY TOWARDS MINORITIES

Until it came to power, the Rumanian Communist Party had always claimed that it alone could solve the minorities problem. As has been seen, between the two world wars it went so far as to adopt an irredentist policy advocating 'self-determination up to secession'. It also claimed that in a 'classless' society national problems are solved automatically. Yet soon after it came to power, and especially after the promulgation of the new constitution, the party was faced with difficulties, since its policy and administration failed to satisfy even sympathizers among the Hungarian, German, and Jewish minorities, not to speak of the majority, who were opposed to communism *per se,* on religious, social, and legal grounds. With the passage of time it was clear that one of the communists' most ironic failures lay in their relations with the minorities. Simultaneously the party adopted a more nationalistic and 'rumanianized' line, often accompanied by authoritarian methods.

The total population of 17,489,450, according to the official census of 21 February 1956, was made up as follows:

Ethnic Rumanians	14,996,114
Hungarians	1,587,675
Germans	384,708
Gipsies	104,216
Jews	146,264
Ukrainians & Ruthenians	60,479
Serbs, Croast, & Slovenes	46,517
Russians	38,731
Czechs, Slovaks	35,152
Tatars	20,469
Turks	14,329
Bulgarians	12,040
Unspecified	42,756

Source: RPR, *Statist. Pocket Book, 1962*, p. 28.

The Hungarian minority is thus clearly by far the largest and most heavily concentrated, more than a quarter of a million living in the Cluj area, almost the same number in the Oradea region, nearly 150,000 around Timisoara, over 100,000 around Brasov, 37,000 in the Hunedoara region, and over half a million in the Magyar Autonomous Region in eastern Transylvania. Here the proportion of Hungarians was 77.6 per cent, although in the country as a whole the Rumanian proportion was 65 per cent in 1956.

As has been seen, the impact of the Hungarian revolution was considerable among the Hungarian minority in Transylvania, and once Kadar was in power, joint action between the two governments was decided upon. Gheorghiu-Dej and Stoica led two delegations to Hungary in November 1956 and January 1957. The object of these visits seems to have been to persuade the new Hungarian leaders to renounce any claims to Transylvania and to denounce those who had taken part in the revolution as chauvinists and nationalists with irredentist aims. This Kadar did when he visited Rumania in February 1958. In particular, the Hungarian students were rebuked,[4] and at a party regional meeting in Cluj,

[4] *Sc.* 16 & 17 Oct., 1957.

Professor Lajos Jordaky confessed that he had been guilty of 'nationalism' and 'bourgeois chauvinism'. On returning from the Twenty-First Soviet Party Congress Gheorghiu-Dej on 19 February 1959 again rebuked 'reactionary elements' who were disseminating nationalist-chauvinist ideas among youth, and on the 21st the Rector of the Bolyai University, Professor Lajos Takacs, regretted the 'national isolation' which made this possible and asked the party organs, 'our ministry', to look into the value of having two separate universities in Cluj. The decision to merge the two universities was announced in June 1959 after a meeting of professors and students had 'unanimously' approved it.[5] The Rector of the new university is the former Rector of the Babes University, and two of his pro-Rectors are Hungarians. Courses in most faculties are held in both languages, but advanced studies in Rumanian. At the same time a gradual merging of the Hungarian with the Rumanian medium schools was begun.

This gradual policy of assimilation cannot be assumed to meet with the united opposition of the Hungarian minority. Many of the young, eager for wider horizons, are likely to accept the greater opportunities afforded by assimilation. Without losing their Hungarian identity, they would have a wider field for their talents than before.

On 24 December 1960 the government announced that they had prepared a plan for territorial reorganization, which was placed before the National Assembly at the end of the month. Three districts were added to the Magyar Autonomous Region, which now became the Mures-Magyar Autonomous Region, article 19 of the constitution, referring to the region as made up of a 'compact Hungarian group', being amended by the deletion of this phrase.[6] Two districts with heavy Szekeles populations were transferred from the Mures-Magyar to the Brasov region.

Policy towards the Jews centred in the question of exit visas to Israel, where the vast majority continued to wish to go. In September 1958 a flood of exit visas was granted, giving rise to angry interventions in the Middle East, especially from the United Arab Republic. On 17 February 1959 its Foreign Minister, Dr Mahmoud Fawzi, announced that his country was dealing with the problem through official channels, and at the end of Feb-

[5] Ibid. 3 July 1959; *New York Times,* 10 June 1959.
[6] *Sc.* 25 Dec. 1960.

ruary he summoned the Rumanian Ambassador to present his views. The situation was further complicated by the Soviet overtures to the Middle East countries at that time. The Rumanian régime replied through Agerpres, denying any suggestion of 'mass emigration' and assuring the Arab nations of their sympathy with regard to Israeli 'aggressive deeds'. The emigration was then stopped, and Jews who had sold all they had and given up their jobs found themselves without any hope of exit visas. A certain unrest resulted and several prominent Zionist leaders were arrested, while Jews released from imprisonment for Zionism were again imprisoned. However, in 1960 a trickle of emigration was again permitted, which has continued up to the present, although it has not been encouraged, and pressure has been brought to bear to prevent applications. In 1961, on payment of a large sum to the authorities, Jewish families were granted visas provided they gave as their destination a Western European or Latin American country or Cyprus. From there they went to Israel, thus giving the Rumanian Foreign Office the opportunity of denying that they were encouraging emigration to Israel.

Policy towards the German minority has also centred in the question of emigration, or rather repatriation to Germany. In 1956 negotiations were opened by the West German Red Cross for the repatriation of 12,500 German nationals. Some kind of agreement was reached, and in 1957 and the spring of 1958 several Germans were repatriated. When, however, the flow diminished, the Federal Government applied economic sanctions, as a result of which trade between the two countries fell by DM 21 million in the first six months of 1959. The sanctions were dropped later in the year, when it was reported that the Rumanian government had resumed issuing exit permits. Between 1 January and 30 September 1960 nearly 15,000 Germans were repatriated.[7]

THE COLLECTIVIZATION DRIVE

As has been seen, the concessions made after the Hungarian revolution included the continuation of the New Course modified collectivization. Nevertheless in 1957 the 'socialized' sector of agriculture as a whole increased quite strikingly, but mainly

[7] See Radio Free Europe, German Affairs Sect., 'German-Rumanian Trade and Repatriation Problems', 20 Nov., 1959; *The Times* and *Manchester Guardian*, 16 Jan. 1959; *New York Times*, 26 Nov. 1959.

because of the increase in the area covered by the agricultural associations. There was a slackening off in 1958 mainly due to the need for some consolidation after the 'leap forward' of the previous year. The following figures show the position at the end of 1958.

Collective farms

(*a*) Families: 12.8 per cent of the total, a gain of 7.7 per cent over the 1956 total, of which 5.1 per cent was achieved in 1957.
(*b*) Arable land: 17 per cent of the total, a gain of 8.8 per cent over 1956, of which 4.8 per cent was achieved in 1957.

Agricultural associations

(*a*) Families: 38.5 per cent of the total, a gain of 32.8 per cent over 1956, of which 16.4 per cent was achieved in 1957.
(*b*) Arable land: 24.3 per cent of the total, a gain of 20.3 per cent over 1956, of which 12.4 per cent was achieved in 1957.

Source: Sc., 4 Apr. 1959.

It was obvious that the régime was postponing its full collectivization drive and concentrating on getting the peasants into the less unpopular associations as the first step. On entering the associations, the peasants retained a substantial proportion of their cattle in private ownership. Nevertheless, during the campaign as a whole, some of the methods of persuasion were far from fair. Indeed, Gheorghiu-Dej, speaking at a press conference in Constanta in April 1958 to celebrate the complete collectivization of that area the previous November, admitted that some methods had violated the principle of free consent. On the other hand in the same speech he drew attention to the abuse of their model statute by many of the agricultural associations, in which the peasants 'continued to carry out some or all of their agricultural work individually, in separate plots', as a result of which the production and revenue of the associations could not reach the levels of co-operative agriculture. In consequence the government began to promote a gradual transfer of associations into collectives. Various measures were adopted such as financial regulations which favoured the co-operativized and harmed the private peasant. The less land the peasant brought into the agricultural association the more highly he was taxed. It was made increasingly difficult for a peasant to leave the association, and so on. The screw was being tightened and the peasants knew it. Many resigned themselves to joining the associations in the hope of postponing the day when they would have to join the collectives. At their elbow, helping them to make up their minds, were the teams of propagandists who swarmed over the countryside and who pointed to the constant help being given by the state to their co-operativized colleagues.

Progress was therefore made, but it was tempered by pragmatism and prudence. There was no *Sturm und Drang*, as in the case of Bulgaria and China. This had evidently not passed unnoticed in Moscow. It was certainly no coincidence that Khrushchev, at both the Bulgarian Party Congress in June 1958 and the East German Party Congress in July did not refer to Rumanian agriculture while praising developments in Bulgaria, Albania, East Germany, Czechoslovakia, and North Korea.

The year 1959 saw another big drive forward. On 26–28 November 1958 the party Central Committee held a plenum which, in retrospect, has shown itself to be one of the most important in its recent history. It decided on both a resumption of industrialization and on a more urgent pace of socialization in the villages. The latter decision had its counterpart in Hungary, when it was decided to begin the first stage of complete collectivization at a party plenum in October. The first half of 1959 saw another considerable 'step forward' in Rumania. In May a Deputy Minister of Agriculture and Forestry, Eugen Alexe, said, in an interview to the *New York Times* that, with the same tempo, the complete socialization of the countryside 'within the next three years' would easily be attained. Alexe claimed that in the first five months of 1959 there had been an increase of over a million hectares of agricultural land in the co-operative sector. An example of how that sector was increasing during this period was given by *Scinteia* on 30 July.[8] The party daily then reported that this sector then stood at 5.87 million hectares which, if the figures were to be believed, represented an increase of 340,000 hectares in something under six weeks. The same article announced that 68.5 per cent of the total agricultural land was in the socialist sector (an increase of 17.5 per cent over the end of 1957). Some seven weeks

[8] Quoted in Radio Free Europe, *Report on Rumania*, Dec. 1959.

later, on 22 August, Gheorghiu-Dej stated that 'more than 70 per cent' of the total arable land was in the socialist sector. (At the end of 1957 the figure was 51 per cent.) The Minister of Agriculture, Ion Cozma, in an article in *Romania libera* of 15 December 1959, stated that the socialist sector on 1 December covered 71.3 per cent of the total agricultural area and 72.2 per cent of the total arable area. The co-operative sector covered 6.3 million hectares, some 63.3 per cent of the total agricultural land of the country, and included 2,610,000 families (72.5 per cent of the total number). The extent of the progress achieved is brought out in the following table.

	1956	*1957*	*1958*	*1959*
No. of state farms	323	377	487	525
Agr. area (000 ha.)	979	1,168	1,327	1,632
No. of co-operatives	10,710	14,608	15,776	15,310
Agr. area (000 ha.)	1,837	3,607	4,442	6,422
No. of collectives	8,130	11,733	12,747	11,482
Agr. area (000 ha.)	770	2,025	2,550	3,424

Source: Dezvoltarea agriculturii RPR (1961), table 15.

There were two special factors contributing to this increase which deserve mention. The first was land reclamation, on which the régime had laid great stress. In 1958 alone some 830,000 hectares had been reclaimed. The second was a decree of March 1959 expropriating all land not directly cultivated by the owner and his family, and prohibiting sharecropping, leasing of land and hired labour. This was, of course, the final blow to the last remaining kulaks and also to a considerable number of middle peasants owning between 20 and 50 hectares who, at least up to 1956, had been prospering. It is not possible to say just how much land was obtained by this expropriation decree, but it must have been considerable since in the first half of 1959 the rate of increase for the collective area was, for the first time since 1952, greater than for the associations.

This development continued in the second half of 1959. At the end of 1960 'socialist agriculture' comprised 81.9 per cent of the total agricultural area. This was made up of 'state agricultural units' totalling 29.4 per cent, co-operative farms totalling 52.5

per cent, and individual farms totalling 18.1 per cent. State farms comprised 11.8 per cent of the 'state agricultural units' and collective farms 31.5 per cent of the co-operatives.[9] Thus at the Third Congress (1960) Dej was able to say that the tasks set by the Second Congress, to ensure the preponderance of the socialist sector in terms of acreage and marketable produce, had been fulfilled. He admitted that 680,000 peasant families, owning 1.8 million hectares of arable land, were still outside the socialist sector, but said that these were mainly in the mountainous localities. He stated that the collectivization of agriculture would be completed by 1965.[10]

This seemed even then to be a conservative estimate. But several factors probably explained this conservatism at the time. First there was the nature of the area which was still in private hands. It was mostly mountainous and inhabited by a very tough breed of people who would take a good deal of 'persuading' of the merits of collectivization. Then there were the remaining agricultural associations to be transformed into co-operatives. But, most important, there were the problems of production and economic efficiency in the collectives. Rumania has proved no exception to the rule that agriculture has been communism's greatest failure. The Second Party Congress in 1955 had set a target for 1960 of 15 million tons of cereal grains. The closest approach to this target was in the very good harvest year of 1957, when about 11 million tons were achieved. The Third Party Congress of 1960 set for 1965 a target in cereal grains of 14–16 million tons, or the same as the Second Congress had set for 1960. It will be difficult to achieve this. The régime therefore still hesitated between collectivization and production. In 1960 there was only an addition of 8.9 per cent of arable area to the socialist sector. This denoted a prudent policy of gradualism so as not to harm the interests of production.

The economic inefficiency of the collective sector had been a cause of disquiet for the régime since socialization began. At the end of 1960 there were about 5,000 collectives in the country and a great many of these were still not solvent units with a sufficient basic fund and with money to buy sufficient machinery. Many of

[9] *An. Stat. 1962*, table 93.

[10] Rep. to Third Congress, 20 June 1960 (*Sc.* & *Agerpres Inf. Bull.*, 25 June 1960).

the state farms, supposed to be models of agriculture, were in a similar position. In February 1960 in the Bucharest region, one of the most fertile and financially favoured regions, only 36 out of 70 state farms were paying their way. The situation has, of course, improved and will continue to improve. The state has made great efforts to assist the socialist sector in machinery and in trained men. But there is still a shortage of both, and it will take several years for the socialist sector to be well enough equipped, manned, and organized to be considered efficient. Whether it will ever command the will of its members to work is another matter.

But, as will be seen, the trend towards collectivization which set in in 1959 proved enduring. It went on uninterruptedly till the spring of 1962 when, as previously in Hungary, East Germany, Bulgaria, and Czechoslovakia, the Rumanian government was able to announce that it had achieved total collectivization.

FOREIGN TRADE

In its efforts to open up markets and secure much needed raw materials in the west, the Rumanian government has shown considerable initiative and resource. Ever since the beginning of the 'new course', Rumanian commercial teams have been touring the world in search of trade. Between 1950 and 1959 the total volume of trade exchanges with Western Europe increased considerably from $455 millions in 1950 to $1,024 in 1959.[11] In 1959 in particular trade relations with the west improved in an almost spectacular way. In June of that year an important delegation led by Alexandru Barladeanu, a vice-premier, and the RPR's chief Comecon delegate, Gheorghe Gaston Marin, President of the State Planning Commission, Mihai Florescu, Minister of the Oil and Chemicals Industries, and Mihai Petri, Deputy Foreign Trade Minister, arrived in Paris to begin an unofficial visit to six Western European countries: France, Great Britain, Italy, Switzerland, Belgium, and Holland. The most important contracts signed during the tour concerned a £7½ million contract signed in Britain with 'Rustyfa', an Anglo-American concern, for a tyre plant and several contracts signed in Switzerland with Sulzer Press and Brown Boveri. It was estimated at the time that the contracts signed during the tour amounted to more than $60 million and

[11] *The Times*, 12 June 1959.

that it was hoped to push the amount up to $100 million. It was also reported that, in addition to the contracts already mentioned, a $20 million contract with French and Italian enterprises for petro-chemical equipment, a $15 million contract for a factory to make special bags for cement, and a $7 million contract in France for two sugar factories had been signed.

During the recent years the United States has also been a particular target of Rumanian appeals for more trade. In February 1958 Rumania declared her willingness to buy U.S. industrial equipment to a total value of over $100 million. But it was objected that the fabrication process of such plants takes longer than the six months for which American export licences are generally accorded, and the régime made it clear that if the United States would not ensure the proper delivery of the equipment, the RPR would be obliged to turn to Great Britain, France, or Federal Germany. In November of the same year a representative of the *Washington Post* was told by Premier Chivu Stoica that there was a growing interest among western business groups in developing commercial relations with the RPR, which was receiving many offers from companies in Great Britain, the German Federal Republic, France, Italy, and Canada, and that several reliable western companies would also be ready to grant credits to the RPR. This was an evident attempt to prod the United States.

Up to 1959 trade with important western countries such as France, Britain, and the United States was severely handicapped by Rumanian refusals to settle the financial claims of these countries arising from the nationalization of property after the war. In March 1959, however, an agreement was signed with France, on very generous terms for the Rumanians. In 1960 an agreement with the United States and a partial agreement with Britain were signed, again on very favourable terms for the Rumanians. Trade with the German Federal Republic has increased enormously despite temporary restrictions imposed by Bonn in 1959 because of Rumanian recalcitrance on the question of the repatriation of ethnic Germans. Farther afield Rumanian trade with the under-developed and emerging countries has greatly increased. Here the commercial efforts have also some political overtones.

All in all, the figures for the total volume of RPR foreign trade were, in millions: 1958=$950; 1959=$1,024; and 1960=$1,365. The distribution by countries was as follows:

Percentage Distribution of trade

	1959		1960	
	Exports	*Imports*	*Exports*	*Imports*
Soviet Union	47.9	46.8	39.2	41.1
Eastern Europe	23.6	27.1	26.6	26.9
Other centrally planned economies	7.1	6.4	4.0	4.4
Western Europe	16.4	15.1	22.1	22.8
Rest	5.0	4.6	8.1	4.8

Source: UN, *Econ. Bull. for Europe,* vol. 13, no. 2, 1961, p. 95.

There was a substantial increase in the trade with the free world; and an even more substantial decrease in the trade with the socialist camp. Within the latter figure, there was a definite decrease in the trade with the Soviet Union whose share, according to some unofficial calculations, fell from some 46 per cent in 1959 to some 40 per cent in 1960. It was, however, a relative decrease, because in absolute figures the trade with Soviet Russia increased from year to year. The growth in the volume of trade was responsible for this evolution. The most spectacular advance among all the western countries was that of the German Federal Republic. Trade with Yugoslavia also showed an increase. As far as the structure of the RPR foreign trade was concerned the figures showed that it was still in the category of raw materials, semi-finished goods, and oil which represented two-thirds of the volume, although there was evident progress in the export of machinery, tools, and vehicles.

But despite this often successful initiative of the RPR in the west, it must be stressed that up to and including 1960 its trade commitments towards the Soviet Union and the Soviet bloc have left relatively little margin for manoeuvre. Many of the efforts made in the west are for goods which Rumania's Comecon partners cannot supply. In 1960 the planned value of the volume of Rumanian foreign trade was $1,000 million. Of this, some 70 per cent was planned with the Soviet bloc and some 40 per cent with the Soviet Union alone.

The RPR's dependence on Soviet Russia for her imports of iron ore, ferro-alloys, copper, synthetic rubber, metallurgical coke, chemical industry equipment, aluminium, &c, was once more confirmed. Rumania was scheduled to deliver more oil products, installations, and equipment for oil refineries, wood products, furniture (so scarce in Rumania itself), textiles, and so forth. In the rest of the Soviet bloc, Czechoslovakia and Eastern Germany were the most important trade partners of the RPR. With both these countries trade increased in 1959 by 17 and 25 per cent respectively. Both countries are also partners to certain quadripartite Comecon operations, as for example the cellulose factory in the Danube delta. Moreover in the agreement of 3 October 1959 with Czechoslovakia, it was stipulated that the Czechs would deliver on credit to the RPR, between 1961 and 1965, two thermal power stations which the RPR will pay for by exporting electric power to Czechoslovakia over an unspecified period of years. With Poland it was agreed on 2 December 1959 that trade between the two countries would increase by as much as 25 per cent, the main exchanges being oil and coal.

With China a three-year agreement (1959–62) was based on the increasing exchange, achieved in 1962, of Chinese pig-iron for Rumanian oil products.

The promising beginning of a more independent foreign trade policy showed some striking results in 1961, when the figures are interesting in the light of the present conflict between Rumania and Comecon, in which Rumania is opposing the projects of supranational integration sponsored, and now proposed, by the Soviet Union.[12]

Foreign Trade, 1958 and 1961: Main Countries
(million lei)

	1958		*1961*	
	Exports	*Imports*	*Exports*	*Imports*
Total	2,810.0	2,890.0	4,755.0	4,888.0
Eastern Europe	504.1	636.3	1,010.7	1,262.3
USSR	1,412.0	1,522.8	2,107.2	1,792.9
Albania	16.7	3.1	7.8	2.4
Yugoslavia	30.1	21.3	58.8	74.6
China	155.1	99.6	55.7	118.4
UAR	68.1	63.7	83.1	94.7
Western Europe:				
Austria	35.7	34.2	101.4	87.7
Switzerland	37.7	15.9	98.0	85.6
U.K.	39.0	44.6	137.7	308.0
France	92.4	94.3	130.8	152.2
W. Germany	157.7	134.2	300.1	380.4
Italy	66.5	48.7	173.2	144.0

Source: An. Stat. 1962, table 172.

[12] See below, p. 339.

The proportion of trade with the Eastern bloc remained at about two-thirds, compared with about one-third with the West; Rumania thus had a lower proportion of trade with the bloc than that of any other member country other than Poland. Moreover 1961, and especially 1962, saw a feverish effort by the Rumanian Foreign Trade Ministry and organizations to expand the volume of trade with the West as much and as quickly as possible, either by concluding new agreements (as in the case of the Federal Republic of Germany, with whom Rumania, shortly after Poland, asked to have an official trade delegation) or by increasing bilateral trade with the countries with which exchanges had steadily progressed over the last seven or eight years, as in the case of Great Britain, France, and especially Italy, with whom the trade agreements signed on 11 April 1962 called for a 40 per cent increase in volume (Rumanian trade with Italy had increased four times since 1955). The stated reason for this increased trade with the West was that Rumania's ambitious industrialization plans (not entirely approved by Comecon) needed massive imports of machinery and equipment which either could not be provided by the industries of the bloc, or which could be found more quickly, cheaply, and of better quality in the West.

THE RESUMPTION OF INDUSTRIALIZATION

The slowing down of the pace of industrialization which started in January 1957 ended with the November 1958 plenum. Two important announcements were made by Gheorghiu-Dej in his speech to this plenum. The first was that in the view of the party and of the government, the country was now ripe for a new effort towards industrialization and more rapid production. The second was that the second Five-Year Plan would be reduced to a Four-Year Plan, ending in 1960, since a new Six-Year Plan (1960–6) was to start simultaneously with the Soviet plan. The figures he released were relevant only for the final year of the abridged second plan, and he implied that the directives for the next Six-Year Plan would be published in due course. When, however, at the enlarged Central Committee plenum held on 3–5 December 1959 Gheorghiu-Dej spoke again, he produced only the figures for the first year of the new Six-Year Plan, which should have been the last of the former Five-Year Plan. This surprising announcement, coupled with the postponement of the party congress, confirmed the suspicion that the party had not yet worked out its new long-term plan.

The course of the second Five-Year Plan had been chequered. After the two-year 'pause' in 1957 and 1958, progress was stepped up in 1959. But it was quite obvious that many of the targets for the plan, as approved at the Second Congress in 1955, would not be achieved by the end of 1960. This was one reason why the last year of the plan was transformed into the first year of the new Six-Year Plan. The other reason, and perhaps the most important one, was to avoid the clash of the Rumanian planning cycle with Soviet and Comecon plans generally.

The limited capital investment target for the second Five-Year Plan was for a total investment of 170–180 milliard lei for the whole 1956–60 period. The actual investments, in billions of lei, for the whole period was as follows:

1956	*1957*	*1958*	*1959*	*1960* (planned
14.48	13.77	15.02	17.64	22.89

Source: An. Stat.

Including the planned figure for 1960, this amounts to 83.5 billion or about 80 per cent of the target.

The failure of the investment plan had a decisive bearing on the results of the plan altogether. Yet the increased investment forecast for 1960 could not be found in hitherto untapped sources. Had such sources existed, they would have been used to help the second Five-Year Plan succeed. The optimism of the party leaders was based mainly on a sounder financial assessment of the possibilities in each individual enterprise. At the November 1958 plenum, Gheorghiu-Dej criticized the attitude of some cadres in the ministries who put forward plans of production which did not 'mobilize the ultimate reserves and did not take into account the fact that an increase in production can be obtained not only through investments but also through using the full capacity of each enterprise'. It was therefore probable that future planning would be based on rather optimistic calculations of reserves and production in all enterprises. It was also clear that the prospects for increased raw materials, and especially the rate of production due to the new technical norms, were thought to be the major causes for increased production and for a faster rate of capital growth. Over and above this, some financial juggling had to be expected, especially over the dividing line now drawn between what is called capital investment and what is called routine investment. The funds obtained by enterprises and plants are to be divided on a fifty-fifty basis between these two categories. Only the sums earmarked for capital investment would go towards new projects and building or equipment plans. These projects and plans would moreover have to be approved directly and solely by the Central Planning Commission. Local and decentralized authorities would be able to draw more freely upon the sums for routine investment but only for continued production and maintenance purposes. The sums saved from routine investments would be returned to the central authorities, who would afterwards put them into the general pool of the increased amounts available for investments. Finally, some of the imported plants or installations from Soviet Russia, Czechoslovakia, and East Germany, which will be paid for over a long period, were counted in the final reckoning of achieved investments, in the same way as were plants for the chemical industry lent by Soviet Russia in 1956–8.

In 1960 the total share of industry was planned at 59 per cent, an increase of almost 6 per cent over the share of industrial investments in the lean years 1957–8. Out of this, the fuel and power industries (which in this context include electric power, coal, oil, and methane gas) were to receive 39 per cent, ferrous and machine-building industries 19 per cent, and the chemical industry 21 per cent. It should be noticed that only the latter had shown a continued increase in investment over the five years: 9.5 per cent in 1956, 11.2 in 1957, 16 in 1958, 20 in 1959, and 21 in 1960. The fuel and power industries received a decreasing share in investments, from 44.6 per cent in 1956 to 29 in 1960: so did the ferrous, non-ferrous, and machine-building industries, from 24 per cent in 1956 to 14 in 1960. With regard to both these industries, however, it must be borne in mind that since the overall scale of investments is higher than in the previous year, their intrinsic share is equal to, if not higher than, those of previous years, and also that investments in previous years may help to maintain an increased production.

As far as production was concerned, the main results of the second Five-Year Plan (as reduced to four years), compared with 1958 (the turning point of the new upwards trend) were:

Principal products	*Production, 1959*	*% over 1958*
Crude oil (000 tons)	11,438	101
Nat. gas (m. cu. metres)	5,782	114
Electric power (m. kwh)	6,824	110
Steel (000 tons)	1,420	152
Pig iron (000 tons)	846	115
Iron ore (,, ,,)	1,460	143
Coal (,, ,,)	7,977	108
Chemical fertilizer (tons)	52,077	180
Caustic soda (000 tons)	74	157
Cement ,, ,,	2,851	111
Tractors (units)	11,000	157
Rolled metals (000 tons)	822	..

Sources: production: *Statist. Pocket Book 1962*, table 44; percentages: Radio Free Europe, Suppl. F-134.

According to the Directives for the 1960–5 plan, in the period 1956–9 gross industrial output showed an annual average rate of increase of 10 per cent. If, however, one compares production in 1960 with the level at which it was originally planned for the end of the period 1956–60 in the directives of the second Five-Year Plan, one finds many branches of production below the target.

So much for the 1956–60 plan. Its curtailment thus marked the end of a phase. The Rumanian party leadership was now impatient to start on the new path of 'quick and many-sided industrialization'. This slogan, constantly repeated since 1959 in the main resolutions, theoretical organs, and speeches of the party leaders, was the economic postulate with which the Rumanian party was to identify itself from then on: the abolition of the differences of level of economic development between the socialist countries. Rumania, the argument ran, a country rich in raw materials, should not remain among the backward countries of the bloc. Therefore it should and could undergo a rapid overall industrialization based on machine-building: a new big steel plant to be set up in Galati became the symbol of this *élan*. This, by then, was much more in accord with the Chinese advocacy of the equality of all communist countries than with, say, the East German and Czechoslovak theses that the component countries of Comecon should proceed to integrate their economies at the existing levels and 'specialize' their production on the basis. By then, too, the Rumanian foreign trade delegations were confident that the equipment needed for industrialization could be purchased in the West. The Rumanian leadership may still have hoped that the Soviet Union would back and assist their plans: economic negotiations lasted during most of 1960. Or they may have hoped to persuade Comecon to start supranational planning only *after* Rumania had attained the new level. But when it became clear to them, even before the end of 1960, that neither Comecon nor the Soviet Union were going to approve or back their industrialization plan, the Rumanian communist leaders determined to go ahead with its implementation. Seen in retrospect, it is apparent that in this and in other instances they were now animated by a new spirit of self-confidence. There were political reasons for this. The policy of coexistence maintained world peace. Within the Soviet bloc Russia's monocentric control could be, and already was, questioned. The economic reasons were, abroad improved trade relations with the West, and at home better results obtained in industry by the new cadres of managers, engineers, technicians, foremen, and skilled workers. Rumanian industry was already showing signs of the buoyancy which became one of the few developments of note in Eastern Europe in the next few years.

One of the accompanying effects of this steady evolution in industry was also a more rapid social stratification in the workers' class. A New Class was indeed appearing, which was constantly increased by new contingents of more contented layers of workers, foremen, and especially technical intelligentsia. This new layer of people with vested interests, of whom more will be said in a further section, brought with it into the otherwise unchanged grim perspectives of Rumanian life under communism the only touches of social prosperity, gaiety, and relative enjoyment.

MORE BAIT FOR THE INTELLECTUALS

The writers too shared in this new prosperity. Their salaries, appointments, and privileges as writers, artists, and entertainers were (and are) somewhere between four and ten times the average wage of a qualified worker. They were given the best flats or houses, allotted the best quarters in holiday resorts, allowed to run private cars, authorized to travel abroad with their expenses paid. Their contracts were generous, regardless of whether their books were sold or piled up in the basements of the publishing house.

However, from 1957 the general stiffening of the party line

towards intellectuals in all the countries of Eastern Europe was also to be remarked in Rumania. The price which the régime exacted for its munificence was total acceptance of party guidance in their creative work. This meant not simply a negative avoidance of party taboos but a positive response to the themes which the party insisted should be part of socialist writing: what and how to write, which problems to treat, what kind of *dramatis personae* to present, what solutions to give to moral and sentimental conflicts, &c.

A new campaign for the 'education of the writers and artists of the people' began with the conference sponsored by Agitprop, now completely dominated by Rautu, held on 4 May 1958 to discuss the 'struggle against bourgeois ideology'. There Rautu called upon the party itself to see to it that this struggle was successful. A party Central Committee plenum held between 9–13 June 1958 discussed these problems and passed the following resolution:

that the party organizations would continue the fight against revisionism and any foreign ideologies whatever their manifestations, against nationalism, idealistic conceptions, reactionary bourgeois aesthetics, manifestations of bourgeois morality, &c. The party organs directing the ideological activities as well as the communists who are acting within the party and state education system in the press and publishing houses, in art and activities on the careful study of Marxism–Leninism are to increase their combativeness and watchfulness in the face of any manifestations of foreign ideology.[13]

A few weeks later, on 18 and 19 July 1958, there appeared two long articles in *Scinteia* summing up Rautu's and Beniuc's basic principles on the artist's duty. For once the two mentors had thought fit to describe in detail the categories of 'cultural deviations' which may be committed by the writer, intellectual, or artist. 'A-politism' was the first of these deviations. This was and has remained the régime's most recurrent complaint against the Rumanian writers. Even at the Writers' Union congress of January 1962 'a-politism' was the *bête noire*. The writers were not taking sides. They refused to look seriously into the political realities of the moment as described by the party. They, and especially the poets, produced works deprived of any contemporary interest. In 1958 a poet of the importance of Geo Bogza was criticized for

[13] *Sc.*, 27 June 1958.

his 'a-political' lyricism. Another deviation was 'negativism'. This, of course, was graver in the sense that it described the developments in Rumania only critically, stressing the defects and not putting the overwhelmingly good results in a sufficiently enthusiastic light. Two women poets, Doina Salajan and Ana Novak, were particularly guilty of this sin. 'Neutralism' and 'eclecticism' were other cultural deviations to which apparently the critics were the most dangerously addicted. There were critics who either did not take a sufficiently aggressive attitude to foreign conceptions of art or who advocated general 'aesthetic' points of view, as if there could be beauty outside the canons of socialist realism. Finally, there were the deviations of 'obsequiousness' and 'literary snobbery'; these were widespread; writers would show their respect towards non-Russian great writers and would try to keep abreast of new ideas, trends, and movements in world literature and art. Against all these deviations, the Rautu–Benuic manifesto upheld the infallible tenets of socialist realism and of Marxism–Leninism.

That these warnings were not taken to heart in the ensuing eighteen months is shown in a speech made by Gheorghiu-Dej on 12–13 March 1960 at a pre-Congress regional meeting in the intellectual stronghold of Cluj. Dej said that the party should fight even more against the 'backward conceptions' that had been circulating in the past among intellectuals, conceptions which some men of culture had not got rid of completely. 'The conceptions were based on idealistic and mythical philosophical systems' and 'on various theories with nationalistic backgrounds in problems of history, language, and literature'. The party organizations, he continued, must fight against the detachment manifested in the work of some writers and artists, the feeble reflection of the world of socialist building and its heroes, the common people of our fatherland, and against tendencies to seek refuge in the past or in narrow themes excluding current trends, or to neglect the content of the work in pursuing an alleged originality in form. He concluded by saying, with obvious impatience, that the party had the means of unmasking the attitude of the individual intellectual opposed to socialism and the working people and of dealing with them as with other 'ghosts of the past'.

This indicated that during the previous eighteen months the party had achieved anything but success. During this period some writers continued their defiant attitude, others—the majority—lapsed more deeply into 'a-politism', while many talented writers chose the rigours of a literary career in the west rather than continue. The case of Dumitriu has been mentioned. In February 1959 he and his wife escaped through Berlin, although this meant leaving behind their small daughter. In his book *Rendez-vous au jugement dernier,* published in 1961, Dumitriu describes the reasons for this escape. In August 1958 the historian Gheorghe Haupt and his wife remained in France. He was the leading young historian, and like Dumitriu, had benefited from the régime's favours over the entire last decade. The exceptionally brilliant philosopher and theologian, the monk Scrima, also remained in a Dominican monastery in the West, after he had been given various missions abroad by the Rumanian patriachate. The most successful musicians of the new generation, the pianist Mandru Katz and the conductor Silvestri did the same. And through the Jewish emigration, which is now being permitted, the RPR is losing many intellectuals of outstanding talent.

But the great bulk of the intelligentsia are those who do not resist openly, cross the frontiers, or accept the party rules and conditions entirely. It is formed of those who continue to play cat and mouse with the régime, by allowing it to publish their soulless and uninspired works and yet refusing to throw themselves into the fray as the party demands. The expression 'internal exile' piquantly describes the situation of the creative intelligentsia in the RPR. If the party during this period could not stimulate the writers, it could repress them. This it tried to do by keeping an exaggeratedly close watch on the literary journals. The Writers' Union weekly *Gazeta literara,* in which Jar had published some of his defiant interviews before his disgrace, was thoroughly reorganized. Under Benuic's watchful eye it became completely docile. A new literary bimonthly, *Luceafarul,* dedicated to the literature of 'socialist realism', was designed to reinforce *Gazeta literara* in the régime's offensive. Two monthly journals which had shown strong signs of defiance were among the main targets of this offensive. *Viata romaneasca* in Bucharest and *Steaua* in Cluj. *Viata romaneasca* was given the same treatment as *Gazeta literara.* It proved fairly easy to infiltrate mainly because, unlike *Steaua,* it was not the product of a united literary group with a broadly similar approach to the problems of literature and life.

For this reason *Steaua* proved a much tougher nut to crack. The leader of the group around it, A. E. Baconsky, was both a poet of great gifts and a man of strong character. The Cluj group was also inspired by the well-known poet, philosopher, and anthropologist Lucian Blaga, whose firmness against régime pressure earned him tremendous respect. In common with Blaga, the Cluj group of young socialist writers had especially an uncommon interest in Dacian history. The party often castigated the *Steaua* writers for their preference for Dacian symbols and allegories. The Dacians, who were the aboriginal element in the region before the Roman legions arrived and produced the new Rumanian people by intermarriage with Dacian women, were an austere people more preoccupied by death, which they described as a 'wedding with nature', than by their worldly goods. When the Romans conquered them their leaders preferred to die as heroes in their mountain fortresses rather than to be taken prisoner. The recurrent Dacian allegories in some contemporary Rumanian poetry may well be interpreted as a symbol of refusal to the last to yield to foreign occupation, pressure, and colonialization.

Individual authors, dramatists, and artists who transgressed the narrow limits were also attacked, usually at the periodic meetings of the Writers' Union. The novelist Zaharia Stancu, the critics Paul Georgescu and Chromalniceanu, the dramatists Aurel Baranga and Ana Novak were all openly attacked. Similarly a new group of historians at the Academy was severely castigated by the Central Committee's theoretical monthly *Lupta de clasa* in March 1958 for wrongly directed and oriented historical research.

When it considered the need arose, the party could exhibit a cynical viciousness and brutality in dealing with recalcitrant intellectuals. In the spring of 1959 public opinion was genuinely shocked by the news that 'at a public meeting of intellectuals and workers of the Bucharest district' three well-known cultural figures had been exposed to open denunciation and instant 'trial'. They were Mihai Andricu, an Academician and well-known composer and teacher, Milita Patrascu, a well-known sculptress, and Professor Marius Nasta, a prominent physician. Their crime was that of passing derogatory remarks about the RPR at a reception at which foreigners were present. Andricu in particular was humiliated and was instantly stripped of all titles and decorations.[14]

By far the most promising development in Rumanian cultural life during the years 1960–2 was the conclusion of cultural agreements with various western countries, especially with the United States, France, Italy and, in 1962, with Great Britain. Unlike the cultural exchanges established by the various western countries with Poland in the 'spring in October' of 1958, when representatives of western universities and foundations went straight to their opposite numbers in Poland and concluded working agreements with only the acknowledgement of the state, the Rumanian cultural agreements were concluded on an inter-state basis, like those with the Soviet Union, which they followed.

Even so, and in spite of the RPR government's reluctance to conclude such agreements and lack of enthusiasm in carrying them out, the fact that American, French, Italian, and British books, films, plays, professors, students, records, and exhibitions started once more to go to Rumania made a considerable difference from the Stalinist years of total isolation. An even greater difference was made by the fact that, with obvious scarcity when compared with the freedom to travel in the west of the Polish and even of the Hungarian and Czechoslovak intellectuals, a few Rumanian professors, artists, graduates, and undergraduates succeeded in travelling to the west every year, returning with a rapidly accumulated knowledge which they smuggle into the country more easily than the trunks of books which they also try to bring back with them. The western country with which the present-day Rumanian intellectuals have the most active links is France, although the young prefer to learn English rather than French. Italy comes second, but it is obvious that the United States and Britain are increasingly becoming centres of attraction for the young intelligentsia. As for carrying out other aspects of cultural exchanges, there is evidence that the régime tries to play them down as much as possible. Thus no western periodicals or newspaper can be found in Bucharest or other towns on the newsstands or in bookshops. Periodicals dealing with literary criticism, such as *The Times Literary Supplement*, the *New York Times Book Review*, or *Les nouvelles littéraires*, can be obtained only with difficulty. The prospective reader is thus unable to know which books to order and which reviews to follow. Visas to travel abroad are given to

[14] *Contemporanul*, 1 May 1959.

people whose records with the party are clean. Foreign professors or lecturers invited to take up the few lectureships opened through the cultural agreements are told what to teach and their syllabuses have to be approved by the respective universities. Contact with individual Rumanians was still very difficult in 1960.[15]

Nevertheless, thanks to the thirst Rumanian intellectuals have had for the few drops of western culture that have fallen their way, many of them have caught up with the years during which they have been so drastically cut off. From recent visits to Rumania have come reports of a real intellectual effervescence. Writers, philosophers, and artists are producing remarkable new works which they cannot yet make public. These works represent their real ability, their real outlook and creativity.

[15] The situation seems to have improved recently. See e.g. a report in the *Neue Zürcher Zeitung*, 2 June 1962, where the author states that he found it relatively easy to have discussions and conversations with intellectuals and artists.

14
The Third Rumanian Congress, 1960

THE SINO-SOVIET CONFLICT

THE Third Congress of the RWP held between 20 and 28 June 1960[1] was one of the most crucial events in communist history, for it was here, at the now famous communist 'little summit', that the serious rift between the Soviet and Chinese Communist Parties became open and accepted.

The leadership of the Rumanian party viewed the Sino-Soviet controversy with considerable uneasiness. Its loyalty to the Soviet Union was undoubted, but it never welcomed Khrushchev's policies wholeheartedly. Nevertheless, then the cautious Dej implicitly toed the Moscow line, and there is no reason to believe that in the secret meetings at Bucharest or at those which came later, the RWP played anything but a supporting rôle.

The Congress was the most purposeful and successful ever held by the party. The top leadership was united, there were some industrial achievements to boast of, there was Khrushchev's presence and ostentatious personal blessing of Dej and the whole party. There was a Six-Year Plan and a longer-term economic programme to present. In particular, the Congress was a personal triumph for Dej, and it was no surprise when, the following March, he was elevated as the head of the newly instituted Council of State.

In the speeches at the Congress a broad series of successes was claimed on every front, but there were no references to any progress in destalinization. Nor did the elections to the Central Committee and Politburo show any changes of personnel which might herald any change in policy. The results seemed the same mixture as before, but rather more of it. One effect of this preservation of the top men was the inevitable conservatism shown by Dej and his colleagues in making changes in junior or minor positions.

[1] *Sc.*, 21–29 June 1960. See also E. Crankshaw, *The New Cold War* (1963).

Only one man was dropped from the Politburo, although he was something of an institution. Constantin Parvulescu, the Nestor of the party, lost his posts not only in the Politburo but in the Central Committee and as chairman of the party Control Commission as well. The following March he was also removed as chairman of the National Assembly. The real reason was made known only at the November–December 1961 plenum of the Central Committee when, as has been said, he was denounced for carrying on factional activities with Constantinescu and Chisinevschi. Although he was present at that plenum and was exhorted to apologize and confess, he did not do so satisfactorily. Thus ended the career of a man who had been in the forefront of the party for forty years without making any noticeable impression on it.

The man who replaced him in the Politburo and who in March 1961 became Prime Minister was Ion Gheorghe Maurer. His rise had been rapid indeed. Maurer had studied law and in his youth had been a state prosecuting lawyer, especially in political trials based on the findings and allegations of the police. After a time he had chosen to become a defence lawyer and became a close associate of Patrascanu. He acted as defence council in several trials of important communists in the 1930s. He showed talent and eagerness, and although he probably became at that time a member of the party, he remained an intellectual and a *mondain*. During the war he was used by the Communist Party as one of their spokesmen and, again as an associate of Patrascanu, in the negotiations with the democratic parties for the creation of an opposition bloc. It was also during the war that he struck up a friendship and understanding with Gheorghiu-Dej that eventually was to pay handsome dividends. At the First RWP Congress in 1948, he became a full member of the Central Committee but soon afterwards suffered a severe eclipse, either because of his past associations with Patrascanu, who at the time started his rapid final fall or, as seems even more probable, because of the suspicion with which Pauker and Luca viewed Dej himself and his friends. At the Second Congress in December 1955, after a period of prolonged inactivity, he emerged again down-graded to candidate member. Soon afterwards, however, he became much more active in the field of diplomacy and in June 1957 was appointed Minister of Foreign Affairs. In January 1958, on the death of Groza, he became chairman of the Presidium of the Grand

National Assembly and thus titular head of state. In June 1958 he became a full member of the Central Committee and at the Third Congress in June 1960 he entered the Politburo over the heads of four candidate-members. In March 1961, when Dej became head of state, he assumed the much more important post of Prime Minister, which combined with his seat in the Politburo gave him a certain amount of power. He is at present obviously in the inner group of the leadership, along with the perennial Gheorghe Apostol, already promoted to first Deputy Premier, Nicolae Ceausescu, the watchdog of the party and as such the potential rival of Maurer, 'the outsider', Mihai Dalea, the former ambassador to Moscow, promoted at the Third Congress to the only vacant place on the Secretariat, and Corneliu Manescu, the young but active Foreign Secretary. Maurer for Parvulescu in the Politburo and Mihai Dalea for Vladimir Gheorghiu in the Secretariat were the only changes in the top leadership. Stability was therefore confirmed and the intended impression of continuity was conveyed.

THE PARTY

As expected, party numbers had certainly grown appreciably since the Second Congress. In his report,[2] Dej announced that there were in June 1960 834,600 members, of whom 148,000 were candidate-members; this was over 40 per cent higher than at the Second Congress in 1955. The greatest increase was registered among candidate-members, who numbered 56,583 in 1955. This increase was one indication of pre-Congress recruitment by the party organizations. The numerical strengthening of the party was confirmed also in the number of basic organizations. There were now over 35,000 such organizations, or 5,600 more than in 1955. The party *Aktiv,* which Gheorghiu-Dej had always described as the core of the party, had now reached 150,000, a third more than the minimum of 100,000 which he had wanted to have in 1955. In it were to be found the best elements of the party, and especially the young 'native' managers recruited by Dej since the beginning of the economic plans in 1950. As far as sheer quantity was concerned, the Rumanian party had done well. It represented in 1960 4.6 per cent of the whole population. This

[2] *Sc. & Agerpres Inf. Bull.*, 25 June 1960.

percentage was almost the same as for Poland and Hungary, but less than for Czechoslovakia and Bulgaria.

Qualitatively, however, the party still left a good deal to be desired. As far as social composition were concerned, it had hardly reached the minimum percentage of workers demanded by the party in its resolutions of 1952 and 1955. Indeed, only by adding the whole suspiciously large number of candidate members, could the Congress statistics demonstrate that workers were in a majority of 1 per cent (51 per cent) of the whole party. Without this artificial calculation, the percentage of worker members would still have remained in the minority. The reluctance of the workers to join the RWP remains a reality. Considering the increase in the number of workers employed in industry and, within this large category, the increase of skilled workers and foremen, one would have expected a much higher increase. Those workers who did join were often not of the right kind.

> When selecting people [Dej complained], some Party and state bodies do not always pay sufficient attention to analysing their activity according to the results they have obtained in carrying out the tasks entrusted to them and urged by immediate requirements, promote people who have neither an adequate political and professional knowledge nor prospects of development; occasionally these bodies pass lightly over harmful actions and manifestations in the life and activity of such people.

In the countryside too the results were not satisfactory. Some 280,000 party and candidate members worked in the state and co-operative sectors of agriculture, nearly all being members of collective farms and agricultural associations, Dej reported. But this showed an increase of only 37,000 members since the Second Congress. There again, considering the steady growth in the number of collective farms, one might have expected a higher percentage than the 34 per cent which included candidate members.[3] Moreover in this layer Dej once more acknowledged a lack of quality in the recruitment. He said that 'great attention must be paid to the improvement of political and educational work in the villages.' He also drew attention to the low percentage of women members and the need to intensify political and educational

[3] At the CC meeting of June 1962 the policy was reversed. Acknowledging that the party had still only some 51 per cent of worker members, the need was stressed to recruit more collective farmers and members of the intelligentsia, for whom admission to the party was also made easier.

work among women. Even among the intellectuals, of whom 23,000 had been added to the party since 1955, Dej stated that there should be more party work to attract people with higher professional and political qualifications.

Chronic difficulties in political and indoctrinational work were once more revealed. Of the 1,150 delegates to the Congress, it was reported that one-quarter had had practically no Marxist–Leninist education.[4] It was also revealed that 670,000 members and candidates were then attending party courses. Finally, it was stated that only 25,000 activists in the party, in the state administration, and in mass organizations and the economy had graduated from party schools in the last five years. These figures again confirmed the party's weakness in ideological knowledge and preparedness.

These failures in political work were also reflected in the Congress reports dealing with Agitprop activities and with the front organizations which were the transmission belts of the régime. Under Leonte Rautu's acknowledged leadership, the Agitprop department was to concentrate on mobilizing the masses for the implementation of the economic targets of the Six-Year Plan; it was also to compile social science textbooks for the party and state educational network. Rautu was given 150,000 party activists and 650,000 non-party activists so that he could carry on the work more efficiently than his predecessors because, Dej said, 'at present ideological activity, the work to eliminate the influence of bourgeois education on people's consciousness, is the main arena of the class struggle'. The fight against the revisionists' anti-Marxist outlook was all-important because 'peaceful coexistence' not only did not include 'but necessarily implies a battle of ideas between socialism and capitalism'. He said that the press had attained a circulation of over 900 million copies and radio sets had increased from 884,794 in 1951 to 1,283,046 in 1960 and were expected to increase even more dramatically in 1961. In 1959 there were also 81 theatres and 2,621 cinemas.

The régime made it clear at the Congress that repression was the mainstay of its political propaganda activities. The Minister of the Interior, Alexandru Draghici, said that 'the fight against trespassing against social rules' was gradually being taken over from the administrative organs of the state by communal organs,

[4] Report of the Credentials Commission, *Sc.*, 21 June 1960.

i.e. 'the comradely councils of judgment, the general assemblies of the workers'. This appeared to be something akin to mob judgment. No wonder that, as Draghici added, there were many cases when those faced with such a trial preferred to go to the people's courts.

THE SIX-YEAR PLAN

The Congress approved the report on the past Five-Year Plan and the draft of the new Six-Year Plan as well as a long-term economic programme extending to 1975.

The draft Six-Year Plan described in detail the 'speedy many-sided industrialization' of Rumania; at its centre stood the key to the entire operation, the project for the steel plant to be built at Galati in the following years. Khrushchev, for whom the separate industrialization of Rumania was later to become the main stumbling-block in the way of the regional integration to be carried out by Comecon, did not criticize it at the 1960 Congress. The East Germans and Czechoslovaks had not yet objected. The Soviet Union had already decided to limit its specific contribution to the Galati project to something very small. Moreover at the time Comecon itself had no great say in such matters; it was still merely a kind of loose consultative organization of sovereign states. It was only later that Khrushchev attempted to convert it into a supranational planning body which would co-ordinate the economies of the member states, and failed because of the stubborn opposition of the Rumanians.

The new Six-Year Plan and the sketchy fifteen-year programme (the first satellite programme of its kind) showed the trend which had been clear since November 1958 towards the speedy build up of heavy industry. There was a contrast with the second Five-Year Plan, which placed the emphasis on industries which could be supplied by the country's own raw materials and which especially stressed the chemical industry. Indeed in some respects the new Six-Year Plan was more like the first Five-Year Plan. Like that plan it heralded an overall industrialization with the machine-building industry as the 'pivot' and complete collectivization of agriculture as the goal, and was thus inspired by the conception of economic autarky. But the ten years which had elapsed between the two plans made for a substantial difference in their actual provisions. In industrial planning the integration and specialization undertaken by Comecon in the intervening years had left their mark. In 1960, while again emphasizing industrialization, the plan was drawn up within the general satellite economic framework, within which Rumania's main rôle was still primarily that of an agricultural producer with a highly developed chemical and oil industry. Heavy industry was to provide it with the means necessary for increasing production in earmarked sectors of the economy. In agriculture the new plan emphasized 'the socialist transformation of agriculture', but collectivization rather than co-operativization was the aim; political and organizational work to speed up the formation of new agricultural associations and collective farms was to be carried out on the basis of 'strict adherence to the principle of free consent'. The following is a breakdown of the investments scheduled in the plan:

	1960–5		*% increase 1960–5 over 1954–9*
	000 m. lei	*per cent*	
Total investment	170–180	100	198–209
of which:			
Agriculture	22–23	13	191–202
Transport	16–17	9.2	198–211
Socio-cultural	20–21	11.6	184–195
Industry	100–106	58.8	210–222
of which:			
Producer goods	(89–95)	(89.3)	(212–225)
Consumer goods	(11)	(10.7)	(195–206)

Source: Rep. of CC to 3rd Congress (*Agerpres*, 25 June 1960), p. 27.

The fuel and power industry was earmarked to receive 32 per cent of the total investments, the metallurgical industry 23 per cent, and the chemical industry 23 per cent.

In terms of the annual average increase in production, the Six-Year Plan forecast an increase of 12.3 per cent for consumer goods and 14 per cent for producer goods, but considering the continuous advance of the latter over the past ten years, this was another indication of the priority given to heavy industry which was emphasized in Dej's report. The greatest planned rate of increase was to be achieved in the electric power industry (234 per cent), followed by chemistry, rubber, cellulose, paper (230 per cent), steel (130 per cent), machine-building (120 per cent), and ore extraction (120 per cent). The special attention to the development of the chemical industry was the main feature the new plan had in common with the previous one. Indeed the cumulative effect of the advance achieved in this industry since the previous plan and the targets of the new plan made it the industry which had made the most spectacular advance since the advent to power of the communists. This was natural since most raw materials for this industry are locally situated, because of its usefulness for the development of agriculture, where the shortage of fertilizers was still one of the causes of stagnating production, and because of the possibilities it afforded for exporting to other countries.

The insistence on the speediest possible advance of the machine-building and metallurgical industries was due to the theoretical premise that the development of the economy of a communist country should begin with the establishment of heavy industry. But here the insufficiency of raw materials in the country itself, and especially of the indispensable iron ores—a problem which has been discussed—would assuredly make the Rumanian economy more dependent on Russian exports. It was announced that between 1961 and 1963 Soviet Russia had agreed to send to Rumania 7,100,000 tons of iron ore, 2,800,000 tons of coke, and 2,800,000 tons of ferrous laminates.[5] As more industrial plants and furnaces would be built, the need for raw materials would increase. A further solution is probably to be found in the active trade between the RPR and India, the RPR delivering entire industrial installations and especially oil refineries to India and getting in exchange massive deliveries of iron ore. Another partial solution was pointed to in the forecast of the Six-Year Plan that by 1965 Rumania's own production of iron ore would increase 3.8 times, from 1,418,800 tons in 1959 to 4 million tons in 1965. This, if achieved, would make Rumania the leading iron-ore producer in Central and Eastern Europe. It is believed

[5] In 1959 Rumania had imported 419,000 tons of coke, 803,000 tons of iron ore, and 479,000 tons of rolled steel from the USSR (U.N., *Econ. Bull. for Europe*, vol. 13, no. 2).

that this optimistic forecast is based on the hope that the Dobruja, the old south-east region lying between the mouth of the Danube and the coast of the Black Sea, holds enormous geological reserves of iron ore. This, of course, explains why the most ambitious individual project of the plan, the big iron and steel centre to be built in the six years, and which in 1970 should reach a production capacity of 4 million tons, was to be located in Galati, a port on the Danube. If this is confirmed, the shortage of iron ore which was partly responsible for the slow growth of the metallurgical industry in Rumania would be largely removed. But this, to many independent observers, still seemed a gamble at the time when the Six-Year Plan was announced.[6] The other gamble lay in the tremendous investments planned for heavy industry. The hope expressed that during the plan period savings due to the reduction of production and turnover costs would attain a total of 80–82 million lei did not come true. In spite of increased production and foreign trade, costs went up.

But it cannot be denied that industrial progress has been great since the beginning of 1959. By the end of 1961 the RPR was showing the fastest industrial growth rate in Eastern Europe. Two factors have contributed to this progress. One was the better ordering of industrial production as a whole by the régime and its managers and technicians. Severity combined with competence, seriousness coupled with more flexibility have led to greater efficiency. The ambitious targets of the Six-Year Plan were projected upon an industry which had never been in such good condition. More skilled workers, more technicians and specialists, more and better machines kept in better control and state of repair and, last but not least, under better and freer management brought about wholesome changes in industrial life. The second factor was the active participation of the free world in the process. Although, generally speaking, the United States, Great Britain, France, and West Germany did not export to Rumania capital goods, installations, or raw materials which would be of direct help to heavy industry, it can be believed that a great many of the industrial projects especially in the chemical industry could not have been commissioned so quickly had they not been imported

[6] In the spring of 1962 it was learned that the Rumanian foreign trade officials were doing their utmost to purchase the main industrial installations from Western Europe, particularly from Great Britain, Western Germany, and Austria (see Paul Underwood in *New York Times*, June 1962).

on long-term credits from the industrial west. The collaboration with the west, diligently exploited by the Rumanian government within the quota it could reserve for trade and economic exchanges with non-communist countries, was in 1961 one of the most obvious reasons for the 'boom'.

PEOPLE WITH VESTED INTERESTS

The success of industrialization led to some important social developments. During these years Rumania's own 'new class' has appeared as a social and economic, if not yet a political, force to be reckoned with. In its Rumanian setting it is perhaps better to refer to this class simply as an expanding category of people with vested interests.

In general, the régime has been unsuccessful in inducing sections of the population to identify themselves with it, its policies, or even its achievements. Its front organizations, the trade unions, the youth movements, the women's organizations, &c—even the people's councils—have been of little help in mediating between party and people, despite the constant exhortations and criticisms. But in one sphere it has been more successful. There has appeared in recent years a constantly growing number of people essential to the party for the fulfilment of its economic, social, and administrative tasks. So obviously essential have these people proved that the régime has had to grant them considerable material privileges and at least a certain freedom to get on with their jobs with the minimum of interference and immediate supervision. Many of these people do not belong to the party and apparently share only in its 'national' purposes. But they are dependent on the party for their professional opportunities, their material well-being, and their privileged status in society, and the party, of course, is dependent on them for their skills and ability. Were they ever to sever their links with the party, they would be relegated to the great anonymous mass. Were the party to be removed from power they might get hurt in the process. Finally, many of them are indeed sons of peasants and workers, educated by the present régime and to a certain extent conditioned by it. Who are these people? How numerous are they? What social percentage do they represent in the country?

They are, first, the non-manual wage-earners. Of a total of

3,208,400 wage-earners at the census of 31 December 1960[7] there were 2,215,000 industrial workers, respectively 69 per cent of the total, and 985,900 non-manual workers, or 31 per cent of the total. Not all are, however, members of the intelligentsia. From a strictly educational point of view, out of almost 1 million non-manual wage-earners, nearly one-half, or 474,651, had received either university degrees (165,449) or high school, technical, teacher-training, or economic education (309,202).[8] If one adds the *apparatchiki* to these—the white-collar workers, the highly skilled workers, and other categories—one arrives at a total of roughly 700,000 people who form the new network of people in higher positions and with a different way of life, mentality, and outlook. Viewed from another point of view, the percentage of non-manual wage-earners is almost equal to that of another privileged layer of the population—the urban population, which in 1960 still contributed only 32.1 per cent of the total population. But this is a slightly misleading calculation since on the one hand the great majority of manual workers live in towns, and on the other many of the people with vested interests must live in the countryside where they occupy managerial or technical positions.

Coming now to their occupations and their own professional divisions, the list of intelligentsia as accepted in the Soviet Union, and thence in the RPR and other people's democracies, gives the clearest breakdown. This includes: executives; technical-industrial personnel; technical-agricultural personnel; scientific workers (professors, &c); teachers; cultural workers (journalists, librarians, &c); physicians; intermediate medical personnel (nurses, midwives); planning and accountancy personnel; judiciary staff; university and college students; other groups of intelligentsia.

This catalogue of the communist intelligentsia as used by the Soviet census of 1956[9] is not very different from that read by Molotov in January 1947 at the Eighteenth Congress of the CPSU, and which in turn was the model for the list of 'positions of responsibility' adopted by the RPR in 1950 when it was drafting its skeleton of posts necessary for the fulfilment of the Plans. The same pattern, reproduced vertically from top to bottom of

[7] *An. Stat., 1961*, table 46.
[8] Ibid.
[9] Quoted by L. Labedz, 'The Soviet Intelligentsia', in R. Pipes, ed., *The Russian Intelligentsia* (N.Y., 1961).

the scale, and multiplied by thousands and thousands of the communal employees, indicates the size of this vast social group.

Since 1956 most of the members of this new vested-interest group have been educated under the Soviet imported system known as 'polytechnization'. In the main year of 'the thaw' the régime had introduced two new regulations in its schools. One, through the decision of July 1956[10] on 'improvement of the general culture', involved the extension of the duration of schooling from 10 to 11 years and of elementary schooling to 7 years, so that the 'new man' could be better prepared from a general cultural point of view. The other was this system of 'polytechnization', by which is meant the interlocking of classroom teaching with production activities through multilateral training. In all schools and in each class since 1956–7 the teaching of elementary industrial production has been introduced, and each school has its workshops for practical tuition. Also at the end of the school year each pupil has to spend at least two weeks on an industrial site for on-the-job training. A professional qualifying test is compulsory. Through this method the régime is preparing cadres to fill the many openings which the economic expansion of the country is affording. At the end of 1958, of 165,449 wage-earners with university degrees, 54,408 had attended technical faculties, 21,057 economic faculties, 14,177 law schools, 25,258 medical and hygiene schools, and 46,611 teacher-training schools. By the end of 1960 it was announced that 30.8 per cent of the students were in technical schools and 11.6 per cent in agricultural and forestry schools.[11] The aim of the new Six-Year Plan is to have 80,000 engineers by the end of 1965. In the same way the plan lists the number of doctors, teachers, journalists, nurses, midwives, tractor drivers, mechanics, librarians, accountants, &c required for the expanding economy. The young graduates step directly from the polytechnics and the technical faculties or high schools into the 'field of production' where the job awaits them and they enter positions of responsibility at once. Here, if they show the necessary skill and quality of leadership, they are reasonable sure of professional advancement without too much harassment from the party. In the RPR it is probable that less than 50 per cent of

[10] *Sc.*, 13 July 1956. [11] *An. Stat. 1961.*

the holders of responsible posts are party members and that the proportion decreases with every new yearly intake of cadres.

The party controls them through the more ingenious means of 'nomenclatura' derived from the Soviet term. This is the system whereby the party compiles lists of the more important posts and people who might be considered suitable candidates for these posts, from the local party committees to the regional, republic, and all-Union party committee. The 'nomenclatura' comprise only the key positions and the key people. It is also the means by which the party exercises its direct control over these groups, regardless of whether they are party-members or not. For if the position is awarded and maintained by the respective party secretary who dominates and controls the 'nomenclatura', the appointee knows only too well that he is ultimately responsible to the party. The 'nomenclatura' exist in towns and in villages; there are various 'nomenclatura' in each geographic or economic unit: party, industry, agriculture, Agitprop, trade schools and scientific institutions, culture and education. In each of them the local party secretary or activist is the man who decides. As the jobs get fewer towards the apex of the pyramid, the 'nomenclatura' get progressively more selective, up to the 'nomenclatura' of the party Central Committee, through which are appointed the men in the top positions of the national life, political, administrative, economic, cultural, and artistic.

The man or woman appointed through the 'nomenclatura' is certainly at the mercy of the party. But if the individual needs the party, the party needs him to run the enormous job of the state employer, and thus the technical intelligentsia are a power in society. There accordingly exists the basic objective condition for a *modus operandi*. But within this basic framework there exist conflicts, or at least dangers of conflicts. One kind of conflict is vertical, between the hierarchy of the intelligentsia and the hierarchy of the party, and there the conflict is on general principles and methods of work. The other is horizontal, between a particular manager in command and his equivalent counterpart in the party. In this latter case there are probably considerable conflicts at the lower level which may be accentuated or modified according to the personalities or temperaments of the people involved. There is, however, at the time of writing no reason to believe that in Rumania the forces tending to make for conflict are gaining the upper hand over those which, out of mutual need, are binding them together. But as high policy in the RPR becomes more and more dictated by considerations of economics and efficiency, as this technical intelligentsia becomes more sure of itself and convinced of its own indispensability, it is obvious that it will demand more say in the framing of policy and come more and more into conflict with the party. If so, this would be a clash between the empirical and the dogmatic attitude of mind. All the communist régimes are, of course, aware of the problem and are trying by their hybrid systems of education to blend the two approaches—the essentially dogmatic approach of the communist with the practical approach of the engineer or technocrat—into one and the same socialist man. At the highest level in the party there are men such as Alexandru Barladeanu and Gheorghe Gaston Marin who are both 'good' communists and good technocrats, and a man such as Maurer probably has considerable sympathy with the new intelligentsia. But with these men the party and its often non-economic dictates come first. It is doubtful whether that order of priority will ever be accepted by the new vested-interest groups.

One important source of conflict, this time at a lower level, has been over the question of decentralization. The decentralization carried out in Rumania in 1957 and again in the wake of Khrushchev's decentralization in Soviet Russia has led to a greater control by the party organizations at local or regional levels over the work of enterprises and of the people's councils. The ministries, directorates, and other authorities in Bucharest were criticized for slowness, red tape, and lack of flexibility. But the criticisms were made by the party; and it was the party which was asked to help at local and regional levels to get the work done. When in March 1960 it was decided to set up regional economic councils which would be attached to the people's councils and which, as stated in the draft presented to the Third Congress, were created to 'help the regional party committees and the regional people's councils in co-ordinating economic activities at the local level', both the party and technical intelligentsia profited from the setting up of these new bodies. The party got a greater control in the regional economic work, planning, and execution of plans. But as in the case of the Soviet *sovnarkhozes,* it was decided that the new economic councils would be formed mostly by technocrats, engineers, technicians, economists, scientists, &c. This was a salutary recognition by the régime of the importance of the technocrats. Nevertheless, if these bodies are ever to function properly, it is difficult to see how they can avoid clashing with the local party organizations.[12]

Such conflicts, however, may take some time before they become a basic problem for the régime. In the meanwhile the technocrats continue in their material prosperity—a prosperity which has not been shared to anything like the same extent by the workers. The technocrats' salaries are on an average three or four times higher than those of the average skilled workers. Also since the major increase in the wages of technical, scientific, and teaching personnel of 1955, they have been covered by all wage increases and adjustments since then, constantly increasing the differential between them and the workers. Moreover the reduction in prices of consumer goods, introduced in 1959 and 1960, mostly affected goods which could not in any case be bought with the average worker's wage. It is, therefore, this ever-growing class which is seen at the good restaurants or buying from the well stocked shops. They have privilege, prosperity, and incentive which the mass of wage-earners in this dictatorship of the proletariat are still far from having. However, as the number and range of the people with vested interests is continually expanding, and as their appearance on the social scene has coincided with a substantial improvement since 1959 in the real wage of the workers of all categories, the effect in the general atmosphere of the country, and especially of the towns, was to the good. More people, with more money, better fed and better dressed, healthier and gayer began to be seen. Restaurants, shops, holiday resorts, even night clubs came back to life. The press and other media adopted a less sombre attitude towards the idea of enjoyment itself. It published reports and articles, made pictures and films

[12] A new situation was created in the spring of 1962 when the Ministries of Agriculture and Culture were replaced by Higher Councils, from which the regiona and district councils, in collaboration with the people's councils at that level take their orders. Although the two presidents of these Higher Councils are important members of the party, the largest number of lower-echelon presidents and members are technicians and experts, appointed primarily for their competence and only secondarily for their party status. It may thus be expected that within these councils the struggle between party and technocrats may take a new turn, the latter being in a relatively stronger position than before.

of the people who, by working well, earn well and live well. An atmosphere of stimulation replaced the general reprobatory attitude of the party towards any sign of personal prosperity. This time the underlying propaganda *motif* was that comfort, ease, and happiness are attainable in the present society provided one follows the party prescriptions for getting them. The palpable results of the industrialization plan and the national stand taken by the party in its defence helped towards better relations between the two teams.

15
After the Twenty-Second Soviet Congress, 1961

THE Twenty-Second Soviet Congress, held from 17 to 31 October 1961, was most memorable for the public denunciation by Khrushchev of the execution of innocent people under the Stalin régime, for his renewed denunciation of the Soviet anti-party group, including further revelations of their attempt to seize power, and for the heightening of the Sino-Soviet conflict through the attack on the policy and methods of the Albanian leaders, who had begun to depart from the 'common agreed line of the communist movement of the whole world' on major issues. The Congress also approved a report on the new party programme, including policies for industry and agriculture, and voted for the removal of Stalin's body from the Lenin Mausoleum.

The Rumanian delegation to the Congress consisted of Gheorghiu-Dej, Bodnaras, Ceausescu, Chivu Stoica, and Rautu; it was a strong delegation, and strongly dogmatist too on the home front. But at the time, until the end of 1962, the RWP did not waver in their loyalty to the CPSU, though they disliked its revisionism. Until the end of 1962 Dej kept quietly on the defensive, as one of the survivors of an era now anathematized. The report he made on his return, at the CC plenum of November 1961 (summarized below), again carried the same justifications: 'We destalinized during Stalin's time'. But at the end of 1963, incensed by Khrushchev's disregard of Rumania's economic aims and by the centrifugalism accentuated by the Sino-Soviet conflict, he calmly operated a triple disengagement. He extricated Rumania from Comecon's growing controls; the party from the automatic endorsement of the Russians; and he refurbished his own Stalinist ideology into a kind of dynamic national dogmatism, as will be seen later.

The plenum was held from 28 November to 5 December 1961[1] and proved to be a massive exercise in diversion. For the first time the party leadership decided to have the main speeches published in *Scinteia* (but not broadcast, thus showing once more a preference for not ventilating problems too widely: *Scinteia* is read by the party members, while the radio is listened to everywhere). Dej's report was not unlike the one following the Twentieth CPSU Congress in laying the blame for Stalinism in the RPR on others, and the substance of what he had to say in effect repeated what he had said at the 1956 Central Committee and Stalin district meetings. The party had done its own destalinization in 1952–3 when it got rid of Pauker, Luca, and Georgescu, who formed a Stalinist ring which was more powerful than himself. In 1957 the final remnants of Stalinism were purged by the removal of Miron Constantinescu and Chisinevschi. After this the party lived in an entirely different atmosphere, of inner-party democracy and collective leadership. It had abolished the unlawful practice of having its members controlled and under constant surveillance by the secret police. It had restored social peace by forging the alliance between working peasants and the workers, an alliance which had been seriously endangered by Ana Pauker and Vasile Luca through their brutal methods of collectivization. What Dej now added to the 1956 statements were declarations of solidarity with the CPSU and some further interesting details on the situation in the party and in the country during the Stalinist era. He castigated the Albanian leaders for attacking 'the general line guiding the communist parties in the main problems of our days' and said they now libelled the CPSU and its Central Committee as well as other Marxist-Leninist parties. 'The leaders of the Albanian Party of Labour assume a heavy responsibility for their line, which is harmful to the interests of building socialism in Albania and to the interests of the socialist camp and of the world communist movement.' He also stated that he shared the opinion expressed at the Soviet Congress that if the Chinese comrades desired to make efforts to normalize the relations between the Albanian party and the fraternal parties, no one could make a better contribution to the solution of that task than they.

In his series of revelations about the state of affairs during the

[1] *Sc.*, 7–19 Dec. 1961; extracts from Dej's report in *Agerpres Inf. Bull.*, 10 Dec. 1961.

Stalinist régime Dej drew a sharp distinction between the '*émigrés* from Moscow', Pauker and Luca, whom he linked with the Soviet anti-party group and especially with Molotov, and between himself and his friends who had sweated it out in Rumanian jails. As has been seen, he asserted that the '*émigrés*' opposed the withdrawal of the Rumanians from the war and preferred to have the whole country occupied by the Soviet armies under whose shield the Communist Party would have come to power immediately and alone. The moment they returned to Rumania, he said, they claimed that they should be given the leadership of the party, considering him as merely the symbolic leader. And they did actually run the party; as a result of orders given by Pauker 'the organs of the Ministry of the Interior, which were not under the control of the Party leadership, began to put Party and state cadres under surveillance, to tap telephone conversations, measures from which not even the Secretary-General of the Party's Central Committee was excepted'. The group ignored the Politburo and the Central Committee. The Secretariat, 'where they had the majority and where the General Secretary in many of the most important problems was put in a minority', ran everything. They terrorized the old party members, and especially those who had fought in Spain during the civil war and in France in the resistance during the world war. In the sectors of the state administration of whose activity they were in charge, such as foreign affairs, finance, internal affairs, agriculture, and trade, they hampered economic reconstruction, industrialization, the development of agriculture, and the raising of living standards. In agriculture Pauker organized forcible collectivization by terror: 80,000 peasants were arrested and 30,000 were brought to public trials in order to terrorize the rest. Once Ana Pauker, Luca, and Georgescu had been expelled, the dead hand of Stalinism was lifted, and now there were 'no grave injustices to be forgiven and nobody to rehabilitate post-mortem'. A few years later two survivors of the Stalinist era, disciples of Pauker, Constantinescu and Chisinevschi, had also to be purged because they tried to distract the attention of the party from the examination of the deeds of the Pauker-Luca group and 'intended to give the discussion on the documents of the Twentieth Congress . . . a direction towards the encouragement of an anarchical and petty bourgeois spirit'. He also mentioned that Parvulescu had joined the Chisinevschi–Constantinescu cabal and had not yet confessed his faults. He concluded his remarks on Stalinism by proposing that the practice of giving names of living persons to streets and institutions should be abolished; he had earlier promised to take steps to remove the many statues of Stalin erected during a period in which there was no single statue of Lenin in Rumania.

The speakers who followed, Bodnaras, Moghioros, Gheorghe and Chivu Stoica, Maurer, Valter Roman, Gaston Marin, and Ana Toma simply produced variations on the same theme, some insisting on Patrascanu's crimes, some on the plight of the 'Spaniards' during Pauker's rule, some on the part played by the party in the 23 August coup d'état, some attacking Parvulescu and Chisinevschi more sharply than Dej had done so. Only two asked that Constantinescu's party membership would be reexamined; demands for Chisinevschi's expulsion were much more frequent.

TOTAL COLLECTIVIZATION

By the beginning of 1962 96 per cent of the total arable land had been brought into the 'socialist sector', comprising state farms, collective farms, and the diminishing agricultural associations.

It is obvious that the state of mind of the peasantry also played a part in the fall of the last redoubt of the scattered individual farmers. The will to resist of the Rumanian peasants had been strengthened throughout this decade by the instinctive hope that some event would occur in the international sphere which would remove from their country, and particularly from their village, a régime which from the first they had known to be an alien imposition. This hope lost most of its ground when after 1958 the communists succeeded in consolidating their position through the manoeuvre of peaceful coexistence. Slowly depression spread in the countryside where harassment and chicanery was the lot of each individual farmer visited by the hordes of activists, propagandists, and controllers.

In less than four months the whole thing was over, four years earlier than had been forecast. Rumania became the last country in the Soviet bloc, with the exception of Poland, to achieve collectivization. But the fact that in April 1962 the Rumanian Workers' Party proclaimed that collectivization had been achieved did not *ipso facto* solve the problems to which it had given rise. These were how to organize collectivized agriculture without endangering the already inadequate production, and how to find some way of adapting the Soviet model so that it might correspond to certain basic aspects of the Rumanian agricultural economy.

Both these problems reappeared in the text of the bill for the reorganization of agriculture passed by the Grand National Assembly on 30 April 1962.

The most striking features of the new organization were the replacement of the Ministry of Agriculture by the Higher Council of Agriculture and the setting up of regional and district agricultural councils under the respective people's councils, but taking their orders and directives from the Higher Council. At first glance the Rumanian reorganization seemed to copy the Soviet agricultural reorganization of 22 March 1962. But there are basic differences. The Soviet text made it clear that the party was directly responsible for the new management of agriculture at all levels: the regional agricultural council is headed by the local regional party First Secretary. In Rumania, however, the head of the regional council is a vice-president of the people's council.

Armed with this new organization, the Rumanian government and party prepared to attack the main problems of collectivized agriculture. The first problem was to ascertain how much of the collectivization was genuine and how much still on paper. A collective farm cannot be decreed; it has to be established. The measure of the success of the establishment of such a farm lies in the growth of the common fund, in its yearly balancing of the budget as a sign of its viability, and in the raising of its production level. None of these three conditions were to be found in the majority of the collective farms previously established in Rumania. It is difficult to believe that they will be found for many years to come in the hurriedly established collectives of 1961.

The second problem was that of mechanization. Although some progress had been made, the fact remained that by the beginning of the new phase Rumania had only one tractor to 190 hectares, compared with one to 135 hectares in Soviet Russia, to 79 hectares in Czechoslovakia, and to 16 hectares in Great Britain. In Poland the party authorities insisted that collectivization should be begun only when mechanization had reached the needed level and could ensure high productivity. When Rumania embarked on total collectivization, while she remained in quantity the most important agricultural producer in Eastern Europe after Russia, she showed the lowest productivity per hectare.

Another main problem was that of the cadres. Indeed, the party's main preoccupation in connexion with the new organization was the dispatching to the countryside of all available technicians and experts. Pressure, promises, and propaganda were brought to bear on the young technicians to induce them to accept posts in the villages; they were also invited to join the party without any further conditions or even delays. Yet there was still not a sufficient number of technicians and experts for the swollen needs of the new agricultural management. Moreover the reluctance of the members of the 'new class' to return to the primitive standard of living from which they had hoped that they had emancipated themselves was obvious. The party had evident difficulty in gathering this task force.

Finally, there was the perennial problem of the peasants' reaction to the new system of production. From this point of view it was indicative that Gheorghiu-Dej in his report on the conclusion of collectivization and the reorganization of agricultural management presented to a special session of the National Assembly on 27 April 1962 emphasized the importance of the collective farmers' private plots, which included 862,000 hectares of agricultural land, over 1 million cows, over 2 million pigs, c. $5\frac{1}{2}$ million sheep, and c. 30 million head of poultry. He said that great attention must be paid to making full use of this personal husbandry so as to obtain a maximum rise in the production of meat, milk, poultry, eggs and vegetables, in order to meet the needs of the collective farm families and create a surplus to be turned to good account mainly by means of state contracts. It appeared from this that collectivization in Rumania has had to make concessions to the principle of private ownership; the Rumanian farmer is shown at his best only when he is allowed the supreme incentive for his work—private ownership of his land and his livestock.

RESISTANCE TO COMECON

But the most important development in the history of the Rumanian Workers' Party in the last years of this survey, and one that could have far-reaching consequences, became apparent only at the end of 1962 and was exposed with glaring publicity by the world press in 1963. This was Rumania's difference with Comecon and consequent isolation within the East European bloc. This estrangement from 'proletarian internationalism' and emancipation from the docility towards the Soviet Union observed by the régime and party for the first fifteen years of their rule had three facets.

The first and most significant was the differences on economic policy. As has been seen, since the Third Congress Rumania had drawn up ambitious plans of industrialization pivoting on the machine-building industry, based in its turn on the great iron and steel combine to be built at Galati, the Rumanian Nova Huta or Stalinvaros. These plans had been acclaimed at the Congress by Khrushchev and by all the other East European leaders attending it, and it may be assumed that they had been previously approved by Comecon (although the Soviet Union promised only limited help for this operation, in contrast with massive help and encouragement for the development of the Rumanian chemical industry).[2] It was obvious that the resumption of a kind of autarkic industrialization in Rumania since 1958 was not consonant with current policy in the bloc which, especially since the rapid progress made by the West European Common Market, had been under special instructions from Khrushchev to speed up regional integration through specialization and supra-national planning. Thus while the Rumanian party claimed that Rumania was entitled to attain a higher level of industrial development and to cease being a mere supplier of raw materials, Comecon, under the aegis of the Soviet Union, had entered a phase in which it was vital to integrate the economies of the component countries on the basis of division of labour and specialization. The other bloc countries, in particular East Germany and Czechoslovakia, in consequence pointed out that if Rumania was allowed to build her own steel industry, this would duplicate the industries of the more advanced countries, which naturally expected to continue to be the main industrial producers in the bloc (after the Soviet Union), a position emphasized in the new set of economic plans. As a result of continuing discussions at various Comecon executive

[2] It was noticed during Khrushchev's visit to Rumania in the summer of 1962 that he visited and praised the chemical industry centres but bypassed and paid only lip-service to the steel industry centres, nor did he visit or mention Galati.

committee meetings, the Rumanian resistance to Comecon policy hardened progressively and proportionately with two other developments: the successful Rumanian negotiations with the West for the acquisition of the equipment needed for the heavy industry plants, and the aggravation of the Sino-Soviet conflict, with the telling corollary of Albania's successful defiance of the Soviet Union.

The Comecon executive committee meeting of 15 February 1963 may be considered as the occasion on which the breach between Rumania and the Comecon countries, especially the Soviet Union, came into the open. At this meeting Alexandru Barladeanu, the Rumanian delegate and chief planner, made it unmistakably clear that while his country would continue to collaborate on a bilateral and even multilateral basis with Comecon, Rumania would not accept any real modification of her industrial plans for the sake of regional integration. Socialist division of labour was acceptable to Rumania only if it did not prevent her from faster development, aimed at catching up with the more advanced countries.[3] But the conflict came into the open in another way as well. For once the reticent and somewhat arrogant leadership considered it absolutely necessary to break its silence towards the rank and file and decided to inform the population in general of the new problems which lay ahead through a series of meetings held at all levels. An exceptionally long and well attended meeting of the party Central Committee was held in Bucharest between 5 and 8 March 1963 to discuss the results of the February Comecon meeting and to endorse and approve the stand taken at it by the Rumanian delegates. This endorsement was itself unprecedented and obviously expressed the Central Committee's desire to demonstrate that this was a basic decision.[4] Moreover the Central Committee communiqué went further in stressing that

> the main means of successfully developing and deepening the socialist international division of labour was co-ordination of the national economic plans in the spirit of the principles proclaimed by

[3] *The Times*, 27 June 1963.

[4] It was rumoured at the time that Gheorghiu-Dej himself had written to Khrushchev informing him that this was the ultimate limit to which the party and government would go in their collaboration with Comecon, and that if forced to alter their national plans, Rumania would have no alternative but to leave Comecon.

the 1960 Moscow statement of observance of national independence and sovereignty, of full equality of rights, comradely mutual aid and mutual benefit.[5]

This formula has become the *leit-motif* of all speeches of the leaders and officials of the party, addressing foreign or national audiences. Indeed, so far as the latter were concerned, the enlarged Central Committee meeting was followed during the whole month of March by a series of meetings of the party and administration, held at all levels, by which the party cadres, the technical intelligentsia, and the workers were told that, although the friendship and collaboration between Rumania and the Soviet Union in all other fields were as strong as before, on the economic problem there were serious differences of view.

The second facet of the conflict is the political aspect, principally the relations between the Russian and Rumanian parties. For a long time it had been rumoured and then confirmed that slowly but thoroughly, quietly but inflinchingly, Dej and the greater part of his team had embarked on the operation of removing the Moscow-trained officials from the apparatus and of replacing them by younger people exclusively loyal to the Rumanian party leadership. This had been made possible by the uninterrupted flow of newly trained cadres, of which more was said in previous chapters. While at the top there still remained some representatives of the former 'Bessarabian' and Soviet-controlled wing (of whom it cannot be known whether they gave Dej sufficient proof of their solidarity or whether they survived, less and less powerful and active, until a good opportunity for eliminating them might occur), in the lower echelons Moscow-trained people were deprived of influence and control. It is clear that without taking such steps in advance (which had not passed unnoticed by the Russians),[6] Dej and the Rumanian leadership could not have risked a public stand of disobedience to the Soviet Union, and it must be assumed that the reshuffle was carried out with special care in the security apparatus. At the same time the assertion of a more independent line towards the Soviet Union was becoming publicly clearer. It had already been noticed that

[5] *Sc.*, 9 Mar. 1963.

[6] 'Whether this was intended as a gesture against Moscow is not known because the turnover of personnel was carried out without any publicity, but it is said that the Russians were concerned about what they considered were disturbing signs of Rumanian nationalism' (*The Times*, 27 June 1963).

in presenting some new bills and laws the RPR government emphasized that these were specifically Rumanian measures. For example, the reorganization of the administration of agriculture differed from the Soviet pattern and was claimed to be deliberately *ad hoc*. A Soviet historian was rebuked in a Central Committee publication for giving the impression that Rumania's liberation was the work of the Red Army and the occasion was used to hammer home the point made by Dej on his return from the Twentieth and Twenty-Second Soviet Congresses, that it was the native Rumanians who wished to liberate their country through the popular rising against the Germans, while the Muscovites would have preferred liberation by the Soviet army. In the new official Soviet history of the war the Dej version of the liberation of Rumania was ultimately adopted.

The third facet was the ideological one. Rumania was defending her economy against Comecon injunctions; but the RWP produced, in defence against Khrushchev's revisionism, its new national dogmatism.

The events which followed the 5–8 March 1963 Central Committee meeting are to be seen in the context of the three facets of the Rumanian position which have been outlined above. On 24 May 1963 an important CPSU delegation, headed by Nikolai Podgorny and including among others A. A. Yepishev, the former Soviet Ambassador to Rumania—during whose tenure of office there Pauker and Luca were purged—arrived in Rumania for an exchange of views of the Rumanian party to attempt to iron out differences, but the visit was inconclusive, Rumania continuing to insist that Comecon was a grouping of sovereign countries. The Rumanian press and radio then, on 22 June, were conspicuous as the only official media in Eastern Europe—with the exception of Albania—to publish a summary of the Chinese letter of 14 June to the CPSU attacking Soviet policy on twenty-five points of principle prior to the Sino-Soviet conference in July; the Soviet party had publicly announced that the text of this letter would not be published in the Soviet Union. But the letter contained at least one point relevant to the Rumanian case. 'It would be great-power chauvinism', it said, 'to deny these basic principles and, in the name of "international division of labour" or "specialization", to impose one's will on others'.[7] This gave

[7] *Peking Review*, 21 June 1963.

the Rumanians a leverage in the Comecon dispute, for the last thing Khrushchev wanted was to have another Albania on his hands. In fact the Albanians were acting as a link between the Rumanians and the Chinese. Rumania sent back her ambassador to Tirana in March 1963; the RWP was treated with noticeable deference by the Albanian party.

Even more significantly, Rumania at the same time met with a warm response to its overtures to Tito. On 12 June, after declining to participate in various investment-starved Comecon projects, Rumania announced that she had concluded a £140 million navigation and hydro-electric project with Yugoslavia, a non-Comecon country, in respect of the Iron Gates of the Danube. When later, in November, Gheorghiu-Dej paid a state (but not a party) visit to Belgrade, he was more highly honoured than Khrushchev, who had been there in August. Dej was the first communist leader invited to address the Yugoslav National Assembly. This exceptional mark of respect could not be explained only by the mutual distrust of Comecon of the two régimes; it is more likely to have indicated Yugoslav welcome for the Rumanian opposition to the monocentrism of the CPSU.

Neither Dej himself nor any notable Rumanian attended the meeting of the First Secretaries held in East Berlin on 29 June on the occasion of Ulbricht's 70th birthday, which Khrushchev utilized for consultations with the other bloc parties before the Sino-Soviet confrontation arranged for 4 July. The Rumanian action was the clearest indication of their refusal to line up with the other parties, as well as a calculated snub to Ulbricht.[8] However, Dej attended the next meeting of the First Secretaries, held in Moscow between 24 and 27 July, to discuss Warsaw Pact and especially Comecon matters. In regard to the former, he found it easy once more to endorse the Soviet policy of 'coexistence and disarmament': not only did he approve of the Nuclear Test Ban Treaty, which had provoked furious reaction from the Chinese, but Rumania was one of the first countries to sign it. As for Comecon matters, the special communiqué of 27 July stressed the progress made in the collaboration of member countries 'on

[8] The East Germans had led the ideological attack on Rumanian industrialization as breaching the socialist division of labour. From this point of view the two most important texts are a study by Huber in *Wirtschaftswissenschaft,* Apr. 1963, and one by Rachmuth in *Probleme economice,* July 1963, both on the subject of economic underdevelopment in socialist countries.

the basis of the principles of equality of rights and strict observance of national sovereignty'. It spoke of co-ordination and not integration of the plans, and even then only of the 1966–70 ones. All these were Rumanian formulae. Nothing was said of Khrushchev's 'supranational planning board' which he had attempted to set up in November.[9] This represented a victory for the RWP and was also a heavy blow for Comecon, which suffered a great loss of prestige.

Rumania next proceeded to remove the marks of her excessive subordination to Soviet influence in other fields as well. On 15 September 1963 the Institute for Russian Studies in Bucharest was converted into one of the four faculties of the newly created Institute for Foreign Languages. The Universal Bookshop replaced the Russian Bookshop, and many streets, buildings, and institutions exchanged Rumanian for Russian names. At the same time there was an increase in cultural exchanges with the West. In August the jamming of the Rumanian-language broadcasts of the western stations was discontinued. Plays, books, films, exhibitions, lecturers, and tourists from Britain, the United States, France, and Italy were received in greater numbers. Some works which had been banned, such as Iorga's histories or Eugène Ionesco's plays, were released. Finally, Rumania caused a slight stir at the United Nations when for the first time she voted with the non-communist countries on a proposal to proclaim Latin America a nuclear-free zone.

It was above all in the ideological realm that the Rumanian Workers' Party tried to ascertain its own position. While it was true that the party had in common with Yugoslavia and Poland the new determination to resist Khrushchev on national matters, it had in common with the Chinese and Albanian parties the determination to oppose him on the structure and evolution of the communist state and society. This line, which for want of a better name might be defined as national-dogmatism, was now projected by the party in the open communist debate. In an article published in the November issue of *Problems of Peace and Socialism* and in *Lupta de clasa,* Ion Gheorghe Maurer, the Prime Minister, writing on the anniversary of the 1960 Moscow declaration (the last ideological document signed jointly by the

[9] See his article in *World Marxist Review,* Sept. 1963 and his report of 19 Nov. 1963.

Soviet and Chinese parties) appeared much as a self-appointed arbiter. One the one hand he restated his party's approval of coexistence and disarmament; on the other he stressed the 'full equality of rights of the brotherly parties', among which there are no 'superior or subordinate parties', and in the relations of which mutual interference was 'inconceivable and inadmissible'. He considered universality as the necessary basis of the communist movement, and drew the conclusion that Comecon too should be open to all socialist countries. This proposal could hardly be welcome to Khrushchev, who, on the contrary, wished to make Comecon a compact and exclusive economic unit. When, later in January-February 1965, the CPSU undertook a round of consultations with the East European parties about the new Chinese attacks, the Rumanians were not included.

At the end of February 1964 the Rumanians accepted a Chinese invitation to send a delegation to Peking to discuss 'problems of the unity of the Socialist camp'. Headed by Maurer, and including Bodnaras, Ceausescu, and Chivu Stoica, the Rumanian party was welcomed by the Chinese President, Liu Shao-chi, on 2 March; Mao Tse-tung himself emerged from seclusion to meet the party. But a curt announcement after the talks had lasted a week merely stated that the two sides had exchanged views on questions of common concern.[10] After visiting North Korea too, the Rumanians held talks with Khrushchev in the Crimea on the way home in order to convey the outcome of their negotiations with the Chinese and North Koreans. It is generally believed that the Chinese were unyielding, while the tone of the Crimean communiqué was, comparatively, warmer.

Finally, on 26 April, the RWP CC issued a concluding 'Declaration'. They rejected Khrushchev's supranational Comecon because of their concern for their own national sovereignty. On the other hand they appealed once more to him and to Mao to avoid the schism—which was already, by then, a *fait accompli*.

But the fact is that once again the Rumanian Workers' Party remained in the middle, still aloof and with room for manoeuvre, but increasingly concerned to see how the growing gap between the two giant parties will split its own precarious doctrinal positions.

[10] *Guardian*, 12 Mar. 1964, *Hsinhua News Agency*, 12 Mar. 1964.

16
Conclusion

THIS history of communism in Rumania in some ways acknowledges some progress. Heavy industry and foreign trade have been comprehensively developed and the urban standard of living has improved in recent years. From a Marxist-Leninist point of view there is more on which the present leaders can congratulate themselves. Private ownership has been abolished with the collectivization of agriculture. In economic and ideological matters the régime has lately shaken off its perennial attitude of docility towards the Soviet Union and the CPSU. This has helped to enhance its reputation at home and abroad and to improve its trade and cultural relations with the West.

Internally a new generation has come to the fore. It has a new mentality and is more easily reconciled to the political asperities of the régime. The country is also recovering some of its traditional gaiety and initiative.

But a success story should mean much more than this. From the point of view of an observer wishing to assess the depth and durability of communism in Rumania, the picture is less satisfactory. The position has been held and can, in similar conditions, be held in the future. But the foundations are insecure.

They are insecure because the imported Soviet system has shown its basic irrelevance for the small and tradition-conscious Eastern European countries. They are especially insecure in Rumania because, until very recently, of the excessive dependence of the régime on the Soviet Union. This dependence has resulted partly from the chronic weakness of the Rumanian party, and partly from the Soviet Union's particular concern for a country which is strategically and economically important to her, but by political instincts and general tradition has been one of the most impermeable to her influence. Thus in spite of the successes which few could deny, the Rumanian régime remained probably more opposed to liberalization than all its other neighbours. Its conservatism or, from another angle, its quasi-Stalinism; its lack of originality or again its failure to suggest or impose a Rumanian road to socialism; its obscurantism or its distrust of any experimentation, within the ideological framework, in exploring problems arising from its relationship with the people; its isolation, or its lack of 'transmission belts' which could help towards mutual questioning between some strata of the people and some cadres of the party, have all derived from the fact that in the beginning the party had agreed to apply a foreign mould to Rumania and had barely tried to adapt it to the realities of the country.

Only in the first years of the 1960's, the last of this study, have two new trends been detectable. The first is that a new social class is beginning spontaneously to play the role of national middlemen. These are the new 'technocrats', those who have been defined as people with 'vested interests'. The party could not accuse them of any original 'social sin', since they were sons of workers and peasants, which it itself had selected. In any case the party needed their services and their knowledge if the complex state machinery which now runs industry, agriculture, culture, and all other activities was indeed to run at all. They are individually as much under the pressure of the party as any other group in a totalitarian dictatorship. But as a group or number of groups they can exert pressure on the party and have done so for the last few years. The first structural reforms which spokesmen of the régime for the first time described as being 'a genuine Rumanian solution',[1] and which differed at least on paper from the Soviet model, were the establishment of the regional agricultural and cultural councils, the members of which have mainly been appointed for their specialized knowledge. In other words, in the first reforms claimed to be Rumanian in origin, the originality has lain in underplaying the rôle of the party and enlarging that of the experts, technicians, and intellectuals. This, if indeed it is to become a durable and significant trend, is a hopeful development.

It could progressively reduce the supremacy of the party which is the root of the tyranny. It is remarkable that while in many

[1] Maurer in his speech of 27 Apr. 1962 introducing the bill for the new agricultural management.

more advanced communist countries the 'withering away' of the state is being at least discussed, this formula is preferred even for utopian discussions to that of the 'end of the monolithic party'. Yet between the two the monolithic party serves a much less useful rôle and does greater harm to the natural growth of society than the state, which is a much more diffuse term. Djilas's final solution was to end the monolithic party and to recognize the right of at least one other opposition party. But this was too much even for the Yugoslav communists and is too much for any Leninist. Djilas's conflict was not with Tito or Khrushchev or even with Stalin; it was with Lenin, who had already experienced once and for all in March 1921 the bitterness of the 'conclusion that the time has come to put an end to opposition, to put the lid on it',[2] if the communists were to remain in power. Yet life, even in the dark maze of the totalitarian societies, proves Lenin to be ever more wrong. The monolithic party cannot do everything alone; and has to acknowledge other, alien bodies, if the state, which is its ultimate responsibility, is to function. In the year 1962 there have been different national variations on the theme of the collaboration between the party and the intelligentsia in the various European communist countries. Tito, Gomulka, and Kadar have allowed and even encouraged free collaboration with non-party technicians. Khrushchev was still confident that the party should be in ultimate and open control of all their activities. In Rumania Dej was proposing to transform as many of the best intellectuals as possible into party members and allowing the formation of agricultural and cultural councils in which there was a risk of the party being overruled. These were all signs of the inevitable erosion of the monolithic rule of the party and of Djilas's dilemma proving itself to be more and more true.

Perhaps in Rumania, more than in any other Eastern European country, the only way to pacify the population and to heal some of the open wounds is the progressive and substantial reduction of the power of the party. If, within the present imposed framework, Rumania is to function more normally, this will only be in the proportion to which the rule of the party recedes into the background and allows other bodies to take responsibilities, to express opinions, and to make rules. In these circumstances the gradual emergence of the country's intellectuals and experts would

[2] Quoted in L. Shapiro's *Origin of the Communist Autocracy* (1955), p. 316.

restore, albeit gradually, some of the now long eclipsed originality and authenticity to Rumanian society and culture. One need not be a Rumanian to aver that Rumanians are a most talented people and to point to the fact that in the years in which Rumanian culture was silenced at home, it has blossomed in other European cultures. In Rumania too, in the first years of the 1960's, the effect of some interpenetration with western culture and the stimulating effect of more freedom in information and inspiration has produced an instantaneous effect of creativity. Like all Eastern European peoples, the Rumanians are strongly nationalist and this led in the late 1930's to some deeply regrettable excesses. The passing of these excesses will be lamented by very few, but the communists in the first decade of their rule have cynically trampled on all legitimate national pride and patriotism

The Rumanian people, following once more the ancestral 'withdrawal from the path of the invaders', withdrew in silence and apparent apathy. During these fifteen years westerners have questioned why the Rumanians, a dynamic people, have shown less active resistance to the Soviet communist administration than the Poles or the Hungarians. The explanation has ranged from the special severity of the Russian quasi-occupation in Rumania to the absence of a rallying-point, as was and is the Catholic Church in Poland and to a lesser degree in Hungary. But one should always remember that the historic reflex of this people, which has miraculously survived for 2,000 years with its distinctive Latin language and culture, was just such a tacit and supremely cautious withdrawal in order to survive. Such a withdrawal connotes neither surrender nor betrayal, but a biding of time.

The spirit of Rumania rests with the new young generation that has grown up in the communist era. In spite of the indoctrination and the awesome propaganda apparatus, this generation, sometimes apparently cynical, has kept a strong grip on reality. In many a young Rumanian it is possible to see a patriotism devoid of nationalist excess and tempered by geo-political realism, which only a romantic would call into question. Internally, a free Rumania, ruled by constitutional means and governed by western values, is the choice; externally, a free association with other Balkan and East European nations seems to be their ideal.

These are the opinions of the majority of young Rumanians to whom this author has talked. One can only hope that they will in the end triumph.

The second new trend was the crystallization of a difference of opinion between the Rumanian Workers' Party and the rest of the Eastern European parties—and implicitly and explicitly with the CPSU—on economic and political problems. The fact that for once the leadership of the Rumanian party admitted and explained to the rank and file that the Soviet Union and the Eastern European block were steering a course contrary to Rumanian basic interests, which should be defended by a firm line of national resistance, was an innovation which could never be forgotten or reversed. The fact that in some respects the Rumanian party adopted at least a kind of neutrality on one basic issue in which the Soviet Union was involved also demonstrated that such attitudes can be taken if the party is courageous enough, and therefore might be taken in future on other problems as well. The fact that in such moments of conflict and tension Rumania found more understanding and help in the west than in the 'fraternal parties' of the east was also a lesson not to be forgotten. These three significant facts bore within them the seeds of possible hopeful developments for the future. For while it is true that Gheorghiu-Dej and his group played their rôle unassumingly and ambiguously, taking firm positions in an almost furtive way, with the minimum of words spoken, and while it is also true that they profited from the conflict to maintain and consolidate their national-dogmatist line, the cumulative effects on a new and less inhibited generation, in a régime which of its own accord has chosen to loosen the former close ties with the Soviet Union and end its slavish imitation, may be profound. When a new generation takes over, the Rumanian régime will of necessity be more independent of the Soviet Union, and at the same time it is this younger generation that aspires to more internal freedom and responsibility. The combination of internal and external emancipation could be of great consequence.

BIOGRAPHICAL NOTES

APOSTOL, Gheorghe (b. 1912, Moldavia). Turner and railway worker, son of a railway worker. Joined CP 1930; active in youth organizations. Arrested 1936, released Aug. 1944. President of General Confederation of Labour Central Committee, 1944–53; member of Politburo 1948; Deputy Premier and for a time Minister of Agriculture May 1952–Apr. 1954; First Secretary of RWP 19 Apr.–2 Oct. 1955. Considered as one of possible successors to Dej.

BODNARAS, Emil (b. 1904, Bukovina). Father Ukrainian, mother German. Officer in Royal Rumanian Army 1928–32; deserted to Russia 1933 and spent war years there. Returned to Rumania over front line spring 1944; active as liaison between the Soviet command and the Moscow wing of the CP—Ana Pauker, Vasile Luca, Gheorghiu-Dej and the other 'Rumanians' from the prisons. After dismissal of Foris and before Dej's release from prison was the most important member of the 'troika' formed by him, of himself, Parvulescu, and Ranghet, which led the party. Supervised Patrascanu's negotiations with the king and the democratic parties before the armistice. Head of Council of Ministers' Political Information Service 1945–7; Minister of Armed Forces 1947; Deputy Premier Aug. 1954 to 1957, and then again in 1959. Member of CC and Politburo. One of the strongest influences in the party as head of the group of political generals.

BORILA, Petre (b. 1906, Bessarabia). Took part in Tatar Bunar revolt 1924. Remained in USSR until 1936 when he was sent to Spain, returning to USSR in 1940. During the war was in command of the Tudor Vladimirescu division, with which he returned to Rumania in 1944. Head of Bucharest party organization 1944–7; member of CC 1948; Chief of Army Political Directorate 1948–50; Minister of Construction 1950; Chairman of State Control Commission 1951; member of Politburo May 1952; Minister of Food Industry 1953; Deputy Premier 1954. Member of RWP delegations which went to Moscow 1960 and to the U.N. Head of Bessarabian wing of the party since Chisinevschi's fall. Remains one of the strongest men in the present ruling group.

CEAUSESCU, Nicolae (b. 1918, Pitesti). Joined CP 1932; Secretary Union of Communist Youth 1940; Brigadier-General 1945. Candidate member CC 1948; full member 1952; Secretary of

CC and candidate member Politburo 1954; full member Politburo 1955. Through his unimpeachable career and continuous rise in the party hierarchy and because, although relatively young, he is virtually in control of the *Apparat* and is a Rumanian, Ceausescu is the most probable successor of Dej within the party.

CHISINEVSCHI, Iosif (b. 1905, Bessarabia). White-collar worker. Joined party 1928; arrested 1928, released 1930. Worked in Agitprop; arrested 1933, released 1936. Active in trade unions. Spent some years in Moscow. Elected to CC 1940; arrested same year. Member CC 1946. Head of Agitprop. Member Politburo 1948, in charge of Agitprop. Deputy Premier. Purged 1957; allegedly died 1962.

COLIU, Dumitru (b. 1907, Bulgaria). Regional secretary of Dobruja before Second World War. Spent war in USSR and returned to Rumania with Tudor Vladimirescu division. Member CC 1948; candidate member Politburo 1952. Secretary-General of Bucharest party organization 1953; Chairman State Control commission 1955 to date. Strong influence in party and in its relations with Soviet and Bulgarian CPs.

CONSTANTINESCU, Alexandru (b. 9 Mar. 1873). Upholsterer. After peasant revolt of 1907 became known for strong speeches delivered at workers' meetings in support of the peasants. Representative of Rumanian workers at 2nd International Congress, Stuttgart, 1907. During First World War remained in Bucharest, setting up in 1916 the 'Committee for the Fight Against the War'; 1917 took part in organization of 'clandestine groups' in the part of Rumania under German occupation. Was sent by these groups to Moscow. Later played important part in formation of the CP until 1923 when he fled abroad, allegedly to France and the USSR. Returned to Rumania 1937, a broken man after the purges in which Rakovsky, Dobrogeanu-Gherea, and Marcel Pauker were liquidated, playing no further active part in the party; d. 1949.

CONSTANTINESCU, Miron (b. 1917, Muntenia). Of middle-class family, related to George Diamandi, one of the young aristocrats who founded the Socialist Party and was afterwards Rumanian Ambassador in Paris and Moscow. Doctor of Philosophy and Economics. Joined Communist Youth 1935; their Secretary 1939. Arrested in 1939 and remained in prison until 1944, his wife being killed in prison in 1942. Member CC 1946; Director of *Scinteia* 1947–9; Secretary-General of interdepartmental Economic Commission. President of State Planning Commission 1949–55; signed convention of dissolution of Sovrom companies. Member Politburo 1948; Secretary of RWP 1952–54; Deputy Premier 1955–7; purged 1957. Allegedly works at Rumanian Academy.

DALEA, Mihai (b. 1917). Joined youth organization of Rumanian CP during Second World War; sent to staff of Moscow Embassy 1947. Vice-Chairman of State Control Commission Nov. 1949-June 1952; Secretary of CC Apr. 1959; Chairman of State Commission for Agricultural Products 1955; Ambassador to Moscow May 1956; Secretary (for Agriculture) of CC June 1960; Chairman of National Assembly for Agriculture 1961 and of Higher Council for Agriculture May 1962.

DOBROGEANU-GHEREA, Alexandru. Eldest son of C. Dobrogeanu-Gherea. A philosopher and sociologist, Alexandru exercised a strong influence upon the party as a whole and particularly upon the intelligentsia. Of a violent and revolutionary temperament, he moulded himself upon the early (Trotskyist) belief in world revolution and in the impossibility of achieving full communism unless and until the main Western European states, especially Germany, had produced their own revolutions. Until 1928 he monopolized the party press and publications. Together with Marcel and Ana Pauker, Lucretiu Patrascanu, Vasilescu Vassia, Fabian, and other 'intellectuals', he was the main communist theoretician, fanatically opposed to the Social Democrat doctrine and yet quite far from Leninist and especially Stalinist doctrine. Shot in Russia during 1936–7 purges.

DRAGHICI, Alexandru (b. 1919, Moldavia). Joined CP in 1930s; sentenced with Ana Pauker in 1936 to 20 years' imprisonment from which he emerged 1944. Member of CC 1948; First Secretary of Bucharest party organization 1949; Deputy Minister of Interior 1951; Minister 1952. Full member of Politburo since 1955. Being in control to date of the security forces, Draghici has considerable power in state and party affairs.

FAZEKAS, Ianos (b. 1920 Transylvania). Of Hungarian origin. Member of CC and Secretariat 1954, taking Moghioros's place in this body as the traditional representative of the Hungarian wing. Strong influence in the *Apparat*.

GEORGESCU, Teohari (b. 1908, Bucharest). Printer; socialist; joined CP 1929; arrested 1933, remained in prison until 1944. Member of CC 1946 and one of the four party Secretaries; Minister of Interior 1947. Purged 1952.

GHEORGHIU-DEJ, Gheorghe (b. 1908, Moldavia). Son of worker, himself a worker from very early age. Joined CP at time of first congresses. Railway worker in 1926. Transferred for disciplinary reasons in 1931 to town of Dej, whence his name. Allegedly member of party CC 1932. Took prominent part in Grivita incident 1933. Sentenced to 12 years' imprisonment from which he emerged 1944. Minister of Communications 1944 and First Secretary of CP 1944 and continuously since, with a short interval when Prime Minister between 1954 and 1955. Operative in denunciation of Patrascanu 1946 and abdication of King Michael 1948. Rapporteur at anti-Tito Cominform 1948–9, although reported to be in eclipse because under suspicion of Titoism between 1949 and 1951. Complete victor in party after purge of Pauker-Luca-Georgescu wing, later defined by him as 'Muscovites'. Head of state 1961.

GROZA, Petru (1884–1958, b. in Transylvania). Lawyer. As a junior minister before the war had to abandon political career in the 1930s because of grave frauds comitted in his department. Later founded the Ploughmen's Front, a radical peasant organization based on the local electorate in Hunedoara and on an association with the Communist Party. Prime Minister 1945; President of the Presidium of the Great National Assembly 1952, a position which he held until his death.

LUCA, Vasile (b. 1898, Transylvania). Of Hungarian family; worker. Joined Bela Kun's revolutionary army 1919; afterwards joined communist groups in Rumania. Head of communist organization in Brasov. Regional secretary of party 1924; arrested same year and spent three years in prison. Elected to CC 1928; in charge of trade unions in Transylvania. Arrested again 1933, remained in prison until 1938. Arrested again 1940 in Cernovitz; was liberated by Soviet troops and went to Moscow where he remained until end of war. Returned to Rumania 1944. One of the four secretaries of the Secretariat, in charge of industrial and financial problems. Minister of Finance 1947. Purged May 1952 and sentenced to 20 years' imprisonment. Died soon afterwards.

MARIN, Gheorghe Gaston (b. 1917, Transylvania). In 1937 left for France, where he took degree in electronics and married a French woman. Joined French CP 1941; fought in resistance. Secretary to Gheorghiu-Dej at Ministry of Economy; later worked in foreign trade and planning institutions. Member of CC 1960; President of Planning Commission 1962.

MAURER, Ion Gheorghe (b. 1907, Transylvania). Degree in law; appointed State Prosecutor 1930; resigned official position and came to bar. Frequently took defence in communist trials, among them that of Ana Pauker. Arrested 1942; released 1943. Joined Bodnaras and Patrascanu in their action to create the opposition front. Visited Dej in prison and effected the liaison between the prison wing and the rest of the party. Full member of CC 1948; in eclipse 1948–52; candidate member of CC 1955; Minister of Foreign Affairs 1957; Chairman of Presidium of Grand National Assembly (head of state) 1958; full member of CC 1958; member of Politburo 1960; Prime Minister 1961.

MOGHIOROS, Alexandru (b. 1917, Transylvania). Of Hungarian origin. Joined CP 1930; in 1935 arrested with Ana Pauker, sentenced to 10 years' imprisonment, from which he emerged in 1944. Full member Politburo 1948 with direct functions in organizational work. Opposed Ana Pauker and Vasile Luca over organization and agricultural problems. Deputy Premier in charge of agricultural organization Apr. 1954. At present head of the powerful 'Hungarian wing'; is one of the most influential members in the present ruling group.

PARVULESCU, Constantin (b. 1895, Oltenia). Member of CP since foundation congress and of the CC since 1929; Secretary-General for a while in 1930. Arrested 1934, escaped and before the war went to USSR where he remained for its duration. Returned in 1944 and with Bodnaras and Ranghet was responsible for the activities of the party while Dej was in prison and Ana Pauker in the USSR. Chairman of party Control Commission 1945–61; chairman of Grand National Assembly 1953. Lost both positions in 1961 after being criticized at CC plenum of Nov.-Dec. that year for ideological vacillation and complicity with Chisinevschi and Miron Constantinescu.

PATRASCANU, Lucretiu (b. 1900, Moldavia). His father D. D. Patrascanu was a well-known satirical writer and was in the group under Stere who founded the review *Viata romaneasca*. Doctor in law and economics, which he studied in France and Germany. In the Rumanian Communist Party since 1921. Led the communist lawyers and organized the defence in the most important trials of communists. Wrote studies and essays in many Rumanian reviews; arrested many times. In 1933 was elected deputy on the lists of the Workers' and Peasants' bloc. During the war was the communist spokesman in negotiations with the democratic parties. In September 1944 was the communist member in the Rumanian delegation at the armistice talks in Moscow. Minister of Justice 1944–8. Purged in 1948, tried in May 1954 and, according to the official version, executed on 17 May 1954.

PAUKER (RABINOVICI), Ana (b. 1893, Moldavia). Joined Socialist Party 1915; noticed in 1917 for revolutionary actions during occupation of Bucharest by German troops and during strike of 13 Dec. 1918. Married Marcel Pauker; together joined communist groups and reorganized newspaper *Socialismul*. Elected to CC at 2nd Congress (1922). Arrested during period of illegality first in 1925; escaped during trial and went to Russia to work in Comintern. Returned 1934 and appointed one of the Secretaries of the party 1935. Arrested 14 July 1935; sentenced to 10 years' imprisonment. Exchanged for a Bessarabian patriot detained in USSR in 1940 and left for USSR. In 1943 organized Tudor Vladimirescu division. Returned to Rumania Sept. 1944. As one of the four secretaries was in charge of organization, recruitment of members, and statutes. Minister of Foreign Affairs 1947. Responsible in Politburo for agricultural collectivization; purged May 1952. Died 1960.

PAUKER, Marcel (b. Bucharest 1901). Son of wealthy and cultured family. After completing studies at Lutheran School, Bucharest, and taking his doctorate in political science, he joined the CP at the foundation congress of 1921; at same time married Ana Rabinovici, by whom he had two children. His career was more successful in the sphere of international communism than in the Rumanian CP which he despised and which he led from outside and above. A favourite of Rakovsky, he exerted an influence on the intelligentsia of the party. Gheorghe Stoica, a veteran of the party and himself a Rumanian Jewish intellectual, was asked to draw a full-length portrait of Marcel Pauker at the CC plenum of Nov.–Dec. 1961 for the benefit of the present party members. He said that he and his companions in prison after the Dealul Spirei congress were indignant to learn how Marcel Pauker, on his own initiative, dismissed the 'collective' which was in charge of the leadership of the incipient party and assumed it himself. He said that this occurred because Marcel had been sent, with Ana Pauker, to Switzerland to report on the results of the congress to certain secret contacts. He then formed a 'directorate' with himself as leader. Stoica confirmed that Marcel Pauker was afterwards re-elected to the CC at the 2nd Congress (Ploesti), but said that this was the last time he was in the CC. His influence between 1922 and 1936 must have been due to the fact that, as another speaker declared at the same meeting (N. Ceausescu), 'Marcel Pauker was very high in the Comintern hierarchy and in charge of Rumanian affairs.' He was shot during the 1936–8 purges in Moscow.

PINTILIE, Ilie (b. Feb. 1903). Probably the most popular worker in the railwaymen's group. Early orphaned, he was an apprentice at Iasi at the time of the Russian Revolution of 1917. Member of the Socialist Youth 1919 and of the maximalist group 1921. Active in the trade unions 1929. Elected, with Gheorghiu-Dej, to the Committee for Action of the railwaymen 1931. Led strike at Iasi and was sentenced to a year's imprisonment. Co-opted member of party CC 1933. Friend of Patrascanu. Arrested and sent to Doftana, where the other workers (Dej, Chivu Stoica, &c.) were also imprisoned, Sept. 1939. In Oct. 1940 the building was shaken by an earthquake and Pintilie was buried in the ruins.

RANGHET, Iosif (b. 1904, Transylvania). Joined Rumanian CP 1930; Secretary-General of Cluj regional committee 1933–4; later secretary of Banat and Jur Valley. One of the triumvirate (with Pirvulescu and Bodnaras) in charge of party during period 1 Apr.–23 Aug. 1944; member of CC 1945; Director of cadres 1945–8; deputy member of Politburo 1948; d. 1 Sept. 1952.

RAUTU, Leonte (b. 1910, Bessarabia). Active in Agitprop work in 1930s; spent war years in USSR. Active in Rumanian broadcasts of Radio Moscow. Member CC 1948; Director of Agitprop 1951; candidate member Politburo Dec. 1955; chief of Directorate of Propaganda and Culture of CC since 1958. In control of all cultural activities. One of members of Rumanian delegations to Moscow 1960 and to U.N. Most controversial and attacked member of ruling group.

SALAJAN, Leontin (b. 1915, Timisoara). Of Hungarian origin (Szilaghi). Joined party 1930; member CC 1945; chairman of Army Verification Committee 1949; Deputy Minister of Armed Forces 1950; Minister 1956 to date. Candidate member of Politburo 1955. Strong influence within inner circle of 'political generals' and the Hungarian wing.

STEFANOV, Boris. Became known when he led 1920 general strike; main qualities seem to have been especially those of an agitator. His articles lacked the brilliance of Alexandru Dobrogeanu-Gherea or the depth of Marcel Pauker. According to his present-day critics (see speech by Rautu at CC plenum of Nov.-Dec. 1961), he was an 'opportunist', totally under the influence of Gherea's theories which 'he carried out all his life in the party'. Like Cristescu, he concentrated upon the Bucharest organization which was the most advanced and which played a decisive role in undermining the old Socialist Party and in the efforts of the 'communist groups' to bring about the affiliation of the party to the Third International. Elected a deputy on the lists of the 'Socialist-Communist' party in 1922 elections. Arrested 1926 and with Vasile Luca was tried and sentenced; later escaped from prison and reappeared in the 1930s in Moscow as a Rumanian spokesman. Although after the war nothing was heard of him either from Soviet or Rumanian sources, and it was generally believed that he had died a long time ago, on 10 June 1963 Radio Sofia reported that he was present at a commemoration of Georgi Dimitrov held in Sofia at that date and delivered a speech. He was introduced as the former First Secretary of the CC of the Rumanian CP during the period 1935–40.

STOICA, Chivu (b. 1908, Muntenia). Railway worker. Sentenced with Dej after Grivita incident to 15 years' imprisonment, from which he emerged in 1944. Member CC 1945; candidate member Politburo 1948; full member 1952 to date. Minister of Industry 1948–9; of Metallurgical and Chemical Industries 1949–55. Deputy Premier since 1950; Prime Minister 1955–60 (Oct.). Currently holding important position in Secretariat and one of the incontestable seniors in the hierarchy.

STROICI, Gheorghe. Early leader of social-revolutionary movement. Was a docker in port of Chilia Nova when on 13 Jan. 1918 Russian sailors and harbour workers tried to organize a revolution and seize the harbour. Escaped to Odessa. Returned to Rumania summer 1918 and arrested in August of that year. Died, allegedly in prison, 1928.

SELECT BIBLIOGRAPHY

I. *Works in Rumanian**

(*Note:* ESPLP = Editura de Stat pentru Literatura Politica.)

1. *Collections of Documents and Surveys*

Academia Republicii Populare Romane. *Catalog*, 1948–54, 1954–.

Includes books and periodicals.

—— *Documente privind istoria Romaniei*, A: *Moldova*; B: *Tara romaneasca*; C: *Transilvania* (Documents concerning the history of Rumania, A: Moldavia; B: Wallachia; C: Transylvania). 1951–.

Bibliografia Republicei Populare Romane, Seria A: *Carti, Albume, Harti* (Bibliography of the RPR, A: Books, Albums, Maps).

Published monthly by the Central State Library; includes new editions of books previously published as well as current works.

Bibliografia Republicei Populare Romane, Seria B: *Bibliografia periodicelor*.

Indexes major studies in the main journals and reviews published in the RPR.

Enciclopedia Romaniei. 1938–41. 4 vols.

Golopentia, Anton. *Populatia Republicii Populare Romane la 25 Ianuarie 1948; rezultatele provizorii ale recensamantului* [*de*] *A. Golopentia si D. C. Georgescu*. Inst. central de statistica, 1948.

Golopentia, a young but illustrious statistician who 'disappeared' after the communists came to power, and Georgescu, both directors at the Central Institute of Statistics, published this brief but clear analysis of the census undertaken in difficult conditions in 1948, which was the first serious attempt to bring the census of 1930 up to date after a similar attempt undertaken by the Institute in April 1941, also in difficult conditions and a truncated territory.

Haseganu, Mihai. *Geografia economica a RPR* (Economic geography of the RPR). Editura stiintifica, 1957.

Based on the 1956 census; an attempt to popularize the main data thus made available.

Partidul Comunist din Romania. *Documente din istoria Partidului Comunist din Romania* (Documents from the history of the Rumanian CP). 2nd ed. ESPLP, 1953.

First published in May 1951, this is a selection of what the present leadership of the party considers to have been the most important and characteristic documents of the party in its illegal years, 1917–44. It is an abridgement of the larger series of documents still being published (see below under Partidul Muncitoresc Romin), which in its turn is a severely purged and interpreted collection.

* Published in Bucharest unless otherwise indicated.

Partidul Muncitoresc Romin. *Congresul II-lea al PMR, 23–28 Dec. 1955*. ESPLP, 1956.

—— *Congresul al III-lea al PMR, 20-25 Iuni 1960*. ESPLP, 1960.

—— Comitetul Central, Institutul de Istorie a PMR. *Documente din istoria Partidului Comunist din Romania*. ESPLP, 1953–.
i: *1917–22* (1953); ii: *1923–8* (1953); iii: *1929–33*, pt. 1 (1953); iv: *1934–7* (1957).

See note under Partidul Comunist din Romania, *Documente* . . .

—— —— *Hotarirea Biroului Politic al CC al PMR cu privire la unele masuri de imbunatatire a muncii politico-educative in randul studentilor, 22 Iune 1956* (Decision of the Politburo of the CC concerning some ways of improving the political-educational work among students). ESPLP, 1956.

—— —— *Hotarirea CC al PMR asupra muncii pe taramul construirii gospodariilor agricole colective si al intovarasirilor agricole, 18 Sept. 1951* (Decision of the CC concerning the work for the building of collective farms and agricultural associations). ESPLP, 1951.

—— —— *Reolutii si hotariri ale Comitetului Central al PMR* (Resolutions and decisions of the CC). 2nd ed. ESPLP, 1952.

After the formation of the RWP in February 1948 by the merging of the CP and some elements of the Social Democratic Party, the party CC decided to publish texts of its resolutions and decisions in book form. This is the first volume of the series.

—— —— *Statutul* (Statute). ESPLP, 1955.

Rumania, Directia centrala de statistica. *Recensamantul general al populatiei Romaniei din 29 Decembrie 1930*. 1938–. 10 vols.

In spite of the obvious shortcomings of statistical work in Rumania in the 1920s, this massive work provided the basic data on demography, economics, social structure &c. used between the two world wars.

—— Institutul central de statistica. *Anuarul statistic al RPR*.

Beginning in 1957, this statistical yearbook is becoming more complete every year, although it is to be noted that compared with statistical data not only of western countries but even of Czechoslovakia, Hungary, and Poland, Rumanian statistics are scarce and not always reliable.

—— —— *Breviarul statistic al RPR* (Statistical summary). 1957–.

Same material by the same authors, but abridged and condensed.

—— Ministerul Justitiei. *Colectia de legi, decrete, hotarari si dispozitii* (Collection of laws, decrees, decisions, and orders).

Bimonthly; contains texts and references to laws, decrees &c. issued over the period.

Statutul Sindicatelor din RPR (statute of the trade unions). 1954.

2. *Works most frequently consulted*

Arcadian, N. P. *Industrializarea Romaniei*. 1933.

Dobrogeanu-Gherea, C. *Neo-Iobagia*. 1910.

Duca, I. G. 'Liberalismul', *in* Institutul Social Roman, *Doctrinele partidelor politice.* 193 .
Gheorghiu-Dej, Gh. *Articole si cuvantari.* ESPLP, 1952.
Giurescu, C. Constantin. *Istoria romanilor.* 1944.
Gusti, D. *60 Sate romanesti.* 1943.
Iordan, D. I. *Venitul national al Romaniei.* 1929.
Madgearu, Virgil. *Evolutia economiei romanesti dupa rasboiul mondial.* 1940.
Manuila, Sabin. *Demografia rurala a Romaniei.* 1940.
Partidul National Taranesc. *Principiile, programul si statutele.* 1926.
Patrascanu, Lucretiu. *Problemele de baza ale Romaniei.* 1944.
Petrescu, C. Titel. *Istoria socialismului in Romania.* 1944.
Roller, Mihai. *Istoria RPR.* 1952.
Rumania. *Trei ani de guvernare, 6 Septembrie 1940–6 Septembrie 1943.* 1943.
An official publication of the Antonescu government.
Stere, Constantin. *Social democratism sau poporanism in Viata romaneasca.* Iasi, 1907–8.
—— *In preajma revolutiei.* 1933–8.
Titulescu, N. *Dinamica pacii.* 1930.
Visoianu, Constantin. 'N. Titulescu', *in Jurnalul de dimineata,* 1945.

3. *Other works*

Balteanu, Boris. 'Romania in ajunul instalarii regimului popular-democratic', *Studii,* no. 2, 1957.
Bratianu, Gh. *Traditia istorica despre intemeerea statelor romanesti.* 1945.
Campus, Eliza. 'Despre politica externa antinationala a guvernelor burghezo-mosieresti din Romania', *Studii,* no. 5, 1952.
—— 'Despre politica externa a guvernului reactionar roman in etapa tradarii dela München', *Studii,* no. 6, 1952.
Chirculescu, I. 'Organizarea si distribuirea muncii GAC', *Lupta de clasa,* no. 10, 1951.
Codreanu, C. Z. *Pentru legionari.* 1940.
Constantinescu, Miron. *Despre patrie si patriotism.* PMR, 1946.
Constantinescu-Iasi, P. *Organizatii de masa legale conduse de Partidul Comunist din Romania.* 1952.
Cresin, Roman. *Agricultura din judetul Arges.* 1945.
Darvicu, S. 'Conferinta dela Iasi a grupurilor comuniste din Romania, Martie 1921', *Analele,* no. 3, May-June 1956.
Farcasanu, Mihai. *Monarhia sociala.* 1938.
Farcasanu, Sergiu. *C. Dobrogeanu-Gherea, editura de stat pentru literatura si arta.* 1955.

Gaston Marin, G. 'Ajutorul economic dat de URSS in constituirea socialismului in RPR', *Probleme economice,* no. 10, Oct. 1951.
Gheorghiu-Dej, Gh. *30 de ani de lupta a partidului sub steagul lui Lenin si Stalin.* 1952.
—— *Raport de activitate al CC al PMR la congresul II, 23 Dec. 1955.* ESPLP, 1956.
Goldberger, N. *Lupta Partidului Comunist din Romania.* 1952.
—— *Lupta Partidului Comunist din Romania in perioada stabilizarii relative a capitalismului, 1923–9.* ESPLP, 1953.
Groza, Petru. *In drum spre socialism.* 1960.
Haupt, Gh. 'Despre influenta miscarii revolutionare ruse asupra inceputurilor miscarii muncitoresti din Romania, 1828–81', *in Studii si referate despre istoria romaniei.* 1954.
—— *Din istoricul legaturilor revolutionare romano-ruse, 1849–81.*
Hutira, Ervin. 'Despre controlul muncitoresc in Romania, 1944–48', *Studii,* no. 3, 1953.
Inceputul raspandirii marxismului in Romania. ESPLP, 1959.
Iorga, N. *Istoria romanilor.* 1939.
Lenin si Stalin despre Romania. ESPLP, 1954.
Liveanu, V. 'Influenta revolutiei ruse din Februarie 1917 in Romania', *Studii,* no. 1, Jan.–Feb. 1956.
Lorincz, I. 'Experienta sovietica in creiarea unui nou aparat de stat', *Iustitia noua,* no. 5, 1953.
Luca, Vasile. *Despre congresul dela Timosoara al sindicatelor unitare.* 1949.
—— *Dictatul dela Viena si resolvarea problemei nationale.* PMR, 1946.
—— *Lupta PCR impotriva fascizarii Tarii, pentru faurirea Frontului Popular antifascist, 1934–8.* 1957.
Manuila Sabin, G. D. C. *Populatia Romaniei.* 1938.
Matei, Pompiliu. 'Miscarea muncitoreasca in Romania, 1918–21', *Studii,* no. 5, 1957.
Marghiloman, Al. *Note politice.* 1931. 5 vols.
Mihalache, Ion. *Noul regim agrar.* 1925.
Palaghita, Stefan. *Garda de Fier, spre reinvierea Romaniei.* Buenos Aires, 1951.
Papadopol, V., ed. *Codul Penal al RPR.* ESPLP, 1950.
Partidul Muncitoresc Romin. *Amintiri despre primul congres al partidului.* Editura Tineretului, 1956.
—— *Partidul Muncitoresc Romin, partid de tip nou, forta conducatoare si indrumatoare a popurului nostru.* 1954.
—— *Probleme ale literaturii noi in RPR.* 1952.
Popovici, V. V. *Organizarea muncii in gospodariile agricole colective.* 1954.

Radulescu, G. 'Desvoltarea comertului exterior in RPR', *Probleme economice,* no. 12, Dec. 1953.
Radulescu-Motru, Constantin. *Taranismul, un suflet si o politica.* 1924.
Rautu, Leonte. 'Statul popular-democrat si functiunile sale', *Scinteia,* 29 Dec. 1951.
Roller, Mihai. *Scrieri istorice si social-politice.* ESPLP, 1951.
—— *In legatura cu miscarea muncitoreasca in Romania.* PMR, 1945.
Rumania. *Pe marginea prapastiei.* 1941.
Varga, V. A. 'Din istoria solidaritatii revolutionare a masselor populare romane si ungare', *Analele,* no. 3, May-June 1957.
Vasiliu, Ion. *Industrializarea agriculturii romanesti.* 1941.
Vianu, Tudor. *Probleme de stil si arta literara.* 1955.
Voinea, Serban. *Marxism oligarhic, contributie la problema desvoltarii capitalismului in Romania.* 1926.
Zeigher, S. *Primul si al doilea plan de stat al RPR.* ESPLP, 1950.
Zeletin, S. *Burghezia romana, origina si rolul ei istoric.* 1928.

4. *Periodicals*

Analele Institutului de istorie a Partidului de pe langa CC al PMR.
Contemporanul (organ of the Ministry of Culture).
Cronica romaneasca (published by Free Europe Committee, New York, 1949–57).
Gazeta literara.
Luceafarul.
Lupta de clasa; organ teoretic si politic al CC al PMR.
Ortodoxia; Revista Patriarhiei romane.
Probleme economice; Revista lunara de studii si documentare.
Romania (published by Rumanian National Committee, New York, 1955–).
Steaua; Revista a Uniunii scriitorilor. Cluj.
Studii, revista de istorie.
Viata romaneasca.

II. *Works in English and other languages*

1. *Collections of Documents and Surveys*

Cour Internationale de Justice, mémoires, plaidoyers et documents. *Interpretation des traités de paix conclus avec la Bulgarie, la Hongrie et la Roumanie.* Leyden, 1950.
Degras, J. D., ed. *The Communist International, 1919–43; Documents.* London, RIIA, 1955.

Great Britain, Foreign Office and U.S. Dept of State. *Documents on German Foreign Policy, 1918–45, from the archives of the German Foreign Ministry, Series D, 1937–45*. London, HMSO, 1949.

Royal Institute of International Affairs. *Survey of International Affairs, 1939–46:*

America, Britain and Russia; Their Co-operation and Conflict, 1941–6, by W. H. McNeil. 1953.

A very courageous study of the hasty and fateful decisions taken by the three powers during and after the war.

'Eastern Europe', by Martin Wight, in *The World in March 1939*. 1952.

Although very short, this is undoubtedly one of the most understanding works by a western historian on Eastern Europe between the two wars.

United Nations, *Economic Survey of Europe*. Geneva, 1951–.

United States, Dept. of State. *Evidence of violations of Human Rights Provisions of the Treaties of Peace by Rumania, Bulgaria and Hungary, submitted . . . to the Secretary General of the United Nations pursuant to the Resolutions of the General Assembly of 3 November 1950*. Washington, 1951. Publl. 4736.

—— *Nazi-Soviet Relations, 1939–41: Documents from the Archives of the German Foreign Office,* ed. R. J. Sontag and J. S. Beddie. Washington, 1948. Publ. 3023.

—— *Treaties of Peace with Italy, Bulgaria, Hungary, Roumania and Finland*. Washington, 1947. Publ. 2743.

Zinner, Paul. *National Communism and Popular Revolt in Eastern Europe; a selection of Documents on Events in Poland and Hungary, Feb.-Nov. 1956*. New York, Columbia UP, 1956.

2. *Works Most Frequently Consulted*

Churchill, Sir Winston. *The Second World War,* vi: *Triumph and Tragedy*. London, 1954.

Ciurea, E. C. *Le traité de paix avec la Roumanie du 10 février 1947*. Paris, 1954.

The complete work on the subject.

Council on Foreign Relations. *The United States in World Affairs, 1945–7*. New York, 1947.

An exposé of the American attitude towards world problems after the Second World War, with a lucid section on Eastern Europe.

Cretzianu, A., ed. *Captive Rumania*. New York, 1957.

Useful for the years 1944–54.

—— *The Lost Opportunity*. London, 1957.

First-hand account of Rumanian efforts and actions to get out of the war.

Deakin, F. W. *The Brutal Friendship*. London, 1962.

Contains new sources on the period 1941–4 which allows the author to retrace authoritatively even if incidentally the history of Rumania during the war.

Fischer-Galati, S., ed. *Romania*. New York, Mid-European Studies Center of the Free Europe Committee, 1956.

A useful symposium for the years 1944–55, many chapters by the editor himself.

Gafencu, G. *Les préliminaires de la guerre à l'Est*. Fribourg, 1946.

By now a classic on the inevitability of the Soviet-Nazi clash on Eastern Europe.

Hillgruber, Andreas. *Hitler, König Carol und Marschall Antonescu*. Wiesbaden, 1954.

Based on German documents, published and unpublished, this is an indispensable description of Rumanian-German relations.

Markham, Reuben. *Rumania under the Soviet Yoke*. Boston, 1949.

Mitrany, D. *The Land and the Peasant in Rumania*. Cambridge UP, 1924.

The basic work on Rumania's agriculture up to the 1930s.

Moore, W. E. *Economic Demography of Eastern and Southern Europe*. Geneva, League of Nations, 1945.

Reitlinger, Gerald. *The Final Solution*. London, 1955.

An indispensable study of the fate of the Jewish population in Europe under Hitler, with a complete examination of this problem in Rumania during the Antonescu regime.

Roberts, Henry L. *Rumania; Political Problems of an Agrarian State*. Harvard, Yale UP, 1951.

This work took up the examination of the agrarian problem where Mitrany left off and carried it to the mid-1940s. By interweaving social, economic and political considerations together with national and international developments, it provides an exceedingly thorough background to the reasons for the communist seizure of power.

Rura, M. J. *Reinterpretation of History as a Method of Furthering Communism in Rumania*. Washington, Georgetown UP, 1961.

A penetrating analysis.

Schieder, T., ed. *Dokumentation der Vertreibung der Deutschen aus Ost-Mitteleuropa*, iii: *Das Schicksal der Deutschen in Rumänien*. Bonn, Bundesministerium f. Vertriebene &c, 1957.

Seton Watson, H. *Eastern Europe between the Wars, 1918–41*. London, 1946.

—— *The East European Revolution*. London, 1951.

—— *The Pattern of Communist Revolution*. London, 1951.

These three works together describe the passing of the Eastern European countries from Nazi to Soviet domination. The author combines exceptional knowledge of the countries with a profound interpretation of communism.

U.N., 'Economic Developments in Rumania', *Economic Bulletin for Europe*, vol. 13, No. 2, 1961.

Wolff, R. L. *The Balkans in Our Time*. Cambridge, Mass., Harvard UP, 1956.

Although it starts with the fourth century, it contains a wealth of documentary material on Balkan developments up to 1953.

3. *Other Works*

Amery, Julian. *Sons of the Eagle*. London, 1948.

Antonescu, M. A. *Im Dienst des Vaterlands: 6 September 1940 bis 6 September 1942*. Bucharest, 1952.

Barbul, G. *Memorial Antonescu: le 3e Homme de l'Axe*. Paris, 1950.

Bolitho, H. *Rumania under King Carol*. London, 1938.

Bova Scoppa, Renato. *Colloqui con due dittatori*. Rome, 1949.

Bratianu, G. I. *Origines et formation de l'unité roumaine*. Bucharest, 1943.

——*Un énigme et un miracle historique: le peuple roumain*. Bucharest, 1942.

Brannen, B. 'The Soviet Conquest of Rumania', *Foreign Affairs*, Apr. 1952.

Burks, R. V. *The Dynamics of Communism in Eastern Europe*. Princeton UP, 1961.

Campbell, J. C. 'The European Territorial Settlement', *Foreign Affairs*, Oct. 1947.

—— 'French Influence and the Rise of Rumanian Nationalism', unpublished Ph.D. thesis, Harvard UP, 1940.

—— 'N. Iorga', *Slavonic & East European Review*, Nov. 1947.

—— 'Diplomacy on the Danube', *Foreign Affairs*, Jan. 1949.

Comnene, P. N. *Preludi del Grande Dramma*. Rome, 1947.

Cretzianu, A. 'The Soviet Ultimatum to Rumania', *Journal of Central European Affairs*, Jan. 1950.

—— 'Rumanian Armistice Negotiations', *Journal of Central European Affairs*, Oct. 1951.

Dallin, A., ed. *Diversity in International Communism*. New York, 1963.

Djilas, Milovan. *The New Class*. New York, 1957.

Dugan, J. and Carroll, S. *Ploeshtii, the Great Ground-Air Battle of 1 August 1943*. New York, 1962.

Dumitriu, Petre. *Rendez-vous au jugement dernier*. Paris, 1961.

—— *Incognito*. Paris, 1962.

Fabre, H. G. *Théorie des démocraties populaires*. Paris, 1950.

Friessner, Hans. *Verratene Schlachter*. Hamburg, 1955.

Gafencu, G. *Les dernier jours de l'Europe*. Fribourg, 1946.

Gheorghe, Ion. *Rümaniens Weg zur Satellitenstaat*. Heidelberg, 1952.

Gluckstein, Y. *Stalin's Satellites in Europe*. London, 1952.

Gormsen, M. *Short Introduction to the Principal Structural Problems of Agriculture in Rumania*. Bucharest, 1945.

Ileana (princess of Rumania). *I Live Again; memoirs*. London, 1952.

International Reference Library. *Politics and Political Parties in Rumania*. London, 1936.

Ionescu, G. 'The Governing Personnel in the Popular Democracies',

paper read at Soviet Affairs Seminar, School of Slavonic and East European Studies, London, 1955.
—— 'Social Structure: Rumania under Communism', *Annals of American Academy of Political and Social Sciences,* May 1958.
—— 'The Evolution of the Cominform', *World Today,* May 1950.
Jordan, C. N. *The Romanian Methane Gas Industry.* New York, 1955.
—— *The Rumanian Oil Industry.* New York, 1955.
Konrad, G. I. *Die Wirtschaft Rumäniens, 1945–52.* Berlin, 1953.
Lee, A. Gould. *Crown Against Sickle.* London, 1950.
Leon, Gh. N. *Struktur und Entwicklungsmöglichkeiten der rumänischen Volkswirtschaft.* Jena, 1941.
Luca, Vasile. *Über den Kongress der Einheits Gewerkschaften in Temesvar.* Bucharest, 1952.
Lukacs, J. A. *The Great Powers and Eastern Europe.* Chicago, 1953.
Madgearu, Virgil. *Rumania's New Economic Policy.* London, 1930.
——*La politique économique extérieure de la Roumanie, 1927–38.* Paris, inst. International de la coopération intellectuelle, 1939.
Marczewski, J. *Planification et croissance des démocraties populaires.* Paris, 1956. 2 vols.
Melbourne, M. R. 'Rumania: Nazi Satellite; a Study of the Politics and Propaganda of the Antonescu Régime', unpublished thesis, Harvard Univ., 1948.
Mitrany, D. *Marx Against the Peasant.* London, 1951.
Moorad, G. *Behind the Iron Curtain.* London, 1947.
Moore, W. *Economic Demography of Eastern and Southern Europe.* Geneva, 1945.
Mosely, P. E. *Face to Face with Russia.* Foreign Policy Ass., Headline ser., no. 70, July–Aug. 1948.
—— 'Is Bessarabia Next?', *Foreign Affairs,* Apr. 1940.
—— 'Transylvania Partitioned', *Foreign Affairs,* Oct. 1940.
—— 'Hopes and Failures: American Policy towards East-Central Europe, 1941–7', *Review of Politics,* Oct. 1955.
Nano, F. 'The First Soviet Double-Cross', *Journal of Central European Affairs,* 1952.
Pavel, P. *Why Rumania Failed.* London, 1945.
Prost, H. *Destin de la Roumanie, 1918–45.* Paris, 1954.
Royal Inst. of International Affairs. *The Balkan States.* 1. 1936.
Rotschild, J. A. *Rakovsky.* St. Antony's College Seminar Paper. Oxford, Feb. 1957.
Rumania, Min. of Foreign Affairs. *The Aggressive Policy and Machinations of American Imperialism against the Rumanian People's Republic.* Bucharest, 1952.

Rumanian National Committee. *Suppression of Human Rights in Rumania*. Washington, 1949.
—— *Persecution of Religion in Rumania*. Washington, 1949.
—— *Perversion of Education in Rumania*. Washington, 1950.
Rumanian Workers' Party. *Ana Pauker*. Bucharest, 1951.
—— *Documents concerning Right-Wing Deviations in the RWP*. Bucharest, 1952.
Schapiro, L. B. *The Origins of the Communist Autocracy*. London, 1955.
Sima, Horia. *Destinée du nationalisme*. Paris, 1951.
Sporea, C. 'Enstalinisierung in Rumänien', *Osteuropa*, Dec. 1962.
Spulber, N. *The Economics of Communist Eastern Europe*. Indiana, 1957.
Sud-Ost Institut (Munich). *Südosteuropa Bibliographie*, vol. i: 1945–1950.

The Rumanian section of the part of this bibliography devoted to Czechoslovakia, Rumania, and Bulgaria contains works published in Rumania or abroad between 1945 and 1950. The second volume, 1950–55, is in the press. By the courtesy of Dr C. Sporea, one of the editors, I was able to consult this volume in manuscript.

Tappe, Eric, 'Rumania', *in* RIIA, *Central and South Eastern Europe*, ed. R. Betts. London, 1951.
Titulescu, N. 'Rumania and Bessarabia', *Nineteenth Century and After*, June 1924.
United States, House of Representatives, Special Committee. *Investigation of Communist Aggression: Rumania*. 83rd Congress, 2nd sess. Washington, 1954.
Warriner, Doreen. *The Economics of Peasant Farming*. London, 1939.
Wilmot, Chester. *The Struggle for Europe*. London, 1952.

Index